FUNDAMENTALS OF COLLECTION DEVELOPMENT AND MANAGEMENT

Second Edition

Peggy Johnson

AMERICAN LIBRARY ASSOCIATION

Chicago   2009

Peggy Johnson is associate university librarian at the University of Minnesota Libraries. She edits two journals, *Library Resources and Technical Services* and *Technicalities: Information Forum for the Library Services Practitioner*. She has written or edited six books, including *New Directions in Technical Services: Trends and Sources (1993–1995)* (ALA, 1997), *The Searchable Internet Bibliography: An On-Disk Annotated Guide to Timely Materials about the Internet* (ALA, 1996), and *Collection Management and Development: Issues in an Electronic Era* (coedited with Bonnie MacEwan; ALA, 1994).

The paper used in this publication meets the minimum requirements of American National Standard for Information Sciences—Permanence of Paper for Printed Library Materials, ANSI Z39.48-1992. ∞

Library of Congress Cataloging-in-Publication Data
Johnson, Peggy, 1948–
    Fundamentals of collection development and management / Peggy Johnson. — 2nd ed.
       p. cm.
    Includes bibliographical references and index.
    ISBN 978-0-8389-0972-0 (alk. paper)
      1. Collection development (Libraries) 2. Collection management (Libraries) 3. Collection development (Libraries)—United States. 4. Collection management (Libraries) —United States. I. Title.
    Z687.J64 2009
    025.2'1—dc22
                                                                        2008019989

ISBN-13: 978-0-8389-0972-0

Printed in the United States of America
13 12 11 10 09   5 4 3 2 1

CONTENTS

Additional material can be found at www.ala.org/editions/extras/Johnson09720.

FIGURES

PREFACE TO THE SECOND EDITION

The goals I have in this second edition of *Fundamentals of Collection Development and Management* are the same as I had for the first edition. I hope this book will serve as an introduction to the topic for both students and experienced librarians with new or expanded responsibilities and as a refresher and resource for those currently performing collection development and management. I have sought to combine history, theory, and practice, drawing from literature outside library and information management when relevant and useful. Although the book focuses on libraries in the United States, the theories and practices presented here are relevant to libraries and librarians wherever they are.

Much in libraries and their collections, in the roles of collections librarians and in the environments in which they operate, has changed since the first edition. Selecting and providing access to digital resources are no longer novel responsibilities, though they remain challenging. The roles of collections librarians are expanding in new and exciting ways. In many libraries of all types, collection development and management are part of a suite of challenging responsibilities. Questions of accountability and impact are put to all types of libraries and their librarians. Reaching out to user communities to understand their needs and interests and to gauge success is more important than ever. This edition aims to recognize the ways that collection development and management are intertwined with all library activities and woven throughout the work librarians do.

When I began work on the second edition, I wanted not only to update the content but also to improve it. To that end, I read published reviews of the first edition and contacted graduate school faculty members who were using it. Critiques of the first edition focused on failure to address collection development and management in all types of libraries evenly. I have sought to make this edition more relevant to public, school, and special librarians. Although electronic resources were new enough when I wrote the first edition to warrant a separate chapter, teaching faculty recommended that this topic be integrated throughout the book, which I have done. I have added a new chapter on scholarly communication, both because faculty requested it and because I believe this topic—access to the results of scholarship—is of critical importance to all librarians regardless of the type of library in which they work. Finally, in response to requests, I have added more practical information that is intended to aid in the day-to-day work of collection development and management.

As in the first edition, all chapters have supplemental suggested reading lists. These have been extensively revised to reflect print and online literature produced since 2004 and to be more inclusive of all types of libraries. The glossary has been updated and expanded. This edition has four appendixes: A, "Professional Resources for Collection Development and Management"; B, "Selection Aids"; C, "Sample Collection Development Policy Statements"; and D, "Contracts and Licensing Terms." The case studies that accompany chapters 2 through 9 are new. The examples are fictional but represent real challenges librarians face daily. I hope these can serve not only as class assignments but also as catalysts for discussion among practicing librarians.

My aim is to provide a comprehensive examination of the key issues in collection development and management today. Each topic could be explored in greater depth, and most warrant and have received book-length treatment, many of which the reader can find in the supplemental reading lists. I hope all readers find useful, practical information in this revised edition of *Fundamentals of Collection Development and Management*.

PREFACE TO THE FIRST EDITION

Writing a book on collection development and management offers two challenges —what to include and what to exclude, not unlike the practice of collection development and management itself. Entire books can be and have been written on the topics addressed in each chapter in this book. Within the limitations of a single book, my goal is to introduce the theory and practice of collection development and management and to present each of the responsibilities that fall within it. In addition, chapters contain a brief history of how these responsibilities and topics have evolved along with the major influencing factors.

Collection development and management are the meat and potatoes of libraries. If you don't have a collection, you don't have a library. In the earliest libraries, people concentrated on building collections and locating materials to add, though the need for preservation has been with us for the duration of libraries. Medieval monks often spent their entire lives copying manuscripts to preserve them—and creating questions about the mutability of content similar to those that trouble us today.

By the late 1970s, the idea of collection development and management as a professional specialization and as more than "selection" (if ever it was just that) was gaining acceptance. Over the last thirty years, collection development and management have come to encompass a suite of responsibilities. This book aims to address this breadth of responsibilities. Chapter 1 presents an introduction to and an overview of collection management and development. Chapter 2 addresses the organization and assignment of collection development and management responsibilities within libraries. Chapter 3 looks at planning activities, including policies and budgeting. Chapter 4, "Developing Collections," introduces various topologies for defining types of materials and explores the selection process and selection criteria, sources for identifying titles and acquisition options, and selection challenges.

"Managing Collections," chapter 5, examines the responsibilities that come into play after an item is added to a collection: decisions about weeding, storage, preservation and conservation, serials cancellation, and protecting materials from theft and damage. The very important responsibilities of reaching out to and understanding a library's user community are the topic of chapter

6. Electronic resources are addressed in every chapter; however, their special nature and the unique challenges as well as opportunities they present are considered in chapter 7. Chapter 8 considers library cooperation and its increasing importance to those with collection development and management responsibilities. The final chapter covers collection evaluation (Is it a "good" collection?) and assessment (Does it serve the community for which it is intended?). Two appendixes provide suggested selection aids and a library-centered glossary of terms used in this book.

The work of collection development and management is being profoundly changed by the Internet and increasing options for resources in digital format. Librarians select print materials that will be digitized, remote e-resources to which they will subscribe, e-books and CD-ROMs that they will purchase, and free web resources to which they will direct their library community. Decisions about e-resources cannot be separated from the decisions that librarians make on a daily basis—selecting, budgeting, planning, assessing and evaluating, canceling and withdrawing, and so on. To that end, I have aimed to integrate digital with more familiar, traditional formats in each chapter. Nevertheless, e-resources continue to present unique challenges, and a separate chapter addressing these remains necessary.

Collection development and management does not exist in a vacuum. It is done well only when its practitioners interact constantly with others within a library and with the collection's users and potential users. Librarianship, regardless of the specialty or range of responsibilities or the library in which it is practiced, cannot be separated from other areas of professional research and theory. To reiterate that point, I have sought to introduce the reader to relevant theories and resources outside the traditional literature of librarianship and information management. References are made to experts and their research in sociology, organizational behavior, communications, history of science and technology, and business and management. A list of suggested readings accompanies each chapter. For the most part, I have recommended more recent resources, electing not to provide literature reviews unless a landmark article or book provides a historical context for current discussion.

Each chapter, excluding the first one, concludes with a case study. The reader is presented with a fictional library situation that illustrates the topics covered in that chapter. Each case includes pertinent facts needed to analyze the issue and make recommendations or solve a problem. The reader should consult materials presented in the chapter's "Suggested Readings" for additional resources that will assist in responding to the problems presented in the case study. My intent is to ground theory and recommended practices in the reality of situations librarians encounter every day and to foster analysis either through group discussion or individual exploration. To this end, questions, outlined in an "Activity" section, accompany each case.

All URLs referenced in this book were valid as of late summer 2003. The URLs at the website of the American Library Association are continuing to change; therefore, I have provided directions (a sequence of steps) for locating sources within this website.

This book is intended for those with little experience in collection development and management—students preparing to enter the field of librarianship and experienced librarians with new or expanded responsibilities. I hope that the combination of history, theory, current thinking, and practical advice also will be of interest to seasoned selectors, who may value a work that aims to present a contemporary perspective on important issues.

ACKNOWLEDGMENTS

Many people provided advice as I prepared this revised edition and gave generously of their time and expertise. I thank especially Ginny Brodeen, Karen Folden, and Gail Mueller Schultz, who shared their perspective on the collection management and development activities of public libraries and school media centers. Many graduate school faculty members (too numerous to name here) who used the first edition with their classes provided thoughtful suggestions for improvement. Especially helpful were comments from Robert P. Holley, Sheila S. Intner, and Cindy Mediavilla. My deep appreciation goes to Karla Hahn and Bonnie MacEwan, who reviewed early drafts of chapters 4 and 9. This book would not have been possible without the support of my husband, Lee English, and my gratitude to him is boundless and eternal.

CHAPTER ONE

Introduction to Collection Management and Development

This chapter begins with an introduction to terms and concepts, followed by a capsule history of the practice of collection development, focusing on the United States. A brief look at the history of collection work and the libraries in which collections were developed is useful because contemporary practice builds on that of the past. Selectors work with library collections that have been created over time in accordance with past understandings and conventions. Topics introduced in this chapter are explored in more depth in subsequent chapters.

The first issue to be addressed in a book devoted to collection development and management is an understanding of what this phrase means. *Collection development* came into wide use in the late 1960s to replace *selection* as a more encompassing term reflecting the thoughtful process of developing a library collection in response to institutional priorities and community or user needs and interests. Collection development was understood to cover several activities related to the development of library collections, including selection, the determination and coordination of selection policy, assessment of the needs of users and potential users, collection use studies, collection analysis, budget management, identification of collection needs, community and user outreach and liaison, and planning for resource sharing. In the 1980s, the term *collection management* was proposed as an umbrella term under which collection development was to be subsumed. In this construct, collection management includes collection development and an expanded suite of decisions about weeding, canceling serials, storage, and preservation. Also of concern in collection management are the organization and assignment of responsibilities for its practice.

Collection management and *collection development* now often are used synonymously or in tandem, a practice followed in this book. For example, the professional organization within the American Library Association's (ALA) Association for Library Collections and Technical Services that focuses on this topic is called the Collection Management and Development Section. The Reference and User Services Association's section is called the Collection Development and Evaluation Section, more commonly referred to as CODES. The tasks, functions, and responsibilities now understood to be the portfolio of collection development librarians include selection of materials in all formats, collection policies, collection maintenance (selection for weeding and storage, preservation, and serials cancellation), budget and finance, assessment of needs of users and potential users, liaison and outreach activities related to the collection and its users, collection assessment and evaluation, and planning for cooperation and resource sharing.

A literature sampling provides a clearer understanding of how collection development and management are understood by practitioners:

> Simply put, collection management is the systemic, efficient and economic stewardship of library resources.[1]

> The goal of any collection development organization must be to provide the library with a collection that meets the appropriate needs of its client population within the limits of its fiscal and personnel resources. To reach this goal, each segment of the collection must be developed with an application of resources consistent with its relative importance to the mission of the library and the needs of its patrons.[2]

> Collection management is defined as a process of information gathering, communication, coordination, policy formulation, evaluation, and planning. These processes, in turn, influence decisions about the acquisition, retention, and provision of access to information sources in support of the intellectual needs of a given library community. Collection development is the part of collection management that primarily deals with decisions about the acquisition of materials.[3]

> Collection development is a term representing the process of systematically building library collections to serve study, teaching, research, recreational, and other needs of library users. The process includes selection and deselection of current and retrospective materials, planning of coherent strategies for continuing acquisition, and evaluation of collections to ascertain how well they serve user needs.[4]

Those who practice collection management are called variously selectors, bibliographers, collections librarians, subject specialists, subject liaisons, collection development librarians, collection managers, and collection developers. Additional titles for those who build and manage collections also are used. This book uses these terms interchangeably to mean a library staff member who is responsible for developing, managing, and teaching about collections. In many libraries, collections responsibilities are part of a suite of responsibilities for which the librarian is responsible. The responsibilities that constitute collection management include one or more of the following: selecting materials for acquisition and access, weeding, storage, and preservation; writing and revising collection development policies; promoting, marketing, and interpreting collections and resources; evaluating and assessing collections and related services; community liaison and outreach responsibilities; managing budgets; liaison with other libraries and cooperative collection development; and soliciting funds to supplement the money allocated to collection development and management. Although their assignment and importance vary from library to library, these elements are universal in the practice of collection management. For that reason, this book does not contain separate chapters for various types of libraries.

All these responsibilities imply a knowledge of the library's user community and its fiscal and personnel resources, mission, values, and priorities along with those of the library's parent organization. Collection management cannot be successful unless it is integrated within all library operations and the responsible librarian has an understanding of and close relationship with other library operations and services. Important considerations for the collection management librarian include who has access to the collection on-site and online, circulation policies, types of interfaces the library supports, quality of bibliographic records and the priority given to their creation, and the extent to which the local catalog or access portal reflects access to online resources. A constant theme throughout this book is the importance of the environment, both internal and external, to the library, within which the collection management librarian practices his or her craft.

Historical Overview

Selection of materials for libraries has been around as long as libraries have, though records of how decisions were made in the ancient libraries of Nineveh, Alexandria, and Pergamum are not available. One can assume that the scarcity of written materials and their value as unique records made comprehensiveness, completeness, and preservation guiding principles. In the 800s, Al-Mamun, caliph of Baghdad, collected as many classical works from the Byzantine Empire as he could, had them translated into Arabic, and kept them in the House of Wisdom.[5] Libraries served primarily as storehouses rather than as instruments for the dissemination of knowledge or a source for recreational reading. Comprehensiveness, completeness, and preservation have continued as library goals through the growth of commerce, the Renaissance, invention of movable type, expanding lay literacy, the Enlightenment, the public library movement, and the proliferation of electronic resources. Size continues today to be a common, though only one, measure of a library's greatness.

Systematic philosophies of selection were rare until the end of the nineteenth century, though a few early librarians gave written attention to selection. Gabriel Naudé, hired by Cardinal Mazarin to manage his personal library in the early 1600s, addressed selection in the first modern treatise on the management of libraries. He stated, "It may be laid down as a maxim that there is no book whatsoever, be it never so bad or disparaged, but may in time be sought for by someone."[6] Completeness as a goal has been balanced by a desire to select the best and most appropriate materials. In 1780, Jean-Baptiste Cotton des Houssays stated that libraries should consist only of books "of genuine merit and of well-approved utility," with new additions guided by "enlightened economy."[7] Appropriate criteria for selection have been a continuing debate among librarians and library users for centuries.

Collection Building in the United States

Libraries developed first in the American colonies as private collections and then within institutions of higher education. These early libraries were small for three reasons: relatively few materials were published in the New World, funds were limited, and acquiring materials was difficult. Even as late as 1850, only six hundred periodicals were being published in the United States, up from twenty-six in 1810.[8] Monographic publishing was equally sparse, with most works being religious in nature.

ACADEMIC LIBRARIES

Academic libraries seldom had continuing budget allocations in their first centuries and, therefore, selection was not a major concern. Most support for academic libraries' collections came from gifts of books or donations to purchase them. Less than a tenth of the holdings of colonial American college libraries were added through direct purchase.[9] Most gifts were gladly accepted. Any institutional funds came from the occasional actions of the trustees or boards of regents rather than from recurring allocations. Student library fees were charged at several institutions, on either a per-annum or a per-use basis.[10] Even by 1856, when John Langdon Sibley became librarian of Harvard, the total fund for library acquisitions and binding was only $250 per year.[11] In purchasing power, this is equals approximately $6,100 in today's dollars (using the Consumer Price Index as the indicator). In comparison, Harvard spent $27,569,823 on acquisitions and access in fiscal year 2006.[12] Even with funds in hand, acquiring materials was challenging. Everything had to be purchased on buying trips to book dealers in large East Coast cities and in Europe.

Collections grew slowly. By 1790, Harvard's library had reached only 12,000 volumes. It had averaged eighty-two new volumes per year in the preceding 135 years. The College of William and Mary's library collection numbered only 3,000, and it was the second largest in the country. The academic libraries added, on the average, only thirty to one hundred volumes per year before 1800. Most additions, because they were donations, were irrelevant to the educational programs of the time.[13] By 1850, only one U.S. academic institution had a collection larger than 50,000 volumes: Harvard College collections had reached 72,000 volumes.[14] At the middle of the century, total holdings for the approximately seven hundred colleges, professional schools, and public libraries in the United States totaled only 2.2 million.[15]

College libraries reflected American education's priorities of the time: teaching rather than study, students rather than scholars, and maintaining order and discipline rather than promoting learning and research. Reflective thinking and theoretical considerations were unusual in any college discipline before the American Civil War. As a consequence, academic libraries had only limited significance in their institutions and still functioned as storehouses.

After the Civil War, academic libraries and their parent institutions began a period of significant change. Libraries gained greater prominence as universities grew. The period 1850–1900 witnessed a fundamental change in the structure of American scholarship, influenced by ideas and methods imported from German universities, which had become centers for advanced scholarship. The move to lectures and seminars as replacements for textbooks, memorization, and recitation and the increasing importance of research had far-reaching consequences for libraries. Passage of the Morrill Act in 1862, which created the land-grant colleges, introduced the concept that these institutions were obligated to produce and share knowledge that would advance society. A direct result was a tremendous increase in scholarly journals and monographs. The needs and working habits of the professionalized and institution-centered scholars were quite different from those of their predecessors. Scholars' attitudes toward the academic library experienced a basic reorientation. The institutional academic library became a necessity. The scholarly profession was no longer confined to those who had the private wealth to collect extensive personal collections. A mounting flood of publications meant that even those few scholars with private means could not individually keep up with and manage all the new information available. They needed the institutional library to consult and to have access to all the materials necessary for research. As the library became increasingly important to higher education, the process of creating collections gained a higher profile.

Well into the 1900s, most selection in academic libraries was handled by faculty members. When Asa Gray was hired as an instructor at the University of Michigan in 1838, he went first to Europe to acquire books for the library. The president at Ohio Wesleyan traveled to New York and Europe in 1854 to purchase library books.[16] German university libraries were unique in placing selection as the direct responsibility of librarians and staff, with less faculty input. A primary advocate of the role of librarians in the development of library collections was Christian Gottlob Heyne, the librarian at the University of Göttingen in Germany from 1763 to 1812.[17] In 1930, faculty members in the United States still were selecting as much as 80 percent of total university library acquisitions, and librarians were choosing 20 percent.[18] This ratio began to shift in the 1960s at universities and had reversed by the late 1970s; faculty continue to have an important selection role in many smaller institutions, often collaborating with librarians, who may have responsibility for some types of materials and portions of the collection. The change can be linked to an increasing professionalism among librarians, the burgeoning volume of publications, a growing number of librarians with extensive subject training, and the expanding pressure on faculty of other responsibilities, including research and publication. As the responsibility for building library collections shifted from faculty to librarians—or to a shared responsibility—selection emphasis changed from selecting materials primarily to meet the needs and interests of specific faculty members to building a unified collection to meet both current and future institutional priorities.

PUBLIC LIBRARIES

Academic libraries preceded public libraries in the United States. Established in 1833, the Peterborough Town Library in New Hampshire is usually identified as the first free, publicly owned and maintained library in the United States.[19] A library established in Franklin, Massachusetts, through funds from Benjamin Franklin to purchase 116 volumes, was opened to all inhabitants of the town in 1790.[20] Though public, it was not supported by public funding. Social libraries, limited to a specific clientele and supported by subscriptions, had existed in the colonies for more than a century. One of the better known is the Philadelphia Library Company, founded by Benjamin Franklin in 1731 and supported by fifty subscribers to share the cost of importing books and journals from England. Less known are the literary society libraries formed by free African Americans in the northeast United States between 1828 and 1860. One of the earliest, the Colored Reading Society of Philadelphia, founded in 1828, directed that all income from initiation fees and monthly dues (excluding that devoted to rent and light) be spent on books.[21] The Phoenix Society of New York, established in 1933, aimed to "establish circulating libraries in each ward for the use of people of colour on very modest pay—to establish mental feasts."[22]

Other social libraries were established and supported by philanthropists and larger manufacturers to teach morality, provide a more wholesome environment, and offer self-education opportunities to the poor and uneducated drawn to cities. Circulating libraries were commercial ventures that loaned more popular materials, frequently novels, for a fee. When considered together, these early libraries were furnishing the collections that libraries provide today—materials that are used for information, education, and recreation.

Boston was the first major community to establish a public library, in 1852. The trustees defined the purpose of the public library as education and, though they had no plans to acquire novels, they were willing to include the more popular respectable books. In their first report, the trustees wrote, "We consider that a large public library is of the utmost importance as the means of completing our system of public education."[23] The responsibility of libraries to educate their users and to bring them to the better books and journals has been a theme guiding selection in public libraries since their establishment, and the definition of appropriate materials has been the source of constant debate.

Trustees or committees appointed by trustees selected materials in early public libraries. By the end of the 1800s and as librarianship evolved as a profession, John Cotton Dana was advising that book selection be left to the librarians, directed by the trustees or a book committee.[24] The present practice of assigning collections responsibility to librarians is the result of a slow transformation. In the United States, public librarians generally acquired selection responsibilities before those in academic libraries. The shift happened in public libraries earlier because college and university faculties retained a more active interest in library collections than did the members of public library boards or trustees. The rise of library schools and the professionalization of librarianship led librarians to expect expanded responsibilities for selection and made trustees and, ultimately, faculty members more willing to transfer them to librarians.

After the Second World War, increased funding for both education and public libraries at the national, state, and local levels led to a period of unparalleled expansion in all types of library collections. The seemingly endless possibilities for growth broadened the librarian's collection responsibilities. Moving beyond individual book evaluation and selection, librarians began to view building coherent collections as an important responsibility. Soon they were seeking and acquiring materials from all over the world, and the scope of collections expanded to include Asia, Africa, the Middle East, and Eastern Europe as well as Western Europe.[25]

Collections theory began to focus on who should be selecting materials for the library, how selection decisions were made and the appropriate criteria, and alternatives to individual title selection for building collections. The emphasis during this period was on growth and how to handle it effectively. In 1944, Fremont Rider made his famous statement that research library collections were doubling every sixteen years.[26] In 1953, Kenneth J. Brough wrote that the mission of Harvard's library was the "collection and preservation of everything printed."[27] During the 1950s, vendors and jobbers began offering services that freed librarians from ordering directly from the publisher. Many of these service agencies began supplying materials through approval and blanket plans, freeing selectors to concentrate on identifying and obtaining more esoteric resources.

Funding for public libraries began to hold steady or to decline in the late 1970s. Pressures to contain taxes at all levels of government reduced the flow of funds to libraries as municipalities began to make difficult choices about how to allocate limited resources. Libraries, in turn, faced choices about their priorities and where scarce funds should be directed—to hours of operation, staffing, services, or collections. Many public libraries closed branches and reduced the purchases of duplicate copies of popular titles. Book vendors began to offer rental collections that provided a rotating collection of popular titles, often with multiple copies, to help libraries manage limited collections budgets. The average total per-capita operating revenue in the United States for public libraries was $31.65 in fiscal year 2005, ranging from $13.50 (Mississippi) to $56.65 (District of Columbia).[28] These funds had to cover all expenses, not just collections. Financial stringency felt doubly painful as libraries sought to expand their collection through the addition of more media (CDs, VHS tapes, DVDs) and access to online electronic resources.

SCHOOL LIBRARIES

Dorothy McGinnis traces the origins of school libraries and the idea that these centers should provide a variety of media to 1578, when an ordinance was passed in Shrewsbury, England, according to which schools should include "a library and gallerie . . . furnished with all manner of books, mappes, spheres, instruments of astronomye and all other things apperteyninge to learning which may be either given to the school or procured with school money."[29] School libraries were present in the early private schools in New England in the late eighteenth century.[30] Their collections primarily comprised reference books and were supported by donations. Public school libraries in the United States were first proposed in legislation recommended to the state legislature by New York governor DeWitt Clinton in 1827, with funds finally appropriated in 1839.[31] By 1876, twenty-one states had passed legislation to support public school libraries.[32] Books were selected by school board members, superintendents, trustees, and occasionally those directly responsible for the school libraries. The debate over appropriate materials seen in public libraries continued in school libraries. School superintendents were complaining about the presence of novels in New York school libraries in 1843.[33] The emphasis was on acquiring materials that would further students' education and excluding "pernicious publications."[34]

The roles and responsibilities of school librarians began to be formalized with the establishment in 1896 of the School Library Section within the National Education Association. Mary Kingsbury was appointed librarian at the Erasmus Hall High School, Brooklyn, in 1900, and has been identified as the first library school graduate appointed to a high school library position as well as the first professionally trained librarian to be employed full time in a school.[35] In 1914, the ALA Council approved a petition from the ALA Roundtable of Normal and High School Librarians to form the School Libraries Section, which held its first meeting at the June 1915 ALA annual conference. In 1951, this section became the American Association of School Librarians (AASL), a separate division in ALA. Despite this recognition within the profession of school librarianship as a specialty, most materials were added to libraries into the 1950s through lists prepared by state education boards.

The first standards for school libraries were published in 1918 and were endorsed and republished by the ALA in 1920 as *Standard Library Organization and Equipment for Secondary Schools of Different Sizes*. This document directed school librarians to select books on the basis of what was needed for classrooms, students' recreational and cultural needs, and curricular needs and recommendations by teachers—but all selection was subject to the approval of the school principal. This first standard stated that "freedom of access to the library must imply, not only freedom to consult books for reference and for supplementary collateral study, but also freedom to read books for recreation and pleasure."[36] *Elementary School Library Standards* followed in 1925, and in 1954, the ALA published *School Libraries for Today and Tomorrow*, the first quantitative and qualitative standards for K–12.[37]

In the early 1940s, only 18 percent of public schools nationwide reported having a centralized library.[38] By 1953, 36 percent of all public schools had library media centers; library media centers were more common in secondary public schools, with 95 percent having them, whereas only 24 percent of public elementary schools had them.[39] Early standards supported the creation of a separate library media facility within schools, but elementary school libraries did not exist in most states until the 1958 National Defense Education Act (NDEA) and the 1965 Elementary and Secondary Education Act (ESEA).[40] Initially, libraries were not specifically mentioned in NDEA, which was enacted in response to the Soviet Union's launch of Sputnik in 1957. Books and materials (especially in sciences, foreign languages, and mathematics) could be purchased with NDEA funds, but often these were not placed in libraries. Some school administrators did not see libraries as having a primary instructional role, and selection of materials often was not handled effectively.

Program guidelines were issued and changes were made to NDEA which, over time, strengthened the role of libraries and librarians, including the latter's responsibilities for selecting materials. ESEA Title II provided $100 million in direct federal assistance for the acquisition of school library resources and other instructional materials. As a result of ESEA Title II, school library media staff were expected to provide leadership in selecting, acquiring, organizing, and using instructional materials.[41] ESEA had a profound affect on the establishment of school media centers. During the years 1965–68, 12 percent of all public schools established a school library, and approximately 193,600 library expansion projects were funded during the same period.[42]

ESEA was reauthorized at five-year intervals until 1981, when ESEA Title IV was consolidated with other educational programs in the Education Consolidation and Improvement Act to create one funding block program, the Chapter 2 block grant. The resulting block grants were distributed to states, which allocated funds to school districts that determined their own priorities. The result has been a decrease in grant funds specifically targeted at school libraries.

The most common use of Chapter 2 funds was for computer applications. By 1984/85, only 29 percent of the local block grant funds were being used for library and media center support.[43] The consistent growth in library media center collections seen over the previous twenty years had come to an end.

The No Child Left Behind Act of 2001 was intended to address a portion of the lost funding by providing grants to local schools districts in which at least 20 percent of the students were from families with incomes below the poverty line. In the first year of the program (fiscal year 2002), $12.5 million was available for grants, and ninety-four grants were awarded.[44] This amount seems modest compared to the $100 million made available annually in the early days of ESEA II.

The second half of the twentieth century saw a change in the nature of school library collections as well as their size. School libraries were beginning to include alternative media in the 1960s. In 1960, AASL updated the outdated 1945 *School Libraries for Today and Tomorrow*.[45] The new 1960 *Standards for School Library Programs* included audiovisual materials but provided no recommended quantitative measures.[46] The 1960 quantitative standard for print materials was a minimum of six to ten thousand books for schools with 200–999 students and ten books per student for school with 1,000 or more students. The 1969 revision, developed in cooperation with the National Education Association Department of Audiovisual Instruction, was titled *Standards for School Media Programs*.[47] The name change signaled a shift from the terms *school libraries* and *school library programs* to *school media centers* (or *school library media centers*) and *school media programs* (or *school library media programs*) and stressed the importance of providing a variety of formats to support instruction and learning. The quantitative standard changed to a minimum of six to ten thousand book titles or twenty volumes per student for schools with 250 or more students. For the first time, modest quantitative standards for audiovisual materials were present.

The next revision, *Media Programs: District and School*, appeared in 1975.[48] This document focused on qualitative goals but continued to include quantitative measures. The minimum collection for schools with 500 or fewer students was twenty thousand items, or forty items per student. Items were defined as books, serial subscriptions, audiovisual materials, or associated equipment. Schools with more than 500 students could have fewer than forty items per student.

Information Power: Guidelines for School Library Media Programs, published in 1988, continued the movement toward qualitative measures, with quantitative data provided in an appendix.[49] These guidelines were revised in 1998 with the *Planning Guide for Information Power: Building Partnerships for Learning*, which dropped the quantitative data completely and shifted the focus to information literacy.[50] Although size of collections is not the only measure of a school library media center's value, recent data suggest that the loss of federal funds has had a profound effect. In fiscal year 2004, only 65 percent of schools had a full-time certified library media specialist, and the average holding per 100 students was

1,891 items—slightly less than twenty items per students.[51] The encouraging news was that 95.1 percent of school library media centers had connections to the Internet, although the number of computer stations averaged only 2.3 per 100 students.

Marilyn L. Shontz and Lesley S. J. Farmer report that local school library media center budgets remained steady during the period 2002–5.[52] Book expenditures kept pace with rising prices, but spending for audiovisual materials, computer software, CD-ROMs, and web-based subscriptions remained unchanged. Most funding came from local sources, but one quarter of those responding to the survey reported receiving federal funds through grants.

Fiscal Stringency

By the 1970s, library budgets in all types of libraries began to hold steady or to shrink. Libraries were unable to keep pace with rapidly increasing costs and growing numbers of publications. Librarians began to look for guidance in how they could make responsible decisions with less money. The goal of comprehensive, autonomous, self-sufficient collections became less realistic. Interest grew in developing guidelines for downsizing serials collections and mechanisms for increasing library cooperation. Collection development policy statements became more common as libraries sought guidance in managing limited financial resources amid conflicting demands. The Research Libraries Group was founded in 1974 as a "partnership to achieve a planned, coordinated interdependence in response to the threat posed by a climate of economic retreat and financial uncertainty."[53] OCLC Online Computer Library Center, established in 1967 for academic libraries in Ohio, opened its membership to all types of libraries regardless of location and facilitated the sharing of resources as well as bibliographic records.

Financial stringency has had a profound impact on the growth of library collections. Between 1986 and 2001, the Association of Research Libraries (ARL) documented a 5 percent decline in serials purchased and a 9 percent decline in monographs purchased by its member libraries. During that same period, serial unit costs increased 215 percent while expenditures increased 210 percent, and monograph unit costs increased 68 percent and expenditures for monographs increased 66 percent.[54] During the twenty years from 1986 through 2006, serials expenditures (for both print and electronic) increased by 321 percent and monograph expenditures increased by 82 percent. These large academic libraries are now investing a major portion of their budgets in serials, including electronic resources, and a lesser portion in monographs.

Interlibrary lending became essential in response to libraries' inability to meet users' needs locally. Librarians began to debate ownership versus access via interlibrary loan and document delivery. The older idea of building comprehensive collections "just in case" a particular item might be needed lost favor. Some librarians suggested that a more responsible use of budgets might be supplying materials to meet users' needs "just in time." In 1988, Maurice B. Line wrote:

> Before World War 2, interlending was regarded as an optional extra, a grace and favour activity, to be indulged in sparingly; any research library considered it an admission of failure to have to obtain any item from elsewhere. Now every library, however large, accepts that it cannot be self-sufficient, and some of the largest obtain the most from elsewhere.[55]

Several pressures, both external and internal, buffeted libraries in the final twenty-five years of the twentieth century. Rapid changes in user community expectations and the makeup of those communities, the publishing industry, telecommunication technology, copyright law, and scholarly communication are among the most significant. Collections librarians in all types of libraries are now seeking to cope with scarce financial resources, preservation and conservation needs, cooperation in collection building and resource sharing, serials cancellation projects, and weeding and storage decisions. Financial austerity, which has characterized libraries for more than two decades, coupled with the need to readjust priorities continually is a primary reason the term *collection management* has become more meaningful to the profession.

Another challenge for libraries emerged in the late 1980s—digital information. Some academic libraries had been acquiring data files on magnetic tapes and punched cards for several years, but widespread adoption of microcomputers presented libraries of all types with a variety of information resources on floppy disks, followed soon by CD-ROMs. The growth of the Internet and ubiquitous access added online resources to the choices to be considered. Librarians selecting electronic resources faced new decisions about licenses, software, technical support, operating systems, interfaces, and hardware. User expectations about ease of access and ubiquity have continued to increase. Purchasing the rights to access online electronic resources has meant that collection management librarians have had to master the language of contracts and license agreements. Much of the literature in the early twenty-first century has focused on the challenges libraries face operating in both print and electronic environments simultaneously.

Nevertheless, this is an exciting time to work in libraries, especially for those charged with developing and managing their collections. Users continue to visit libraries in person and online to meet their information and recreational needs. Drawing on data collected in five surveys of 1,000–1,600 individuals each, an IMLS study, completed in 2008, examined how adults in the United States search for information in the online age and how this affects the ways they interact with public libraries and museums, both online and in person.[56] The research team, led by José-Marie Griffiths and Donald W. King, found that libraries and museums are the most trusted sources of online information among adults of all ages, education levels, races, and ethnicities. Libraries and museums rank higher in trustworthiness than all other information sources including government, commercial, and private websites. The explosive growth of information available online appears to stimulate Americans' appetite for more information. Further, Griffiths and King found that the Internet is not replacing in-person visits to libraries and museums and may increase on-site use of libraries and museums. The *InterConnections* report provides evidence that public libraries and museums are thriving in the Internet Age as trusted providers of information to people of all ages.

Theories of Selection

The origins of collection management and development can be traced to theories of selection. The first American guide to selection was prepared by Thaddeus M. Harris, Harvard librarian, in 1793. In his introduction to a catalog of books suggested for a "small and cheap" library to serve common readers at a distance in the country, he wrote that "books have become so exceedingly numerous . . . that the greatest caution is necessary in selecting those of established reputation from the many that are indifferent or useless."[57] Until the 1960s, most theories of selection promoted in the United States focused on choosing materials for public libraries. Libraries of all types have experienced a continuing tension between demand and value, and much of the literature on selection has focused on this tension between what people want and what librarians believe is good for them. This has been particularly true in public libraries, which have seen the education of citizens as a primary goal. Part of the demand-value controversy has been the question of what to do about fiction. The public's preference for novels was troubling to early library leaders, in part because of the long-term effects of Puritan condemnation of fiction reading. Writing to the *Library Journal* in 1899, Lucious Page Lane (New York State Library School, class of 1899) quoted a school principal who stated that "the voracious devouring of fiction commonly indulged in by patrons of the public library, especially the young, is extremely pernicious and mentally unwholesome."[58] Many early librarians took a paternalistic, even elitist position about selection and collection building.

Librarians as Arbiters of Quality

Such early legends in American librarianship as Melvil Dewey, John C. Dana, Herbert Putnam, and Ainsworth Spofford insisted that libraries' primary role as educators implied that their responsibility was to provide only the highest-quality materials—with *quality* defined, of course, by librarians.

Many librarians were proud of their role as censors, by which they meant arbiters of quality. Arthur E. Bostwick explained the positive role of public librarians as censors in his 1908 ALA presidential address. He stated that they had a responsibility to censor anything that was not Good, True, and Beautiful.[59] In contrast, other leading librarians of the time, including William F. Poole, Justin Winsor, and Charles Cutter, supported the selection and provision of more popular materials.

One of the most powerful early statements in support of popular reading materials in public libraries was written by Poole, first head of the Chicago Public Library. He voiced the still widely held view that reading less sophisticated materials leads readers to more cultivated works. In 1876, Poole wrote:

> To meet, therefore, the varied wants of readers there must be on the shelves of the library books which persons of culture never read, although it is quite probable they did read such books in some stage of their mental development. Judged from a critical standpoint, such books are feeble, rudimentary, and perhaps sensational; but they are higher in the scale of literary merit than the tastes of the people who seek them; and, like primers and first-readers in the public schools, they fortunately lead to something better.[60]

Not all librarians were confident they could select the Good, True, and Beautiful or identify the primers that would lead readers to a higher level. As the profession of librarianship developed, librarians turned to their professional associations and librarian authorities for guidance in selecting individual titles. Several reviewing tools appeared in the early 1900s to help librarians select the best books, including *ALA Booklist* (1905), *Book Review Digest* (1906), and *Fiction Catalog* (1908). The first edition of *Guide to the Study and Use of Reference Books* (now *Guide to Reference*) was published in 1902 by the ALA.

Despite the theoretical debate among library leaders over value versus demand, the volume of fiction in American public libraries continued to increase. By 1876, practically all American public libraries offered at least some fictional materials, though it was often of the "better" kind. During the First World War, the opponents of fiction in U.S. public libraries felt that the serious mood of the country provided a logical argument against the frivolity of popular fiction. Cornelia Marvin, state librarian of Oregon, suggested a new librarian's slogan: "No new fiction during the war."[61] All the same, many librarians selected materials for military camp libraries and were not hesitant about choosing fiction to entertain and distract the troops.[62]

After the First World War, the controversy about the role of fiction in public libraries continued. Many wanted libraries to be as attractive as possible to returning soldiers. Nevertheless, with the declining economy of the Great Depression resulting in reduced library funding, fiction continued as a point of contention among librarians. Some library leaders felt that the 1930s was a time for libraries to focus on educational reading. Carl B. Roden of the Chicago Public Library asked, "Who among us would not rather supply the books and competent guidance for ten self-students than the latest novels for a thousand fiction readers?"[63] Others felt that libraries had an obligation to provide fiction as part of their public mission. The debate over suitable library materials is documented in Esther Jane Carrier's two volumes on fiction in U.S. public libraries, which gives a detailed picture of the arguments for and against fiction and its rise as part of collections.[64]

Evolution of Selection Theory

The first comprehensive American works on book selection were textbooks written by Francis K. W. Drury (1930) and Helen Haines (1935). These early works are reflections of their times—with statements such as Haines's "Consider what books mean in individual development: in the formation of character, in the activation of intelligence, in the enrichment of resources, and in the deepening of sensitivity"—and a testament to the continuity of guiding principles in collection management.[65] Drury's goals have relevance today, with a few exceptions that seem amusingly dated. For him, the purposes of a course in book selection and, by implication, the goals of selectors were

- to analyze the nature of a community;
- to recognize the various uses to which books of varied types are to be put;
- to consider the character and policy of a library in adding books;
- to cultivate the power of judging and selecting books for purchase, with their value and
- suitability to readers in mind;
- to become familiar with the sources of information;
- to renew acquaintance with books and writers from the library angle;
- to develop the ability to review, criticize, and annotate books for library purposes;
- to decide where in the library organization book selection fits;
- to learn how to perform the necessary fundamental tasks of book selection; and
- to scrutinize the mental and personal fitness of the selector.[66]

According to Drury, "A qualified selector, acquainted with the demand from his community and knowing the book and money resource of his library, chooses the variety of books he believes will be used, applying his expert knowledge."[67]

The continuing tension between demand and value was a recurring theme in the professional literature on selection. A vigorous proponent of value was Leon Carnovsky, who framed his position by saying that public libraries should provide materials that were true.[68] Before the Second World War, he offered a scholarly position that supported internal censorship. He held a strong conviction that the public library should be a force for truth on vital issues. He advocated censorship of local prejudice and opinion and said the library is "acting democratically when it sets up the authority of reason as the censor."[69] The political implications of the Second World War, combined with a loss of confidence in librarians' knowledge and ability to choose what is true and what is not, caused Carnovsky to moderate his position in the 1950s and 1960s.

The debate over popular materials in public libraries continued. The Public Library Inquiry of the late 1940s once again raised serious questions about the place of light fiction. Funded by the Carnegie Corporation and conducted by the Social Science Research Council, the inquiry focused on describing libraries and their services, collections, and users. Bernard Berelson wrote the summary volume, in which he held to an elitist view of public libraries, recommending that the library's purpose is to be "serious" and its proper role to serve the culturally alert community members rather than to try to reach all people.[70]

Other librarians responded that a public library's duty was to supply its users with the books of most interest to them. They believed that democratic principles should operate in libraries as well as in society. These librarians were increasingly conscious of the importance of the freedom to read and the right of each reader to find what he or she liked best. In 1939, the ALA adopted the first Library Bill of Rights to provide an official statement against censorship and to oppose pressures on the freedom of citizens to read what they wished. Lester Asheim, in his 1953 paper "Not Censorship but Selection," stressed the concept of selection as choosing good books instead of excluding bad ones.[71]

Librarians in the second half of the twentieth century began promoting the ideal that subjects should be covered evenly or equally within collections. Balanced coverage has meant seeking to select materials that represent all viewpoints on important and controversial issues. Librarians have become increasingly aware of their responsibilities to be attentive to both content and format in selection of library materials.

Collection Development and Management as a Specialization

As selection of materials shifted to librarians, the responsibility often fell to acquisitions librarians. The early acquisitions librarians found their professional home in the ALA Board of Acquisition of Library Materials, created in 1951. The ALA Resources and Technical Services Division (RTSD) was created in 1957, and the Board of Acquisition of Library Materials became the Acquisitions Section within RTSD.

A preconference held before the ALA annual conference in Detroit in 1977 is often identified as the landmark event in the recognition of collection development as a new specialization separate from acquisitions in librarianship. Conducted by the then new Collection Development Committee of the Resources Section of the ALA RTSD, the preconference and the section were created and organized by a group of forward-looking librarians including Juanita Doares, Sheila Dowd, Hendrik Edelman, Murray Martin, Paul H. Mosher, and David Zubatsky.

The volume of new publications was increasing rapidly, the publishing world was becoming more complex, and acquisitions budgets had slowed libraries' expansion. Part-time faculty selectors and librarians without special expertise could no longer manage selection adequately. The planners of the 1977 preconference, who were primarily academic librarians, saw a need to develop research collections in a more solid, conscious, planned, and documented manner. They called this new specialization *collection development* to distinguish it from acquisitions. The goal of the 1977 preconference was to educate the library profession about this new subdiscipline—its nature, components, and functions. The first *Guidelines for Collection Development*, published by the Collection Development Committee, followed soon after the preconference.[72] This 1979 publication has since been revised and published as several more focused numbers in the Collection Management and Development Guides series.

The first Collection Management and Development Institute, sponsored by RTSD's (now Association of Library Resources and Technical Services) Collection Development Committee, was held at Stanford University in 1981. Planners were increasingly aware that the management of collections—not just their development and growth—was the primary issue for the future of this new specialization. They focused on boundary-spanning aspects, including the integration of collection management with acquisitions and other internal library operations and services, and on working closely with interested constituents. They sought to define collection management in ways that had meaning to librarians in all types of libraries.

Many professional groups were focusing on collection development and management in the early 1980s. The Public Library Association sponsored a preconference in 1984.[73] The ARL established its Collection Development Committee, the Research Libraries Group initiated the Collection Management and Development Committee, and other divisions within ALA, including the Reference and Adult Services Division (now Reference and User Services Association), the Public Library Association, and the Association of College and Research Libraries formed committees that concentrated on collection development and management. Whereas collection development had always been closely associated with acquisitions, these two functions began to be separated in larger libraries, with acquisitions more typically associated with technical services units and collection development and management as separate or, perhaps, allied with public services.

In the late 1970s and 1980s, the profession took up collection management as a cause célèbre. Numerous textbooks, manuals, overviews, and journal articles were published. Specialized journals, including *Collection Management* (1976), *Collection Building* (1983), and *Library Collections, Acquisitions and Technical Services* (previously *Library Acquisitions: Practice and Theory;* 1977), began publication. Several textbooks on collection development, which was more broadly defined than acquisitions or selection, appeared in the 1970s. Research in the field was summarized in the important *Collection Development in Libraries: A Treatise.*[74] By the mid-1980s, most professional library schools were offering one or more courses that focused on collection development and management. Richard Kryzs identified the topics covered in a basic collection development course of the time; these included the historical background of books and libraries, types of libraries and their communities, library materials, publishers and publishing, selection of materials, acquisition of material, and collection evaluation, which covered storage, weeding, preservation, and replacement decisions.[75] By the mid-1980s, the position of collection development librarian was firmly established.[76]

Collection Development and Management since 1980

The 1980s were a challenging period for libraries of all types as librarians became increasingly concerned about the condition of collections built during the periods of prosperity. Libraries were running out of space and collections were deteriorating because of heavy use, poor environmental conditions, and highly acidic paper. Many large libraries established preservation departments with conservation laboratories to address the fragile materials, with collection development librarians playing a role in selecting materials for treatment. The National Endowment for the Humanities funded numerous cooperative microfilming projects that aimed to preserve the contents of thousands of brittle books. *Slow Fires* introduced librarians and the nation to the fragility of acidic collections.[77]

The right to read, censorship, and intellectual freedom became important concerns. The ALA initiated Banned Books Week in 1982 to highlight the challenges to books in school and public libraries. Librarians sought to raise awareness that materials on potentially controversial topics including politics, religious beliefs, sexuality, and social philosophies have a place in many libraries. The need to represent diverse communities, a pluralistic society, and world perspective in collections drew attention. The ALA Ethnic Materials Information Exchange Round Table (renamed the Ethnic and Multicultural Information Exchange Round Table in 1998) was created as a source of information on ethnic and multicultural collections, services, and programs.

Nonprint media (audio and video recordings, slides, films, photos, drawings, filmstrips, and realia) remained a hot topic in the 1980s but were overshadowed by the arrival of computer software, computer files, and CD-ROMs. The latter were still considered nontraditional formats, and librarians debated whether libraries should acquire them, whether the acquisitions budget (still often called the "book budget") should be used for them and for supporting hardware, and what the appropriate criteria were to evaluate them. Librarians had their first experiences with license agreements as publishers sought to protect their products. Collection development librarians began a continuing relationship with lawyers as they questioned what the licenses and contracts meant, how to revise them, and who could sign them.

The most traumatic issue before collections librarians at the end of the 1980s was the escalating cost of journals, often referred to as the "serials crisis." The ARL began tracking both serial and monograph unit costs, expenditures, and number of titles purchased against the consumer price index. Librarians in all types of libraries were preoccupied with journal pricing projections, journal cancellation projects, electronic publishing ventures that might affect pricing, and perceived unfair pricing practices. How best to allocate limited funds among different subject areas and formats and demonstrate financial accountability concerned collections librarians.

The consolidation of publishers and vendors has profoundly changed the marketplace in which collection development librarians make their decisions. Six groups (Reed Elsevier, Taylor and Francis Informa, Wolters Kluwer, Candover and Cinven, Wiley Blackwell, and Verlagsgruppe George von Holtzbrinck) now control more than forty major publishers, with Reed Elsevier controlling 24.6 percent of the market as of 2007.[78] With mergers have come price increases. When Elsevier Reed purchased Pergamon, Pergamon's journal prices increased 27 percent; when Kluwer purchased Lippincott, Lippincott's prices increased 30 percent.

The impact of automation on the nature and meaning of collections—and on the processes and decisions of managing collections—joined the challenge of coping with constantly increasing serial prices in the last decade of the twentieth century. When the 1980s began, many librarians still relied on labor-intensive manual searching in *Books in Print*, publishers' catalogs, and national bibliographies to identify titles to acquire. They typed five-part order forms on electric typewriters—or manual typewriters, if they were less fortunate. Within the decade, Tim Berners-Lee had proposed a global hypertext system (the Web) and initiated technological developments that now support communication with publishers and vendors—and information creators—around the world.[79] The rapid development of the Web provided access to and delivery of content, forever changing the nature of collections and the role of those who build and manage them.

The term *digital library* made its appearance and was defined as

> organizations that provide the resources, including the specialized staff, to select, structure, offer intellectual access to, interpret, distribute, preserve the

integrity of, and ensure the persistence over time of collections of digital works so that they are readily and economically available for use by a defined community or set of communities.[80]

Collection development librarians began to explore how technology—that is, expert systems, in-house web pages, automated collection analysis tools, and other vendor products (including online selection)—could support their activities. They continued to ponder criteria for selecting electronic resources and struggled with the question of how to move these materials (including those available on the Internet) into mainstream practices.

The number of electronic journals swelled. The first issue of the *Directory of Electronic Journals, Newsletters and Academic Discussion Lists* (1991) listed 110 journals and newsletters and 517 academic discussion lists, or e-conferences, and by 1997 the count had grown to more than 3,400 journal and newsletter entries and more than 3,800 e-conferences.[81] Most of the growth occurred in 1996 and 1997, when large commercial publishers such as Academic Press, Chapman-Hall, Elsevier, and Springer-Verlag began publishing e-journals. At the time, librarians had hopes that e-journals would provide an alternative to the high cost of serials facing libraries. The end of the 1990s introduced the "Big Deal," in which commercial publishers bundled packages of e-journals for a single price with the promise that cost increases would be controlled if libraries accepted the package, often with conditions prohibiting cancellations.

Licenses and contracts to acquire or access online electronic resources became a major issue for libraries and librarians who had little or no experiences in this area. Several organizations offered workshops to help librarians with licenses and contracts for e-resources. In 1996, Yale launched Liblicense (www.library.yale.edu/~llicense/), an educational website to assist librarians in negotiating licenses. This site continues to serve the librarian and publisher community, providing standard license terms and definitions, suggesting language to use and language to avoid, and presenting a model license among other tools and resources.

The 1990s introduced the debate over ownership versus access. Librarians pondered the shift from traditional ownership of print collections to an increasing reliance on online electronic formats. They worried about the consequences of canceling print with the electronic version now available and preferred by users. Leasing access provided no guarantee of perpetual access, unless negotiated in the license. Licenses for electronic content also often included restrictions on its use for interlibrary loan, hindering cooperative collection development. These and other troubling areas led librarians to consider which contractual clauses should be considered deal breakers.

The need to manage the reality of serials cancellations and to negotiate the best price for e-content revitalized interest in cooperative collection development. Library consortia took on new life, often negotiating agreements that provided several (if not all) consortium members a discounted subscription cost. The International Coalition of Library Consortia (ICOLC), intended to foster communication among consortia and with publishers and vendors, was organized in 1997. In 1998, ICOLC issued its "Statement of Current Perspective and Preferred Practices for the Selection and Purchase of Electronic Information."[82] ICOLC monitors new electronic information resources, electronic content provider and vendor pricing practices, and related issues of interest to consortium directors and governing boards. Negotiating costs and licenses became a new and continuing responsibility for collections librarians.

Other legal issues, in addition to contracts and licenses for e-content, captured the attention of collection development librarians in the last decade of the twentieth century. They learned about intellectual property and copyright law, digital rights management, open access to works, copyright exceptions for libraries and archives, orphan works, fair use and electronic reserves, and protecting children from harmful materials on the Internet. The Communications Decency Act (Title V of the Telecommunications Act of 1996) sought to regulate both obscene and indecent materials on the Internet but was ruled unconstitutional by the U.S. Supreme Court for violating the First Amendment. Eventually, the attempt to regulate obscenity was addressed in the Children's Internet Protection Act (CIPA), which became law in December 2000. CIPA requires schools and public libraries to use Internet filtering software on computers with Internet access to protect against access to visual depictions that are obscene, child pornographic, or harmful to minors. If a library receives federal E-rate funds (discounts to assist most schools and libraries to obtain affordable telecommunications and Internet access), this provision applies only to adults; if a library receives only LSTA (Library Services and Technology Act) grant funds, the provision applies to all patrons. Public librarians protested against CIPA, which they viewed as infringement on the right to read and a form of censorship. The ALA challenged the law as unconstitutional in 2001, but the Supreme Court upheld it in 2003.

The Digital Millennium Copyright Act (enacted into law in 1998) criminalizes production and dissemination of technology intended to circumvent measures taken to protect copyright, not merely infringement of copyright itself, and increases the penalties for copyright infringement on the Internet. It amended Title 17 of the U.S. Code to extend the reach of copyright while limiting the liability of online providers from copyright infringement by their users. The Copyright Term Extension Act of 1998—also known as the Sonny Bono Copyright Term Extension Act and as the Mickey Mouse Protection Act—extended copyright terms in the United States by twenty years. Before the act, copyright would last for the life of the author plus fifty years, or seventy-five years for a work of corporate authorship. The act extended these terms to life of the author plus seventy years and ninety-five years, respectively. The act also affected copyright terms for copyrighted works published prior to January 1, 1978, increasing their term of protection by twenty years. The library community expressed concerns that such protection of copyright holders disenfranchised libraries and their ability to retrospectively digitize materials for preservation and access while increasing protection and rights of authors and producers.

The 1990s introduced the idea of scholarly communication as an information food chain: academic libraries purchase the resources that researchers use, researchers write up their findings, which they give to journal publishers, who then publish the research in journals and sell them to libraries. Librarians began to question this system, which placed libraries at the low (and expensive) end of the food chain and potentially reduced the dissemination of scholarship. In 1997, the ARL started SPARC, the Scholarly Publishing and Academic Resources Coalition (www.arl.org/sparc/), an alliance of universities, research libraries, and professional organizations, as a constructive response to market dysfunctions in the scholarly communication system. Collections librarians in academic libraries joined to raise the consciousness of their faculties about their own roles and responsibilities in the creation and dissemination of knowledge.

As the 1990s drew to an end, the concept of "pure" bibliographers, subject specialists whose sole responsibility was collection development and management, began to fade as libraries of all types placed emphasis on outreach and liaison roles within the context of subject responsibilities. Conversely, many librarians (reference librarians and technical services librarians) who had not selected materials and managed collections were assigned these responsibilities.

Responsibilities for managing e-content (books, journals, indexes and abstracting sources, reference materials, media, archival materials, etc.) continued to expand in the twenty-first century. The number of e-journals was estimated to be between 25,000 and 50,000 in 2007, with libraries spending an average of 35 percent of their acquisitions budgets on electronic products and services.[83] The proliferation of e-resources is changing the nature of collection development. Research conducted in 2003 by Daniel G. Dorner verified that the levels of responsibility and time spent on activities related to digital resources had increased compared to five years previous.[84] Keeping track of these contracts and licenses, their renewal dates, terms and conditions, and access and copyright restrictions has become overwhelming for collection development librarians and serials staffs. Several libraries initially developed in-house, stand-alone tools, now called electronic resources management (ERM) systems, to manage licenses, but these required duplicate data entry and were seldom linked to existing automated library systems. Soon, commercial vendors began offering turnkey systems, often integrated with integrated library systems or subscription agent services.

The proliferation of e-journals led to the development of link resolvers, which provide context-sensitive links between indexing databases and the electronic full text in both aggregated databases and online publisher sites.

This technology links catalog users directly to the e-resource from within the catalog with a single click. Many link resolvers come packaged as a suite of services that include searchable A–Z e-journal lists, e-journal title collection tools, and MARC record services. The combination of these tools allows librarians to manage access to their full-text resources centrally and can help them make electronic full-text collection decisions.

Link resolvers are part of the emphasis on bringing together through a single interface, portal, or federated search mechanism the ability to locate, identify, and access all the resources selected by librarians. The goal is to aggregate content or information about content for local library users. Selecting this content and these sources is often the responsibility of collection development librarians, who continue to select resources appropriate to a particular user community. Enterprise-level solutions such as Primo (from ExLibris) and Endeca aim to facilitate discovery and delivery of institutional resources and materials from different types of collections (digital and print, local and online) through one user interface. They can provide librarians with the ability to select repositories and websites to be harvested or crawled while normalizing and enriching data harvested from various applications. By combining targeted web crawling and collocation in a single catalog-like solution, these systems can be powerful collection development tools.

Digitization projects and the preservation of digitized and born-digital content are a pervasive theme of the twenty-first century. In 2001, the Research Libraries Group and OCLC issued a joint report, "Attributes of a Trusted Digital Repository: Meeting the Needs of Research Resources," and conversation continues about the long-term persistence of digital content.[85] Libraries are moving from small, boutique digitization projects to coherent collections containing print resources digitized for preservation and access. Defining a sound and consistent plan for digitizing content owned by the library is often the responsibility of collection development librarians. Google's move into mass digitization in December 2004 may be the biggest story for collection development so far in this century. Google began the project by announcing partnerships with the University of Michigan, Harvard University, Stanford University, the University of Oxford, and the New York Public Library through which approximately fifteen million volumes will be digitized. The project plans to digitize all library holdings, including copyrighted works. Since the initial announcement, other libraries in the United States and abroad have joined the project. Publisher and author associations quickly challenged through the courts Google's plans to digitize titles still under copyright. Google's project spurred a group led by Yahoo to begin a parallel project, the Open Content Alliance (www.opencontentalliance .org), to digitize works in the public domain and make them freely available.

Simultaneously, academic libraries have begun developing institutional repositories to collect and preserve the intellectual output of their parent institutions in digital format. Called digital depositories, repositories, and conservancies and most often located at academic institutions, these digital libraries contain electronic versions of published research journal articles by institutional faculty, along with other digital assets created at the institution; these can include administrative documents, course notes, learning objects and other education materials, numeric and other forms of born-digital research data, multimedia (audio, video, etc.) products, and theses. These repositories are intended as archives to store and preserve digital assets and to provide open access within the institution to these resources. Collection development librarians and archivists generally have an important role in identifying and securing content and in encouraging faculty members to deposit their publications and research.

Summary

The theory and practice of collection development and management have their origins in the selection of materials for library acquisition. In early U.S. libraries, a combination of limited budgets and a small volume of publications caused selection per se to receive little attention. Decisions about what to acquire were in the hands of faculty and trustee boards for colleges and universities, trustees and library boards for public libraries, and school boards, trustees, and school superintendents for school libraries. As acquisitions budgets and the amount of material being published increased and librarianship developed as a profession in the second half of the nineteenth century, selection responsibilities shifted to librarians in public libraries. After the Second World War, the same transition occurred in large academic libraries. Simultaneously, the shift to shared responsibility between librarians and faculty members for developing college library collections began. The move to selection by librarians for school libraries began earlier—in the 1920s.

A tension between collecting as much as possible and collecting only the best and most appropriate has been a constant feature of library selection. This is coupled with defining what is good and appropriate and balancing user demand against librarians' perception of value. Public librarians have struggled with the place of popular fiction in their collections and how to fulfill their mission as a public institution, funded to serve the public interest. Much early theory of selection for public libraries focused on the responsibilities of libraries to lead their readers to the "better" works. In the twentieth century, librarians began to consider the implications of intentional and unintentional censorship and libraries' responsibilities for guaranteeing intellectual freedom and the right to read what one wishes. Librarians began to strive for broad and even coverage in collections. Balancing immediate need and long-term responsibilities to develop collections remains a troubling issue.

Collection development and management as a specialty can be traced to the 1970s, when professional associations, conferences and institutes, and professional literature began focusing on a variety of collections responsibilities in addition to selecting materials. Collection development and management are now understood to include selection; the determination and coordination of selection policy; assessment of the needs of users and potential users; collection use studies; collection analysis; budget management; identification of collection needs; community and user outreach and liaison; planning for resource sharing; decisions about weeding, storage, and preservation; and the organization and assignment of responsibilities for its practice.

Tremendous and continuing growth in worldwide publications, rapidly inflating prices for information in all formats, and library budgets unable to accommodate either have stressed libraries and collections librarians since the late 1970s. Simultaneously, deteriorating print collections are requiring decisions about appropriate preservation expenditures within already strained budgets. These pressures have been compounded by the electronic information explosion and associated legal issues and concerns about preservation and perpetual access. User expectations about the services, collections, and access that libraries should provide are profoundly affecting collection development and management.

Notes

1. Paul H. Mosher, "Collection Development to Collection Management: Toward Stewardship of Library Resources," *Collection Management* 4, no. 4 (1982): 45.

2. Bonita Bryant, "The Organizational Structure of Collection Development," *Library Resources and Technical Services* 31 (1987): 118.

3. Charles B. Osburn, "Collection Development and Management," in *Academic Libraries: Research Perspectives*, ed. Mary Jo Lynch, 1–37, ACRL Publications in Librarianship no. 47 (Chicago: American Library Association, 1990), 1.

4. Michael R. Gabriel, *Collection Development and Evaluation: A Sourcebook* (Lanham, Md.: Scarecrow, 1995), 3.

5. Kanwal Ameen, "Developments in the Philosophy of Collection Management: A Historical Review," *Collection Building* 24, no. 4 (2005): 112–16.

6. Gabriel Naudé, *Advice on Establishing a Library*, with an introduction by Archer Taylor (Berkeley: University of California Press, 1950), 17.

7. Jean-Baptiste Cotton des Houssays, *The Duties and Qualifications of a Librarian*, English translation (Chicago: A. C. McClurg, 1906), 43.

8. Howard Clayton, "The American College Library, 1800–1860," *Journal of Library History* 3 (April 1968): 120–37.

9. Louis Shores, *Origins of the American College Library, 1638–1800* (Nashville, Tenn.: George Peabody College, 1934).

10. Arthur T. Hamlin, *The University Library in the United States, Its Origins and Development* (Philadelphia: University of Pennsylvania Press, 1981).

11. Orvin Lee Shiflett, *Origins of American Academic Librarianship* (Norwood, N.J.: Ablex, 1981).

12. Association of Research Libraries, "ARL Statistics Tables 2005–06," www.arl.org/stats/annualsurveys/arlstats/arlstats06.shtml.

13. Shores, *Origins of the American College Library.*

14. George Livermore, *Remarks on Public Libraries* (Cambridge, Mass.: Boils and Houghton, 1850), 17.

15. Michael K. Buckland, "The Roles of Collections and the Scope of Collection Development," *Journal of Documentation* 45, no. 3 (1989): 213–26.

16. Shiflett, *Origins of American Academic Librarianship.*

17. Margaret Ann Johnson, "Christian Gottlob Heyne as Librarian" (master's thesis, University of Chicago Graduate Library School, 1973).

18. U.S. Office of Education, *Survey of Land-Grant Colleges and Universities*, Bulletin no. 9, 2 vols. (Washington, D.C.: U.S. Government Printing Office, 1930).

19. Jesse H. Shera's *Foundations of the Public Library: The Origins of the Public Library Movement in New England 1629–1855* (Chicago: University of Chicago Press, 1949) is the classic history of public libraries and the source of information presented here.

20. James C. Baughman, "Sense Is Preferable to Sound," *Library Journal* 111 (Oct. 1986): 44.

21. Elizabeth McHenry, "Black Readers and Their Reading Rooms," in *Institutions of Reading: The Social Life of Libraries in the United States*, ed. Thomas Augst and Kenneth Carpenter, 99–108 (Amherst, Mass.: University of Massachusetts Press, 2007).

22. *Address and Constitution of the Phoenix Society of New York, and the Auxiliary Ward Association* (1833), reprinted in Dorothy Burnett Porter, comp., *Early Negro Writing, 1760–1837* (Boston: Beacon Press, 1971), 144.

23. Boston Public Library, *Upon the Objects to Be Attained by the Establishment of a Public Library: Report of the Trustees of the Public Library of the City of Boston, July, 1852* (Boston: J. H. Eastburn, City Document no. 37, 1852; reprint, Boston: Hall, 1975), 8–9.

24. John Cotton Dana, *A Library Primer* (Chicago: Library Bureau, 1899).

25. Edward G. Holley, "North American Efforts at Worldwide Acquisitions since 1945," *Collection Management* 9 (Summer/Fall 1987): 89–111.

26. Fremont Rider, *The Scholar and the Future of the Research Library* (New York: Hadham, 1944).

27. Kenneth J. Brough, *Scholars Workshop: Evolving Concepts of Library Service* (Urbana: University of Illinois Press, 1953), 99.

28. National Center for Education Statistics, *Public Libraries in the United States: Fiscal Year 2005* (Washington, D.C.: U.S. Department of Education, 2007), http://nces.ed.gov/pubs2008/2008301.pdf.

29. Dorothy McGinnis, "Instructional Materials Centers—Something New?" *California School Libraries* 34, no. 1 (1962): 4.

30. Cheryl Ann McCarthy, "Progress in School Library Media Programs: Where Have We Been? Where Are We Now? And Where Are We Going?" *Advances in Librarianship* 30 (2006): 271–97.

31. Tim J. Cole, "The Origin and Development of School Libraries," *Peabody Journal of Education* 37, no. 2 (1959): 87–92.

32. U.S. Bureau of Education, *Public Libraries in the United States of America: Their History, Condition, and Management; Special Report* (Washington, D.C.: U.S. Government Printing Office, 1876).

33. Frank Hermann Koos, *State Participation in Public School Library Service* (New York: Columbia University Teachers College, 1927).

34. Josiah W. Leeds, *Concerning Printed Poison* (Philadelphia: Printed by the author, 1885), 7.

35. Cole, "Origin and Development."

36. Casper Carl Certain, *Standard Library Organization and Equipment for Secondary Schools of Different Sizes* (Washington, D.C.: National Education Association, Department of Secondary Education, 1918), 7.

37. Casper Carl Certain, *Elementary School Library Standards* (Chicago: American Library Association, 1925); American Library Association, *School Libraries for Today and Tomorrow: Functions and Standards* (Chicago: American Library Association, 1945).

38. Joan Michie and Barbara Holton, *Fifty Years of Supporting Children's Learning: A History of Public School Libraries and Federal Legislation from 1953–2000* (Washington, D.C.: National Center for Education Statistics, U.S. Dept. of Education, Institute of Education Sciences, 2005).

39. National Center for Education Statistics, *American Public School Libraries: 1953–2000* (Washington, D.C.: NCES, 2005), http://nces.ed.gov/pubs2005/2005324.pdf.

40. McCarthy, "Progress in School Library Media Programs," 271–97.

41. U.S. Department of Health, Education, and Welfare, *An Evaluative Survey Report on ESEA Title II: Fiscal Years 1966–1968* (Washington, D.C.: U.S. Government Printing Office, 1972).

42. U.S. Department of Health, Education, and Welfare, *School Library Resources, Textbooks, and Other Instructional Materials; Title II, Elementary and Secondary Education Art of 1964, Third Annual Report, Fiscal Year 1968* (Washington, D.C.: U.S. Government Printing Office, 1971).

43. Michael S. Knapp et al., *The Education Block Grant at the Local Level: The Implementation of Chapter 2 of the Education Consolidation and Improvement Act in Districts and Schools* (Menlo Park, Calif.: SRI International, 1986).

44. Michie and Holton, *Fifty Years of Supporting Children's Learning.*

45. Mary Peacock Douglas, *School Libraries for Today and Tomorrow: Functions and Standards* (Chicago: American Library Association, 1945).

46. American Association of School Librarians, *Standards for School Library Programs* (Chicago: American Library Association, 1960).

47. American Association of School Librarians and National Education Association, Department of Audiovisual Instruction, *Standards for School Media Programs* (Chicago: American Library Association, 1969).

48. American Association of School Librarians, *Media Programs: District and School* (Chicago: American Library Association, 1975).

49. American Association of School Librarians, *Information Power: Guidelines for School Library Media Programs* (Chicago: American Library Association; Washington, D.C.: Association for Educational Communications and Technology, 1988).

50. American Association of School Librarians and Association for Educational Communications and Technology, *Planning Guide for Information Power: Building Partnerships for Learning* (Chicago: American Association of School Librarians, American Library Association, 1999).

51. National Center for Education Statistics, Digest of Education Statistics, table 416: "Selected Statistics on Public School Libraries/Media Centers, by Level and Enrollment Size." From U.S. Department of Education, National Center for Education Statistics, Schools and Staffing Survey (SASS), Public School Library Media Center Questionnaire, 2003–04 (Sept. 2006), http://nces.ed.gov/programs/digest/d06/tables/dt06_416.asp.

52. Marilyn L. Shontz and Lesley S. J. Farmer, "Expenditures for Resources in School Library Media Centers, 2005," in *Bowker Annual: Library and Book Trade Almanac 2007*, 52nd ed., Dave Bogart, ed. (Medford, N.J.: Information Today, 2007), 445–58.

53. Jeanne Sohn, "Cooperative Collection Development: A Brief Overview," *Collection Management* 8, no. 2 (1986): 4.

54. Association of Research Libraries, "Monograph and Serial Expenditures in ARL Libraries, 1986–2006," www.arl.org/bm~doc/monser06.pdf. Information at this site is updated annually as ARL member libraries' statistics are added.

55. Maurice B. Line, "Interlending and Document Supply in a Changing World," in *Interlending and Document Supply: Proceedings of the First International Conference Held in London, November, 1988*, ed. Graham P. Cornish and Alison Gallicao, 1–4 (Ballston Spa, England: IFLA Office for International Lending, 1989), 1.

56. José-Marie Griffiths and Donald W. King, *InterConnections: The IMLS National Study on the Use of Libraries, Museums and the Internet: Public Libraries Report* (Washington, D.C.: Institute of Museum and Library Services, 2008), http://interconnectionsreport.org; José-Marie Griffiths and Donald W. King, *InterConnections: The IMLS National Study on the Use of Libraries, Museums and the Internet: Conclusions Summary* (Washington, D.C.: Institute of Museum and Library Services, 2008), http://interconnectionsreport.org/reports/ConclusionsSummaryFinalB.pdf.

57. Thaddeus M. Harris, *Seleced* [sic] *Catalogue of Some of the Most Esteemed Publications in the English Language. Proper to Form a Social Library, with an Introduction upon the Choice of Books* (Boston: I. Thomas and E. T. Andrews, 1793), ii.

58. "Monthly Report from Public Librarians upon the Reading of Minors: A Suggestion," *Library Journal* 23 (Aug. 1899): 479.

59. Arthur E. Bostwick, "Librarian as a Censor," *Library Journal* 33 (July 1908): 257–59.

60. William F. Poole, "The Organization and Management of Public Libraries," in *Public Libraries in the United States of America: Their History, Condition, and Management; Special Report*, Part I, by the U.S. Bureau of Education (Washington, D.C.: U.S. Government Printing Office, 1876), 479–80.

61. Cornelia Marvin, "No New Fiction during the War," *Public Libraries* 23, no. 6 (1918): 269.

62. American Library Association, "Our Libraries and the War," *Library Journal* 42 (Aug. 1917): 606–11.

63. Carl B. Roden, "The Library in Hard Times," *Library Journal* 56 (Dec. 1, 1931): 981–87.

64. Esther Jane Carrier, *Fiction in Public Libraries, 1876–1900* (New York: Scarecrow, 1965); and *Fiction in Public Libraries, 1900–1950* (Littleton, Colo.: Libraries Unlimited, 1985). For explorations of the manner in which librarians' cultural and social attitudes and biases have affected their theories of selection and service, see Lee Garrison, *Apostles of Culture: The Public Librarian and American Society, 1876–1920* (New York: Free Press, 1979); and Evelyn Geller, *Forbidden Books in American Public Libraries, 1879–1939: A Study in Cultural Change* (Westport, Conn.: Greenwood, 1984).

65. Helen Haines, *Living with Books: The Art of Book Selection* (New York: Columbia University Press, 1935), 3.

66. Francis K. W. Drury, *Book Selection* (Chicago: American Library Association, 1930), xii–xiii.

67. Ibid., 2.

68. Leon Carnovsky, "The Role of the Public Library: Implications for Library Education," in *The Intellectual Foundations of Library Education*, ed. Don R. Swanson, 13–23 (Chicago: University of Chicago Press, 1965).

69. Leon Carnovsky, "Community Analysis and the Practice of Book Selection," in *The Practice of Book Selection*, ed. Louis R. Wilson, 20–39 (Chicago: University of Chicago Press, 1940), 27.

70. Bernard Berelson, *The Library's Public: A Report of the Public Library Inquiry* (New York: Columbia University Press, 1949).

71. Lester Asheim, "Not Censorship but Selection," *Wilson Library Bulletin* 28 (Sept. 1953): 63–67. See also his "Selection and Censorship: A Reappraisal," *Wilson Library Bulletin* 58 (Nov. 1983): 180–84.

72. David L. Perkins, ed., *Guidelines for Collection Development* (Chicago: Collection Development Committee, Resources and Technical Services Division, American Library Association, 1979).

73. Judith Serebnick, ed., *Collection Management in Public Libraries: Proceedings of a Preconference to the 1984 ALA Annual Conference, June 21–22, 1984, Dallas* (Chicago: American Library Association, 1986).

74. Robert D. Stueart and George B. Miller Jr., eds., *Collection Development in Libraries: A Treatise*, 2 vols., Foundations in Library and Information Science, vol. 10 (Greenwich, Conn.: JAI Press, 1980). A new collection of essays updated this publication—Charles B. Osburn and Ross Atkinson, eds., *Collection Management: A New Treatise*, 2 vols., Foundations in Library and Information Science, vol. 26 (Greenwich, Conn.: JAI Press, 1991).

75. Richard Kryzs, "Collection Development Courses," in *Internationalizing Library and Information Science Education: A Handbook of Policies and Procedures in Administration and Curriculum*, ed. John F. Harvey and Frances Laverne Carroll, 201–14 (New York: Greenwood, 1987); John M. Budd and Patricia L. Brill, "Education for Collection Management: Results of a Survey of Educators and Practitioners," *Library Resources and Technical Services* 38, no. 4 (1994): 343–53; Paul Metz, "Collection Development in the Library and Information Science Curriculum," in *Recruiting, Educating, and Training Librarians for Collection Development*, ed. Peggy Johnson and Sheila S. Intner, 87–97 (Westport, Conn.: Greenwood, 1994).

76. Karen Schmidt, "Past Perfect, Future Tense: A Survey of Issues in Collection Development," *Library Collections, Acquisitions, and Technical Services* 28, no. 4 (2004): 360–72.

77. American Film Foundation, *Slow Fires: On the Preservation of the Human Record*, sponsored by the Council on Library Resources, Library of Congress, and National Endowment for the Humanities (Santa Monica, Calif.: American Film Foundation, 1989).

78. University of California–Berkeley Library, Library Collections, Hot Topics—Publisher Mergers (2007), www.lib.berkeley.edu/scholarlycommunication/publisher_mergers.html.

79. Tim Berners-Lee, "Information Management: A Proposal," www.w3.org/History/1989/proposal.html.

80. Daniel Greenstein, "DLF Draft Strategy and Business Plan," public version 2.0 (Washington, D.C.: Digital Library Federation, 2005), www.diglib.org/about/strategic.htm.

81. Dru Mogge, "Seven Years of Tracking Electronic Publishing: The ARL Directory of Electronic Journals, Newsletters and Academic Discussion Lists," *Library Hi Tech* 17, no. 1 (1999): 17–25.

82. International Coalition of Library Consortia, "Statement of Current Perspective and Preferred Practices for the Selection and Purchase of Electronic Information" (March 1998), www.library.yale.edu/consortia/statement.html.

83. Richard W. Boss for the Public Library Association, "eContent," PLA Tech Notes, April 4, 2007, www.ala.org/ala/pla/plapubs/technotes/technotes.cfm; Richard W. Boss for the Public Library Association, "Evaluating Electronic Products and Services," PLA Tech Notes, www.pla.org/ala/pla/plapubs/technotes/evaluatingelectronic.cfm.

84. Daniel G. Dorner, "The Impact of Digital Information Resources on the Roles of Collection Managers in Research Libraries," *Library Collections, Acquisitions, and Technical Services* 28, no. 3 (2004): 249–74.

85. RLG and OCLC, "Attributes of a Trusted Digital Repository: Meeting the Needs of Research Resources," RLG-OCLC report, draft for public comment (Mountain View, Calif.: RLG, 2001), www.oclc.org/programs/ourwork/past/trustedrep/attributes01.pdf.

Suggested Readings

Agee, Jim. *Acquisitions Go Global: An Introduction to Library Collection Management in the 21st Century.* Oxford, England: Chandos, 2007.

Atkinson, Ross. *Community, Collaboration and Collections: The Writings of Ross Atkinson.* Edited by Robert Alan and Bonnie MacEwan. Chicago: Association for Library Collections and Technical Services, 2005.

Bishop, Kay. *The Collection Program in Schools: Concepts, Practices, and Information Sources.* 4th ed. Westport, Conn.: Libraries Unlimited, 2007.

Blake, Virgil L. P. "Navigating the Parallel Universe: Education for Collection Management in the Electronic Age." *Library Trends* 48, no. 4 (2000): 891–922.

Branin, Joseph. "Shifting Boundaries: Managing Research Library Collections at the Beginning of the Twenty-first Century." In *Cooperative Collection Development: Significant Trends and Issues*, edited by Donald B. Simpson, 1–17. New York: Haworth, 1998.

Branin, Joseph, Frances Groen, and Suzanne Thorin. "The Changing Nature of Collection Management in Research Libraries." *Library Resources and Technical Services* 44, no. 1 (2000): 23–32.

Brodie, Carolyn S. "A History of School Library Media Center Collection Development." In *The Emerging School Library Media Center: Historical Issues and Perspective*, edited by Kathy Howard Latrobe, 57–73. Englewood, Colo.: Libraries Unlimited, 1998.

Carrigan, Dennis P. "Toward a Theory of Collection Development." *Library Acquisitions: Practice and Theory* 19 (Spring 1995): 97–106.

Casserly, Mary F. "Collection Management as Risk Management." *Library Collections, Acquisitions, and Technical Services* 28, no. 1 (2004): 79–92.

Clayton, Peter, and G. E. Gorman. *Managing Information Resources in Libraries: Collection Management in Theory and Practice.* London: Library Association Publishing, 2001.

Cohen, Henry, and Mary Minow. "Intellectual Freedom in Libraries: Then and Now." *Advances in Librarianship* 30 (2006): 73–101.

Evans, G. Edward, and Margaret Zarnosky Saponaro. *Developing Library and Information Center Collections.* 5th ed. Westport, Conn.: Libraries Unlimited, 2005.

Hughes-Hassell, Sandra, and Jacqueline C. Mancall. *Collection Management for Youth: Responding to the Needs of Learners.* Chicago: American Library Association, 2005.

Jenkins, Clare, and Mary Morley, eds. *Collection Management in Academic Libraries.* 2nd ed. Aldershot, Hampshire, England, and Brookfield, Vt.: Gower, 1999.

Johnson, Peggy, and Bonnie MacEwan, eds. *Virtually Yours: Models for Managing Electronic Resources and Services: Proceedings of the Joint Reference and User Services Association and Association for Library Collections and Technical Services Institute, Chicago, Illinois, October 23–25, 1997.* ALCTS Papers on Library Technical Services and Collections no. 8. Chicago: American Library Association, 1999.

Kerby, Mona. *Collection Development for the School Library Media Program: A Beginner's Guide.* Chicago: American Association of School Librarians, 2006.

Latrobe, Kathy Howard, ed. *The Emerging School Library Media Center: Historical Issues and Perspectives.* Englewood, Colo.: Libraries Unlimited, 1998.

Lougee, Wendy Pradt. *Diffuse Libraries: Emergent Roles for the Research Library in the Digital Age.* Washington, D.C.: Council on Library and Information Resources, 2002.

Lukenbill, W. Bernard. *Collection Development for a New Century in the School Library Media Center.* Westport, Conn.: Greenwood, 2002.

McGregor, Joy, Ken Dillon, and James Henri, eds. *Collection Management for School Libraries.* Lanham, Md.: Scarecrow, 2003.

Miller, Ruth H., "Electronic Resources and Academic Libraries, 1980–2000: A Historical Perspective." *Library Trends* 48, no. 4 (2000): 645–70.

Obama, Barack. "Bound to the Word." *American Libraries* 36, no. 7 (2005): 48–52.

Osburn, Charles B. "Toward a Reconceptualization of Collection Development." *Advances in Library Administration and Organization* 2 (1983): 175–98.

Pankake, Marcia. "From Book Selection to Collection Management: Continuity and Advances in an Unending Work." *Advances in Librarianship* 13 (1984): 185–220.

Raber, Douglas. *Librarianship and Legitimacy: The Ideology of the Public Library Inquiry.* Contributions in Librarianship and Information Science no. 90. Westport, Conn.: Greenwood, 1997.

Stephens, Claire Gatrell, and Patricia Franklin. *Library 101: A Handbook for the School Library Media Specialist.* Westport, Conn.: Libraries Unlimited, 2007.

Sudduth, Elizabeth A., Nancy B. Newins, and William E. Sudduth, comps. *Special Collections in College and University Libraries.* CLIP Note no. 35. Chicago: Association of College and Research Libraries, 2005.

Sullivan, Michael. *Fundamentals of Children's Services.* Chicago: American Library Association, 2005.

Toor, Ruth, and Hilda K. Weisburg. *New on the Job: A School Library Media Specialist's Guide to Success.* Chicago: American Library Association, 2007.

Turner, Philip M., and Ann Marlow Riedling. *Helping Teachers Teach: A School Library Media Specialist's Role.* 3rd ed. Westport, Conn.: Libraries Unlimited, 2003.

CHAPTER TWO

Organization and Staffing

Collection development and management comprise many responsibilities. This chapter offers an overview of these responsibilities and how collection development and management may be organized within a library. Subsequent chapters explore these tasks, functions, and responsibilities in greater depth. Also addressed in this chapter are desired competencies, the effects of automation of the work of collections librarians, a phenomenon known as deskilling, on-site training for collections librarians, ethical issues associated with the practice of collection development and management, and performance evaluation.

Responsibilities and Their Assignment

Collection development and management encompass a suite of activities. Not all collections librarians have all responsibilities that can fall under the heading of collection development and management. However, most librarians who have a title of or an assignment as selector, bibliographer, subject or area specialist, subject liaison, collection development or collection management librarian, or collections librarian perform several of these functions. In smaller libraries an individual may handle these responsibilities along with many others, including placing orders, receipting and cataloging materials, providing reference service, teaching information literacy, supporting circulation, and various other duties. The usual list of responsibilities follows:

Selecting:
- Choosing current materials in one or more formats for acquisition and access
- Selecting access methods for digital resources
- Deciding upon retrospective materials for acquisition and access
- Choosing which gift materials to accept
- Evaluating free websites and web-based resources for possible inclusion in a library's catalog or accessible through a library's portal

- Selecting materials to withdraw, store, preserve, digitize, and cancel
- Identifying and soliciting materials for inclusion in a digital depository

Budgeting:

- Requesting and justifying budget allocations
- Expending and managing allocated funds
- Working with donors and potential donors of in-kind and cash gifts
- Writing grant proposals and managing grants

Planning and organizing:

- Coordinating collection development and management activities with others within the library
- Monitoring and reviewing approval plans
- Monitoring and reviewing exchange agreements
- Evaluating and assessing collections and related services
- Fostering cooperative collection development
- Writing and revising collection development policies

Communicating and reporting:

- Serving on internal and external committees that deal with collections issues
- Keeping administrators (principals, directors, etc.) and other stakeholders informed about library challenges, accomplishments, and activities
- Promoting, marketing, and interpreting collections and resources
- Performing liaison and outreach activities in the user community
- Connecting with other libraries and librarians
- Advising readers, often called readers' advisory service, and giving book talks

One possible responsibility not listed in this summary is the preparation of bibliographies, once routinely taught in library school courses. Although some collections librarians do prepare both analytical and enumerative bibliographies of varying lengths, this function is not as common as those identified above.[1] Developing a library website that is subject- or user-based and that lists and points to related resources is beginning to replace the preparation of bibliographies.

Assignment of responsibilities and placement of collections activities within the organization vary with the size of the library and its budget, its mission, and its user community. In small libraries, all activities may be handled by one individual. In larger libraries, responsibilities may be highly centralized or widely dispersed according to subject responsibility, user community, physical location of staff members, or subset of functions within the many that are considered collection development and management activities.

The contemporary understanding of collection development and management as an inclusive set of coherent activities mandates close coordination between activities when they are handled by different individuals or by different units. When a single individual does not perform all functions identified in the list above, he or she usually works closely with those who handle these related tasks. For example, a preservation unit may identify items in need of treatment and recommend alternatives but rely on the collection management librarian to decide if the item should be withdrawn, replaced, preserved, or conserved. Choosing an approval plan vendor may be the joint responsibility of the acquisitions unit and the collection development unit. A collections librarian cannot develop and manage a collection effectively without in-depth knowledge of everything affecting that collection.

Academic Libraries

The idea of subject specialist positions responsible for portions of the collection was developed in Germany in the 1800s. German academic libraries began the practice of placing selection in specific fields in the hands of library staff with academic credentials in those areas.[2] U.S. libraries did not begin to employ subject specialists (sometimes called area specialists) widely until after the Second World War, when selection in academic libraries began to shift from faculty members to academic librarians.[3] Subject specialists were seen to be most appropriate in libraries with complex bibliographic, linguistic, acquisition, and processing problems that required specialized expertise to solve. Some have seen the shift of selection decision making from teaching faculty to librarians as both a force toward and an indication of the professionalization of librarianship.[4] For a time, the phrase *subject specialist* or *subject bibliographer* was understood to mean a librarian who was assigned full time to collections activities. This has changed, and now a librarian who is called a subject specialist or bibliographer often has additional library responsibilities, such as reference service, cataloging, or user community outreach using his or her unique language or subject expertise.

In many smaller academic libraries, faculty continue to play a major role in selecting materials, though collection management activities are generally handled by librarians. Teaching faculty may identify new materials for acquisition through review of approval plan notification slips (print or electronic) or new approval plan receipts. They may make recommendations, with final authority for approving orders residing with the library. Smaller academic libraries seldom have the breadth and depth of specialized subject expertise found in larger libraries, and relying on the proficiency of faculty members active in the field is reasonable. The success of faculty-based selection depends on faculty members' interest in and involvement with the library. In such environments, librarians typically have responsibility for reference collection development and management and, perhaps, more general materials.

The evolving nature of subject specialists mirrors a trend in academic libraries of all sizes toward assigning librarians at least one other primary responsibility along with collection development and management. A 1994 study of eighty-six ARL member libraries found that the most frequent model was a decentralized staff composed, in part or wholly, of librarians having responsibilities in collection development as well as other areas.[5] More than half the responding libraries in this survey reported having no full-time staff members assigned to collection development. Selection is now commonly one of several responsibilities held by librarians in most academic libraries.

Traditionally, assignments in academic libraries have combined reference services and collection development and management. Although subject specialists or bibliographers often have provided specialized reference service, they now more frequently serve as part of a reference or public services unit with reference, liaison, and information literacy responsibilities. An additional trend in large research libraries is to assign collections responsibilities to staff members from nonpublic service units, such as cataloging.[6] The result is that many librarians in academic libraries are now doing some selection and collection management— whether it be a major or a minor assignment among many responsibilities. Regardless of the number of librarians handling collections responsibilities, all activities must be carefully coordinated or the collection loses focus and coherence.

A debate continues in some large academic, research, and public libraries over the advantages and disadvantages of full-time bibliographers compared to librarians with collections responsibilities as part of a suite of responsibilities. Full-time selectors (the term used here to cover the full range of collection development and management functions) are championed because this model is seen to assure that collections responsibilities are not subordinated to other library responsibilities. Full-time academic bibliographer positions were, from their beginning, perceived as a special class of scholar-librarians, intended both to replace faculty selectors and to appease faculty members with appropriate replacements within the library.[7] This model has been promoted as more effectively positioning selectors to establish formal communication with teaching faculty members because of their credibility as scholars. In public libraries, the position of full-time collections librarian is often seen as the most effective and efficient use of staffing. Without distractions such as assigned reference desk hours or a backlog of cataloging, the full-time selector is seen as better able to focus on building and managing the collection.

The full-time selector model has been criticized as elitist and distanced from everyday library services, concerns, and problems. Full-time academic bibliographers have the potential of becoming too closely affiliated with the departments or schools they support. Any full-time bibliographer faces the risk of losing sight of the overall goal of building and maintaining a balanced collection. The independent nature of full-time bibliographer work can result in internal cultural and organizational problems and in positions that do not fit comfortably into the library's organizational structure.[8] Even if a library has moved from a traditional bureaucratic organizational structure to a flattened, less rigid model, the solitary character of full-time selections work can isolate the bibliographer.[9] Other staff members may perceive the full-time bibliographer as uninvolved and outside the collaborative interaction that has come to characterize library planning and problem solving. Public librarians may feel that the centralized collections librarian is too removed from the day-to-day business of working with the public and understanding their needs and interests. School librarians in districts with centralized selection may have the same perception about managing selection through a district office that does not understand the variations from school to school.

The alternative to full-time selectors is positions in which collection development and management are part of a suite of many responsibilities. This might be seen as a shift from artisan collection development to a holistic approach to developing and managing collections. This model stresses the value of regular contact with collection users such as occurs through reference and outreach or liaison work. This contact can provide direct information about user interests and needs. A frontline librarian has firsthand experience with and understanding of the importance of continually balancing needs and reassessing priorities. Many academic libraries have given these holistic librarians the position title "subject liaison" or "departmental liaison." Catalogers with in-depth subject background and language expertise may have more knowledge and skills in certain areas than other librarians on the staff. Assigning collections responsibilities to such capable individuals can be the best use of staff resources and lead to outstanding collections. Having many librarians with collections responsibilities can, however, make coordination more challenging. The primary criticism of part-time selectors is that collections work has a tendency to become a secondary responsibility and can be slighted as librarians try to fit it in among the constant pressures of other daily activities. Some public library and school systems have addressed these tensions by handling most selection centrally but allocating a portion of the collection budget to individual locations to be managed on site.

The need to balance collections responsibility assignments between librarians and multiple responsibility assignments within a single position has motivated the profession to try to determine the time or staffing levels needed to expend budgets and manage collections. Several writers have argued that such calculations are impossible because collections work is too complex and neither objective nor observable.[10] Bonita Bryant notes the "difficulties in measuring the results of collection development and management qualitatively and in measuring the process itself quantitatively."[11] One solution to this dilemma is to make clear the priorities assigned to various tasks.

One successful project to develop a pragmatic, objective, and quantitative means of estimating collection development workload in an academic library with part-time bibliographers is described by Paul Metz.[12] Metz proposes a formula of weighted parameters, with weights to be assigned different values according to the library in which the formula is applied. The five parameters are (1) number of academic departments and key centers for which a bibliographer is responsible, (2) number of full-time tenure-track faculty in assigned departments or centers, (3) number of orders in all the bibliographer's firm order budget accounts for the previous fiscal year, (4) call number responsibilities measured as total inches in the shelf list or via automated title count, and (5) number of standing orders and continuations in all the bibliographer's accounts. Although no one has been able to figure out how much time it takes to be a successful selector, Metz lists four significant components that make up collections work in all types of libraries: outreach and liaison, selecting items to order, managing an existing collection, and managing serials, continuations, and standing orders.

Public Libraries

Larger public libraries may use full-time or part-time collections librarians or a combination of both types of assignment. Large public libraries may have a centrally located collections coordinator, collections officer, or collection development officer who manages the collections budget and either coordinates or directly supervises the work of several subject specialists located in a central library and larger branches, if they exist. Cynthia Orr suggests that public libraries increasingly are instituting centralized collection development as a cost-saving measure.[13] Many collections librarians in public libraries also have responsibilities for reference work and other public services and may manage a major subject- or user-based unit (e.g., music, children's services, or a branch library). Subject specialists and unit heads may have responsibility for monitoring review aids and selecting materials in their specialty. Another frequent division of selection responsibilities is according to publishers or formats, or both. For example, one selector may be responsible for selecting materials from major publishers and another from small presses. Some large public libraries have one or two individuals who handle all selection work, while collection management is handled at the service points. Many public libraries have a selection committee with rotating membership.

Public libraries with one or more branch libraries may assign some responsibility for selecting materials to a librarian working in an individual branch so that a collection can be developed that meets the needs of that particular user community. For example, a branch library patronized by senior citizens may have more large-print materials or more materials on health care. A branch library patronized by an immigrant population may have more materials in a language not extensively collected in the main library. Even in libraries with centralized selection or a selection committee, librarians not charged with selection or not members of the committee can usually make suggestions for new titles. In public libraries in which selection responsibilities are widely distributed, the centrally located coordinator is usually responsible for monitoring and circulating reviews, acquiring review copies, and coordinating approval plans (if they are used).

The trend in public libraries is toward more use of centralized selection. This permits redirecting additional staff time to public services. The justification for this reassignment of responsibility is supported by research showing that the variations between user interests and circulation at different branches is minimal because so much of contemporary reading is influenced by popular media—which reaches a wide audience.[14] Centralized selection and ordering of multiple copies can speed the delivery of new materials to the branches, increase branch collection diversity, and reduce biases in individual collections. Many library systems with several branches have daily or biweekly delivery service to the branches, facilitating the movement of materials to the pick-up location requested by patrons. Research conducted in 1995 by Ann Irvine in ninety-one public libraries reported that 81 percent of libraries with budgets more than $100,000 and 43 percent of libraries with budgets less than $100,000 had centralized a portion of the selection process.[15] In these libraries, librarians in branch libraries continue to make recommendations and, occasionally, make some selection decisions locally.

All librarians are more likely to participate in collection development and management in medium-size and smaller public libraries in order to distribute the work and take advantage of librarians' formal education and interest areas. Selection and collection management are typically coordinated by the head librarian, who has direct budgetary responsibility. Of course, the smaller the budget, the less is expended on collections, though selection decisions require more scrutiny. In smaller public libraries, collection development and management are normally handled by a single individual, usually the head librarian. In the past, a small acquisitions budget also meant limited access to print review sources. Now, if the library has Internet access, a host of online review sources can be at the librarian's fingertips.

School Library Media Centers

The assignment of collections responsibilities in school library media centers mirrors that found in public libraries. Large systems usually have a district coordinator who supervises the activities of librarians in the several schools that make up the system. In some systems, one person or a committee selects items that go to all of the schools, with variations depending on grade levels (i.e., elementary, middle, and high school). This arrangement can relieve some of the demands on individual librarians, but it does not permit addressing the unique needs within each school. Even in some school systems, each librarian may have responsibility for developing collections within his or her school, in consultation with the school's teachers and in response to student needs and interests. A typical process in school districts is to place orders and receipt and process items centrally at the district office, even when selection is handled at the school level. If the school librarian is not part of a system or works in a school system without a district office, then these responsibilities fall to the individual.

One aspect of collection development and management in school library media centers not present in other types of libraries is the number and variety of groups that may be engaged in decisions. These groups may include teachers, school administrators, school boards, parents, students, individuals in the community, and community organizations. As W. Bernard Lukenbill notes, these varied stakeholders both help and hinder logical, well-considered selection decisions.[16] He goes on to advise school media center librarians to accept this involvement and recognize the inherent complexity it brings to the selection process. Educating others about the selection process, stressing the professional nature of making good selection decisions, and using generally accepted selection tools and aids can strengthen the position of the school media center librarian.

Some schools have a standing curriculum and media committee to deal with library selection and collections issues. A typical committee might consist of a teacher from each grade level, a student representative, a special education teacher, an ESL teacher, and perhaps other faculty members. If the school media center has a selection policy, the standing committee may be responsible for reviewing it and setting goals and priorities for the media program. The committee may be involved with other media center policies, including those that address Internet use (or acceptable use), copyright, gifts, weeding, intellectual freedom, and responding to challenges to materials. In addition, the committee may preview suggested media, discuss requests for materials and equipment, make recommendations for purchases and online access, and evaluate and review challenged materials.

Special Libraries

Special libraries present a unique environment for collection development and management for several reasons. First, special libraries have a specific mission and narrow user community. Second, they may be staffed by only one librarian, who is responsible for all functions. Third, collection building may consist primarily of placing orders submitted by the special library's users. In larger special libraries with several librarians, each librarian may have a clear and narrow area of specialization within which he or she manages the collection.

Skills and Competencies

Libraries expect newly hired librarians to have certain skills and competencies learned in a graduate school program. These are supplemented with on-the-job training and experience gained through the practice of collection development and management over time. Library and information schools provide the conceptual learning. These are the skills, principles, and concepts of librarianship and provide the building blocks or mental models for its practice. They represent the theory that lies behind the practice of collection development and are important to the master as well as the novice. For masters, they are points of reference that aid the continual refinement of their practice and help them explain it to others. For novices, they give an understanding of the rationale that guides collection development and management.

A library school curriculum should include basic functional principles. George J. Soete has called these "assumed competencies,"[17] which include

- reasons for building library collections and a commitment to resource sharing
- importance of knowing the library's users
- factors that make for effective selection and collection management decisions
- tenets of intellectual freedom and respect for diverse points of view
- importance of building and preserving collections for the future as well as the present

Conceptual learning also involves skills and practices—basics that are as important as the philosophical underpinnings. A selector needs knowledge of the subject, formats, and users for whom he or she will select. He or she needs a basic understanding of the targeted user community and knowledge of the techniques to learn about the specific local community being served. This means, at a minimum, expertise in the literature if the selector is not an expert in the subject or discipline. Ideally, a subject specialist is familiar with specialized terminology, understands the basic concepts and importance of the field, is aware of current controversies, recognizes the names of prominent researchers and authors, knows of historical milestones and the names associated with them, and understands how the field relates to other fields and disciplines. A librarian who plans to work with collections used by children and teenagers, for example, should be familiar with the history of children's fiction and nonfiction, understand children's interest and reading levels and the types of materials that match these, be aware of current theories about the use of literature in the curriculum, and know the names of prominent authors, illustrators, and award-winning books.

A library expects a new selector to understand the publishing industry and the factors a publisher considers in making decisions about what to publish, the types of materials in which major publishers specialize and quality of their publications, and major publishers' reliability, pricing practices, and general reputation. The new selector should have studied publishing trends, production statistics, and pricing behavior. Equally important is knowing how materials are provided to libraries and how to select the appropriate means of acquiring various materials types. This includes familiarity with distribution and acquisitions mechanisms (vendors, agents, scholarly societies, approval plans, firm orders, standing orders, etc.). The student should have a basic understanding of intellectual property rights, copyright law, and licensing agreements and their functions in acquisition of and access to resources. Those who plan to become academic librarians should understand the changing nature of scholarly communication and academic research.

John M. Budd and Patricia L. Bril found that collection development practitioners ranked the ability to identify and use key materials as selection sources as the most important skill gained in graduate education.[18] The new selector should have a firm grasp of sources of information (book reviews, bibliographies, publishers' catalogs, web pages, publishers' reputations, key authors) for selecting resources and methods of finding authoritative reviews when needed.

Automation and emerging information technologies are affecting how collections librarians do their work as well as the resources with which they work. Being comfortable in an increasingly technology-driven environment is essential. Library automation and access to bibliographic networks and Internet resources support collections activities such as selection of materials, individual item verification, order preparation, claiming, collection evaluation and assessment, budget management, cooperative collection development, and communication with library staff members and others outside the library, including publishers, vendors, and other suppliers. In-house automated library systems often can produce various useful reports and provide information on demand about fund balances, units and costs, circulation activity, supplier performance, and other statistical compilations that can be manipulated on personal computers. Vendors and agents provide various reports that can help evaluate their performance. Many of these reports can be accessed online at no cost and are part of the services provided by the supplier.

Some libraries and librarians are creating web-based resources or locally designed online toolkits specifically to aid in the practice of collection development and management. A locally developed site for collections librarians typically provides links to useful external sites prepared by other librarians, such as home pages of vendors and publishers frequently used by the library and links to local policies, procedures, and forms. AcqWeb (www.acqweb.org) provides links to resources of interest, including verification tools and directories of publishers and vendors, to acquisitions and collection development librarians. Some local sites include links to bibliographic tools, like *Books in Print*, to which the library has contractual access, and to relevant professional association pages. Other types of information often provided are budgets and fund allocation, a selectors' directory with their subject responsibilities, a currency converter, and management and statistical data. Contributing to and, perhaps, maintaining a local selectors' home page is now a common selector's responsibility.

Working with electronic information resources requires different skills and expertise. Collections librarians must understand licensing and contract negotiation for electronic resources, copyright in the digital environment, and new types of consortial agreements for cooperative purchasing. More library staff members may be involved in evaluation and selection decisions because of the boundary-spanning nature of managing and servicing both local and online electronic information.

Various authors and professional associations have identified additional competencies that new librarians should bring to their first jobs, including these:[19]

- ability to control information bibliographically
- ability to understand and assess the needs of the community to be served
- knowledge of assessment and evaluation techniques, both quantitative and qualitative
- understanding of collection development policy and procedures
- knowledge of general business practices, including financial analysis and budget management
- knowledge of and ability to analyze currency fluctuations around the world, economic trends, and world market forces
- knowledge of digital technology and the appropriate means for providing access to needed online resources
- abilities in critical analysis, problem solving, and critical decision making
- commitment to continuous learning and professional development
- negotiation skills
- managerial and supervisory skills
- salesmanship
- understanding of organizational behavior, power, and politics
- understanding of administrative practices
- knowledge of grant writing and administration

Many of these competencies are not normally part of a library school curriculum. Students should consider taking courses in other professional school programs, such as a business school, education department, or public policy program, to gain the skills needed in contemporary collection development and management practice.

Nancy M. Cline, a university librarian, has provided a set of attributes she views as essential for collections librarians and that supplement the competencies that should be learned through formal study:[20]

- commitment to change
- ability to think innovatively, creatively, and strategically
- commitment to high-quality services
- commitment to professionalism
- skills in analytical reasoning
- adaptability, flexibility, and resilience
- vision
- resourcefulness
- intellectual curiosity
- excellent communication and interpersonal skills
- keen sense of political contexts
- ability to tolerate ambiguity

Karen Schmidt adds the qualities of leadership, risk taking, emotion, and a collaborative approach as essential for successful collections librarians.[21] This suite of attributes can apply to anyone who aspires to a successful career as a professional librarian.

The previous paragraphs identify a set of core or assumed competencies consisting of principles, concepts, and skill that libraries expect a newly hired collection development and management librarian to have learned in a course of graduate study. Not all librarians will have taken courses that cover each of these topics, and certain ingredients in successful collections work cannot be taught in library school. Much is mastered while on the job. Some skills are specific to the individual's library and are learned once he or she begins a new position. These include learning the selector's responsibilities (which depend on the job description), the library's collection (on-site and online), and local procedures. In the latter category are how to prepare orders, how to interact with various library units, and how the local budget and financial system operate. To this can be added learning about the local culture or organizational environment, including what is acceptable behavior and what is not, how decisions are made, and how autonomously individuals operate.

Learning and Mastery

Peter M. Senge has explored the difference between learning and mastery, with these conclusions:[22] Successful collections work can be mastered only by practice—by actually doing the work. The distinction rests on the difference between theory, which can be learned, and practice. Practices are the most evident aspect of any profession in the sense that they are what define the field to those outside it. Practices are also the primary focus of individuals when they begin to follow a new career or discipline. The novice requires "discipline" in the sense of conscious and consistent effort because following the practices is not yet second nature.

The new selector working with mental models of how to develop and manage a collection must attempt to identify the assumptions he or she is making and the skills and competencies that guide them. Over time and with experience, the practices of a discipline become more and more automatic. This is why it is sometimes hard for an experienced selector to explain what goes into a selection or collection management decision and how one weighs pros and cons to select or not to select, replace, withdraw, or cancel a title.

The novice is tempted to think that understanding certain principles means one has learned all about the discipline. This confuses intellectual understanding with mastery. A student of the French language may know French grammar and vocabulary but has not mastered the language until he or she speaks French automatically and without first mentally translating every word from English to French. Senge relates this distinction to the essence of a discipline. The essence of a discipline cannot be gained by focusing conscious attention and effort on it. The essence of a discipline is the state of being that is experienced naturally by individuals with high levels of mastery in that discipline.

This perspective suggests that the successful collection development librarian *is* a collection developer instead of one who *does* collection development. The distinction reflects the growth from a linear understanding (knowing the building blocks) to a nonlinear, internalized understanding of collection development as a whole. This is the mastery that cannot be learned in library school. The new collections librarian has learned everything he or she can through an educational program, but only through experience does the whole become greater than the sum of its parts. Collection development is sometimes called both an art and a science. It combines creativity with empirical knowledge. Practice gives meaning to theory, refines performance, and builds mastery.

Training on Site

If fortunate, a newly hired selector is provided with a formal on-site training program, supported by a bibliographer's manual. Although library and information science education teaches the elements of collection development and management, each library has unique practices and expectations. A librarian, even one who has worked in another library, comes to a new position equipped with collection development and management principles, guidelines, and typical procedures but must learn how to operate in the new environment. Most new collections librarians learn the details of a new position through individual instruction, mentoring, and on-the-job experience.

A manual provides the documentation necessary for carrying out collection development and management activities in a specific library.[23] It describes local practices in a systematic way and provides a planning tool for individual selectors to measure progress of their work or improve its quality. Other in-house training materials may include library-specific collection development policies, procedures for the acquisition process, guidelines for collection analysis, procedures for using an automated library system, and goals for collection development work.

A collections librarian should be prepared to develop his or her own training program. Without a formal local program, the new librarian might consult the *Guide for Training Collection Development Librarians*, which lays out the skills and expertise specific to a library in which a new librarian needs training.[24] Even with a formal on-site program, a newly hired selector should develop a personal self-education plan in consultation with his or her supervisor. This plan will include learning

- how the library and its parent organization are organized and the scope and emphasis of its programs
- who the library's staff members are and what they do
- the individuals and groups outside the library with whom he or she will work
- the library's holdings and their strengths and weaknesses
- how patrons use the collections
- how the materials budget is allocated, monitored, and spent
- reports available from the local automated system or generated manually
- the library's collection development policies
- any cooperative collection development agreements
- how the library chooses, uses, and evaluates vendors, and the vendors used
- local procedures for selecting, ordering, and processing materials

As libraries move toward assigning their staff members multiple responsibilities, many librarians who have not handled collections responsibilities previously are being asked to assume them. This is a particular challenge for two reasons. The librarian may have completed his or her graduate education some time ago and, even if he or she remembers the content of collection management courses, that information likely is out of date. Second, supervisors and coworkers may erroneously assume that the new selector is familiar with in-house policies, procedures, and performance expectations. A carefully designed training program is as important for an existing staff member who assumes collections responsibilities as it is for a newly hired librarian.

Effective performance of collection management and development activities requires continual learning, both in the theories and practices of this specialty and in the areas for which one is responsible. A commitment to self-education, along with intellectual curiosity, energy, and time, is essential.

Understanding the User Community

Collection development and management in all types of libraries require close contact with users, and this may be reflected in the assignment of selection responsibilities. Special libraries, as noted above, rely primarily on their users to identify new acquisitions. Academic libraries serving smaller academic institutions often rely heavily on faculty for selection decisions. School library and media centers may rely on committees composed of librarians, teachers, administrators, and sometimes students and parents. Coordination, communication, and cooperation are always crucial.

Technology's Influence on Skills

Harry Braverman introduces the concept of *deskilling* and explores it in his *Labor and Monopoly Capital*.[25] He suggests that capitalism, combined with technology, results in degradation of work by pushing the skills necessary for doing a job down in the organization or profession. Capitalism is, according to Braverman, geared toward profit and finding more economical ways of delivering goods and services. The increasingly sophisticated responsibilities assigned to nurse practitioners and physician's assistants, who handle many medical practices previously performed only by physicians, are examples. Braverman's work has been the source of extensive research, numerous articles, and endless debate by economists, sociologists, and historians.[26] Many analyses on the effects of new, computerized technology on work have tended to characterize them as a continuation of the deskilling process described by Braverman. On the other hand, some analysts see new technologies as having *enskilling* effects as well—in some cases, automation changes the nature of a position by requiring more sophisticated knowledge and skills.[27]

Understanding the nature of skill and distinguishing between skill in individuals and the skill required in particular positions are two aspects of the debate surrounding Braverman's thesis. Individuals can learn the skills needed to perform routine tasks through experience and on-the-job training, but different degrees of awareness are required to perform certain activities. Advanced education and extensive experience prepare individuals to cope with unfamiliar situations for which existing routines are inadequate. Even in environments in which automation is causing significant changes, autonomous, skilled employees continue to have an important role.

The blurring of distinctions that traditionally separated professional librarians from library support staff or paraprofessionals might be seen as deskilling. Over the past twenty-five years, paraprofessionals have taken on more diverse and higher levels of responsibilities.[28] Complex activities are moving downward in the library hierarchy. One distinguishing aspect of a profession is the ability of its practitioners to exercise control over the knowledge base of the field, including control over the criteria for entering that field.[29] Librarians and their professional associations have been unable to maintain exclusive control over the qualifications needed to perform library work. This is caused, in part, by shrinking staffs and the need of libraries to use all current employees effectively. In addition, automation has broadened the skill base needed to work in libraries. In the area of collection development and management, the increasing use of approval plans and automation has reduced the emphasis on selecting individual titles in many libraries.

Nevertheless, most libraries continue to assign certain collections responsibilities to professional staff members. Selection at the individual title level has traditionally remained the purview of professional librarians—at least in academic libraries—but this distinction is not as rigorously maintained as previously. Academic libraries may assign selection to a staff member without a graduate library degree if that individual has extensive subject knowledge gained through either formal study in the discipline or extensive experience with the local collections and their users. The collections-related areas that remain the responsibility of librarians are distinguished by their complex and abstract nature, significant impact on the future of the library, and influence on how the library is perceived by its user community, stakeholders, partners, and service and materials providers. Allen B. Veaner calls these *programmatic responsibilities.*[30] Such areas include collection development program planning and articulation, budget allocation, collection development policy preparation and revision, departmental and community liaison, and work with suppliers, vendors, and consortia.

Organizational Models

Who performs various functions or activities, how these individuals are coordinated, and how they communicate among themselves and with others both within and outside the library define the library's collection development and management organizational structure. Much of the professional literature on organization of collections activities addresses academic libraries and, specifically, large academic and research libraries. This focus reflects the greater tendency of libraries with larger staffs, collections, and budgets to develop large, complex, and variant organizational structures.

No single collection development organizational model predominates. Defining the components of an optimal structure that assures successful accomplishment of goals has proved impossible. No specific model is perfect. Variations, as with the assignment of collections responsibilities, are influenced by the size of existing collections, staffing levels, budget, local assumptions about the goals of collection management and development, and the preferences of the current library administrators.

Bonita Bryant suggests that one or more of three conditions makes some sort of collection management organizational structure necessary.[31] These are when the decision of what to purchase and the responsibility for expenditure of the materials budget is no longer the direct responsibility of the library director, when the library acknowledges that neither technical services (where funds have been managed) nor public services (where selection and user liaison have occurred) allow the necessary combination of fund management and patron contact for systematic collection development and management, and when inconsistencies among collection growth, collection use, and patron needs are discovered.

Libraries handle reporting lines and assignment of responsibilities in various ways, depending on their size, history, and individuals on their staffs. Two models predominate and can be seen as two ends on a continuum, with variations falling in between. In the *functional model*, staff members with collection development and management responsibilities are grouped in a single organizational unit. This unit may be called a department, division, or team. The subject specialists, who may not work in this unit full time, may then be assigned part time to other units according to subject responsibilities, user community, or physical location of their offices, collections, or libraries.

In the *geographic* or *client-based model*, collection development librarians are part of a unit that consists of staff members with various responsibilities who are grouped according to the user community they serve or a geographic location shared by members of the unit. Again, the librarians may be assigned full or part time to collections work. As with the functional model, members of a geographic or client-based unit may be assigned to smaller subunits. In this case, the smaller units may be functional or subject based.

The functional model has the advantage of improved communication and coordination among librarians with similar responsibilities, which can enhance the development of a coherent collection and make working on shared projects, such as serial cancellations or collection analysis, easier. The role of the collection development officer is less complicated because he or she has direct authority as well as responsibility for the collections librarians. Disadvantages include the potential of isolation from other librarians and distance from the user community.

The geographic or client-based model can be particularly effective in focusing on the needs and expectations of a specific user group. In addition, collections librarians work more closely with staff members, including catalogers, circulation units, and interlibrary loan staff, whose work is integral to effective collections work. Planning and problem solving may be easier. The main difficulty with this model is in coordinating collections activities across a large library with many geographic or client-based units. Balancing needs and goals can be a challenge.

Few libraries are organized into either of these "pure" models. Most fall somewhere between them. A large academic library may have a functional unit of full-time bibliographers under an assistant director or assistant university librarian for collection development and a client-based unit with part-time selectors under an assistant director for science and engineering. A large public library system may have a central division of collection development librarians with system-wide responsibilities and several branch libraries with librarians who have multiple responsibilities including collection development and management. These hybrid models can have all the advantages of each of the pure models and all of their problems as well. Regardless of the organizational structure employed, the most important consideration is coordination of collection activities and their proper attention within the library's mission and priorities.

Many libraries have one or more standing committees to improve communication across departmental or divisional lines. Typical committees are a general collection development coordinating committee, a serials review committee, a discipline- or user-based committee (e.g., a committee of science selectors or children's librarians), and a committee that addresses electronic resources. Many of these committees include staff members from other library units because of the boundary-spanning nature of collections work. A general coordinating committee may include, for example, representatives from the library's fiscal office, cataloging unit, or interlibrary loan operation. Committees that deal with e-resources almost always include members from throughout the library—acquisitions and cataloging staff members, automation librarians, reference librarians, an individual charged with managing and monitoring contracts—whose expertise is essential in making responsible, informed decisions about acquisition and access. Libraries with distributed selection responsibilities may have a standing committee or working group that pulls together everyone with selection responsibilities for regular meetings to address shared concerns and pertinent topics. Ad hoc committees may be appointed to address a finite issue or project, such as choosing a new serials or approval plan vendor. The goal of all these committees is to improve communication and decision making by drawing together the individuals and library units with appropriate expertise and those who will be affected by the decisions.

Libraries in which several staff members have collections responsibilities generally have an individual who coordinates their activities. In academic libraries these individuals are often called collection development officers (CDOs). By 1994, 82 percent of ARL member libraries responding to a survey reported that they had a senior CDO reporting directly to the head librarian.[32] In other types of libraries, this person may be called collections officer, collections team leader, collections coordinator, head or director of collection development, assistant or associate librarian for collection development and management, assistant director for collections, media coordinator, or a variation of one of these. A separate senior position is found most commonly in large and medium-size public, academic, and research libraries. This person generally coordinates collection development activities, manages the overall collections budget, and may or may not have direct supervisory responsibility for all staff members with collection management and development assignments.

In large libraries of all types, the collections officer often has senior administrative responsibility for additional operations or services, such as information services, public services, technical services, reference, planning, document delivery and interlibrary loan, development of external funding sources, all aspects of e-resources, and preservation. A direct linkage with acquisitions—either through placing acquisitions within the collection development and management division or combining senior administrative responsibility for technical services (of which acquisition is a subunit) and collection development and management—is seen frequently.[33] This arrangement provides direct control over budget expenditures. These alignments reflect both the boundary-spanning nature of collection development and management and a reduction in the number of senior administrators through consolidation of responsibilities. The collections officer is often a member of the library's administrative group and participates in library-wide policy development and planning. He or she works with other administrators and unit heads to develop mutually agreed-upon processing priorities.

The collections officer role varies depending on the span of control and responsibilities within the library and the library's collection development and management operation. As the administrator responsible for library-wide collection development and management, the collections officer is normally charged with preparing budget requests for staffing and collections and allocating and monitoring the budget—expenditures and balances in the funds assigned to various selectors. Additional responsibilities normally include recruitment, training, assignment of responsibilities to staff members, supervision, and evaluation of that portion of work assignments considered under his or her purview.

The collections officer oversees all aspects of collection building and management for all formats. Under this heading fall coordinating the creation and revision of collection development policies, ensuring that those policies are upheld, and coordinating collection assessment and evaluation, preservation and conservation decisions, and withdrawals, transfers, and journal cancellations. The collections officer is one of several library administrators who may be charged with negotiating contracts and licenses for acquisition of and access to e-resources. Primary responsibility for and coordination of cooperative collection development and consortial activities and fund-raising through development activities and grant writing are usually assigned to the collections officer. He or she may negotiate with individual donors and review gifts and exchanges and frequently represents the library's collection development program to user groups, governing agencies, and in external forums.

Jasper G. Schad stresses the collection officer's leadership role. He lists team building, articulation of vision and values, continuous formal and informal training, and controlling workload as the four key challenges.[34] These four responsibilities, when effectively executed, enable selectors to know what to do and how to do it, realize why it is important, and experience enhanced feelings of competence with less frustration. The collections officer, whether managing a full-time staff or coordinating the work of part-time selectors, has an important role in helping set a realistic agenda that allows selectors to establish priorities, regulate workflow, and accomplish their work. Communication and interpersonal skills are particularly important.

In some libraries, the collections officer may have no direct administrative responsibility for librarians with collection and development assignments. In this environment, the selectors report to another administrator, such as the associate university librarian, the public library's assistant director responsible for technical services or public services, or in the case of school media specialists to the principal in a school.

Ethical Issues

Normative ethics is the set of principles of conduct or standards of behavior governing an individual or profession. Ethics seeks to provide a context for determining what is right and wrong. *Primum non nocere* ("first, do no harm") is one of the principal ethical precepts in the medical profession and is taught to all medical students. Principles or standards can be legal, moral, personal, or institutional. Professional ethics, an applied form of normative ethics, seeks to apply ethical principles to decisions made every day. Professional ethics is sometimes referred to as professional values—an explicit conception of what an individual or group regards as desirable. Professional ethical considerations influence how collections librarians interact with materials sellers, suppliers, and service agents as well as with their user community and coworkers.

Ethical behavior is the result of an internal or personal code and an external context provided by institutional and professional principles. A personal code of ethics may develop out of civic and religious convictions. People do what makes them feel good about themselves and avoid what makes them feel bad. They are also influenced by the frame of reference for behavior developed by the groups of which they are members. In other words, behavior can be a consequence of how one feels others around him or her perceive this behavior. People understand and react to what happens according to the particular frame of reference they are using for ethical behavior.

Lee G. Bolman and Terrence E. Deal identify three principles found in ethical judgments: mutuality (all parties to a relationship are operating under the same understanding about the rules of the game), generality (a specific action follows a principle of conduct applicable to all comparable situations), and caring (an action shows care for the legitimate interests of others). As Bolman and Deal state, "Such questions raise issues that should be part of an ongoing dialogue about the moral dimension of management and leadership."[35] Taking a stance on values, ethical choices, and appropriate behavior is a reflection of principled judgment.

Codes of Ethics in Librarianship

Professional ethics is an additional frame of reference for behavior and the decisions a librarian makes on a daily basis. Professional ethics is behavior set forth, either formally or informally, by the profession of librarianship. Ethical concerns for collections librarians address

- censorship (intentional and unintentional)
- intellectual freedom and freedom of expression
- intellectual property and copyright
- privacy of individuals
- relationships and business practices with vendors, publishers, and subscription agents and avoidance of conflicts of interest
- compliance with library and parent institution requirements and applicable legislation

Several formal statements of ethics for librarianship have been developed. The ALA first provided its "Code of Ethics" in 1938, which was most recently revised in 1995; it is supplemented by "The Freedom to Read Statement" and "The Freedom to View Statement."[36] The Association for Library Collections and Technical Services (ALCTS) has developed a set of guidelines for its members to supplement the ALA "Code of Ethics," according to which,

> Within the context of the institution's missions and programs and the needs of the user populations served by the library, an ALCTS member
>
> 1. strives to develop a collection of materials within collection policies and priorities;

2.   strives to provide broad and unbiased access to information;

3.   strives to preserve and conserve the materials in the library in accordance with established priorities and programs;

4.   develops resource sharing programs to extend and enhance the information sources available to library users;

5.   promotes the development and application of standards and professional guidelines;

6.   establishes a secure and safe environment for staff and users;

7.   fosters and promotes fair, ethical and legal trade and business practices;

8.   maintains equitable treatment and confidentiality in competitive relations and manuscript and grant reviews;

9.   supports and abides by any contractual agreements made by the library or its home institution in regard to the provision of or access to information resources, acquisition of services, and financial arrangements.[37]

Rare book, manuscript, and special collections librarians have also developed a set of standards for ethical conduct, as has the Acquisitions Section of ALCTS.[38]

The ALA first adopted the Library Bill of Rights in 1948; the current version was reaffirmed in 1996:

The American Library Association affirms that all libraries are forums for information and ideas, and that the following basic policies should guide their services.

I.   Books and other library resources should be provided for the interest, information, and enlightenment of all people of the community the library serves. Materials should not be excluded because of the origin, background, or views of those contributing to their creation.

II.   Libraries should provide materials and information presenting all points of view on current and historical issues. Materials should not be proscribed or removed because of partisan or doctrinal disapproval.

III. Libraries should challenge censorship in the fulfillment of their responsibility to provide information and enlightenment.

IV.   Libraries should cooperate with all persons and groups concerned with resisting abridgment of free expression and free access to ideas.

V.   A person's right to use a library should not be denied or abridged because of origin, age, background, or views.

VI.   Libraries which make exhibit spaces and meeting rooms available to the public they serve should make such facilities available on an equitable basis, regardless of the beliefs or affiliations of individuals or groups requesting their use.[39]

An individual's response to situations is guided by a mix of standards or principles from various frames of reference. For example, one may operate within a set of religious or moral principles, legal requirements at the organizational level, and professional ethical standards. When these different frames are mutually inconsistent, the individual attempting to follow them experiences conflict and must decide which code should predominate and guide behavior. When different sources or frames of reference for ethical behavior suggest different decisions or responses, the librarian must resolve the conflict in order to act. This is an individual decision. There are times when one may feel compelled to take an ethical stand that conflicts with one's employer. Situations in which the parent institution or community prescribes censorship of one form or another yet the librarian believes that intellectual freedom is being compromised are examples of personal and professional ethics in conflict with institutional ethics. Conversely, many libraries and librarians find personal and institutional values in conflict with tenets set forth in the Library Bill of Rights. The greatest area of controversy is the bill's Article V: "A person's right to use a library should not be denied or abridged because of origin, age, background, or views." Research by Julian Aiken found that nearly 51 percent of 110 public libraries responding to a survey did not permit free access for minors to nonprint materials.[40] The pertinent question Aiken raises in the face of these data is why the realities of day-to-day decisions and service policies are disconnected from the values and principles promoted by the ALA.

Working with Suppliers and Vendors

Collections librarians can face ethical issues in their relationships with suppliers and vendors. Librarians often develop a congenial relationship with supplier and vendor representatives, fostered by pleasant lunches and conference receptions. This is one reason many libraries and their parent institutions prohibit or place financial limits on the gifts and personal benefits librarians may accept. Librarians should not permit a personal desire to be nice to representatives to interfere with an ethical obligation to manage institutional resources as effectively as possible. Although librarians have an obligation to be honest and fair and to act in good faith with suppliers, they have no obligation to help them succeed. Librarians should keep the financial and service interests of their libraries foremost, seeking to obtain the maximum value for each purchase, license agreement, and service contract.

Another frame of reference may be explicitly or implicitly provided by the library and its parent institution. One university has issued a document called "Code of Ethics," which makes explicit the institution's expectations and values when negotiating with an external supplier. In the terms of this document, the employee agrees to "support and uphold the values, policies and procedures of the University in all my purchasing activities . . . , maintain a high level of ethics . . . [and] strive to obtain the maximum value for each purchase."[41]

Implicit guidance supplements explicit guidelines and codes and is modeled through the behavior of administrators, managers, and peers. Values are conveyed through actions as well as written statements.

A commercial binder who cannot provide binding of the appropriate quality at market prices should not be retained as the library's binder, no matter how long the relationship has continued. A serials agent who has a cash flow problem and fails to pay publishers is not a reliable serials agent with a promising future. A history of friendly relations between librarian and vendor is not the issue. Each service and purchase agreement must be reviewed and all available information evaluated. Each agreement must be continually assessed as a business decision, and the needs of the library must be placed first. A librarian must keep in mind the long-term interests of the communities that his or her decisions affect. One must have the ethical convictions and courage to place these interests above any personal short-term preoccupations. No matter how gracious and charming a service agency's representatives are and how competently the agency has performed in the past, future performance and financial viability are the deciding factors.

Librarians' ethical obligations are twofold: to conduct business with mutual respect and trust, and to serve their own organizations as best they can. Explicit and implicit codes aim for high standards of professional conduct and integrity; they value honesty, trustworthiness, respect, and fairness in dealing with other people and loyalty toward the ethical principles, values, policies, and procedures espoused by a librarian's institution. Librarians have an obligation to consistently demonstrate and carefully maintain a tradition of ethical behavior.

Performance Evaluation

An important aspect of any position is regular evaluation of performance. This may involve an annual formal performance review and should include frequent informal contacts with a supervisor that address performance goals, accomplishments, and problems. This continuous dialogue ensures that the librarian has a clear understanding of expectations and the extent to which they are being met. Performance appraisals, whether formal or informal, should provide constructive guidance. Ideally, performance evaluation begins with an individual's job description, which reflects the relative importance of and anticipated percentage of time devoted to collection activities. The job description may be responsibility based (what the person does) or outcome based.

Evaluations of collection development librarians are complicated because of difficulty in developing performance standards and measuring outcomes. If the librarian has multiple assignments and multiple supervisors, compiling and preparing the evaluation can be challenging. If more than one supervisor is involved, the librarian and supervisors must be in agreement about the priorities of multiple assignments and effort to be devoted to each. Academic libraries may use peer reviews in place of or in addition to supervisor reviews. The librarian being reviewed should be provided with explicit goals within each review period and a clear understanding of performance criteria and what is being measured.

The newly hired collection development librarian should know from his or her first day on the job how performance evaluation is handled. Many libraries require supporting documentation relevant to the employee's performance, and the employee should be assembling this information on an ongoing basis. Some libraries require monthly reports prepared by the staff member. Academic libraries may solicit comments from faculty in academic departments.[42] Part of the annual review process may be the preparation of a self-review reporting on the individual's success or failure in meeting certain specific goals agreed upon at the beginning of the review cycle.

Performance expectations should be consistent with the library's overall mission and goals. They may be very specific and delineate every area of the job description, such as quantity and quality of liaison contacts with users, success in managing budget allocations, quality of new acquisitions, and contributions to the library as a whole. Librarians in academic libraries and some school media centers may also have performance expectations that must be met in order to be promoted and granted tenure or continuous appointment. Academic librarians often have performance expectations that are similar to those of teaching faculty, involving research, publication, instruction, and contributions to the profession. Because most tenure and promotion decisions are based on a cumulative history of performance, the new librarian must work closely with his or her supervisor and the tenure committee or its equivalent to begin building a persuasive dossier from the point of hire.

Summary

Any library activity that relates to library collections both on-site and online may be assigned to the collection development and management librarian. Assignment of responsibilities and placement of collections activities within a library vary depending on the library's size, budget, mission, and user community. In small libraries, all activities may be handled by one individual. In very large libraries, responsibilities may be highly centralized or widely dispersed according to subject responsibility, user community, physical location of staff members, or a subset of functions. The trend is toward combining collections responsibilities with others, though full-time collection development and management librarians are found in larger libraries. Many functions that were once the purview of professional librarians have migrated to paraprofessionals. Those that remain solely the responsibility of collections librarians are programmatic in nature because they have the potential to change the library's direction, create new programs, and influence how the library's constituents perceive it. Typical responsibilities fall under the categories of selecting (and deselecting), budgeting, planning and organizing, and communicating and reporting.

Organizational models for assigning and managing collection development responsibilities vary according to the library's size, type, and mission. Larger libraries of all types often have a senior collections officer. This individual may have direct responsibility for all librarians with collection development and management responsibilities or may serve a coordinating function. The collections officer usually has budgetary authority and provides the guidance essential for coherent, coordinated collection development and management. Many libraries also have committees with permanent or rotating membership that provide coordination, consistency, and help with problem solving by virtue of members representing various units, branches, or divisions. In small libraries, all collections responsibilities may be handled by a single individual.

The skills and competencies a new librarian brings to the practice of collection management and development are extensive. Ranging from knowledge of factors that make for effective selection and collection management decisions and how to analyze a user community to management practices for budgeting, planning, and critical decision making, these skills can be learned and form the building blocks for beginning a career. Other aspects of collections work can be learned only through on-site training and practice. A collections librarian must work closely with his or her supervisor to set performance and mastery goals. Whether newly hired or newly assigned collections responsibilities, a collection development and management librarian must take personal responsibility for his or her professional goals, accomplishments, and career.

Library automation and new technologies for delivering and accessing information are affecting the work of collections development librarians. Some tasks and responsibilities that were once solely those of professional librarians have been assumed by support staff. Computerization is making the identification of resources, placement of orders, and provision of management information faster and easier. Digital information provides new challenges related to complex licensing, new interpretations of copyright and fair use, and the complexities of accessing and servicing different formats. The expansion of electronic information reinforces the importance of cooperation and coordination among library operations and services.

Ethics influence how collections librarians interact with materials sellers, suppliers, and service agents as well as with their user community and coworkers. Collections librarians' ethical obligations concern how they conduct business with vendors and suppliers and how they serve their libraries in all aspects of performing their responsibilities. Honesty, trustworthiness, respect, and fairness in dealing with other people and loyalty toward the ethical principles, values, policies, and procedures espoused by a librarian's institution are essential.

CASE STUDY

Jeff has recently taken a position as the collection development coordinator for a small county library, which has one large main library and one smaller branch library. The collection (all formats) consists of approximately 105,000 items and has increased by 60 percent in the previous five years. The library is heavily used (88 percent of the county residents have library cards) and well supported by the county, receiving reasonable budget increases annually. The total staff numbers seventy, most of whom are paraprofessionals. Before Jeff arrived, the library did not have a collections coordinator. They library does not have collection development policies for either the library as a whole or the various divisions of the collection. Individuals charged with selection do not have written descriptions of their responsibilities, no selectors' manual exists, and the library has neither a formal nor an informal training program for selection responsibilities. Over time and as the budget for collections grew, the assistant director has distributed selection responsibilities to twenty-five staff members, few of whom have graduate library degrees. Responsibilities are assigned variously according to Dewey ranges, formats, language, and fiction genre. This distributed approach, though not as common as a more centralized approach with fewer selectors, has some advantages. Staff members feel engaged, excited, and empowered by the responsibility and are often selecting materials to meet the needs of the community they know well. The problems are lack of coordination, lack of communication, and difficulty managing the overall budget, which is Jeff's responsibility. Some staff members spend little time on selection and collection management activities, and some neglect other duties to focus much of their time on selection. Jeff needs advice on how to control and regulate the distributed selection system.

Activity

Suggest measures that Jeff can employ to improve the coordination of selection. Identify steps that can improve communication between the selectors and Jeff. Suggest ways that fiscal accountability can be improved. If the current system with many selectors should be changed, suggest a more effective system and explain why it is so. List the advantages and disadvantages of the system proposed.

Note: The first edition of this book also provided a case study and associated activity in its discussion on organization and staffing; access it as a supplementary resource at www.ala.org/editions/extras/Johnson09720.

Notes

1. See Robert B. Harmon, *Elements of Bibliography: A Guide to Information Sources and Practical Applications*, 3rd ed. (Lanham, Md.: Scarecrow, 1998), for an introduction to the art of bibliography.

2. J. Periam Danton, "The Subject Specialist in National and University Libraries, with Special Reference to Book Selection," *Libri* 17, no. 1 (1967): 42–58.

3. Russell Duino, "Role of the Subject Specialist in British and American University Libraries: A Comparative Study," *Libri* 29, no. 1 (1979): 1–19.

4. Raven Fonfa, "From Faculty to Librarian Materials Selection: An Element in the Professionalization of Librarianship," in *Leadership and Academic Librarians*, ed. Terrence F. Mech and Gerard B. McCabe, 22–36 (Westport, Conn.: Greenwood, 1998).

5. Gordon Rowley, comp., *Organization of Collection Development*, SPEC Kit no. 207 (Washington, D.C.: Association of Research Libraries, 1995).

6. James E. Bobick, *Collection Development Organization and Staffing in ARL Libraries*, SPEC Kit, no. 131 (Washington, D.C.: Association of Research Libraries, 1987).

7. John Haar, "Scholar or Librarian? How Academic Libraries' Dualistic Concept of the Bibliographer Affects Recruitment," *Collection Building* 12, nos. 1/2 (1993): 18–23.

8. Eldred R. Smith, "The Impact of the Subject Specialist Librarian on the Organization and Structure of the Academic Research Library," in *The Academic Library: Essays in Honor of Guy R. Lyle*, ed. Evan Ira Farber and Ruth Walling, 71–81 (Metuchen, N.J.: Scarecrow, 1974).

9. The traditional bureaucratic organizational structure, as defined by Max Weber, is hierarchical and places decision making and responsibility at the top of the organization. Diminishing amounts of authority are delegated in prescribed portions to lower levels in the organizational pyramid. See Max Weber, "Bureaucracy," in *From Max Weber: Essays in Sociology*, trans. H. H. Gerth and C. Wright Mills, 196–244 (New York: Oxford University Press, 1962).

10. See, e.g., Anthony W. Ferguson, "University Library Collection Development and Management Using a Structural-Functional Systems Model," *Collection Management* 8 (Spring 1986): 1–14; and Dan C. Hazen, "Modeling Collection Development Behavior: A Preliminary Statement," *Collection Management* 4 (Spring 1982): 1–14.

11. Bonita Bryant, "The Organizational Structure of Collection Development," *Library Resources and Technical Services* 31, no. 2 (1987): 111.

12. Paul Metz, "Quantifying the Workload of Subject Bibliographers in Collection Development," *Journal of Academic Librarianship* 17, no. 5 (1991): 284–87.

13. Cynthia Orr, "Collection Development in Public Libraries," in *Encyclopedia of Library and Information Science*, 2nd ed., Miriam A. Drake, ed., vol. 1, 585–90 (New York: Marcel Dekker, 2003).

14. Catherine Gibson, "'But We've Always Done It This Way!' Centralized Selection Five Years Later," in *Public Library Collection Development in the Information Age*, ed. Annabel K. Stephens, 33–40 (Binghamton, N.Y.: Haworth, 1998); Phyllis Sue Alpert, "Effect of Multiculturalism and Automation in Public Library Collection Development and Technical Services," in *Current Practices in Public Libraries*, ed. William Miller and Pita M. Pellen, 91–104 (Binghamton, N.Y.: Haworth, 2006).

15. Ann Irvine, "Is Centralized Collection Development Better? The Results of a Survey," *Public Libraries* 34 (July/Aug. 1995): 216–18.

16. W. Bernard Lukenbill, *Collection Development for a New Century in the School Library Media Center* (Westport, Conn.: Greenwood, 2002).

17. George J. Soete, "Training for Success: Integrating the New Bibliographer into the Library," in *Recruiting, Educating, and Training Librarians for Collection Development*, ed. Peggy Johnson and Sheila S. Intner, 160–69 (Westport, Conn.: Greenwood, 1994).

18. John M. Budd and Patricia L. Bril, "Education for Collection Management: Results of a Survey of Educators and Practitioners," *Library Resources and Technical Services* 38, no. 4 (1994): 343–53.

19. Association for Library Collections and Technical Services, "ALCTS Educational Policy Statement," approved by the ALCTS Board of Directors, June 27, 1995, www .ala.org/ala/alcts/manual/conted/cepolicy.cfm; Maria Otero-Boisvert, "The Role of the Collection Development Librarian in the 90s and Beyond," in *Catalysts for Changing: Managing Library in the 1990s*, ed. Gisela M. von Dran and Jennifer Cargill, 159–70 (New York: Haworth, 1993); Patricia Battin, "Managing University and Research Library Professionals: A Director's Perspective," *American Libraries* 14, no. 1 (1983): 22–25; Edward G. Holley, "Defining the Academic Librarians," *College and Research Libraries* 46 (Nov. 1985): 462–77.

20. Nancy M. Cline, "Staffing: The Art of Managing Changes," in *Collection Management and Development: Issues in an Electronic Era*, ed. Peggy Johnson and Bonnie MacEwan, 13–28, ALCTS Papers on Library Technical Services and Collections no. 5 (Chicago: American Library Association, 1994).

21. Karen Schmidt, "Past Perfect, Future Tense: A Survey of Issues in Collection Development," *Library Collections, Acquisitions, and Technical Services* 28, no. 4 (2004): 360–72.

22. Peter M. Senge, *The Fifth Discipline: The Art and Practice of the Learning Organization*, rev. and updated (New York: Doubleday, 2006).

23. Collection Management and Development Committee, Resources and Technical Services Division, American Library Association, *Guide for Writing a Bibliographer's Manual*, Collection Management and Development Guides no. 1 (Chicago: American Library Association, 1987).

24. Susan L. Fales, ed., *Guide for Training Collection Development Librarians*, Collection Management and Development Guides no. 8 (Chicago: Association for Library Collections and Technical Services, American Library Association, 1996).

25. Harry Braverman, *Labor and Monopoly Capital: The Degradation of Work in the Twentieth Century* (New York: Monthly Review, 1974).

26. See a special issue of *Monthly Review*, vol. 46, no. 6 (1994), commemorating Harry Braverman's *Labor and Monopoly Capital*; and Stephen Wood, ed., *The Degradation of Work? Skill, Deskilling, and the Labour Process* (London: Hutchinson, 1982).

27. Shoshana Zuboff, *In the Age of the Smart Machine: The Future of Work and Power* (New York: Basic Books, 1988).

28. Ron Ray, "Paraprofessionals in Collection Development: Report of the ALCTS/CMDS Collection Development Librarians of Academic Libraries Discussion Group," *Library Acquisitions: Practice and Theory* 18 (Fall 1994): 317–20.

29. Nina Toren, "Professionalization and Its Sources," *Sociology of Work and Occupations* 2 (Spring 1975): 323–27.

30. Allen B. Veaner, "Paradigm Lost, Paradigm Regained? A Persistent Personnel Issue in Academic Librarianship, II," *College and Research Libraries* 55 (1994): 389–402.

31. Bryant, "Organizational Structure of Collection Development," 113–14.

32. Rowley, *Organization of Collection Development*, from unpaged prefatory materials.

33. See Nancy Courtney and Fred W. Jenkins, "Reorganizing Collection Development and Acquisitions in a Medium-Sized Academic Library," *Library Acquisitions: Practice and Theory* 22, no. 3 (1998): 287–93; and Kathleen Wachel and Edward Shreeves, "An Alliance between Acquisitions and Collection Management," *Library Acquisitions: Practice and Theory* 16 (1994): 383–89.

34. Jasper G. Schad, "Managing Collection Development in University Libraries That Utilize Librarians with Dual-Responsibility Assignments," *Library Acquisitions: Practice and Theory* 14, no. 2 (1990): 165–71.

35. Lee G. Bolman and Terrence E. Deal, *Reframing Organizations: Artistry, Choice, and Leadership*, 2nd ed. (San Francisco: Jossey-Bass, 1997), 193.

36. American Library Association, "Code of Ethics of the American Library Association" (adopted June 28, 1995, by the ALA Council), www.ala.org/ala/oif/statementspols/codeofethics/codeethics.cfm. American Library Association, "The Freedom to Read Statement" (adopted June 25, 1953, by the ALA Council and the AAP Freedom to Read Committee; amended January 28, 1972; January 16, 1991; July 12, 2000; June 30, 2004), www.ala.org/ala/oif/statementspols/ftrstatement/freedomreadstatement.cfm; American Library Association, "The Freedom to View Statement" (endorsed January 10, 1990, by the ALA Council), www.ala.org/ala/oif/statementspols/ftvstatement/freedomviewstatement.cfm.

37. Association for Library Collections and Technical Services, "Guidelines for ALCTS Members to Supplement the American Library Association Code of Ethics" (developed by the ALCTS Task Force on Professional Ethics and adopted by the ALCTS Board of Directors, Midwinter Meeting, February 7, 1994), www.ala.org/ContentManagement/ContentDisplay.cfm?ContentID=39659.

38. "Standards for Ethical Conduct for Rare Book, Manuscript, and Special Collections Librarians, with Guidelines for Institutional Practice in Support of the Standards, 2nd ed., 1992," *College and Research Library News* 54, no. 4 (1993): 207–15, www.ala.org/Template.cfm?Section=standards&template=/ContentManagement/ContentDisplay.cfm&ContentID=8969; Association for Library Collections and Technical Services, "Statement on Principles and Standards of Acquisitions Practice" (developed by the ALCTS Acquisitions Section Ethics Task Force, endorsed by the ALCTS Acquisitions Section and adopted by the ALCTS Board of Directors, Midwinter Meeting, February 7, 1994), www.ala.org/ContentManagement/ContentDisplay.cfm?ContentID=162505.

39. American Library Association, "Library Bill of Rights" (adopted June 18, 1948, by the ALA Council; amended February 2, 1961; amended June 28, 1967; amended January 23, 1980; inclusion of "age" reaffirmed January 24, 1996), www.ala.org/ala/oif/statementspols/statementsif/librarybillrights.cfm.

40. Julian Aiken, "Outdated and Irrelevant? Rethinking the Library Bill of Rights—Does It Work in the Real World?" *American Libraries* 38, no. 8 (2007): 54–56.

41. University of Minnesota, "Code of Ethics for Department Staff Responsible for Buying," www.policy.umn.edu/groups/ppd/documents/form/codeofethics.pdf.

42. Jack Siggins, comp., *Performance Appraisal of Collection Development Librarians*, SPEC Kit no. 181 (Washington, D.C.: Association of Research Libraries, 1992).

Suggested Readings

Anderson, Cokie G. *Ethical Decision Making for Digital Libraries.* Oxford, England: Chandos, 2006.

Biery, Susan S. "Team Management of Collection Development from a Team Member's Perspective." *Collection Management* 25, no. 3 (2001): 11–22.

Booth, Heather. *Serving Teens through Readers' Advisory.* Chicago: American Library Association, 2007.

Bucknall, Carolyn. *Guide for Writing a Bibliographer's Manual* [prepared for the Collection Management and Development Committee, Resources and Technical Services Division]. Collection Management and Development Guides no. 1. Chicago: American Library Association, 1987.

Butler, Rebecca P. "The School Librarian and On-the-job Ethics." *Knowledge Quest* 33, no. 5 (2005): 33–34.

Carson, Janet. "Professional Practice and the Labour Process: Academic Librarianship at the Millennium." *Advances in Library Administration and Organization* 21 (2004): 3–59.

Carter, Nancy F. "Bibliographer's Manual: A New Life, a New Process." *Collection Management* 29, no. 1 (2004): 31–41.

Casserly, Mary F. "Collection Management as Risk Management." *Library Collection, Acquisitions, and Technical Services* 28, no. 1 (2004): 79–92.

Eckwright, Gail Z., and Mary K. Bolin. "The Hybrid Librarian: The Affinity of Collection Management with Technical Services and the Organizational Benefits of an Individualized Assignment." *Journal of Academic Librarianship* 27, no. 6 (2001): 452–56.

Finks, Lee W., and Elisabeth Soekefeld. "Professional Ethics." In *Encyclopedia of Library and Information Science*, edited by Allen Kent, vol. 52, supp. 15, 301–21. New York: Marcel Dekker, 1993.

Fisher, William. "Impact of Organizational Structure on Acquisitions and Collection Development." *Library Collections, Acquisitions and Technical Services* 25, no. 4 (2001): 409–19.

Forte, Eric, et al., "Developing a Training Program for Collections Managers." *Library Collections, Acquisitions, and Technical Services* 26, no. 3 (2002): 299–306.

Frazier, Kenneth. "Collection Development and Professional Ethics." In *Collection Development in a Digital Environment*, edited by Sul H. Lee, 33–46. New York: Haworth, 1999.

Gorman, Michael. *Our Enduring Values: Librarianship in the Twenty-first Century.* Chicago: American Library Association, 2000.

Harris, Roma M. "Information Technology and the Deskilling of Librarians." In *Encyclopedia of Library and Information Science*, edited by Allen Kent, vol. 53, supp. 16, 182–202. New York: Marcel Dekker, 1994.

Hazen, Dan. "Twilight of the Gods? Bibliographers in the Electronic Age." *Library Trends* 48, no. 4 (2000): 821–41.

Jenkins, Paul O. "Collection Development and Faculty." In *Faculty-Librarian Relationships*, 37–54. Oxford, England: Chandos, 2005.

Johnson, Peggy, and Sheila S. Intner, eds. *Recruiting, Educating, and Training Librarians for Collection Development.* New Directions in Information Management no. 33. Westport, Conn.: Greenwood, 1994.

Kennedy, John. "Education for Collection Management: Ending before It Ever Really Started, or Only Just Beginning?" *Education for Information* 16, no. 1 (1998): 45–56.

Koehler, Wallace C., and J. Michael Pemberton. "A Search for Core Values: Towards a Model Code of Ethics for Information Professionals." *Journal of Information Ethics* 9, no. 1 (2000): 26–54.

McMenemy, David, Alan Poulter, and Paul F. Burton. *A Handbook of Ethical Practice: A Practical Guide to Dealing with Ethical Issues in Information and Library Work.* Oxford, England: Chandos, 2007.

Mouw, James R. "Changing Roles in the Electronic Age: The Library Perspective." *Library Acquisitions: Practice and Theory* 22, no. 1 (1998): 15–21.

Munroe, Mary, John Haar, and Peggy Johnson. *Guide to Collection Management Administration, Organization, and Staffing.* Collection Management and Development Guides no. 10. Lanham, Md.: Scarecrow; Chicago: Association for Library Collections and Technical Services, 2001.

Neville, Robert, James Williams, and Caroline C. Hunt. "Faculty-Library Teamwork in Book Ordering." *College and Research Libraries* 59, no. 6 (1998): 524–33.

Rabine, Julie L., and Linda A. Brown. "The Selection Connection: Creating an Internal Web Page for Collection Development." *Library Resources and Technical Services* 44, no. 1 (2000): 44–49.

Rubin, Richard R., and Thomas Froehlich. "Ethical Aspects of Library and Information Science." In *Encyclopedia of Library and Information Science,* edited by Allen Kent, vol. 58, supp. 21, 33–52. New York: Marcel Dekker, 1996.

Saricks, Joyce G. *Readers' Advisory Service in the Public Library.* 3rd ed. Chicago: American Library Association, 2005.

Schweinsburg, Jane D. Finks. "Professional Awareness of the Ethics of Selection." In *Encyclopedia of Library and Information Science,* edited by Allen Kent and Carolyn Hall, vol. 63, supp. 26, 247–59. New York: Marcel Dekker, 1998.

Sorgenfrie, Robert, and Christopher Hooper-Lane. "Book Selection Responsibilities for the Reference Librarian: Professional Benefit or Burden?" *Library Collections, Acquisitions, and Technical Services* 25, no. 2 (2001): 171–78.

Stacy-Bates, Kristine K., et al. "Competencies for Bibliographers: A Process for Writing a Collection Development Competencies Document." *Reference and User Services Quarterly* 42, no. 3 (2003): 235–41.

Tucker, James Cory, and Matt Torrence. "Collection Development for New Librarians: Advice from the Trenches." *Library Collections, Acquisitions, and Technical Services* 28, no. 4 (2004): 397–409.

Webb, John. "Collections and Systems: A New Organizational Paradigm for Collection Development." *Library Collections, Acquisitions, and Technical Services* 25, no. 4 (2001): 461–68.

Wengert, Robert G. "Some Ethical Aspects of Being an Information Professional." *Library Trends* 49, no. 3 (2001): 486–509.

Wicks, Don A., Laura Bartolo, and David Swords. "Four Birds with One Stone: Collaboration in Collection Development." *Library Collections, Acquisitions, and Technical Services* 25, no. 4 (2001): 473–83.

Winters, Barbara J. "Ethics in Acquisitions Management." In *Understanding the Business of Library Acquisitions*, 2nd ed., edited by Karen A. Schmidt, 335–45. Chicago: American Library Association, 1998.

Wyatt, Neal. *The Readers' Advisory Guide to Nonfiction.* Chicago: American Library Association, 2007.

CHAPTER THREE

Policy, Planning, and Budgets

Formal or systematic planning and goal-setting activities, along with assessment and evaluation techniques to measure progress toward those goals, have become standard practice in many libraries. Planning would not be necessary in a static environment, but the environment in which every library exists is changing constantly. These changes are on many fronts—sociological, educational, economic, demographic, political and governmental, technological, and institutional. This chapter introduces planning as an organizational responsibility and examines collection development policies and budgeting, two of the most commonly used formal planning tools in libraries. Collection assessment and evaluation are addressed in chapter 7.

Planning in Libraries

Planning is one of many of the librarian's responsibilities. Formal planning should not be viewed as the responsibility of managers and administrators only. Planning should be part of all activities in the library. Planning means devising a method for accomplishing something. Planning takes place every day because outcomes are sought, decisions are made to reach those outcomes, and actions are taken based on those decisions. The distinction is between informal planning, which people do daily, and formal planning, which has a structure within which conscious, intentional planning occurs.

Peter Drucker writes that formal planning is improving the "futurity" of decisions.[1] In an environment of rapid change, formal continuous planning becomes more important. Libraries need to anticipate change and decide how to handle it. Formal planning examines both the probable and the possible future. Ideally, a library will identify several possible futures and then decide which are the most probable. The future is unpredictable, and alternatives need to be on hand so that plans can be modified as needed. Uncertainty is the reason planning is a continuous process. Planning is the process of allocating and reallocating resources in response to change in the environment while keeping in mind the library's mission and priorities.

Consider, for example, the impact of information in digital formats. Librarians recognize its pervasiveness and costs along with increasing user expectations to access it through libraries. A librarian should consider several possible futures. What percentage of information resources will be available electronically five, ten, twenty years from now? What is the impact on the current and projected acquisitions budget? What percentage of the budget might be spent on electronic resources five, ten, twenty years from now and how will this affect acquisition of other formats? Given the forces at play, where would the library like to go and what does it need to do to get there? Laying out alternative scenarios allows the librarian to project alternative funding needs, collection development policies, and service implications.

Formal planning is a form of organizational learning. Planning for the future requires understanding what the library is doing now and what it would like to be doing in the future given certain probable conditions, then choosing the most reasonable path to that future. People involved in planning—and, ideally, planning is broad based in an organization—learn a tremendous amount about their library, their parent organization, the external environment, and their user community.

Planning is also a communication tool. Information is shared within the library as part of the planning process. Equally important, information about present services and programs and future needs, expectations, and hopes is both gathered and shared with the library's clientele and funding bodies. Planning sets a course for the future. It provides a mechanism to inform people about that future and an opportunity for them to buy into it.

George Keller identifies several caveats to consider when planning.[2] Planning is not the production of a blueprint to be followed rigorously. A formal plan is not a set of platitudes and buzzwords. It should not be the personal vision of one individual or a statement by a particularly vocal individual or group. Planning does not work if it is an attempt to avoid or outwit the future. Plans do not eliminate risks, nor are they a surrender to external forces. Planning should not be limited to a once-a-year organizational exercise. Planning will not solve all an organization's problems, and it cannot address all issues at once. Formal planning is a library's guide for continuity. It provides a structured way to envision and move toward a future, anticipate change, maximize its positive effects, and minimize its negative ones.

Planning Models

No single style, method, or model of planning is best. Several types of planning may be in use simultaneously in the same library. The following discussion presents various popular planning approaches but is not exhaustive.

Budgeting, a traditional planning process through which many program-planning decisions are made, is discussed later in this chapter. Budgeting is often a component of the planning approaches described below.

Master planning is top-down planning that begins in the administrative offices. In a college or university, the president's or provost's office begins with an institutional mission and sets out goals, objectives, and time lines with which each academic unit must adhere. City government master planning through the mayor's office or school district planning through the superintendent's office can take the same approach. Unit plans are prepared consistent with the master plan. This model is simple because responsibility for planning is not dispersed and nothing changes unless mandated by the governing body or administrative office. Units and individuals within the organization or institution are seldom satisfied with such an approach. Their knowledge and expertise do not contribute to the planning process, and plans may be crafted in isolation from the reality in which librarians work.

Contingency planning is directed specifically toward preparing for one possible and usually undesirable future. For examples, libraries prepare disaster contingency plans. Such a plan begins by identifying the possible disaster, such as a flood, and consequences for facilities, services, and collections. Contingency plans identify appropriate steps to respond to those circumstances. Collection development librarians should ensure that a disaster response plan is prepared and kept up to date for the library collection.

Formal democratic planning is a cyclic planning process in which all units are requested to formulate their plans for program development on a regular schedule. Plans are reviewed simultaneously to arrive at a complete and coherent plan for the library, college or university, school system, city government, and so on. In this style, the source of ideas rests primarily with individuals and individual units. Contributing units and individuals may be given one or more themes or priorities on which to focus.

Strategic planning has an external focus and requires continual scanning to monitor changes in the environment. Environmental scanning is an important component of strategic planning but equally useful in all types of planning. Strategic planning constantly reviews external conditions, as well as changing internal conditions, and devises an appropriate response. It usually begins with a vision of the organization's future that serves as a guide to planning the goals, objectives, and strategies that form the plan. Strategic planning is broadly participative and often uses small groups to generate strategies that are incorporated into a coherent plan. Strategic planning, although it may look at one- or three- or five-year increments, does not produce a final, static plan. It remains an open-ended, continuous process that seeks to keep the organization in step with its environment. Collection development activities are defined and planned in terms of the environment.

In *scenario planning*, the library develops scenarios that describe alternative futures and formulates plans or strategies for the library in those various futures. Scenario planning can be used in strategic planning and in more focused planning as well. It provides an opportunity to be creative in envisioning the library's future and to consider what is probable, possible, and preferable.

Entrepreneurial planning, also called opportunistic planning, is a laissez-faire, individual approach to program planning that relies on individuals coming forward whenever they have an idea for altering or expanding programs. This approach has no planning constraints, no timetables, and no formal requests for ideas. It implies acting immediately while the opportunity presents itself. The process of choosing remote electronic resources in libraries is often entrepreneurial. If a new resource is suddenly available, the price is favorable, and the user demand is high, the library may choose to purchase access, even though that particular resource or subject focus was not identified as a priority in library planning.

Incentive planning has not been as prevalent in nonprofit organizations as in the corporate sector, though it is being seen more often in higher education, where it may be called *responsibility-centered management*. The institution is viewed as an economic organization. Institutional leaders develop performance benchmarks and an incentive structure that rewards particular types of activities. Each unit or department selects programs to be developed based on the incentive structure. Incentive planning is more likely to be found in academic institutions. For example, units may retain revenue generated through tuition or sales. Since a library has little opportunity to produce income, it is often defined for the purposes of incentive planning as a public or common good. Academic units may be taxed to support the library. In this scenario, the academic library faces pressures to justify its contributions to the institution.

Environmental Scanning

Environmental scanning, a formal method developed in the for-profit sector, can gather information and enhance one's understanding of the library's environment. It is a key component of strategic planning. Environmental scanning has been defined as "a methodology for coping with external social, economic, and technological issues that may be difficult to observe or predict but that cannot be ignored and will not go away."[3] Eileen Abels writes that "all organizations need to monitor at some level what goes on in their environments and recognize their strengths and weaknesses in relation to it. The importance of environmental information depends on the degree to which the success of the organization itself depends on its environment."[4] The purpose of an environmental scan is to detect, monitor, and analyze trends and issues in the environment, both internal and external, in which an organization operates. It is a key component in planning because it positions an organization to set goals and make plans within the framework of an emerging future.

Environmental scanning first received widespread attention in the late 1960s as businesses sought a way to avoid unexpected crises and to prepare for startling and increasingly rapid change. The American auto industry did not anticipate the consequences of smaller families, increasing fuel prices, and declining interest in new car models as status symbols. Consequently, U.S. companies were years behind foreign car manufacturers when they finally entered the small-car market. Ultimately, they realized the necessity of preparing for significant changes in their market and the forces that governed that market. This realization evolved into an awareness that tracking external forces and issues that have great impact on an organization can provide a competitive advantage. An organization that analyzes alternative futures and effectively monitors potential threats and opportunities can take advance action. It can modify present decisions and adapt quickly.

Environmental scanning is distinguished from simple monitoring by its systematic approach. Its four elements are scanning, analyzing, reporting, and crafting an appropriate organizational response. Formal environmental scanning requires the creation of a scanning team, which collects and analyzes information. The environmental scanning team selects the resources to scan, chooses criteria by which to scan, and develops categories of trends to monitor. Team members have individual scanning assignments and meet regularly to review trends. After selecting key trends, they interpret the strategic importance of these trends to the organization. The team is responsible for producing reports and briefings that can inform planning and decision making throughout the organization.

The corporate sector continues to rely on formal environmental scanning, but it is less widely used in nonprofit organizations because its complexities can be overwhelming. C. Davis Fogg maintains that strategic planning is impossible without environmental analysis.[5] Environmental scanning is not, however, an all-or-nothing proposition. A modified approach can provide benefits to the library. Recognizing trends and analyzing their impact can position libraries to assign priorities and make decisions about budget, personnel, and facilities before crises force them into a corner. As planning for alternative futures becomes increasingly important, libraries need all the resources they can marshal to make informed decisions. Anticipating future user community needs, wants, and demands helps the library to design collections and services to meet them.

Many libraries already monitor their internal and external environments, using techniques that can be applied more widely. These monitoring techniques can be combined with analysis and a commitment to link this analysis to planning activities. Typical techniques are reading source materials, monitoring electronic discussion lists, tracking issues through personal contacts, and directly soliciting comments from the user community. Some libraries assemble and route reading files of relevant materials to staff members and routinely forward online announcements and information about reports and documents accessible via the Internet. Source materials may include newsletters and reports from peer and local libraries; pertinent articles and editorials; announcements and newsletters from the college or university, school district, or government body; federal and foundation grant announcements; vendor announcements; and publications from consortia, organizations, and agencies with whom the library has regular contact. Many library science journals have sections devoted to tracking important developments and issues of interest to librarians.

These information sources should be seen as more than a source for current awareness. Classic environmental scanning includes developing a set of categories or a mental model within which trends or issues are organized. This helps draw together dispersed information to form a more complete picture of trends on the horizon. Categories should be tied to organizational concerns. Librarians often already use mental models as they scan the information that crosses their desks. For example, the children's librarian in a public library pays particular attention to information in the local media regarding the increase in day-care homes or changes in competency requirements for advancing to the next elementary grade. He or she notes which books are on banned book lists or the focus of school-parent conflict. Tracking popular topics for local school assignments, local trends in school age population, or growth in non-English-speaking families is important in library planning.

One aspect of environmental scanning often neglected in libraries is analysis. The question is, What do these trends mean for our programs, services, and collections? Trend analysis does not have to be addressed by a special team with the permanent responsibility of collecting and analyzing information. Individuals or small groups of staff members can prepare briefings to guide planning and goal setting. In addition, occasional meetings of the management team and other library committees or teams can be devoted to a review and analysis of hot topics that should be monitored and incorporated into planning.

The goal of environmental scanning is to identify and analyze trends that can inform planning. Just as the corporate sector seeks a competitive advantage through environmental scanning, so too libraries can better position themselves to meet a changing future. Identifying the trends, events, and ideas on which the library can capitalize guides management of financial and personnel resources. Simultaneously, libraries can identify possible events outside their control that are threats and for which they need to plan and seek ways to mitigate. If issues and trends are identified early, librarians can incorporate them in planning. Recognizing and reacting to environmental change before it becomes a crisis are the goals of environmental scanning.

Why Undertake Formal Planning?

The earlier an issue is identified and analyzed, the more successful the response. Planning does not eliminate uncertainty. It does suggest ways an organization can prepare for and respond to possibilities. Foresight, manifested in a plan, can lead to organizational actions that may prevent problems and provide positive opportunities for the organization. Refusing to prepare or delaying preparation of plans does not delay the future or minimize its impact. Such behavior only hinders the ability to respond effectively. Planning should not be viewed only as contingency planning for worst-case scenarios. Proactive planning gives the library a measure of control over the future. Planning offers an opportunity to influence the environment. Preparing plans is more than being prepared.

Planning, by focusing on goals along with the objectives or steps to reach those goals, provides desired outcomes against which progress can be measured. Accountability is increasingly important in nonprofit organizations such as libraries. The library must be in a position to demonstrate and document how it is using its financial resources effectively. By pointing to what it has accomplished, the library can justify continued and perhaps increased funding. Library plans often have subtitles such as "The Library in the Twenty-first Century" or "A Vision for the Future." These should not be seen as grandstanding. A final plan with goals, objectives, and strategies is only one result of formal planning. The process of systematic planning creates its own benefits by creating a vision of the library and engaging people to share that vision.

Any planning activity in a library affects collection development, and collection development planning must occur within the context of the library's overall planning. A collection development policy statement can be written and revised within various planning models. A collection policy is most effective if it has aspects of democratic planning—it should be prepared by the individuals who best understand the issues and will apply the plan.

Collection Development Policy Statements

Libraries without collection development policies are like businesses without business plans. Without a plan, an owner and his employees lack a clear understanding of what the business is doing now and what it will do in the future, and potential investors have little information about the business's prospects. The owner has no benchmarks against which to measure progress. Daily decisions are made without context. Even a library with written policy statements suffers if those statements are not consulted, reviewed, revised, and updated regularly. Collection development policies are also called selection policies, collection statements, or collection development plans—reflecting the reality that they serve as the plan for building and maintaining a collection, both locally held and accessed remotely. Selection, deselection, and priority setting throughout the library occur in isolation and without coordination if the library has no recorded rationale for decisions.[6]

Paul H. Mosher writes that collection development is a process that "should constitute a rational documented program guided by written policies and protocols and should reflect, in a sense, a contract between library users and library staff as to what will be acquired, for whom and at what level."[7] Marjorie L. Pappas declares that "one of the most important policy documents for a school library media center is the selection policy or the collection development policy."[8] A collection development policy describes the collection (on-site and remote access) as it is now and sets out a plan for how it will be developed while defining the rules directing that development. It is a systematic document, both comprehensive and detailed, that serves multiple purposes as a resource for public planning, allocation, information, administration, and training.[9]

Written collection policies became more widespread, particularly in academic libraries, after the Second World War and the tremendous growth of academic libraries' collections. In the decades that followed, libraries of all types began to prepare polices that documented practices and goals. By the mid-1950s, the ALA had recommended that every public library have a written selection and collection maintenance policy. In 1961, the American Association of School Librarians published *Policies and Procedures for the Selection of School Library Materials*.[10]

Policy statements are not general, idealistic, theoretical, or vague, but they are not so detailed and ponderous that they become unusable. Policy statements are not static. Preparing, reviewing, and revising policy statements are continuous processes because the community served, the financial resources available, and the information resources produced are always changing. Robert D. Stueart and Barbara B. Moran identify four characteristics of good policies: they are consistent; they are flexible and change as needs arise; they are guides rather than rules and permit discretion in their application; and they are written.[11] No policy, however well crafted, is a substitute for good collection development and management. A policy statement defines a framework and provides parameters, but it never tells how to select or reject a specific title. No matter how specific and detailed the collection development policy statement is, personal judgment is still necessary.

Purposes and Audience

The many purposes collection policies serve can be divided into two broad categories: to inform and to protect. The audience to whom the policy is directed must also be considered when creating a policy.

INFORMATION

Collection development policy statements inform by first presenting the library's mission and then describing current collections in terms of strengths and weaknesses and setting future goals. By identifying future collection levels, policies provide a benchmark against which to measure success in reaching those levels. To the extent that they match collections to mission, policies can guarantee that the collection being developed serves the educational, entertainment, and research mission of the parent institution or community. A policy "provides a theoretical overview that explains the educational, social, and cultural rationale for the development of the collection."[12] Collection policies provide the information needed to establish priorities for the library. Priorities for collection development and management are an obvious result. Claire Gatrell Stephens and Patricia Franklin state that, despite a perception that a collection development policy is extra work for a busy school library media specialist, it is important for articulating short- and long-term goals to the principal and community.[13] Typically, a collection policy outlines who is responsible for collection development and management. In addition, collection policies can inform decisions about cataloging, retrospective conversion, space allocation, budgeting, and fund-raising priorities. They can guide those individuals responsible for managing personnel, fiscal resources, space, and other resources in support of collections. By establishing collection priorities, policy statements can guide libraries in establishing staffing needs and allocating available personnel.

Policy statements help with budgeting by providing information for external and internal budget preparation and allocation. A well-crafted policy informs a library's governing and funding body about the library's directions and provides a clear and carefully articulated rationale for its collection. It demonstrates accountability by presenting a plan for careful management of fiscal resources and describing the results of funding decisions. A good policy statement can improve the library's ability to compete for resources within a complex and competitive institutional or government environment. A policy can provide supporting information for the preparation of grant proposals, budget requests, and fund-raising and development plans. Policy statements can be used in responses to accreditation surveys and to inquiries about the impact of new academic and research programs or new service mandates.

Policy statements serve as a vehicle for communication with the library's staff, administration, and constituencies. While describing the library collection and its strengths and weaknesses, they also formally document practice. They are contracts documenting the library's commitment, and they express this commitment in writing. Within the library, policy statements serve to coordinate selection when responsibility for selection is dispersed among many selectors and geographically among several physical locations. Policies provide control and consistency.

Because they are used to educate and train librarians responsible for collections, collection development policy statements must not become outdated. As new selectors, librarians, or school media specialists are hired and selection responsibilities reassigned, policy statements can serve as a training tool. If the policy statement is current in describing community service priorities, academic programs and research interests, school curricula, criteria for selection and deselection, collecting levels, and other pertinent areas, it provides the new selector with a baseline of information from which to begin managing the collection.

Policy statements serve a particularly important function to the extent that they document and support cooperative collection development. The policy statement should explicitly identify all current cooperative programs in which the library participates: collection building, resource sharing, regional storage, shared contribution and access to electronic resources, and so on. By documenting what the library does and what it plans to do with collecting levels by discipline or user group, a policy can facilitate cooperative collection development and resource-sharing programs. Using the same policy format and descriptive measures or terms within a consortium or other resource-sharing group can expedite cooperation and coordination.

PROTECTION

Collection development policy statements protect the library against external pressures. Policy statements can serve to protect intellectual freedom and prevent censorship. Many libraries' statements repeat or reference the Library Bill of Rights and other statements of intellectual freedom.[14] Librarians should give care to this significant area, especially with so much public attention focused on library access to the Internet. A library is best served by preparing a statement tailored to its own environment. The policy may include the procedures for handling a complaint against material held by a library. This does not mean that a statement about censorship is totally negative. The policy can be written so that it affirms the library's commitment to intellectual freedom. The process of creating a statement on intellectual freedom provides library staff members with the opportunity to think through these issues and to clarify their position. The presence of a carefully prepared and board-approved policy will not decrease the likelihood of a challenge to a specific controversial title, but it does increase the likelihood that challenged materials will be fairly reviewed and retained. When the library is challenged, librarians are prepared to respond. They have, in effect, rehearsed their response by writing the policy. Many school media center collections policies include a section that lays out the process for requesting reconsideration of materials and the steps followed in response to a reconsideration request. It may include a template or form that the students, parents, and legal guardians can use to object to resources available in the library media center.

Having a policy and process in place protects the library from being accused of inconsistency in responding to challenges.

At the same time that a policy resists the exclusion of certain materials, it can protect against pressure to include inappropriate and irrelevant materials. A statement can protect against undue special interest pressure from those who demand that the library accept gifts or purchase certain materials. A policy makes clear that materials are rejected because of collection guidelines, not because of who may or may not wish their acceptance.

Policies can protect by guiding the handling of gifts. The policy specifies the conditions under which the library accepts and rejects gifts. The gift policy should address the economic, social, and political situation in which a library exists. Libraries are advised not to appraise gifts but to refer potential donors to one or more external appraisers. Gift policies may be written for specific collections within a larger library or library system. For example, special collections may have their own policies for gifts.[15] By defining policy and procedures for accepting or declining, appraising, accessioning, acknowledging, and processing gifts, both the library and the potential donor are protected legally and practically.

In times of decreasing budgets and increasing materials costs, libraries need protection as they plan weeding, deselection, and serial cancellations. Making clear the operating principles under which these decisions are made protects the library from charges of bias and irresponsible behavior. A policy should define the process through which materials identified for withdrawal and cancellation are reviewed and evaluated, and by whom. Any processes for involving members of the user community should be described. This portion of the policy statement should include guidelines for disposal of unneeded materials.

A policy statement can identify issues of confidentiality. By specifying the types of information that are private—for example, about donors, budgets, costs and value of materials—a policy protects the library and its users, the parent institution, and donors.

AUDIENCE

Just as collection development policy statements serve many purposes, they serve many audiences. The library's collection policy is usually designed for use by staff members. The better the policy is, the more frequently it is consulted. Copies should be available for all library personnel, not just those with selection responsibilities. Many libraries post their policies on the library's website, where they can be consulted easily by both staff and other stakeholders.

A collection policy statement often serves a wider audience as well. It can be designed to be meaningful to library users, teachers and parents of students who use a school library media center, and external funding and governing bodies. Collections policies may be official governing board policies, especially in public libraries and schools. Though usually crafted by or in consultation with librarians and school library media specialists, the collection management policy carries the imprimatur—and thus the authority—of the governing board. This credence can be useful in the face of challenges to materials held and accessed by the library. If well written, the policy tells administrators and the user community what the library is doing with its allocated funds and makes clear that the library materials budget is not a "black hole" without definition or dimension. Other libraries can be part of the policy's audience. If the policy is intended to identify and develop cooperative collection building and use initiatives, then it must be shared with actual and potential partners.

Writing the Collection Development Policy Statement

A policy should be considered in terms of format, content, and style.[16] A policy usually conforms to a standard appearance and arrangement. Authors, whether individuals or committees, should keep in mind their primary purpose and audience while writing the policy and tailor the document appropriately. For example, a policy that is to be shared within a consortium and used for cooperative collection development planning should match the style of others in the consortium. A policy statement intended to inform teaching faculties or the parents of K–12 students might incorporate terminology from the curriculum. Format, content, and style can be crafted to meet specific ends and speak to specific audiences. Well-researched and well-written policy statements can address multiple purposes and audiences effectively.

Frank W. Hoffmann and Richard J. Wood identify what they consider the components necessary for good collection development policies, which include these sections or topics:[17]

- purpose statement
- background statement
- responsibility for collection development
- mission, goals, and objectives
- target audiences
- budgeting and funding
- evaluation criteria
- format
- government publications
- treatment of specific resource groups
- special collections
- resources sharing
- services
- selection aids
- copyright
- intellectual freedom
- acquisitions
- gifts and exchange
- collection maintenance
- weeding
- collection evaluation

- policy revision
- definition of terms and glossary

- bibliography
- appendixes

Though all these components may be found in a single policy, such comprehensiveness is not universal or always necessary. Developing and maintaining a policy with so many sections can be daunting and result in either the absence of a policy or failure to use or revise it as needed. Most libraries focus on those areas that best speak to their own priorities and issues.

Policies often begin with an overview or introductory section. A common first element is a statement of the policy's purpose, followed by the library's (or the parent organization's) mission statement. This is followed by a brief description or profile of the user community, including numbers and types of users served and these users' needs. Types of users mentioned in an academic library may include undergraduates, graduate and special students, faculty, distance education students, and the general public. The policy for an academic library might also describe academic programs, degrees granted, and research centers. The policy of a public library describes the citizens and their needs. Types of users might include K–12 students, students at local higher-education institutions, ethnic communities, care facilities residents, local businesses, the elderly, the visually impaired, and prison inmates. A library media center collection policy might identify the user community in terms of ESL students, special needs students, grade levels, teachers, and so on. The description of the user community is followed by a general statement of library priorities related to primary and secondary users. The statements about mission and community served provide information that sets the stage for the policies and guidelines that follow. Guidelines governing the appropriateness of materials, subjects, formats, and language must be coherent with the library's mission.

Limitations affecting collection development and management can be an important part of the policy's introduction. This is the place to note any factors or challenges that may limit the library in achieving its goals. New academic programs may have been added without additional library funding, meaning reduced support for all collection areas. The school enrollment or city's population may be increasing rapidly or changing significantly in ethnic composition. The impact of new technologies for information delivery, escalating monograph and serial prices, and reduced or static budgets may be addressed in this section.

Often, a brief description of the library and the scope of its collections follows. This can consist of the history of the collection or collections, broad subject areas emphasized or deemphasized, and collection locations. The quality and character of existing collections are evaluated in broad terms, as is current collecting practice. A general statement about criteria guiding selection and management decisions usually appears in the introduction. The policy introduction lists any cooperative collection development and resource-sharing agreements. Finally, the introduction describes the library's collection development organization. It locates responsibility for collection building and management. The specific tasks of evaluation, selection, collection maintenance, budget management, user community liaison, and so forth can be identified and assigned.

An overview of system-wide policies and guidelines follows the introduction. Collection development policy statements vary greatly in what they cover, though some areas are addressed more consistently. Policies usually enumerate types of materials that are selected and not selected, referencing those that apply only to certain subjects. A typical list might include statements about books, periodicals, newspapers, textbooks, juvenile materials, reprints, maps, dissertations and theses, textbooks, paperbacks, microforms, pamphlets, popular magazines, artworks, musical scores, audiovisual materials, software, and access to external electronic resources. Other issues addressed in general policies might be special collections and archives, reference materials, and government documents. Policy statements dealing with languages and translations, popular and trade materials, handling of superseded materials, gifts, duplicate copies, and expensive purchases are common. Three topics frequently addressed in collections policies are intellectual freedom, access to collections materials, and reconsideration of library materials. These areas address part of the protection function that a policy can service.

Many libraries find that a policy that contains the information described above is sufficient and can be presented in five or six pages—or less. Policies are often widely available and posted on libraries' public web pages. The policy for the Saint Paul (Minnesota) Public Library, which addresses the critical elements for this library, its community, and governing body, is presented as an illustration in appendix C of this book.

General policies may be supplemented by more detailed policies focused on subjects, user communities, or special collections. A public library may have a general policy augmented by policies for the children's collection, young adult collection, reference collection, adult nonfiction collection, and so on. An academic library or school media center may have supplemental policies addressing various subjects or disciplines—history, chemistry, geography, English language and literature, and so forth. These supplemental collection development policies usually follow one of three formats: narrative, classed analysis, or a combination of elements of these two.

NARRATIVE MODEL

The *narrative model* for a collection developmental policy statement is text-based. It includes a series of narrative descriptions, one for each subject, discipline, or subcollection. The sections may be defined broadly (e.g., Social Sciences, Humanities, and Sciences; or Adult Fiction, Children' s Fiction, and Reference), or each section may have a narrower focus (e.g., subdividing Agriculture into Animal Science, Agronomy, Soil Science . . . ; or Adult Fiction into Mysteries, Romances, Science Fiction . . .). The purpose is to give a focused view of subjects or subdivisions and of collection management as practiced in the library preparing the policy. An advantage of the narrative model is use of terms to describe local programs and collections that are local and immediately familiar.

These policy statements generally follow the outline and content of the overview. Each discusses the specific user community, specific limitations or emphases, types of materials collected or excluded, library unit or selector responsible for this collection, interdisciplinary relationships, additional resources, and other local factors. The Saint Paul Public Library (in appendix C) policy is a narrative policy.

CLASSED MODEL

The *classed model* describes the collection and current collecting levels in abbreviated language and numerical codes, typically according to the Library of Congress or Dewey Decimal Classification scheme. It may also describe preservation levels and future collecting levels. Though often extensive, this model allows one to see the collection as a whole, displayed on charts. This format grew out of libraries' need to develop an effective, consistent way of defining subjects and levels of collecting. The Research Libraries Group (RLG) was a leader in developing the Conspectus, a classed analysis format (examined in detail in chapter 7). Complemented by verification studies and supplemental guidelines, the RLG Conspectus has done much to define concepts, standardize procedures and terminology, and offer consistent techniques for describing and managing collections.[18] The Conspectus model was adopted by the ARL for its North American Collections Inventory Project, adapted by the National Library of Canada for use in that country, and is employed in the United Kingdom, other European countries, and Australia. Though initially intended for use by research libraries, the Conspectus has been modified for use by groups of libraries collecting at less than research intensity for state or regional resource sharing, fund allocations, space allocation and storage projects, accreditation, grant proposals, and preservation priorities. The Conspectus approach to assessing collections through the use of a standard vocabulary, though challenged by some as too dependent on individual perceptions, has become accepted as a tool that is both adaptable and widely applicable.

A library using the classed analysis model should use the same classification system for its collection development policy that it uses to organize its collection. This allows the library to use title counts to verify existing levels and measure changes over time as described in the policy. The library can select the appropriate level of specificity to be used. The original Conspectus uses some 3,400 subject classifications; these can be simplified and contracted into far fewer divisions to describe collections for which broader distinctions between subjects are more appropriate.

In this system, subject categories are defined by classification range and subject descriptors. Each category is assigned a series of numbers for existing collection strength, current collecting intensity, and desired collecting intensity. The numbers, often called collection depth indicators, range from 0 (out of scope—nothing is collected in this subject) to 5 (comprehensive—collecting is exhaustive, inclusive, and intensive). Language codes can be assigned to each category. Scope notes can be used to describe special features of parts of the collection. Librarians should not become too preoccupied with levels. Levels do not imply value. Reporting a level of 4 or 5 does not mean a library is better. The most important part of using collection depth indicators is to understand how the library's selectors are collecting and to reconcile practice with the library's mission, goals, objectives, and available funding. The formal classed analysis, through the use of standardized divisions and terminology, provides a vehicle for verification, comparisons and cooperation between libraries, clear division and coordination among selecting responsibilities, and measurement of progress, and it can define the context in which selection and collection management take place.

COMBINED NARRATIVE AND CLASSED MODELS

A combination of the narrative and classed models borrows the most useful features of each to describe the collecting plan succinctly. It is usually fairly brief, no more than two to four pages, and can serve as a useful tool when reviewed and updated as the environment and available resources change. The policy statement for a collection that supports the dentistry and dental hygiene programs at the University of Minnesota (see appendix C) combines a narrative and a classed analysis, using the National Library of Medicine classification scheme.

The Pennsylvania State University Libraries collection development policy for history (also in appendix C) combines narrative with a variation of the classed model. Instead of classification numbers, it uses brief prose descriptions of the subject areas and assigns Conspectus levels for both collecting intensity and language covers.

Regardless of the model employed, a collection development policy should be well organized, consistent from section to section in use of terminology and elements addressed, detailed, and literate without being wordy. A collection development policy is a formal, official, documented policy of the library, but it should be crafted in such a way that is easy to understand and practical to use. A policy that is well written will be used; one that is not will be put in a file and left there.

SUPPLEMENTAL POLICIES

Other policies may be written to deal with specific issues. They may address procedures for donor relations and other considerations related to accepting and declining gifts and large purchases opportunities. A preservation policy discusses policies and procedures for maintaining the physical condition of the collections. These cover criteria for making decisions about binding, conservation, reformatting, and other treatment options; priorities for allocating preservation resources are covered here. A separate statement about weeding and deselection policy is useful. This defines the policy for review of materials for transfer between collections, transfer to remote storage, and withdrawal. It may include guidelines for canceling periodical subscriptions and disposing of unneeded materials. If appropriate, this section addresses the library's responsibilities as a library of record or resource for the region, district, state, or larger area.

When electronic resources became part of library collections, many libraries developed supplemental policies to address the complexities of selecting and managing them. Over the past few years, many libraries have moved away from separate policies for e-resources, assuming that the same guidelines, practices, and criteria apply to all resources regardless of format or delivery mechanism. Unique requirements for e-resources generally apply to how the library handles contracts and licenses, including who is responsible for their review and negotiation and the role of individual selectors in the process. These issues are more likely to be addressed in an internal procedures document and may record selection and acquisition processes (e.g., who has the authority to review, approve, and sign contracts and license agreements) and any services, conditions, or clauses mandated by the library or parent agency. For example, the library may require that all e-resources provide a certain level and format of use statistics, that use by unaffiliated walk-in library users be permitted, that archival access to the resource be ensured, or that indemnities that obligate the library not be accepted. A new policy focusing on e-resources has appeared recently in academic libraries—a policy on the migration to electronic-only versions of journals. Libraries develop these policies to explain the criteria that must be met in order to acquire only the electronic form of a journal and not acquire a parallel print version. The primary criteria tend to be provision of the full scholarly content of the print equivalent, availability simultaneous to or earlier than the print version's publication, image and graphics quality equivalent to the print version, publisher reliability, and perpetual access to all content for which the library is paying.

Budgeting and Finance

Budget Basics

The word *budget* is used in two ways—as a plan and as an allocation amount. In the planning sense, the library's budget is its plan for the use of money available during a fiscal year and reflects allocations, expected revenues, and projected expenditures. A proposed budget is presented to funding authorities as both a request for funding and a plan for what the library will do with the money it receives. Allocations are the dollar amounts distributed to various fund lines in the budget. This budget also is called a *budget document*. Such a budget may include, in addition to allocations and other sources of revenue, fund balances and encumbrances brought forward from the previous year, if permitted by the parent agency. A fund balance consists of the dollars allocated but unexpended at the end of a fiscal year. Encumbrances represent the projected cost of orders that have been placed but not yet billed. An encumbrance is recorded as soon as the obligation for payment is incurred, that is, when the order is placed. When the item is received and payment approved, the encumbrance is cleared and the actual cost recorded as an expenditure. If encumbrances are present at the end of the fiscal year, unexpended funds must be held in escrow until payments for outstanding orders are made.

Budget also can mean the total amount of funds available to meet a library's expenditures over a fixed period of time. The budget varies from year to year. This use of the term is at play when a librarian reports receiving an increase or decrease in the current year's budget compared to the previous year. Most libraries manage their budgets on a fiscal year, which may or may not parallel the calendar year. Parent institutions determine the fiscal year. Most colleges, universities, schools, public libraries, and many companies run on a July-through-June fiscal year, some follow a calendar year, and the U.S. government's fiscal year begins October 1 and ends September 30.

Once a library's goals and objectives are understood through the planning process, its budget serves both to document those decisions through allocations and to coordinate achieving those goals and objectives. Allocations are a measure of the financial commitment to support activities necessary to reach the goals outlined in a plan. A well-crafted budget becomes an internal control that can measure operating effectiveness and performance. The materials budget, also called the acquisitions budget, collections budget, or resources budget, is one portion of a library's total budget. Eugene L. Wiemers Jr. writes,

> The materials budget is both the plan and the framework that sets the boundaries within which choice will be allowed to operate. The "correct" budget will produce the optimal set of limits on choice that will reflect the library's collection goals and priorities, and provide a mechanism to track the library's efforts to reach those goals.[19]

The materials budget is one part of the overall library budget. A library also has an operating budget, which covers ongoing expenses necessary to operate the library. The personnel budget may be managed within the operating budget, or it may be a third separate budget within the total budget. For many libraries, the split is 20–30 percent for collections, 50–60 percent for personnel, and 20 percent for operating expenses. In some libraries, once funds are appropriated to the library and allocated to the library's materials budget, operating budget, and personnel budget they cannot be moved from one budget section to another. The planning process should make clear which budget covers which types of expenses. The materials budget may be intended to cover the purchase of equipment to house collections, costs to support the technological infrastructure that provides access to e-resources, binding and other preservation and conservation treatments, vendor service charges, catalog records, shelf-ready processing, shipping and handling fees, institution memberships, and shared digital repositories. Some libraries fund document delivery through the materials budget.

A materials budget should be consistent with both the library's long-range and short-range plans. Budgets are most effective and most realistic if they are prepared within the context of organizational planning. Both the overall mission of the library and the goals and objectives of library departments should be considered. Because budgets so often parallel the accounting period, they may focus on short-range planning at the expense of the long-range view. Long-range fiscal planning is difficult because the library's future and that of its environment are so volatile. Libraries face problems in predicting materials costs and the effects of inflation, publication patterns, international currency fluctuations, and availability of funds. In addition, the parent agency may make unanticipated changes that affect the user community and user demands and expectations. Nevertheless, including long-range projections in the total budgeting process is important.

Materials budgets, both the request for funding and the allocations once funds are received, are usually prepared by the librarian with administrative responsibility for collections. In a smaller library, the head librarian may prepare the total budget, of which the materials budget is one portion. In school library media centers, the librarian or media specialist usually prepares an acquisitions budget within the context of the school's or the school district's budget. He or she may have modest input into the amount of funds allocated for acquisitions but usually has some responsibility for how funds are allocated within the acquisitions budget (e.g., amounts allocated by subjects, reading levels, discretionary and nondiscretionary purchases). In larger libraries, the individual with administrative responsibility for collection development and management usually prepares the materials budget, generally in consultation with individual selectors or, perhaps, with a coordinating committee. Individual selectors are usually asked to present annual requests for the level of funding they wish to receive in their fund lines in the next fiscal year. The administrator with responsibility for the entire materials budget rolls these individual requests into the total amount requested for the library.

Budgeting Techniques

Approaches to the budgeting process vary from library to library. The parent institution may mandate the approach and, in some organizations, this may change from year to year. A *zero-based budget* requires a fresh start each year. The library is asked to begin with a blank page and determine how much to spend in each category of the budget. Each funding request is proposed and defended without reference to past practice. Few government and nonprofit organizations take this approach because of the amount of work involved. A *program* or *performance budgeting* approach looks at allocations for specific activities or programs and provides a clear connection with planning documents and the objectives set each year. Some libraries' allocations are determined through *formula-based budgets*, such as those recommended in professional standards or guidelines. One approach might be to determine the allocation as a percentage of the collection value. Another might be to allocate based on a per-capita calculation or as a percentage of the parent organization's or parent agency's operating budget.

Most organizations use a *historical* or *incremental budget* approach, which determines the needed incremental changes in various categories. Combining incremental budgeting with program budgeting is a common practice. The library begins with the previous year's base budget and identifies programmatic priorities that should be funded at a higher level.

The librarian should approach budget preparation in the manner required by his or her parent institution. An effective budget system provides the tools for making reasonable decisions about allocation or reallocation of resources.

A recurring theme in the budget process in today's libraries is accountability. Librarians are expected to be able to demonstrate effective stewardship of the funds they receive and expend. Effectiveness is usually measured by the degree to which the organization's stated goals and objectives are achieved. Whereas a count of materials acquired and current serial subscriptions and e-resources has been a traditional measure of success, increased attention is being given to demonstrated outcomes. If a library has set a goal of expanding large-print books to meet the increasing number of senior citizens, success would be a combination of the number of titles acquired with the number of circulations recorded for these materials. Additional considerations reflecting responsible stewardship include balanced encumbrances and expenditures over the budget year and avoidance of financial misconduct.

Funding Sources

For most libraries, the largest part of the budget is funded through an appropriation from the parent organization. Prior to the end of the fiscal year, most libraries prepare a funding request and, just prior to or soon after the beginning of the fiscal year, receive an appropriation or budget allocation. In many organizations, the budget for library materials is treated as a protected category and may receive extra scrutiny and interest in how it is allocated and spent. This scrutiny underlines the need for linking the budget to a well-crafted and widely supported plan and for being accountable for effective use of the allocated funds. Sources of funding, in addition to an appropriation, include gifts, endowment income, grants, fees and charges, and fines.

Development Activities and Grant Proposal Writing

Supplemental funds are of increasing importance in most libraries. In the broadest sense, fund-raising is the process of seeking additional moneys from sources other than the parent organization; these might include gifts, bequests, and grants. Collections librarians are becoming more involved in fund-raising. They may be called upon to write or present proposals to donors to solicit collections, obtain funds to purchase collections, or create endowments that will generate income to maintain collections. As institutions become more dependent on these sources of funds, they have found that the librarians closest to the collection and its users often can make the most convincing cases to the donor. Their enthusiasm and commitment can be infectious. Successful fund-raisers know their job, their institution, and their donors.[20] Selectors also play a critical role in the stewardship process by ensuring that gifts, whether dollars or collections, are managed well. Donors often mandate how the money is to be spent and expect their gifts to be an addition to the amount currently allocated to that specific purpose. Most donors want to know that their gifts are being used to further the goals of the institution. Selectors are called upon to write letters or meet with donors to thank them, to let them know how their gifts are being used, and to encourage their continued involvement with the library.

Grants can provide additional funding for library collections. Collections librarians may be expected to seek grant funding from private and government agencies. Grant proposals draw upon the selector's knowledge of the collection and its users and require special writing skills. Once a library receives a grant, tracking mechanisms and reporting procedures are specified in the grant guidelines. The reporting dates for the grant may be different from the library's fiscal year. Projects funded through grants should be consistent with the library's planning and reflect its goals.

Material Budget Requests

Prior to the beginning of the fiscal year, the library is asked to submit a budget request. This is usually part of the overall planning process of the parent organization. The library can use this process for two purposes: to request funds and to inform. A well-crafted proposal begins by explaining the library's financial needs in reference to internal and external forces. Ideally, an environmental scan has assembled this information and informed the library's planning document. Through this explanation, the funding body or parent institution learns about pressures, constraints, and expectations the library faces. An initial summary of external and internal conditions sets the stage for a convincing proposal. This information must be presented clearly and succinctly but with enough detail to justify the request.

Internal conditions are those factors in the library's immediate environment. Among these are changes in the population to be served. Many libraries serve user communities that are becoming more diverse, and they are called upon to provide new resources to meet the needs of these changing populations. Special libraries may support new product research and development or other new corporate focal points. School library media centers may have increasing or declining enrollments or new graduation standards. An academic institution may be expected to serve new graduate programs, undergraduate degrees, or research centers. Changing ways of teaching can affect how a collection is used and increase demand on secondary resources or access to online indexes and resources. Such a budget proposal has a programmatic basis—that is, it makes a case for funding based on program areas such as recreational resources, information resources, or new areas of emphasis.

Another internal influence on the budget is the collection mix, that is, the kinds of materials in the collection. A library with a higher ratio of serials to monographs can predict greater financial need. Libraries with a higher proportion of foreign acquisitions are more vulnerable to fluctuations in foreign currency. Budgeting is forecasting future funding needs based on internal and external factors.

Some of the external conditions to which a budget proposal might draw attention are changes in pricing trends in library materials and services, volume of materials published, impact of electronic information, consumer price indices, and value of the dollar on the international market. Over the past twenty years, serial and book prices have increased at significantly greater rates than either the consumer price index or annual increases to most libraries' base allocations. An added pressure is the increase in the volume of materials to be considered for purchase. Attention should also be drawn to the extensive new resources available in electronic formats. Librarians seeking to support user community needs and interests through access to these resources should ensure that funding agencies are aware of the many pressures on materials budgets.

Indexing the materials budget to market prices has been a successful strategy for some libraries.[21] The underlying premise is that supporting a library is part of the operating costs of the parent institution or agency and that increases in materials costs should be covered in the same way that increases in heating and telecommunications are covered. Indexing monitors the levels of book and serial production, fluctuations in exchange rates, and inflation in materials costs and produces a target funding level that maintains a specified rate of acquisitions and access.

Some libraries use the budgets of an agreed-upon set of peer libraries as benchmarks to support their own budget requests. In many cases, the parent institution may have determined a set of peers, and comparing the resources of the library to those held in the other members of the peer group can be useful. No matter the strategy used, a materials budget proposal should make clear the consequences of various funding levels. Using statistical data and meaningful information strengthens the budget proposal and provides an opportunity to inform the parent institution of the library's short- and long-term plans. In the process, the library should take care to present consequences not as threats but as reality.

The school media specialist might seek to demonstrate the need for more funding above the regular budget in order to update the collection and to acquire a higher percentage of the high-quality materials on the market. Ideally, budgets in school systems are developed by school library media specialists at the individual school level and reflect long-range plans for three to five years. Teachers are frequently involved in budget justification.

Several reliable sources provide statistical information about pricing, publishing, and population trends. These include professional library publications, trade publications, and library service vendors:

- *Book Industry Trends*, published by the Book Industry Study Group
- *Bowker Annual Library and Book Trade Almanac*
- "Library Materials Price Index," prepared by the Association for Library Collection and Technical Services, Library Materials Price Index Committee
- "Periodical Price Survey," published annually by *Library Journal*
- *Publisher's Weekly*
- *Statistical Abstract of the United States*, issued by the U.S. Department of Commerce and Bureau of the Census
- reports and projections prepared by serial and monograph service vendors, which can be found on their websites

Allocation of Funds

The allocation of funds within the collection development budget may absorb much of a head librarian's or collection development officer's time in larger libraries. The annual allocation process is an opportunity to create "a successful budget [that] translates competing demands into real levels of financial support."[22] The goal of the allocation process is to reflect the goals and priorities set out in the library's planning process and to create a mechanism to track the library's efforts to reach those goals. The method used to make allocations should be understood clearly by both those within the library and external parties.

Most materials budgets are line-item budgets, with subdivisions or subaccounts within the larger budget. A line-item budget lists allocations and expenditures, classified by type, in a detailed line-by-line format. A line-item budget allows easy comparisons from year to year and promotes accountability. Large libraries may have one hundred or more lines. In academic libraries, budgets typically are allocated first by subject or discipline. Libraries also may allocate by one or more of the following: location (main library, branch library, children's department, remote research site); type of user (children, adult); format or genre (monographs, serials, reference materials, fiction, microforms, online resources, newspapers); or type of publisher (trade presses, academic presses, small presses). Very large libraries may further subdivide allocations. For example, funds allocated to purchase materials for children in a large public library may be subdivided into fund lines for nonfiction, fiction, picture books, and videos. In this way, allocations mirror the organizational structure of the library, the community served, and the collection development policy. Selectors are responsible for one or more fund lines. The details represented in line-item budget divisions provide for accountability and convenience of reporting.

The disadvantage of a line-item budget is the opportunity for scrutiny it provides those outside the library. It simplifies the process of aligning the library's goals with those of the parent institution, but it may heighten the political sensitivity of the process. Citizens, teachers, researchers, or faculty members may question why the library spends more money in one area than another when the funding is allocated into readily identifiable budget lines. It may be difficult to add lines to a budget for new focus areas or to change an existing line item. A very granular line-item budget may limit this type of flexibility, though many libraries have the option of moving funds from one line to another over the fiscal year as surpluses and deficits develop.

Libraries, even those that do not use multiple fund lines, typically divide the annual budget between discretionary and nondiscretionary allocations. Discretionary purchases are individual orders for items. Nondiscretionary purchases are those materials that arrive routinely and automatically without creating individual purchase orders. Libraries with approval plans may have a third type of allocation to cover these expenses, which are nondiscretionary in the sense that a certain amount is set aside to cover books that come through the approval plan and are not selected on a title-by-title basis.

Recent rapid increases in the prices of serials have made keeping track of the ratio between expenditures for serials and monographs especially critical. As serials have inflated in cost, many libraries have reduced the amount they allocate to monographs and other discretionary purchases to maintain current serial subscriptions or to minimize the number of serials canceled. Establishing a ratio between serials and monographs can be useful. Although the collecting goals of each library affect this ratio, a common practice in academic libraries is to maintain a ratio of no less than 30 percent of the budget spent on monographs and no more than 70 percent on serials. Public and school libraries generally aim for something closer to a 50:50 ratio. Special libraries may set a target that accepts spending 80 percent of the budget on serials. Libraries also use ratios to help guide their shift to purchasing electronic resources.

Budgeting for Electronic Resources

Budgeting for e-resources presents several challenges. These include the high cost of some access agreements and increases in percentage of the budget spent on e-resources; a variety of payment options that make comparison difficult; supplemental costs not associated with print and other traditional formats; difficulty in determining cost-benefit comparison between options; shifting expenditures from acquiring capital assets to leasing access rights; and aggregator and publisher packages that make determining costs of individual titles nearly impossible. The percentage of library budgets allocated to e-resources continues to increase, and planning for this shift requires care and attention. ARL member libraries reported spending an average of 25 percent of their budgets on e-resources in 2002/3, an eightfold increase from 1992/93.[23] Although a portion of this shift reflects redirecting dollars to e-journals and other e-resources and reducing their print counterparts, the consequences are significant for managing acquisitions budgets.

Until the mid-1990s, nearly everything libraries acquired was a physical entity and added to a tangible collection. These materials constitute a permanent capital expenditure; that is, the library collection is a fixed asset and—over time—can become the most valuable capital asset on a campus or in a town. Library collections, unlike most capital expenditures, appreciate in value rather than depreciate, especially if they are well maintained. The library's annual financial report shows a direct relationship between the allocations it receives, its expenditures, and growth of the collection's value as a long-term capital asset. Purchasing the right to access a remote resource or leasing a product on CD-ROM that must be returned at the termination of the lease are not capital expenditures. Thus, libraries and their parent bodies are experiencing a shift in return on investment. Money allocated to a library for resources does not increase the net capital value of the library to the extent it has done in the past. Collections librarians should be aware of this trend and be able to explain why it is happening and articulate both cost savings and the less tangible value accruing in improved access to materials and user satisfaction.

Allocating the Budget

Various methods, ranging from using an allocation formula to following a strict historical division of the budget, can be used to allocate the budget to fund lines. Allocation formulas are usually built on supply and demand factors.[24] The supply factors take into account the amount of material published in the subject area and the cost of those materials. Demand factors include number of students, teachers, faculty, courses offered, circulation, registered borrowers, or interlibrary activity. Often, factors are weighted to reflect institutional or community priorities or other factors. For example, the number of doctoral students may be weighted three times the number of undergraduates in the formula to accommodate the specialized resource needs of doctoral candidates. A public library may look at demographic data to determine a formula for allocating funds to different user communities. Another formula-based approach sometimes used in academic libraries, percentage-based allocation, allocates a percentage of the acquisitions budget to disciplines in parallel to the percentage of the total university budget allocated to corresponding academic departments or programs.[25] Though attractive for its simplicity, this approach to allocation does not account for variations in format, publication output, or cost of materials in different disciplines.

A formula provides an easily understandable explanation for allocations and can be useful in a setting where the budget is open to a wide and highly interested constituency of library users. Formulas may shift funds dramatically in response to changes in user demand, such as the creation or elimination of an academic program or a new community emphasis on supporting small businesses. Formulas can be cumbersome because of the extensive data required and the complexity of calculations. Most often, formula-based allocations are adjusted somewhat on the basis of professional judgment and local factors that cannot be quantified completely in a formula.

Another method of allocation is more incremental and based on historical allocation. A senior collection development officer or the director of the library gathers information from selectors and from the parent organization and adjusts the historical allocations in response to this information. The collection development officer often takes into account the same factors used in the allocation formula but brings to bear his or her knowledge of the parent institution or agency, the user community, and the library's longer-term goals in a less rigid manner.

One advantage of this method is that it diminishes the effects of unexpected and short-term shifts in the parent body.

Budget models vary in how they handle allocation of and responsibility for expending funds for e-resources. Some libraries have a single central fund line for all e-resources. This approach can be found in libraries that have a single selector and those that have several. A single separate fund can stress the priority of e-resources to the organization and make tracking expenditures easier, but it can also stress their separateness from other selection and management activities. At the other end of the continuum is the model in which all funds are allocated to subject lines, and individual selectors manage funding for e-resources as they manage funding for more traditional library materials. Selectors may make cooperative purchases with other selectors by pooling funds, but no resources are funded centrally. A middle ground retains some money in a central fund for resources (perhaps a general periodical index and associated full-text file, an encyclopedia, or an aggregator package) of system-wide interest and allocates to the individual subject line level for more narrowly focused titles. If e-journals are part of a package from an aggregator or a single publisher, separating and tracking costs of individual titles are challenging for collection development librarians and library accounting staff. Ideally, responsibility for managing funds should be consistent with policies that assign responsibility for selection and collection management decisions.

Most libraries hold some money aside in a contingency fund, which may be managed by the collection development officer, the library director, or a library committee. This fund can be used to meet unexpected needs, purchase large and expensive items, or balance unexpected fluctuations in user demand. Holding 5–10 percent of the total materials budget in a contingency fund is a common strategy.

Allocating and managing a collections budget require compliance with the parent organization's fiscal and accounting requirements as well as making wise financial decisions. Most nonprofit organizations are required to use fund accounting, a procedure through which funds are classified for accounting and reporting purposes in accordance with the regulations, restrictions, or limitations imposed by the governing board or sources outside the library, or in accordance with activities or objectives specified by donors. For example, moving funds from the operating budget to the collections budget or using collections funds to acquire computer equipment or support data lines for accessing remote resources may be prohibited. Although most libraries have accounting staff or rely on the resources of the larger organization for accounting activities, selectors should understand the regulations, restrictions, and limitations that apply.

Expending the Budget

Once the collections budget is allocated, it must be spent. Expenditures are tracked to inform the planning process and to allow the library to report on its progress to the parent institution or governing body. Many libraries use this information to assess the performance of selectors and of the library as a whole. For example, the parent institution may have a goal of supporting diversity. The library may set a goal of purchasing a certain number of items that support multicultural or diverse populations. The library uses the reports of funds expended to show progress toward this goal. In addition, reports of expenditures are useful when preparing stewardship reports and thanking donors.

Most libraries set targets for expenditures and encumbrances during and at the end of the fiscal year. Institutions that operate on a cash accounting system require that the funds be fully expended by the end of the fiscal year and do not permit unexpended funds to be carried forward into the new year. Some organizations using a cash accounting system do permit carrying forward encumbrances with the funds held in escrow to cover payment when the ordered item is receipted. The accrual system of accounting allows one to carry over unexpended funds in addition to encumbered dollars, which are added to the new year's allocation. Some libraries and their parent organizations discourage developing large cash balances, often called reserves, which can suggest that the library or a particular budget line is overfunded. Figure 3-1 presents a sample budget cycle for a library that is able to carry forward encumbrances.

Figure 3-2 represents the midyear financial status of an academic library that has allocated broadly to three subject areas, with varying ratios in the allocations to discretionary (for title-by-title selection) and nondiscretionary categories (for periodicals, including licenses for e-content), depending on the discipline. The library does not have an approval plan. Note that not all discretionary funds (orders placed plus orders received and paid) have been half spent at the midyear point. The humanities fund has only 15 percent of the initial allocation remaining for the second half of the budget year. The social sciences fund has 62 percent remaining. Nondiscretionary funds do not show encumbrances because the commitments for these resources are known when the initial allocations are made and orders are not placed during the fiscal year. Because most invoices for serials and e-resources are received and paid in the fall (before the start of the calendar year), only modest amounts remain in these fund lines. The contingency fund allocation remains untouched and can be used for special purchases or to address new needs.

In general, libraries experience a significant lag between the date an order is placed and the date the item is received and the invoice paid. For large libraries, this lag can average as long as ninety days. The period between order placement and item receipt of highly specialized materials can be years. Selectors usually have encumbrance target dates that are based on the library's experience with

July	**Fiscal Year Closeout/New Year Startup**
	• Open and partial orders and funds are rolled over for new fiscal year cycle.
	• Preliminary allocations are made and selectors are advised to begin ordering, assuming they have 60% of previous year's allocation (all funds and endowments) and carryover and unexpended gift funds from previous year.
	• Administration notifies libraries about new general funds available for collections.
	• First half-year payment made to vendor to ensure approval plan discount.
August	**New Fiscal Year Allocation Planning**
	• Library Budget Advisory Group meets to determine distribution of general funds.
	• Selectors are advised if serial cancellations required.
	• Head of Collection Unit, in consultation with Collection Development Advisory Group, determines subject and collection allocations.
September	• End-of-fiscal-year documentation is prepared for selectors, including summaries of allocations, outstanding encumbrances, and expenditures by category.
	• Balance of current FY funds (new general funds and endowment funds) is allocated to subject and collection fund lines.
	• Serial title cancellations are due to Serials Department.
	• Selectors submit special purchase requests to the assistant dean, collections.
November	• General monographic funds should be 66% committed.
January	• General monographic funds should be 85% committed.
	• All non–U.S. source orders should be submitted by January 31.
	• Second half-year payment is made to vendor to ensure approval plan discount.
March	• March 15: Deadline for submitting monographic orders (should be 100% committed).
	• March 31: Uncommitted general funds are pooled for special purchases.
April	• Research purchase requests are solicited, final decisions made, and orders placed.
June	• June 30: Endowment funds should be fully committed.

FIGURE 3-1 Budget management cycle. For easy reference, this figure can be downloaded and printed from www.ala.org/editions/extras/Johnson09720.

receiving material and paying bills. The simplest way to accomplish this is to count backward from the end of the fiscal year and end the collection development year on the last day one can expect to receive and pay for the material. Setting interim dates to check the progress of the library toward its goal of fully expending the budget is important. The amount of material published can vary widely from year to year, and there may be a need for midyear adjustments to accommodate these changes to ensure that all funds are spent by the end of the fiscal year.

	Initial Allocation	Encumbrances	Expenditures	Free Balance	% Remaining
Fund Line	7/1/2007	12/31/2007	12/31/2007	12/31/2007	12/31/2007
Humanities					
Discretionary	$100,000	$60,000	$25,000	$15,000	15
Nondiscretionary	150,000	0	130,000	20,000	13
Social Sciences					
Discretionary	75,000	15,750	12,750	46,500	62
Nondiscretionary	175,000	0	170,000	5,000	3
Sciences					
Discretionary	100,000	25,000	25,000	50,000	50
Nondiscretionary	400,000	0	390,000	10,000	3
Contingency	25,000	0	0	25,000	100

FIGURE 3-2 Sample budget report

Most institutions require some separation of selection, acquisition, and payment responsibilities. Depending on the size of the library, it may have three people or three departments. Within a large acquisitions department, separate units may order and receipt materials. In very small libraries, the same person may handle all functions. Whatever the case, the three functions should be clearly defined and distinguished to guard against fraud and malfeasance. Proper handling of these functions is necessary for a successful audit. Audits are reviews of financial records, usually conducted at regular intervals by parties external to the library. They serve to verify that financial records are accurate and orderly, that the library is in compliance with organizational and generally accepted accounting policies and procedures, and that units are operating effectively.

Monitoring the Materials Budget

Several individuals may have responsibilities for monitoring the materials budget. The selector has a responsibility to monitor his or her allocations and to ensure that funds are being expended over the fiscal year in accordance with individual objectives and library goals. The collection development officer, or other librarian with overall responsibility for the materials budget, monitors the total budget to track that balances are being spent down and, when necessary, to reallocate unspent funds. He or she is charged with ensuring that the budget is being spent in a manner consistent with the library's planning documents.

The library's or organization's financial officer oversees procedures to determine that encumbrances and payments are correctly recorded. If any funds are to be carried forward into the next year, as either encumbered or cash balances, the financial officer negotiates and monitors this process. Usually, the financial officer prepares year-end reports, which show balances by fund line and list expenditures and encumbrances. The collection development officer uses this report to see if goals were met and to prepare the next year's budget request with adjusted allocations.

School library media specialists can use year-end budget reports to document per-pupil expenditures in categories such as books, periodicals, audiovisual materials, and online resources. In addition to demonstrating accountability, these data can help the school media specialist determine budget variations over time, compare budget allocations to similar libraries (statewide and nationally), and monitor changes in market prices compared to local budget allocations. Having access to such baseline data is useful for school media specialists with roles in the budget-planning process of the local school district.

Summary

Formal, systematic planning is both an organizational and an individual responsibility in libraries. Plans, by analyzing the library's environment and mission, improve the quality of all decisions. In other words, the library has a better understanding of its desired future and how to apply available resources to obtain that future. Systematic planning may follow one or more models, depending on the particular situation and the methods endorsed by the parent organization. Strategic planning, with its specific focus on understanding and responding to a changing environment through continual revision, is a commonly applied planning model. The process of planning brings librarians to a better understanding of their library's mission and goals. The plan also serves to inform the library's constituents about its desired goals and the objectives designed to reach these goals. It provides both library users and parent agencies benchmarks against which to measure the library's use of financial resources. Planning, though time consuming, is justified by its importance to future success.

The purpose of a library collection development policy, a central planning document, is to inform and protect. It defines the scope of existing collections, relates the library's collecting goals to the resources available to meet them, incorporates the parent institution's mission, and recognizes current and future user needs. A policy protects the library against external pressures, particularly in the areas of intellectual freedom and censorship. The policy's audience is the library's staff, users, and governing or administrative body.

Format, content, and style of policy must be selected in response to the audience. Classed analysis, narrative, or a combination of the two are the most frequently used formats. Most policies contain information on the user community, limitations in meeting the needs of that community, an overview of the library and its collections, descriptions of cooperative arrangements, an overview of how collection development and management decisions are handled, and general policies, guidelines, and criteria. Policies in larger or more complex libraries include detailed statements of particular formats, genres, subjects, and disciplines. All policies should be written clearly and succinctly. A collection policy statement describes—in a public voice—where the collections budget is going and how collections decisions are being made. The most effective policy statements are realistic documents built on a theoretical base. The importance and value of a collection development policy reside in the context it provides for every decision made in a library.

Collections budgets are an important part of the planning process and also a mechanism for tracking effectiveness. A good collections budget is one that reflects the goals of the parent institution. It provides a mechanism to show the library's commitment to its goals in concrete fiscal terms and to monitor progress toward those goals. Good budgeting does not replace good selecting; they are complementary processes. Collections policies and budgeting are part of the planning process that informs collection development and management.

CASE STUDY

Walnut Public Library is located in a small midwestern town and serves a population of 5,500, which is increasing approximately 2 percent per year. Twelve percent of the population is younger than twenty and 18 percent is sixty and older. Library data show 3,680 active patrons; circulation transactions totaled 30,546 in the previous year. Walnut Public Library is part of a regional public library network of eight similar libraries that share a union online catalog and have a twice-weekly delivery service among the libraries. The Walnut Public Library has a collection of 23,726 volumes, 646 videos, forty-four audio recordings, and eighty current subscriptions. Approximately two-thirds of the books are considered adult; the remaining books are considered juvenile. The adult collection is fairly evenly split between nonfiction and fiction; the juvenile collection is one-third nonfiction and two-thirds fiction. Three public terminals provide access to the union catalog and the Internet.

Through the regional library system, on-site patrons can access OCLC's WorldCat and Infotrac SearchBank. The annual cost of accessing these online resources is budgeted separately from the materials budget and considered part of operating expenses. A full-time professional librarian, Marguerite, who reports to the library's six-member board of trustees, manages the library. She has 2.5 full-time staff members, none of whom has a graduate library degree. One assistant, Virginia, has primary responsibility for children's programming and materials selection. Marguerite selects all other materials. The current annual materials budget is $9,850.

Activity

Develop a budget plan for the Walnut Public Library and allocate the current year's materials budget. Decide the types and names of the fund lines to which dollars will be allocated and the amount to be allocated to each. Research price trends for typical public library materials, documenting your sources, and develop a proposal for the next year's budget allocation to be presented to the trustees and town counsel. Indicate where increases may be needed and explain why.

Note: The first edition of this book also provided a case study and associated activity in its discussion on policy, planning, and budgets; access it as a supplementary resource at www.ala.org/editions/extras/Johnson09720.

Notes

1. Peter Drucker, *Management: Tasks, Responsibilities, Practices* (New York: Harper and Row, 1974), 125.

2. George Keller, *Academic Strategy: The Management Revolution in American Higher Education* (Baltimore, Md.: Johns Hopkins University Press, 1983).

3. John D. Stoffels, "Environmental Scanning for Future Success," *Managerial Planning* 31, no. 3 (1982): 4–12.

4. Eileen Abels, "Environmental Scanning," *Bulletin of the American Society for Information Science and Technology* 28, no. 3 (2002): 16.

5. C. Davis Fogg, *Team-Based Strategic Planning: A Complete Guide to Structuring, Facilitating, and Implementing the Process* (New York: American Management Association, 1994).

6. Not all librarians are convinced of the necessity of collection development policies. See, e.g., Richard Snow, "Wasted Words: The Written Collection Development Policy and the Academic Library," *Journal of Academic Librarianship* 22 (May 1996): 191–94, which challenges this assumption.

7. Paul H. Mosher, "Fighting Back: From Growth to Management in Library Collection Development" (unpublished paper delivered at the Pilot Collection Management and Development Institute at Stanford University, July 6–10, 1981), 4.

8. Marjorie L. Pappas, "Selection Policies," *School Library Media Activities Monthly* 21, no. 2 (2004): 41.

9. Joanne S. Anderson, ed., *Guide for Written Collection Policy Statements*, 2nd ed., Collection Management and Development Guides no. 7 (Chicago: American Library Association, 1996), 1.

10. American Library Association, Coordinating Committee on Revision of Public Library Standards, *Public Library Service to America: A Guide to Evaluation, with Minimum Standards* (Chicago: American Library Association, 1956); American Association of School Librarians, *Policies and Procedures for the Selection of School Library Materials* (Chicago: American Library Association, 1961).

11. Robert D. Stueart and Barbara B. Moran, *Library and Information Center Management*, 7th ed. (Westport, Conn.: Libraries Unlimited, 2007).

12. W. Bernard Lukenbill, *Collection Development for a New Century in the School Library Media Center* (Westport, Conn.: Greenwood, 2002), 43.

13. Claire Gatrell Stephens and Patricia Franklin, *Library 101: A Handbook for the School Library Media Specialist* (Westport, Conn.: Libraries Unlimited, 2007).

14. The Library Bill of Rights and other resources on censorship, intellectual freedom and the law, and the ALA's Free to Read initiative can be found in the *Intellectual Freedom Manual*, 7th ed. (Chicago: American Library Association, 2006). The ALA Library Bill of Rights is also available at www.ala.org/ala/oif/statementspols/statementsif/librarybillrights.cfm.

15. Elizabeth A. Sudduth, Nancy B. Newins, and William E. Sudduth, comps., *Special Collections in College and University Libraries*, CLIP Note no. 35 (Chicago: Association of College and Research Libraries, 2005).

16. Several resources on format, content, and style are available. Among these are Anderson's *Guide for Written Collection Policy Statements*; Elizabeth Futas, ed., *Collection Development Policies and Procedures*, 3rd ed. (Phoenix, Ariz.: Oryx, 1995); Frank W. Hoffmann and Richard J. Wood, *Library Collection Development Policies: Academic Public, and Special Libraries* (Lanham, Md.: Scarecrow, 2005); and Frank W. Hoffmann and Richard J. Wood, *Library Collection Development Policies: School Libraries and Learning Resource Centers*, Good Policy, Good Practice no. 2 (Lanham, Md.: Scarecrow, 2007). AcqWeb's Directory of Collection Development Policies on the Web (www.acqweb.org/cd_policy.html) provides example policies from public libraries, community college libraries, college libraries, university libraries, academic library special collections, national and state government libraries, and school libraries.

17. Hoffmann and Wood, *Library Collection Development Policies: Academic, Public, and Special Libraries.*

18. Dora Biblarz, "The Conspectus as a Blueprint for Creating Collection Development Policy Statements," in *Collection Assessment: A Look at the RLG Conspectus*, ed. Richard J. Wood and Katina P. Strauch, 169–76 (New York: Haworth, 1992).

19. Eugene L. Wiemers Jr., "Budget," in *Collection Management: A New Treatise*, ed. Charles B. Osburn and Ross Atkinson, 67–79, Foundations in Library and Information Science, vol. 26 (Greenwich, Conn.: JAI Press, 1991), 67.

20. David Farrell, "Fundraising for Collection Development Librarians," in *Collection Management and Development: Issues in an Electronic Era*, ed. Peggy Johnson and Bonnie MacEwan, 133–142 (Chicago: American Library Association, 1994).

21. Gay N. Dannelly, "Indexing Material Budgets at Ohio State University," in *Collection Management and Development*, ed. Johnson and MacEwan, 121–132.

22. Wiemers, "Budget," 68–69.

23. Mark Young and Martha Kyrillidou, comps., "ARL Supplementary Statistics 2002–03" (Washington, D.C.: Association of Research Libraries, 2004), www.arl.org/bm~doc/sup03.pdf.

24. Charles B. Lowry, in "Reconciling Pragmatism, Equity, and Need in the Formula Allocation of Book and Serial Funds," *College and Research Libraries* 53, no. 2 (1992): 121–38, offers an overview of formulas, including their limits as allocation tools.

25. Wanda V. Dole, "PBA: A Statistics-Based Method to Allocate Library Materials Budgets," in *Statistics in Practice: Measuring and Managing: Proceedings of the IFLA Satellite Conference, Loughborough, August 2002*, ed. Claire Creaser, 98–115 (Loughborough, Leicestershire: Library and Information Statistics Unit, Department of Information Science, Loughborough University, 2003).

Suggested Readings

Anjejo, Rose. "Collection Development Policies for Small Libraries." *PNLA Quarterly* 70, no. 2 (2006): 12–16.

Arora, Anish, and Diego Klabjan. "A Model for Budget Allocation in Multi-Unit Libraries." *Library Collections, Acquisitions, and Technical Services* 26, no. 4 (2002): 423–38.

Bodi, Sonia, and Katie Maier-O'Shea. "The Library of Babel: Making Sense of Collection Management in a Postmodern World." *Journal of Academic Librarianship* 31, no. 2 (2005): 143–50.

Bryson, John M. *Strategic Planning for Public and Nonprofit Organizations: A Guide to Strengthening and Sustaining Organizational Achievement*. 3rd ed. San Francisco: Jossey-Bass, 2004.

Canepi, Kitti. "Fund Allocation Formula Analysis: Determining Elements for Best Practices in Libraries." *Library Collections, Acquisitions, and Technical Services* 31, no. 1 (2007): 12–24.

Carter, Betty. "Leading Forward by Looking Backward." *Library Media Connection* 25, no. 4 (2007): 16–20.

Clayton, Peter. "Managing the Acquisitions Budget: A Practical Perspective." *Bottom Line* 14, no. 3 (2001): 145–51.

Clendenning, Lynda Fuller, J. Kay Martin, and Gail McKenzie. "Secrets for Managing Materials Budget Allocations: A Brief Guide for Collection Managers." *Library Collections, Acquisitions, and Technical Services* 29, no. 1 (2005): 99–108.

Corrigan, Andy. "The Collecting Policy Reborn: A Practical Application of Web-Based Documentation." *Collection Building* 24, no. 2 (2005): 65–69.

Debowski, Shelda, "Collection Program Funding Management." In *Collection Management for School Libraries*, edited by Joy McGregor, Ken Dillon, and James Henri, 281–306. Lanham, Md.: Scarecrow, 2003.

———. "Policies for Collection Management." In *Collection Management for School Libraries*, edited by Joy McGregor, Ken Dillon, and James Henri, 109–34. Lanham, Md.: Scarecrow, 2003.

Evans, G. Edward, Patricia Layzell Ward, and Bendik Rugaas. "The Planning Process." In *Management Basics for Information Professionals*, 161–90. New York: Neal-Schuman, 2000.

Friend, Frederick J. "Policy: Politics, Powers and People." In *Collection Management*, edited by G. E. Gorman, 45–58. International Yearbook of Library and Information Management, 2000–2001. London: Library Association Publishing, 2000.

Gerding, Stephanie K., and Pamela H. MacKellar. *Grants for Libraries: A How-to-Do-It Manual*. How-to-Do-It Manuals for Librarians no. 144. New York: Neal-Schuman, 2006.

German, Lisa, et al., eds. *Guide to the Management of the Information Resources Budget*. Collection Management and Development Guides no. 9. Lanham, Md.: Scarecrow and the Association for Library Collections and Technical Services, 2001.

Hall-Ellis, Sylvia D., and Ann Jerabek. *Grants for School Libraries*. Westport, Conn.: Libraries Unlimited, 2003.

Hallam, Arlita, and Teresa R. Dalston. *Managing Budgets and Finances: A How-to-Do-It Manual for Librarian and Information Professionals*. How-to-Do-It Manuals for Librarians no. 138. New York: Neal-Schuman, 2005.

Hennen, Thomas J. *Hennen's Public Library Planner: A Manual and Interactive CD-ROM*. New York: Neal-Schuman, 2004.

Hoffmann, Frank W., and Richard J. Wood. *Library Collection Development Policies: School Libraries and Learning Resource Centers*. Good Policy Good Practice no. 2. Lanham, Md.: Scarecrow, 2007.

Hughes-Hassell, Sandra, and Jacqueline C. Mancall. "Budgeting for Maximum Impact on Learning." In *Collection Management for Youth: Responding to the Needs of Learners*, 52–65. Chicago: American Library Association, 2004.

———. "Policy as the Foundation for the Collection." In *Collection Management for Youth: Responding to the Needs of Learners*, 19–32. Chicago: American Library Association, 2004.

International Federation of Library Associations and Organizations, Section on Acquisition and Collection Development. *Guidelines for a Collection Development Policy Using the Conspectus Model*. The Hague: IFLA, 2001.

Lankford, Ronald D. *Book Banning*. Detroit: Greenhaven, 2008.

Linn, Mott. "Budget Systems Used in Allocating Resources to Libraries." *Bottom Line* 20, no. 1 (2007): 20–29.

Mack, Daniel C. *Collection Development Policies: New Directions for Changing Collections*. Binghamton, N.Y.: Haworth, 2004.

Maple, Amanda, and Jean Morrow. *Guide to Writing Collection Development Policies for Music*. Technical Reports Series no. 26. Lanham, Md.: Scarecrow and the Music Library Association, 2001.

Matthews, Joseph R. *Strategic Planning and Management for Library Managers*. Westport, Conn.: Libraries Unlimited, 2005.

Mesling, Cris Fowler. "Collection Development Policies in Community College Libraries." *Community and Junior College Libraries* 11, no. 2 (2003): 73–88.

Nelson, Sandra, for the Public Library Association. *Strategic Planning for Results*. PLA Results Series. Chicago: American Library Association, 2008.

Nelson, Sandra, and June Garcia. *Creating Policies for Results: From Chaos to Clarity*. Chicago: American Library Association, 2003.

Packer, Donna. "Acquisitions Allocations: Equity, Politics, and Bundled Pricing." *portal: Libraries and the Academy* 1, no. 3 (2001): 209–24.

Scholtz, James C. "Developing Video Collection Development Policies to Accommodate Existing and New Technologies." In *Video Collection Development in Multi-Type Libraries: A Handbook*, 2nd ed., edited by Gary P. Handman, 245–76. New York: Greenwood, 2002.

Smith, A. Arro, and Stephanie Langenkamp. "Indexed Collection Budget Allocations: A Tool for Quantitative Collection Development Based on Circulation." *Public Libraries* 46, no. 5 (2007): 50–54.

Smith, G. Stevenson. *Managerial Accounting for Libraries and Other Not-for-Profit Organizations.* 2nd ed. Chicago: American Library Association, 2002.

Smyth, Elaine B. "A Practical Approach to Writing a Collection Development Policy." *Rare Book and Manuscripts Librarianship* 14, no. 1 (1999): 27–31.

Snyder, Herbert. *Small Change, Big Problems: Detecting and Preventing Financial Misconduct in Your Library.* Chicago: American Library Association, 2006.

"Spending Smart: How to Budget and Finance." (Special section) *Book Report* 21, no. 1 (2002): 6–24.

Steele, Victoria, and Stephen D. Elder. *Becoming a Fundraiser: The Principles and Practice of Library Development.* Chicago: American Library Association, 2000.

Stephens, Annabel K. "The Public Library Planning Process: Its Impact on Collection Development Policies and Practices." In *Public Library Collection Development in the Information Age*, edited by Annabel K. Stephens, 15–23. New York: Haworth, 1998.

Truck, Lorna. "Plain English Collection Budgets: A Collection Plan for Public Libraries." *Bottom Line* 15, no. 4 (2002): 167–73.

Turner, Anne M. *Managing Money: A Guide for Librarians.* Jefferson, N.C.: McFarland, 2007.

Walters, William. "A Regression-Based Approach to Library Fund Allocation." *Library Resources and Technical Services* 51, no. 4 (2007): 263–78.

CHAPTER FOUR

Developing Collections

This chapter covers the activities that develop or build both on-site and online collections. It might have been called "Selection" in earlier times. Selecting between two or more options is part of nearly every decision collections librarians make as they seek to implement collection development and management goals. Dennis Carrigan writes that "the essence of collection development is choice."[1] This chapter introduces various topologies for defining types of materials and explores the selection process and selection criteria, sources for identifying titles, interaction with the acquisition process, acquisition options, diverse user communities and alternative literature, and censorship and intellectual freedom.

Universe of Published Materials

Selecting among the vast number of materials published each year can seem a daunting task. Book title output increases every year. The *UNESCO Statistical Yearbook* for 1999 reported that more than 900,000 hardbound, trade paper, and mass market paperbound titles were published worldwide in 1996.[2] UNESCO has not updated this information, but others project that worldwide book production is now more than one million titles.[3] Bowker reported that U.S. title output in 2007 increased slightly to 276,649 new titles and editions, up from the 274,416 published in 2006.[4] The number of active periodicals also continues to grow. When consulted in January 2008, Bowker's Ulrichsweb.com (www.ulrichsweb.com/ulrichsweb/) listed more than 300,000 academic and scholarly journals (largely peer-reviewed titles including many open access publications), popular magazines, newspapers, newsletters, and other types of periodicals from around the world.

Librarians are challenged by increasing materials costs as well as the vast number of publications. The costs of materials have been increasing far in excess of U.S. inflation for more than twenty years and usually in excess of most libraries' acquisition budgets. Between 2005 and 2006, the Consumer Price Index (CPI) increased 2.5 percent and the average price of U.S. periodicals increased by 7.3 percent. The average price of North American academic books published in 2005 increased by 6.4 percent over 2004, compared to the CPI increase of 3.4 percent; during the same period hardcover books increased by 9.87 percent and mass market paperbacks by 2.3 percent.[5] Selection becomes more challenging because collections librarians must be increasingly selective.

Separating the universe of published materials into categories facilitates their selection and management. Larger libraries may assign responsibility for these categories to different people. Several topologies have been and continue to be used, many of them overlapping. Format is a typical topology and distinguishes, for example, between print, microforms, video and audio recordings, and electronic resources. Format often guides how the material is handled in the library—who catalogs it and how it is marked, shelved or stored, and serviced or circulated. Other formats are maps, slides, pictures, globes, kits, models, games, manuscripts and archives, and realia.

Genre is often mingled incorrectly with format in discussions of types of materials. Categories within genre include monographs, monographic series, manga and anime, 'zines, dissertations, musical scores, newspapers, application software, numeric data sets, exhibition catalogs, pamphlets, novels, plays, manuals, websites, encyclopedias, ephemera or gray literature, indexes and abstracts, directories, journals, magazines, textbooks, and government documents. A single genre may be presented in several formats. For example, serial publications can be acquired in print, microform, and various digital formats.

Resources may be categorized by subject. These may be broad divisions (humanities, social sciences, sciences), narrower (literature, sociology, engineering), or very refined (American literature, family social science, chemical engineering). Often, the categories are described by divisions in a classification scheme, typically the Library of Congress or Dewey Decimal systems. Some genres are more frequently found within subjects and disciplines. For example, the sciences rely heavily on proceedings and research reports. Tests and other measurement tools are part of the education and psychology literature.

Materials can be subdivided by language in which they are produced or geographic area in which they are published or which they cover. They may be considered by the age of the reader to whom they are directed—children, young adult, adult. These, too, can be subdivided (e.g., picture books, early readers). Some libraries employ categories that reflect their organizational structure. The staff members in the reference unit select reference materials, librarians in the children's services unit select all materials for young readers, librarians in the popular reading group select these materials, and so on. Academic and research libraries may distinguish between primary (source documents), secondary (reviews, state-of-the-art summaries, textbooks, interpretations of primary sources), and tertiary resources (repackaging of the primary literature in popular treatments, annuals, handbooks, and encyclopedias).

Topologies guide how reviews, publication lists, and introductions to the literature are organized or defined. These may reflect format, such as *Film and Video Finder.*[6] They may reflect subject areas (e.g., *Index to Social Sciences and Humanities Proceedings*), reader groups (e.g., *Best Books for Boys*), or genres (e.g., *Public Library Core Collection: Fiction, A Selection Guide*).[7] Appendix B suggests bibliographic tools, directories, and review resources to aid in selection.

Librarians and the reviewing media have tended to focus on traditional print-based resources. Sheila S. Intner calls this a "bibliocentric" stance and recommends a nonbibliocentric approach that looks beyond print materials to include intellectual and artistic expressions in all formats.[8] Stephen Abram describes this approach as being "container and format agnostic."[9] Several formats and genres are of increasing interest to library users and should not be ignored.

Library users and nonusers like audio and video works. Videos and audiobooks are immensely popular with library users. According to the Audio Publishers Association 2007 sales survey, libraries accounted for 32 percent of all audio sales, the highest of any outlet.[10] The Association of College and Research Libraries 2006 "Guidelines for Media Resources in Academic Libraries" begins with these assumptions: "All academic libraries will collect media resources. . . . The principles of collection management that apply to print and other library collections also apply to media resources."[11] The appeal and value of audiobooks are not limited to adults. Arnie Cardillo and colleagues suggest that audiobooks for children and teens have benefits in several areas.[12] They can offer more time for reading, serve as models of verbal fluency, motivate reluctant readers, and improve the English vocabulary development of non-English-speaking students. Children and youth live in an environment dominated by new media—MP3 players, iPods, podcasts, and so on. If libraries fail to respond effectively to the rapidly expanding media environment, patrons will go elsewhere. More important, failing to encompass all formats in collections ignores a tremendous wealth of information and artistic expression.

Graphic novels are another genre with high demand, especially by children and young adults. Graphic novels are book-length comics and, despite being called novels, can be fiction or nonfiction. *Manga*, a term sometimes used instead of *graphic novel*, is generally understood to mean graphic novels created in the Japanese style (*manga* is the Japanese word for comics).[13] Graphic novels are highly visual but not necessarily violent or sexually offensive. They can fulfill various roles in school library media centers and public libraries, from supporting the K–12 curriculum to meeting students' leisure reading interests. Philip Charles Crawford writes that "graphic novels strongly appeal to teens and are an invaluable tool for reading motivation."[14] Graphic novels also appeal to adults and have received critical acclaim. *Maus: A Survivor's Tale* by Art Spiegelman won a Pulitzer Prize Special Award in 1992.[15] Charles McGrath's 2004 article "Not Funnies," in *New York Times Magazine*, considers the literary merits of graphic novels.[16] Graphic novels are increasingly reviewed in the mainstream literature and are the recipients of awards, such as the Harvey Award and the Eisner Award, and the subject of recommended reading lists.[17] The general criteria for evaluation and assessment presented later in this chapter apply to graphic novels as well—with an additional caveat offered by Crawford, who recommends that all graphic novels for children and teens be previewed before adding to the collection.

E-books continue to increase in popularity in all types of libraries and can facilitate information discovery through search features, expand collections, save space, and reduce costs. An e-book is a digital object containing an electronic representation of a book, most commonly thought of as the electronic analog of a printed book. E-books have been around since the early 1980s and were initially delivered via physical media such as CD-ROMs or diskettes. The term *e-book* now most often is used to refer to digital objects specifically designed to be accessible online and read on either a handheld device or a personal computer. A survey of special, academic, and public libraries conducted by Barbara Blummer examined the increase in numbers of e-books in these libraries.[18] At the time of her study (2006), she reported that special libraries were the most likely to have e-books, with the special libraries in her survey reporting 15–60 percent of their collections being e-books. The Association of American Publishers released data showing that e-book sales increased 25.1 percent in the first eleven months of 2007.[19]

E-books can be selected on a title-by-title basis or as part of a package—macro selection. Commercial services that market to libraries sometimes offer both options along with the ability to purchase titles or subscribe for a period of time. Services such as NetLibrary (a division of OCLC), Ebook Library, and ebrary host the content of several publishers for online access. In addition, numerous publishers including Elsevier, Springer, and Oxford University Press have developed their own e-book publishing initiatives through which they host and sell e-books to libraries directly or through vendors. Patrons may have the option of either checking out an e-book, viewing it online, or viewing it offline by downloading it onto their personal computers. The library negotiates access either for one user at a time or for multiple users as part of an e-books license.

One impetus for the growing popularity of e-books as a format was the development of electronic book readers for individual users. Electronic book-reading devices, however, present libraries with the problem of device-specific licensing; digital right management (DRM) is the current strategy used to protect publisher interests. DRM encompasses the technologies, tools, and processes that protect intellectual property during digital content commerce for many kinds of content. If a library or individual downloads and pays for an electronic text for an e-book device, the text is usually exclusively licensed for that particular e-book device. DRM is used to encrypt the e-book so that it can be read only on a single, specific reader. Consequently, libraries more commonly deliver e-books via the Internet, in PDF format, for viewing on a personal computer. Nevertheless, library patrons are constrained and often confused by the lack of interoperability and the need to use multiple e-book platforms.

The International Digital Publishing Forum (IDPF; www.idpf.org) is an international trade and standards organization that aims to address variations in e-book systems. Members are hardware and software companies, publishers, authors, and related organizations working to establish, maintain, and promote specifications and standards for electronic publishing and interoperability. This organization has developed three open standards—Open Publication Structure, Open Packaging Format, and Open Container Format—which allow publishers to produce and send a single digital publication file through distribution and offer consumers interoperability between software and hardware for digital books and other electronic publications. These standards eliminate the need for publishers to reformat their titles for each machine and reduce the inconvenience of DRM.

An early noncommercial initiative is Project Gutenberg (http://promo.net/pg/), which began in 1971 when Michael Hart and a group of volunteers began to convert what Hart called "the world's great literature" to electronic versions and make them widely and freely available. Now providing access to more that 100,000 books through its partners and affiliates, Project Gutenberg offers only books that are in the public domain.

A more recent source of e-book collections is the mass scanning books held by libraries. A prominent player on the e-book scene is Google, which is scanning millions of books held by libraries partnering with Google in the Google Books Library Project. Google Book Search is a tool from Google that searches the full text of books that Google scans and stores. Google Book Search lets the user view pages (if permitted by the publisher) or snippets from the book, offers links to the publisher's and booksellers' websites, and displays information about libraries that hold the book. If the book is under copyright, Google limits the number of viewable pages. If the book is out of copyright or the publisher has given permission, one can see a preview of the book and, in some cases, the compete text. If the book is in the public domain, one can download a PDF copy. In addition to Google, other companies, cooperative projects, and some libraries are creating large collections of scanned books. These include Open Content Alliance (www.opencontentalliance.org) and the Million Book Project (www.ulib.org/index.html). Because all of these programs provide digital books openly on the Internet, no license agreements are required to provide access to library users.

Most libraries merge combinations of material categorizations when assigning and managing selection responsibilities. Academic libraries may use a combination of subject or discipline specialists, geographic area studies librarians, and a government documents librarian. Committees are often used to deal with a specific genre, for example, serials committees. Public libraries may categorize by reader group or discipline or a combination. Some public libraries divide responsibilities according to publisher type (e.g., trade publishers, small presses). School libraries may think in terms of fiction and nonfiction, age of reader, and discipline. Rigidly following topological distinctions in performing collections responsibilities can result in important resources being ignored because they are outside a selector's scope or in a format or genre that is not covered in a familiar catalog or selection tool. The needs of the library and its clientele are best served when the entire collection is viewed as a coherent whole.

The Selection Process

Selection is both an art and a science. It results from a combination of knowledge, experience, and intuition. An experienced collections librarian is hard pressed to explain exactly how he or she decides what to add and what to exclude. John Rutledge and Luke Swindler propose a mental model that assigns a weighted value to each criterion considered. They suggest that a selector works through this mental model and reaches one of three conclusions: the title must be added, should be added, or could be added.[20] Lynn B. Williams explores how the mind works in the decision process, citing the role of recognition, "an automatic or deliberative decision-making process whereby a cue is subjected to some kind of familiarity test and an affirmative or negative response is given."[21] Recognition guides the selector to determining if the item is appropriate and helps answer questions about whether the content is relevant and the author, editor, publisher, or title familiar. Williams notes that recognition capabilities are strengthened as a result of frequent, routine, and repeated collection building. Mastery comes through these activities. Brian Quinn investigated the interaction between affect (feeling) and cognition (thought) in the collection development process and notes that emotion can affect decision making.[22]

Despite the central roles experience, intuition, and sometimes emotion play in collection building, familiarity with the tools selectors use and an understanding of their techniques, processes, and potential problems are essential building blocks for success. The selector must know the appropriate resources for locating suitable materials. He or she needs skills in choosing between various materials and formats, evaluating materials' quality, and balancing costs with funds available.

All selection decisions begin with consideration of the user community and the long-term mission, goals, and priorities of the library and its parent body. Long ago, Francis K. W. Drury stated, "The high purpose of book selection is to provide the right book for the right reader at the right time."[23] About the same time, S. R. Ranganathan proposed his five laws of library science, which include "Every reader his or her book" and "Every book its reader."[24] In the ideal situation, a collections librarian has a written collection development policy that describes the library's mission and user community and provides guidance for developing and managing a collection and the subsection or category for which he or she is responsible. In the absence of a local policy, the librarian aims to understand the informal guidelines for collection building through a review of the collection and consultation with other librarians. Familiarity with the community and the collection guidelines or policy statement is part of the building blocks of good selection. To this is added knowledge of the literature for which the librarian is responsible. When the librarian has a firm grasp of these elements, he or she is equipped to begin selection.

The selection process can be thought of as a four-step process: (1) identification of the relevant, (2) evaluation (is the item worthy of selection?) and assessment (is the item appropriate for the collection?), (3) decision to purchase, and (4) order preparation and sometimes placement. Identifying possible items requires basic, factual information about authors, titles, publishers, and topics. Many tools and resources exist to help librarians identify possible acquisitions.

Identifying the Relevant: Selection Tools and Resources

Bibliographies and *lists* may be issued by libraries, library publishers, school systems, professional societies, and commercial publishers. National bibliographies and trade lists have been standard tools in libraries for decades. Libraries often consult recent accession lists prepared by other libraries. Recommended lists are prepared by library associations and other professional associations. Several sources list books that have received awards, such as *The Pura Belpré Awards* and *The Newbery and Caldecott Medal Books*.[25] Bibliographies published by commercial publishers are usually available as an online resource (which is constantly updated), a print or CD-ROM subscription (which may be updated annually or perhaps quarterly), or a monograph issued in revised editions. Bibliographies and lists provide guidance for filling gaps in existing collections. For example, a librarian seeking to increase a collection of African American literature for children would consult *The Coretta Scott King Awards Book*.[26] Indexing and abstracting resources provide a list of the titles indexed, which can be checked against library holdings. Some resources identify specific types of publications, such as *Graphic Novels Core Collection*.[27] Others focus on both a specific discipline and specific types, such as *Index to Social Sciences and Humanities Proceedings*.[28] Bibliographies and lists are not, however, inclusive, not available in every field, and not always annotated. Even well-respected and long-standing selection guides, such as the *Public Library Catalog* (now the *Public Library Core Collection: Nonfiction, A Selection Guide*), can lack a balanced perspective, because they are developed and maintained by individuals (who have their own points of view and expertise) working together.[29]

Selectors can use *directories* to identify a discipline's professional associations; examples include the *Encyclopedia of Associations* and *Yearbook of International Organizations*.[30] Directory entries usually list the association's periodical publications and contact information to request catalogs and other information on current imprints.

Reviews appear in the library-oriented press, popular media, and discipline-based journals. Public librarians should keep up with popular media because it has a significant influence on reader interests. Each time Oprah selects a new book for Oprah's Book Club, libraries experience high demand for this title. Titles reviewed in the *New York Times Book Review* and appearing in its best-seller lists are always in high demand. An Internet-based resource, Bookwire (www.bookwire.com), indexes book review resources on the Internet and contains thousands of links to book sites worldwide. Many discipline-specific journals provide scholarly and critical reviews of high quality, but these often follow publication by several months or years. Finding reviews of Internet sites is becoming easier. *College and Research Libraries News* has a monthly feature, "Internet Resources," that reviews selected Internet sites on a specific topic.[31] *The Scout Report* (www.scout.cs.wisc.edu), provided by the Internet Scout Project at the University of Wisconsin–Madison, offers thousands of critical annotations for carefully selected Internet sites and mailing lists. Great Web Sites for Kids (www.ala.org/greatsites/) is maintained by the ALA. Remember, though, that the total number of titles reviewed in all sources combined is only a small portion of the world's publishing output.

Publisher announcements (brochures, advertisements, catalogs, websites) provide detailed content descriptions, tables of contents, and author biographies. Sample chapters may be found on publishers' web pages. Evaluative statements in publishers' announcements should be viewed with caution because most of these are solicited by the publisher as part of the promotional process. Announcements are timely—often appearing before or simultaneous with the publication—and are widely used by academic, special, and larger public libraries.

Review or *approval copies* are ideal selection aids. Publishers often provide review copies at exhibits at librarians' conferences and sometimes sell the publication at the same time. Journal publishers often provide a sample issue upon request. Many video suppliers provide a preview copy to be returned if the item is not selected for acquisition. Approval plans, by their nature, provide books "on approval." The approval plan vendor and library aim for a low return rate, but vendors generally permit returning items if the library finds them unacceptable. Many electronic resources offer trial periods during which librarians and users can try the product.

Book fairs and bookstores provide an opportunity to examine materials before purchase. Book fairs bring together many publishers to display and promote their publications. Book fairs may be local, regional, national, or international in scope.

Among the best known are the book fairs in Frankfurt, Zimbabwe, and Madrid. Many professional conferences include publisher exhibitors. Though not book fairs in the true sense, they serve the same purpose of introducing new publications and, often, authors to attendees. Bookstores are particularly useful for locating alternative literature and materials from outside the predominant culture, which are less frequently reviewed in traditional sources.

Web-based tools provide several approaches to locating new and relevant older titles. Librarians can find reviews, out-of-print dealers who offer lists of available titles and search for specific requests, vendor and publisher information, and online stores and catalogs covering all formats. Amazon.com is one of the more familiar online dealers and useful for subject-based searching, reviews, and speedy delivery of items. Amazon.com offers special services to libraries including processing (Mylar covers, MARC records, and labels) and approval slips, though without the discounts provided by traditional approval plan vendors. Alibris.com, an online out-of-print site, promises more that sixty million titles. Publishers frequently provide the table of contents and sample chapters of new books on their websites. Librarians can perform subject searches in national bibliographic utilities and in other libraries' catalogs. Electronic discussion groups and electronic newsletters directed toward collection development and acquisitions librarians can provide information about publishers and resources for specific subject areas and types of materials.

In-house information such as interlibrary loan requests can aid selection. Repeated requests from users for articles from a particular journal suggest that journal should be added to the collection. The same is true for interlibrary requests for a specific book title. Frequent recalls or a long waiting list for a book provide evidence that that title should be considered for duplication. Some academic libraries have added a service that purchases books requested through interlibrary loan for users and adds them to the libraries' permanent collection after the user's loan period.[32] Most libraries accept purchase requests from users; these suggest specific titles that should be considered for addition and may suggest formats, subject areas, or genres to which the library should add materials.

Locating information about *government documents* (the official publications of agencies at the international, national, regional, state, and local levels) can present its own challenges. The aim in selecting documents is the same as that for all types of materials. As Lisa A. Ennis writes, "The goal is to develop the best [documents] collection possible, concentrating on the most appropriate content in the most appropriate formats for your user base."[33] The Government Printing Office provides several online tools for locating U.S. federal documents. The nature of U.S. federal document collecting has changed significantly as more and more of these publications are available in both print and online formats, or only online. In 2006, 94 percent of these publications were born digital and never printed.[34] Some libraries, legally designated as U.S. federal depository libraries in the Federal Depository Library Program, are charged with ensuring that the public has free and open access to the government publications that are received free of charge from the Government Printing Office (GPO) and must acquire all federal government publications. Partial depository libraries build their collections through the creation of profiles, making selections for series and groups of publications in advance of printing lists provided by the GPO and thereby acquiring groups of titles. Nondepository libraries select titles for purchase using standard review sources and tools offered by the GPO, including the *Catalog of U.S. Government Publications* and other tools such as the Basic Collection, which lists basic titles, and Core Documents of U.S. Democracy.[35]

The most effective method for identifying and acquiring state, regional, and local documents is through direct contact with the issuing agency. State government agencies generally provide websites that list publications and links to online resources. Some commercial indexes such as the *Statistical Reference Index*, LexisNexis Statistical (an online product), and *Index to Current Urban Documents* handle state and local documents.[36]

Foreign documents and those published by international agencies may be listed in government and agency catalogs and on their websites; see, for example, the United Nations Publications website (http://unp.un.org). An increasing number of foreign and intergovernmental publications are available free via the Internet. Bernan (www.bernan.com), a commercial source for U.S. and intergovernmental publications, has an extensive online catalog that includes separate lists of publications from Africa and Latin America.

Evaluation and Assessment

Evaluation and assessment assist the collections librarian in deciding if the title should be added. *Evaluation* looks at qualities intrinsic to the item. The item is first considered on its own merits before assessing its ability to meet local needs. In practice, evaluation and assessment generally occur simultaneously. A collections librarian will not devote time to evaluating an item if that item is not appropriate for the user community being served.

EVALUATION

Evaluation criteria vary from item to item and between categories of materials, but generally they include several of the following considerations:

- content or subject
- language
- currency
- veracity

- writing style (e.g., well written, easy to read, aesthetic aspects)
- completeness and scope of treatment
- reputation, credentials, or authoritativeness of author, publisher, editor, reviewers
- geographic coverage
- quality of scholarship
- frequency the title is referenced in bibliographies or citations
- reader or user level to which content is directed
- comprehensiveness and breadth
- frequency of updates or revisions
- access points (e.g., indexes, level of detail in the table of contents)
- ease of use
- external resources that index the publication
- physical quality (e.g., illustrations, paper and binding, format, typography, durability, visual and audio characteristics)
- uniqueness of content, capabilities, or features
- availability of equipment required for hearing or viewing audiovisual material
- cost in relation to quality of the item

Some categories of materials have additional and unique evaluation criteria that should guide selection. For example, a selector of pictures books should give special consideration to the nature and quality of the illustrations. Phyllis J. Van Orden and Sunny Strong recommend that a selector ask if the artwork extends or clarifies the text (or in a wordless book, if the story is clear through the pictures) and consider the artistic elements of color, line, shape, composition, and design.[37]

The nature of e-resources suggests additional criteria for consideration. These include

- licensing and contractual terms, limitations, and obligations
- special pricing considerations, including discounts for retaining or canceling paper subscriptions, restrictions on cancellations, and discounts for consortial purchase
- completeness (if the e-version of a print resource, is the same content provided?)
- currency (the speed with which e-content is added or updated)
- ability to select and deselect individual titles or other content subsets, if offering is a package deal offered by an aggregator or publisher

- local service implications
- compatibility with link resolvers, bibliographic and citation management software, and course management software
- quality of end-user interface
- support for information transfer (output options)
- availability of data to measure use and effectiveness.
- response time
- vendor support and responsiveness
- availability of back files for genres such as e-journals
- publisher preservation arrangements
- permission to access purchased content if a subscription is canceled

For electronic resources involving physical media (e.g., CD-ROMs), these additional criteria should be considered:

- physical and logistical requirements within the library, including space, furniture, hardware, wiring, and telecommunication and data ports
- effective use of technology

Comparing the same e-content delivered several ways can be a challenge. A product may be available in print, CD-ROM, online from several suppliers, and with different pricing packages. For example, PsychINFO can be acquired directly from the American Psychological Association and through EBSCO, Ovid, OCLC, ProQuest, DIALOG, and other vendors. When possible, a library should arrange demonstrations and free trials and involve staff from public services and the information technology unit in reviewing the e-resource. One approach to evaluating similar products is to create a decision matrix into which comparative information, including cost, is recorded for each product.[38] This facilitates comparing similarities, differences, advantages, and disadvantages of the options being considered.

The process of selecting serials and other continuing resources (regardless of format) parallels that for other types of publications. The differences are the need to consider the continuing financial commitment implicit in initiating a subscription or licensing access and the possible need to negotiate a contract for electronic resources. A serial is "a publication in any medium issued in successive parts bearing numerical or chronological designations and intended to be continued indefinitely."[39] Many librarians interchange the terms *serial* and *periodical*. Serials include general magazines, which provide recreational reading and popular sources of information on current social and political issues; scholarly and scientific journals, which are often specialized and directed to a narrow audience; annual reports and house organs of businesses; trade and technology-focused magazines; and "little magazines," which concentrate on literature, politics, or both and often fall within what is known as alternative literature. The term *e-journal* is often used for any serial that is available electronically. *Continuing resources* is gaining favor as an umbrella term for serials (issued successively over time) and all types of integrating resources that continue over time (e.g., indexing and abstracting tools with and without associated full-text articles; online encyclopedias, directories, dictionaries, statistical compendia). According to the first draft of Part 1 of *Resource Description and Access,*

> The term integrating resource refers to a resource that is added to or changed by means of updates that do not remain discrete and are integrated into the whole. An integrating resource may be tangible (e.g., a loose-leaf manual that is updated by means of replacement pages) or intangible (e.g., a website that is updated either continuously or on a cyclical basis).[40]

The term *continuing resource* also indicates the continuing financial obligation implicit in selecting it. The library pays, usually on an annual cycle, for periodicals before they are published and for access to an e-resource for a period of time into the future. A librarian needs to consider the library budget's capacity to accommodate annual increases for these materials often in excess of normal collections budget growth. He or she must be prepared to cancel serials and other continuing resources to operate within available funds and as part of the selection process for new resources. E-resources increasingly are sold through multiyear contracts, and some vendors place strict limits on cancellations, perhaps even requiring the library to reinstate previously canceled subscriptions.

When selecting a serial, the collections librarian must pay particular attention to the purpose of the publication and to where it is indexed. Magazines, trade journals, scholarly periodicals, and so on each have an intended audience, and the evaluation criteria set out in this chapter are generally applicable. For example, part of evaluating a scholarly journal is considering the credentials of the editors and reviewers to determine the rigor with which submissions are analyzed. A public or school library might consider whether a popular magazine is indexed in *Readers Guide to Periodical Literature.*[41]

Because of the continuing financial commitment, many larger libraries use selection committees to evaluate possible new serial titles and continuing resources. The committee can consider several titles at the same time, ranking them in priority order and seeking balanced coverage. School libraries may have a committee composed of teachers and the school media specialist. Academic libraries, school library media centers, and special libraries may seek evaluations from faculty members, teachers, and researchers. Other libraries rely on selectors to balance monographs and serials and other continuing resources within their own separate budgets.

ASSESSMENT

Assessment considers items in relation to user needs, the existing collection, the mission of the library, local policies and practices, and consortial obligations. Does the item support the curriculum, research interests, grants, faculty or teacher specialties, or specific community interests? Methods for answering these questions are suggested in chapter 6. Does the item fall within the parameters of subjects or areas to be covered as defined in the collection development policy? Librarians need to consider if a title is being acquired to satisfy short-term needs and how it might relate to any long-term collection goals. Does the library need an additional work on this subject? Does the item fill a gap in the collection? Is a duplicate copy justified? Is it easily available from another library? If the item requires a contract, are the licensing terms consistent with local policies and practices? Does the library have the ability to handle the title? Will it get prompt cataloging? Does the library have appropriate housing (shelf space, microform cabinets, server capacity), equipment (microform readers, printers, computer workstations, CD-ROM drives), and electrical and telecommunication infrastructure? Are staff members who work with the public prepared to support the title's use and service needs? Does the library have a consortial obligation to purchase the item?

School library media specialists assess materials' ability to match curricular trends. School librarians and media specialists often find themselves playing catch-up as the curriculum and its emphasis and philosophy shift. Lotsee P. Smith identifies three valid primary purposes of school library collections: supporting the curriculum, providing materials for recreational use, and providing professional aids for teaching, with primary emphasis on the first.[42] Achieving these aims requires understanding the intended user community. The current national emphasis on core competencies and meeting basic standards in order to be promoted to the next grade and to graduate are influencing selection activities. School library media specialists often seek to balance building collections that support curricular goals with building a core collection that meets more broad-based goals. Learner-center collection development, a concept and practice explored by Sandra Hughes-Hassell and Jacqueline C. Mancall, aims to accommodate the changing curricular needs and recreational interests of students through broad engagement with teachers and other stakeholders.[43] Hughes-Hassell and Mancall developed a decision-making matrix for school media center librarians that asks whether the resource addresses the information needs of the learning community, matches learner characteristics, fits the teaching-learning context, is consistent with the current knowledge bases, and falls within budget parameters (or is available from partners). If the answer is no to any of the questions, the resource does not meet the requirements of the learning community and should not be selected.

Licensing terms for e-resources must be examined to determine if they meet the specific libraries' policies and practices. The advent of e-resources, first offered on CD-ROMs and now frequently accessed online, brought librarians into a new era of selection and acquisition—one in which licensing and contractual terms, limitations, and obligations became another area requiring evaluation. Libraries no longer purchase all materials outright for addition to a physical collection; they also license access to digital content through contracts with providers. Nearly all publishers and vendors require a signed contract before permitting access to an online resource or providing CD-ROMs to a library. A contract is a formal, legally binding agreement between two or more parties. It is usually in writing, but a verbal contract to which the parties agree can be equally binding. In libraries, a license or license agreement is a contract that presents the terms under which a vendor or publisher grants rights (powers or privileges) to use one or more proprietary bibliographic databases, e-journals, or other online resources, usually for a fixed period of time in exchange for payment. Often the CD-ROMs must be returned, and access to an online resource is terminated if the contract is not renewed. The evaluation process involves careful review of a contract and its conditions before a decision is made to choose the resource.

Many traditional library services and usage policies may be curtailed or disallowed in an e-resource contract, which spells out terms and conditions governing the resource. Because contracts are part of the legal system and subject to contract law, they use legal terminology. Appendix D provides a primer to frequently used terms. Contracts include clauses that

- govern terms of use (e.g., prohibitions against or permission to use the e-content in interlibrary loan and course reserves)
- define authorized users and any limitations on walk-in use and off-site access
- may specify the process of authorizing and authenticating authorized users
- set out the pricing model (which might be based on FTE users, pay per use, or number of concurrent users), often as an appendix
- specify the term or duration of the contract and any prohibitions against cancellation
- describe the renewal and cancellation process
- specify the contractual obligations of both parties and the penalties if obligations are not fulfilled
- specify whether the library has access to the content if the contract is terminated and the form that access might take, often called perpetual access

In theory, everything within a contract can be changed through negotiation. By its nature, a contract must be mutually acceptable before it is signed. The librarian's goal is a contract that allows the user community to pursue its usual activities, renders a fair exchange of money for product and service, and balances the rights, responsibilities, and legal liabilities of all parties. Most libraries work with a list of desirable terms and conditions that they hope to negotiate in their favor (e.g., many libraries prefer to have the contract under the governing law of the state in which the library is located—but do not consider this a show stopper) and a list of terms or conditions that must meet the library's requirements (e.g., the ability to provide unaffiliated users walk-in, on-site access). Contract law is complex, and negotiating contracts can be time consuming. A survey published in 2007 found that respondents estimated spending an average of 229.74 hours of staff time annually in U.S. libraries reviewing contract terms in licenses for electronic content.[44] Librarians should be able to identify the issues that need to be addressed when negotiating a contract. They should know when to call for expert opinion and advice. They should understand the policies of the library and its parent body regarding contracts, leases, purchasing, and accountability to ensure that all contracts and their signing are consistent with these policies.

Several resources are available to help librarians with contracts and licensing for e-resources. *The Survey of Library Database Licensing Practices* presents data from ninety corporate, legal, college, university, public, state, and nonprofit libraries about their database licensing practices.[45] Model licenses can be found at Liblicense and Licensingmodels.com.[46] The International Federation of Library Associations and Institutions and the University of California Libraries have developed licensing principles.[47] *Guide to Licensing and Acquiring Electronic Information* offers a comprehensive but not overwhelming starting point.[48] Additional sources are listed in the "Suggested Readings" section of this chapter.

A new approach to acquiring e-resources without negotiating license agreements is available—the NISO Shared Electronic Resources Understanding Best Practice (SERU).[49] Though SERU is not designed to replace all license agreements, it can be a convenient method to use for inexpensive e-resources, especially those from small publishers that do not have large staffs to negotiate license agreements. SERU is not a license agreement but rather a set of statements that reference existing law (e.g., copyright law) and describe some common practices in working with e-resources. If both the library and publisher agree, a simple reference to SERU can be made in a purchase order and the library then gains access when payment has been made. No license agreement is signed so no negotiation is needed. Libraries and publishers can register with NISO to indicate their willingness to consider using SERU for e-resource acquisition.

Decision to Purchase

Once the selector has considered all relevant evaluation and assessment questions, he or she is ready to add or reject the item. Ross Atkinson refers to the universe of materials not locally owned as the anti-collection. He holds that selection is, "to a great extent, a continuous series of decisions about which items in the anti-collection should be moved into the collection" and goes on to suggest that the selection decision is relatively simple because the selector has only two options: buy or don't buy.[50] Selectors employ a mental model that looks at the potential utility for current and future users. Atkinson believes that the line between accepting and rejecting materials is primarily dependent of the financial resources available to the selector. Given the volume of materials being published and the finite nature of library budgets, librarians always face choices about what not to add as they are choosing what to add.

Order Preparation

The processes and systems of ordering and obtaining library materials after they are selected are termed *acquisition*. The acquisition of materials is closely related to collection development, though in most medium-size and large libraries selection and acquisition are handled by different individuals, who may be located in different library departments or units. Acquisitions responsibilities typically include placing orders (i.e., initiating purchase orders), claiming, canceling, receipting, invoice processing, and preparing requests for proposals (RFPs) from monograph vendors and serials agents and may include payment processing. Typical accounting guidelines require that the responsibility for approval for payment and payment processing be assigned to different individuals. Selection and acquisition may be handled separately in smaller libraries if the staff size makes this reasonable; however, combining the functions of selection and acquisition is common. The ease with which selectors can work directly with suppliers' online databases is blurring the traditional division of work. Selectors may place orders directly online as part of the item identification process.

Usually, the selector is expected to verify title, author or editor, publisher, publication date, and cost before ordering an item. Ideally the selector also provides series, ISBN or ISSN, and perhaps information about the source from which the publication is available. Many libraries request selectors to provide bibliographic information on forms that may be preprinted, retrieved and printed from an online template, or completed online (see figure 4-1). These forms usually require the selector to assign a fund or budget line, identify the collection to which the item will be added, request any special handling, and confirm, if appropriate, that a duplicate copy is desired. If the title being ordered is a serial, the selector identifies the volume with which the subscription should begin and any back files that are to be ordered. A selector can use the sample form in figure 4-1 to relay the specific elements of a book order.

Selector:	
Title:	
ISBN:	
Author:	
Publisher:	
Budget code:	
Begin order with volumes/issue/year (if standing order):	
Location:	
Is a record in the catalog? ❏ No ❏ Yes BIB ID#:	
Price:	
Comments:	

Submit   Reset

FIGURE 4-1 Sample online internal order form. This form is available at www.ala.org/editions/extras/Johnson09720.

The selection and acquisition of e-resources add complexity to the interaction of collections librarians and acquisitions staff for many reasons. Many e-resources are expensive and may require special approval processes. Standard systems that facilitate acquisition of print resources often are lacking for e-resources, and the latter commonly require more direct interaction with the producers or publishers. Many require the added step of negotiating license agreements, which must be signed or approved online by a designated signatory authority within the library or the library's parent agency to acquire or access the resource. In some libraries, the selector shepherds license agreements through the institution's approval process.

In others, a specified collections librarian or library administrator may be charged with the responsibility, or it may be handled by acquisitions staff members. In some school library media centers, especially those that are part of larger school systems, the management and sometimes even selection of online resources are handled by staff in an information technology department.

One of the challenges facing a library after signing contracts for e-resources is managing them and monitoring the terms and conditions specified. E-resource management systems are automated systems used to manage the creation, use, and maintenance of information related to e-resource contracts. These systems may be developed in-house or purchased from a vendor, and they may or may not integrate with a library's automated system. They usually record information about selection, trials, status of contract negotiation, vendor, dates actions are taken, term of contract and renewal dates, cost and fund line billed, and contractual obligations and limitations. Because much of the information recorded duplicates that tracked in an automated acquisitions system, interoperability between an e-resource management system and the local automated system is desirable.

Acquisitions Options

Monographic materials may be ordered from wholesale book vendors, who handle new imprints from a variety of publishers. Book jobbers may specialize in disciplines or subject areas, publishers, or materials for types of libraries (public, school, or academic). Research jointly undertaken by the Association of American Publishers and Association for Library Collections and Technical Services reported that 77.3 percent of the 305 U.S. libraries surveyed in 1999 were placing their orders through vendors.[51] Some types of materials, such as publications from small and alternative presses, may be available only by ordering directly from the publisher.[52] Items that are ordered title by title are called *discretionary purchases* or *firm orders*. A firm order is an order for a specific title placed with a dealer or publisher that specifies a time limit for delivery and a price that must not be exceeded without the library's approval. Selecting individual titles is considered *micro selection*.

The alternative to micro selection is *macro selection*, which adds large quantities of materials to the library en bloc or en masse. Macro selection is managed through mass buying plans—standing orders, blanket orders, or approval plans—or the acquisition of large retrospective collections either through purchase or as a gift. Macro selection has been used more commonly by larger public and academic libraries, but it is increasingly found in smaller academic libraries and in public libraries of all sizes. Several authors have argued convincingly that approval plans are desirable in smaller libraries for the same reasons they are used in larger libraries—efficiency, cost-effectiveness, and well-rounded collections.[53]

Macro selection does involve true selection. It typically uses a group of selectors, who review a range of criteria that guide which titles are supplied. This may be through an RFP process, periodical review of approval plan profiles, or other analyses based on a range of criteria that are fundamentally the same as those used for micro selection. Macro selection programs may have substantial setup costs and do require time to establish, but costs of investing resources up front are offset by selector time savings once the macro selection plan is implemented.

Access to many electronic publications, most commonly e-journals but increasingly e-books as well, is through macro selection—that is, acquiring access to an extensive package of titles from a single publisher or an aggregator. With this model, a package of titles from a single publisher often includes a clause that locks in the total price or caps the annual rate of price increase for a specified number of years. This is sometimes referred to as the "Big Deal," or journal bundling. Although this approach may offer differential pricing or a price discount and provide additional titles, it has disadvantages and has been viewed critically by some in the profession.[54] Selectors can lose the ability to select and deselect individual titles. Tracking titles by discipline and budget line can be difficult. Libraries may be locked into keeping titles that are no longer relevant or of good value. On the other hand, Big Deal arrangements can offer a cost-effective approach to acquiring numerous titles for some institutions. Cecilia Botero, Steven Carrico, and Michele Tennant used comparative data to demonstrate that the University of Florida reduced expenditures through Big Deals because the library no longer had to pay document delivery charges for articles in journals added through the licenses, and the library also gained access to titles not previously represented in its print collection.[55] Other advantages may include a single search interface for multiple titles, a single order and license agreement for multiple titles, and consistent presentation of usage statistics.

Serials can be acquired through subscription agents, directly from publishers (commercial publishers, scholarly associations, etc.), or e-journal aggregators. When possible, most libraries acquire as many serials as possible through one or a few subscription agents because of efficiencies gained. Instead of dozens or even thousands of individual invoices coming from multiple publishers, the agent provides a single invoice for all the titles it handles. Often the invoice is loaded directly into the library's automated system. Serial subscription agents usually offer centralized online ordering, claiming, renewal, cancellation, and reports and charge a service fee calculated as a percentage of the total cost of the serials being handled. Libraries usually issue RFPs for a subscription agent at periodic intervals (perhaps every five years), soliciting proposals from their current agent and competitors. The transition to e-journals is changing the role of serials agents, who are compensating for business lost to publishers' journal bundles by offering additional services (e.g., A-to-Z titles lists, contract negotiation, management of contract access rights and license terms) and reports tailored to the digital environment.

Multipublisher packages and collections of articles from aggregators offer additional options for the acquisition of e-journals. Three examples of multipublisher packages are Project Muse, BioOne, and JSTOR. Project Muse (http://muse.jhu.edu) is a nonprofit collaboration among libraries, more than sixty scholarly publishers, and the Milton S. Eisenhower Library at Johns Hopkins University. Publishers joining the platform contribute the complete content of each journal as it is published, with articles available in HTML, PDF, or both formats. To supplement current issues, MUSE subscribers have access to a decade of back files for selected titles. The MUSE system provides a common search interface and allows libraries to subscribe to many titles through one transaction. This kind of collaboration offers small publishers many of the advantages large publishers obtain from economies of scale.

BioOne (www.bioone.org) is another collaborative initiative, this one among scientific societies, libraries, academe, and the private sector; it offers a package of biological, ecological, and environmental science research journals. Most of BioOne's titles are published by small societies and other not-for-profit organizational publishers and, like Project MUSE, BioOne provides the latest issues and full journal content for titles in the BioOne collection.

JSTOR (www.jstor.org) is a nonprofit organization that provides a somewhat different kind of journal collection. It creates and maintains a trusted archive of important scholarly journals across many disciplines from many publishers and offers several packages of journal titles on a subscription basis. JSTOR creates scanned images of journal issues and pages as originally published and provides full-text searching of the journals based on optical character recognition. JSTOR does not offer access to current issues and employs a moving-wall approach, meaning that the most recently published journal issues are embargoed for one to five years, with only the older issues available. Some journals that participate in Project MUSE or BioOne for their current issues also work with JSTOR to provide access to their older issues.

Aggregator collections are developed by intermediaries that assemble e-journals from multiple publishers and offer them online through a common interface. Producers of many indexing and abstracting databases also offer aggregated article collections and build hypertext links between the full-text electronic documents and the index records, combining index searching with partial full-text access. For example, Academic Search Premier (from EBSCOhost) indexed 8,302 serials and provided full text to 4,655 of these in January 2008. Aggregators' agreements with journal publishers have been volatile, with publishers signing on with an aggregator and then withdrawing from the agreement. The description of Academic Search Premier makes this clear: "Publications included on this database are subject to change without notice due to contractual agreements with publishers."[56] Aggregators rarely offer the full content of a journal up to the most current issues. They sometimes provide selected articles and may not include book reviews, editorials, or advertisements. Embargoes on current content from a few months to a few years are also the norm. Increasingly publishers contribute to multiple aggregator collections and also may offer separate e-journal subscriptions to libraries, which acquire the same content from multiple sources. Aggregator collections can be a convenient and cost-effective approach to providing access to a sizable set of journal articles, but they offer no long-term guarantee of access to the titles in the package.

Taking advantage of various macro selection options, a large academic library allocates anywhere from 65 to 90 percent of its acquisitions budget to nondiscretionary purchases. These include standing orders for monographic series, serials, and other continuing resources; blanket orders with publishers; and approval plans. Order plans usually provide speedier delivery, and some guarantee that titles in small publication runs will be acquired. They make it possible for libraries to expend large budgets effectively and efficiently and to focus selection attention on less mainstream resources. Blanket orders and approval plans provide a discounted price for the materials supplied. Relying on macro selection to supply significant amounts of materials can free selectors to focus their time on identifying and selecting more esoteric materials.

Approval Plans

Monographic approval plans are business arrangements in which a wholesale dealer assumes responsibility for supplying, usually subject to return privileges, all new publications that match a library's collecting profile. Richard Abel is credited with the invention, in the early 1960s, of the approval plan as it is now employed.[57] Approval plan vendors operate in many countries and provide books and services to libraries wherever they are located. An approval profile is defined by the library's collections librarians and specifies the subjects, collecting levels, formats, genres, prices, languages, publishers, and so on to be shipped. The supplier sends on a regular basis materials that fit the profile. Librarians review the items shipped and decide which to buy. Michael Sullivan notes that, "for children's items especially, the ability to hold the item, examine illustrations, glossaries, indexes, and the like is a great improvement over buying from a printed review."[58] Most vendors and libraries aim for a return rate of 2 percent or less. Some approval plans offer paper or online notification slips rather than the publications themselves, and some plans provide a combination of slips and books. Selectors refine and revise the profile as the library's goals, priorities, and budget change.

A blanket order plan is an arrangement with an individual publisher or scholarly society to provide all its publications (or all publications below a specified price) each year, or with a vendor to provide a copy of every book published in a particular country within certain parameters. Blanket order plans do not, in most cases, include return privileges.

The variety of services and enhancements provided by both approval plan vendors and firm order suppliers has grown to include electronic data interchange through which digital order records and invoices can be loaded into a local library automated system, interactive access to the vendor or supplier online database, online order placement, cataloging records (which may be Library of Congress copy, CIP records, or original brief or full cataloging created by the vendor), and fully shelf-ready books. Shelf-ready books come to the library cataloged and processed with spine labels, book plates, and antitheft strips. Thus, vendors are supplementing or replacing functions traditionally performed within libraries. Libraries that contract externally for services previously provided by internal library staff members are outsourcing those services. Librarians have viewed outsourcing as a way to contain costs when library staffing has been reduced and as a way to release staff members for other responsibilities perceived as more important. Approval plans are widely employed because they can provide discounted prices, faster delivery of newly published books, reliable coverage, and reports that enable selectors to monitor plans. They can free selectors to look for more esoteric materials and to do other types of work.

Approval plans are not without controversy and were the source of a major flap in the library profession in the 1990s.[59] In 1996, the Hawaii State Public Library System implemented a radical extension of approval plans and contracted with a vendor who was to have sole responsibility for selecting, cataloging, and processing all materials for the central library and forty-nine branch libraries. Administrators saw this as way to manage a 25 percent budget cut without laying off employees and to release technical services librarians for direct public service. Most of Hawaii's librarians, on the other hand, felt unable to respond to users' needs and saw their collections deteriorating under the plan. The librarians saw this kind of outsourcing as a challenge to the very heart of professional librarianship and moved the debate to a national forum. The Hawaii situation became an emotional issue for librarians across the United States, who resented the use of a vendor in a way that was perceived as causing "commodification, commercialization, and homogenization of books, information materials, and libraries."[60] Selection of materials was seen as an essential function of librarianship. The Hawaii contract with the vendor was terminated two years after it was begun, and selection returned to the librarians.

Exchange Agreements

Some academic libraries use exchanges as a form of en bloc selection.[61] Exchanges are most frequently with foreign exchange partners and can provide materials not available in other ways or more economically than direct purchase. Partner libraries share local institutional publications. Partners may be libraries, scholarly societies and associations, university academic departments, or research academies and institutes. Exchanges may be a viable means of acquiring foreign documents. Exchanges should be established and monitored within the library's collections priorities. Some libraries are reducing their exchange programs, though many libraries continue exchange agreements because they are cost-effective mechanisms for obtaining publications, a cross-cultural activity, and a way of helping other libraries.

Gifts and Other Free Materials

Gifts may bring individual items or a collection of items to the library. A gift is transferred voluntarily without compensation. Gifts may be conveyed to the library through a deed of gift, a legal document that transfers title from the donor to the library without requiring payment. A deed of gift may contain conditions with which the library must comply. Generous donors expect careful stewardship of their gifts. No payment to the donor does not mean that the library has no costs associated with the gift. Costs arise when a gift is reviewed by the selector, cataloged and processed, shelved and reshelved, and repaired and preserved. Gift serial subscriptions have ongoing costs just as paid subscriptions do. Most selection decisions about gifts can be reduced to a trade-off between the cost of adding the item and its value to the library.

Gift materials are desirable because they can strengthen a library's holdings, fill gaps, supply replacements, and provide materials too expensive for the library to purchase or not available through purchase. A collection of many items from a single donor often focuses on a particular area or discipline. It may contain out-of-print items, serial runs in excellent condition, first editions, and other items of intrinsic value. Besides filling gaps, a gift collection can add both depth and breadth to a library's collection. Adding materials can strengthen institutional relations with individuals, who may make additional donations (both materials and funds) to the library and the institution over time. Gift materials can enter the library unsolicited, through direct negotiation with potential donors, or through requests to publishers. Special collections librarians or library development staff members may target individuals with known collections and negotiate a gift. A library may ask to receive all publications of a corporation, a research center, or an academic institution—in effect, a gift standing order.

The same criteria that guide selection of items for purchase should be considered when reviewing gifts. The first decision the selector must make is whether the material fits within the scope of the library's collecting policy or guidelines. The library may have policies about adding or not adding particular types of materials such as textbooks, laboratory manuals, duplicates, vanity press items, realia, reprints and preprints of individual articles, collections of reprinted journal articles, trade paperbacks, popular pamphlets, and commercial publications of a promotional nature.

Many librarians are selecting resources that are accessible without charge on the Internet. Selection of such items is an extension of a librarian's normal collection-building activities and presumes that intellectual access via catalog records and, perhaps, online subject-based finding aids is provided. In many library catalogs, the bibliographic record contains a live link to the web location of the item. The nature and complexity of free web resources suggest an important role for librarians in reviewing, evaluating, selecting, and cataloging websites for library users.[62]

Donors must be considered as part of the selection process. Some gifts are not worth adding to the library precisely because of special conditions insisted on by the potential donor. Donors may offer gifts with conditions about use, housing, or special treatment. Even a library that does not have guidelines for the selection of gift materials may have guidelines that address acceptable and unacceptable donor restrictions. The selector should weigh the value of the gift (and possible future gifts) to the library against any donor restrictions.

The library receiving gifts usually supplies the donor with a letter of acknowledgment. Under the U.S. Revenue Reconciliation Bill in 1993, which modified the 1984 Tax Reform Act slightly, donors are required to provide a written acknowledgment or formal deed-of-gift from the library for any non-cash donation in which they are claiming a deduction of $250 or more. Libraries should not give appraisals or estimates of value to the donor. A letter provides the donor with a record that may be used to claim a tax deduction, creates a permanent record of gifts received for the library, and graciously acknowledges the donor's gift to the library. Such a document eliminates any ambiguity regarding the library's right to use, retain, or dispose of materials received from donors.

If the donor's total deduction for all noncash contributions for the year is more than $500, the donor must file IRS Form 8283 and attach the receiving organization's acknowledgment letter of receipt. The donor is responsible for determining the fair market value of the gift. If the property being contributed is reported as being worth $5,000 or more, the donor must retain a qualified appraiser to determine the gift's fair market value. U.S. tax law requires a recipient institution to retain any gift valued at $500 or above for two years. If the library disposes of the gift or portions of it and thereby reduces the value of the original gift, it must file IRS Form 8282, which affects the donor's original deduction.

Retrospective Selection

Retrospective selection is the process of selecting materials that are old, rare, antiquarian, used, or out of print (OP). It includes seeking replacements for missing or damaged materials and older materials not previously acquired.

Many librarians develop desiderata files of titles to be purchased when funding is available or the item is located. These materials may be needed to fill gaps in the collection or to support new academic programs or community interests. Retrospective selection is more common in larger research libraries. The usual sources for materials are OP dealers' catalogs, auctions, and personal negotiations with a private owner.

Out-of-print titles are those that can no longer be obtained from the original publishers. This can happen rapidly as a result of the limited number of copies printed in some fields. Many used and OP booksellers produce catalogs. These catalogs, either in print or online, usually list only single copies; therefore, the librarian must act quickly to ensure acquisition. Many OP dealers accept lists of titles the library is seeking. Dealers can be located through the *American Book Trade Directory*.[63] Additional suppliers can be found through the Antiquarian Booksellers Association of America (http://abaa.org) and the International League of Antiquarian Booksellers (www.ilab-lila.com). Many university press books no longer go out of print because of print-on-demand, a technology employed by publishers in which new copies of a book are not printed until an order has been received. Print-on-demand is also used by smaller presses and academic publishers to maintain an active backlist of short-run titles.

A specialized area within retrospective selection is filling gaps in serial runs and replacing missing issues. One source is the Duplicates Exchange Union (www.ala.org/ala/alcts/pubs/duplicatesexch/duplicatesexchange.cfm), sponsored by the Association for Library Collections and Technical Services. Libraries prepare lists of periodical issues and books they are willing to supply to member libraries through a cooperative exchange of other duplicate materials. Libraries then check these available issues against their needs. Sometimes a publisher can provide missing issues for a price. Often the library is unable to locate replacement issues and borrows and photocopies issues needed to complete a serial run. The practice of assembling complete back runs of journals is often of less importance to libraries because of the increasing ability to access articles through online sources or interlibrary loan.

Microforms, reprints, and digital collections are viable alternatives in retrospective selection. If the item is too costly to replace in print, the OP title or issues cannot be located, or the item will not see heavy use, microform is a reasonable solution. Some titles are available in reprint editions, which are usually photoreproductions of the original and satisfy most users' needs. Librarians can purchase extensive microform sets of retrospective titles on specific topics, and several publishers and vendors are providing online access to important retrospective collections. *Early English Books Online* (http://eebo.chadwyck.com) is one example of the latter. The more than 125,000 titles published from 1475 to 1661 in this collection are also available in microfilm format.

Diverse Communities and Alternative Literatures

The United States is a multicultural society, reflecting diversity in race, religion, geographic origin, economic status, political affiliation, and personal preference. In 2006, 13 percent of U.S. residents were foreign born, up from 7.9 percent in 1990.[64] In 2003, 40 percent of school children were ethnic minorities.[65] Ethic diversity is increasing faster than had been projected; in 2000, the Census Bureau had forecast that ethnic minorities in schools would not reach the 40 percent mark until 2010.[66] Diverse collections address and respond to the needs and interests of an increasingly diverse society, including individuals with disabilities; single parent and other nontraditional families; gay, lesbian, bisexual, and transgender individuals; and foreign born and nonnative English speakers.

The librarian's professional obligation is to develop balanced collections that reflect and meet the educational and recreational needs of these diverse user communities and are not biased by the librarian's own cultural identity and personal experiences. The ALA provides guidance in "Diversity in Collection Development: An Interpretation of the Library Bill of Rights."[67] Denise E. Agosto writes that school library collections that represent a range of cultures "can serve as a form of advocacy on behalf of students from minority backgrounds by making them feel included in classroom and school environments."[68] Finding materials that are representative and age-appropriate can be difficult. For example, Crystal E. Kaiser writes of the challenging and time-consuming nature of locating current books for children with disabilities and their families.[69] In addition to meeting the needs and reflecting the perspectives of various populations, multicultural collections present opportunities to understand other people, lifestyles, and cultures.

Some publications that are not part of the dominant culture and do not reflect the perspective and beliefs of that culture are considered alternative literature. Generally, these materials are published by small presses, independent publishers, the radical right and left, and other dissenting groups. Many topics that dominate alternative literature are the same topics that are challenged in library collections.[70] These include critiques of public life and the mass media, environmental activism, peace and antimilitarism, human rights (including right to life and free choice), freedom of speech and censorship, creationism, anarchism, situationist literature, critical education and free schools, sexual politics, paranormal phenomena, and literature of extremist groups. Alternative literature includes works of fiction, poetry, art, and music.

Librarians are generally comfortable selecting works that represent diverse cultural and ethnic groups, because this is perceived as the sensitive and politically correct stance. They are less at ease when making selection decisions that are inconsistent with their own social, moral, and political interests.

Personal biases, concerns about accountability to governing bodies, and feelings of responsibility for collection users often result in a subtle conscious or unconscious self-censorship.

Censorship and Intellectual Freedom

Chapter 1 traces how the ideal of freedom to read came to replace a quite different ideology between 1876, when the ALA endorsed the librarian as moral censor, and the 1930s, when the first Library Bill of Rights was adopted by the ALA. Librarians' attitudes toward censorship have changed in line with changing concepts of the public interest and of the library's democratic function. Intellectual freedom and free access to ideas are embodied in the First Amendment as a basic human right. The Library Bill of Rights (see chapter 2) continues to be an important statement for American librarians.

Ensuring intellectual freedom is a major focus of ALA, which maintains an Office for Intellectual Freedom and publishes the *Intellectual Freedom Manual*.[71] The Freedom to Read Foundation, a sister organization to the ALA, was created to protect the freedoms of speech and press, with emphasis on First Amendment protection for libraries and library materials. The Foundation provides support and legal counsel to libraries whose collections are challenged. An added obstacle to intellectual freedom facing librarians is the public's concerns about ease of accessing questionable materials via the Internet.[72]

The ALA and many of its divisions have developed statements and various documents that address intellectual freedom and free access to information, particularly in relation to electronic information. It has prepared "Access to Electronic Information, Services, and Networks: An Interpretation of the Library Bill of Rights."[73] Other examples include the Association of College and Research Libraries' expansion on the Library Bill of Rights in the academic setting, Intellectual Freedom Principles for Academic Libraries, and the American Association of School Librarians' Access to Resources and Services in the School Library Media Program: An Interpretation of the Library Bill of Rights.[74] The ALA's "Freedom to Read Statement" is a further iteration of librarians' commitment to free access to information and ideas:

> Freedom to Read
>
> 1. It is in the public interest for publishers and librarians to make available the widest diversity of views and expressions, including those that are unorthodox, unpopular, or considered dangerous by the majority.
> 2. Publishers, librarians, and booksellers do not need to endorse every idea or presentation they make available. It would conflict with the public interest for them to establish their own political, moral, or aesthetic views as a standard for determining what should be published or circulated.

3. It is contrary to the public interest for publishers or librarians to bar access to writings on the basis of the personal history or political affiliations of the author.

4. There is no place in our society for efforts to coerce the taste of others, to confine adults to the reading matter deemed suitable for adolescents, or to inhibit the efforts of writers to achieve artistic expression.

5. It is not in the public interest to force a reader to accept the prejudgment of a label characterizing any expression or its author as subversive or dangerous.

6. It is the responsibility of publishers and librarians, as guardians of the people's freedom to read, to contest encroachments upon that freedom by individuals or groups seeking to impose their own standards or tastes upon the community at large; and by the government whenever it seeks to reduce or deny public access to public information.

7. It is the responsibility of publishers and librarians to give full meaning to the freedom to read by providing books that enrich the quality and diversity of thought and expression. By the exercise of this affirmative responsibility, they can demonstrate that the answer to a "bad" book is a good one, the answer to a "bad" idea is a good one.[75]

Librarians are charged with preventing censorship of collections and simultaneously ensuring freedom to read and access to diverse viewpoints within collections. Robert Hauptman defines censorship as "the active suppression of books, journals, newspapers, theater pieces, lectures, discussions, radio and televisions programs, films, art works, etc.—either partially or in the entirety—that are deemed objectionable on moral, political, military, or other grounds."[76] In the name of intellectual freedom, librarians are encouraged to select, collect, and disseminate information without regard to race, gender, or other potential discriminators. Ideally, the guidelines for selecting materials are presented in a library's collection development policy, which can protect the library in the face of challenges. The goal is a diverse collection, representing all points of view, including the extreme. A collection is not diverse if it includes only majority, noncontroversial, inoffensive opinions.

According to Herbert N. Foerstel, the history of book censorship has consisted of the suppression of naughty stories.[77] Challenges on the grounds of immoral, obscene, or pornographic content are the most common, but other justifications, such as subversive political or social content, have also been presented over the years. Challenges are most common in school and public libraries. Between 1990 and 2000 (the most recent compilation available), the ALA recorded 8,332 attempts by groups or individuals to have books removed from library shelves and classrooms. Of these, 71 percent were in schools or school libraries and 24 percent were in public libraries. In 2001, the ALA logged 448 challenges and estimated that four times that number of challenges were made but not reported.[78] The following list, compiled by the ALA Office of Intellectual Freedom, identifies the ten most frequently challenged books in 2007:[79]

1. *And Tango Makes Three,* by Justin Richardson and Peter Parnell
2. *The Chocolate War,* by Robert Cormier
3. *Olive's Ocean,* by Kevin Henkes
4. *The Golden Compass,* by Philip Pullman
5. *The Adventures of Huckleberry Finn,* by Mark Twain
6. *The Color Purple,* by Alice Walker
7. *TTYL,* by Lauren Myracle
8. *I Know Why the Caged Bird Sings,* by Maya Angelou
9. *It's Perfectly Normal,* by Robie Harris
10. *The Perks of Being a Wallflower,* by Stephen Chbosky

Types of Censorship

Censorship comes in three varieties: mandated by the law, demanded by individuals or groups, and exercised by the librarian. Legal censorship occurs when national, state, or municipal legislation forbids access to materials deemed immoral or unacceptable (perhaps incendiary or subversive) under the law. Laws in the United States, notably the 1865 Mail Act and the Comstock Law of 1873, have sought to control access to "obscene," "lewd," or "lascivious" publications by controlling the mailing and receiving of such materials. The problem lies in defining these terms. Such Supreme Court cases as *United States v. One Book Called "Ulysses"* (1934), *Roth v. United States* (1957), and *Miller v. California* (1973) have considered obscenity in relation to contemporary community standards and whether a work may be seen to have serious literary, artistic, political, or social value.[80] The Supreme Court has ruled that the states may prohibit the printing and sale of works that portray sexual conduct in an offensive manner. The emphasis has shifted to local standards. When librarians are presented with legislation requiring the removal of materials, they are seldom in a position to contest the law in court. More often, organizations such as the American Civil Liberties Union and the ALA press a case.

Individuals and groups who challenge library materials may be parents, concerned citizens, school and library boards, religious and political organizations, or local police. They may seek to censor by banning books, severely limiting access, or labeling materials for special handling and restricted use. Most challenges revolve around sexual propriety, political views, religious beliefs, and the rights of minority groups (gays, lesbians, persons of color, atheists, etc.). Library publications such as *American Libraries, Library Journal,* and *Newsletter on Intellectual Freedom* regularly report on challenges to libraries around the United States. Censorship frequently becomes an emotional issue and can divide a community because it develops out of personal beliefs, convictions, and value systems. A report issued in 1993 stated that 41 percent of the attempts to remove or restrict access to materials in U.S. schools were successful.[81]

Censorship of material available for children, particularly that of a pornographic or violent nature, continues to have strong and articulate proponents.[82] A strong case grows out of the position that children are different from adults in their abilities to analyze conflicting visions of society and in the extent to which they are affected by materials such as pornography or depictions of violence. Central to much of this discussion are society's responsibility to protect minors and the conditions under which legislation should be enacted to do so. The complication that attends this issue, as with all questionable materials, is reaching agreement on what constitutes pornographic and violent content and what has the potential to be harmful to minors.

Some censorship is unintentional and results from failure to select materials representing a pluralistic society. Librarians can protect against unintentional self-censorship by being conscious of and sensitive to diverse communities and viewpoints. Monitoring bibliographic tools, selection sources, and reviews can improve the multicultural and comprehensive nature of collection building.

Intentional censorship, or self-censorship, by librarians is more troubling. Personal values and standards, fears about potential challenges, or user complaints can lead a librarian to decide not to purchase a title, to limit access to an item, or to remove an item from the collection. When one's employment and source of income are at risk, pragmatism has a way of modifying one's values. Research over the years has demonstrated that, although librarians support the concept of intellectual freedom, many do not stand by these principles in the face of censorship pressures; Ken P. Coley found that 82 percent of the high school librarians in his study group practiced self-censorship.[83] Some scholars writing on this dilemma address it by placing emphasis on the selection process instead of the rejection process.[84] The challenge for librarians is distinguishing between self-censorship and careful selection of materials consistent with appropriate selection criteria.

Censorship should not be confused with refusing to spend limited funds unwisely, to select materials inappropriate to the user community, or to provide illegal or socially detrimental information. One can easily insist that a librarian should never censor or refuse to disseminate information. Nevertheless, all librarians are constrained by their budgets, their professional values, and legislation to exclude some materials. What is the judicious response when a high school student wants books on building pipe bombs, a white supremacist offers a free subscription of a racist newsletter to a public library, or those who deny the Holocaust insist that the academic library purchase materials that argue their point of view? When making decisions about material that is sexually explicit, racist, or dangerous to society, few librarians can take a neutral stance. They can only seek to exercise informed judgment. Free expression, intellectual freedom, and access to information must be protected, yet some materials are inappropriate and detrimental to certain user groups. The tension and the challenge arise in determining what falls within these categories.

Censorship and the Internet

The trend toward providing Internet access in libraries is generating new concerns about censorship and debates over the responsibility of librarians to select what users can and cannot access. School and public libraries receive frequent demands that blocking or filtering software be installed on libraries computers that access the Internet. One problem with filtering software is that useful sites can be blocked along with objectionable ones. State and federal legislation has been passed and court cases have been filed on both sides of the issue. A significant judgment was made in 1997 in *Reno v. American Civil Liberties Union* (Reno I), when the Supreme Court unanimously declared that the federal Communications Decency Act (CDA) was unconstitutional.[85] That law made it a crime to send or display indecent material online in a way available to minors. The court held that the Internet is not comparable to broadcasting and instead, like books and newspapers, receives the highest level of First Amendment protection. Following Reno I, Congress passed the Child Online Protection Act (COPA), which sought to avoid the constitutional issues raised in the CDA. A federal district court in the case *American Civil Liberties Union v. Reno* (Reno II) has more recently determined that COPA is flawed in similar ways to CDA.[86]

The Children's Internet Protection Act (CIPA) and the Neighborhood Children's Internet Protection Act (NCIPA) went into effect in 2001. These laws place restrictions on the use of funds available through the Library Services and Technology Act, Title III of the Elementary and Secondary Education Act, and on the Universal Service discount program known as the E-rate (Public Law 106-554). They require public libraries and schools to install filters on their Internet computers to retain federal funding and discounts for computers and computer access. Because CIPA directly affected libraries and their ability to make legal information freely available to their patrons, the ALA and Freedom to Read Foundation filed a lawsuit to overturn CIPA. In 2002, the Eastern District Court of Pennsylvania held CIPA to be unconstitutional and ruled Sections 1712(a)(2) and 1721(b) of CIPA to be facially invalid under the First Amendment. The court permanently enjoined the government from enforcing those provisions. Public libraries thus are not required to install filters on their computers in order to receive federal funds. The court held the CIPA statute to be unconstitutional, because mandated filtering on all computers results in blocked access to substantial amounts of constitutionally protected speech. The Justice Department, acting on behalf of the Federal Communications Commission and U.S. Institute of Museum and Library Sciences, appealed this ruling.

In June 2003, the Supreme Court reversed the district court's decision and rejected the plaintiffs' facial challenge to CIPA. The stakes of the case were lowered when the government promised, in the course of litigation, that libraries could, and would, remove the filters if users asked them to do so. It also promised that users would not have to explain why they were making the request.

Although six justices voted to uphold CIPA, there was no majority opinion for the Court. The plurality opinion, authored by Chief Justice William Hubbs Rehnquist, was joined by three other justices (Sandra Day O'Connor, Antonin Scalia, and Clarence Thomas). Because it did not have the support of five justices, the reasoning of the plurality opinion is not controlling. Justices Anthony M. Kennedy and Stephen Breyer each wrote concurring opinions upholding CIPA against the plaintiff's facial challenge but on narrower grounds than those stated in the plurality opinion. In cases where no single opinion has the support of the majority of the justices, the narrow concurring opinions typically govern future interpretations and any precedent implied by the case.[87]

The dilemma is that filters can both overblock (block access to protected speech) and underblock (allow access to illegal or unconstitutional speech). The latter is of particular concern when libraries are perceived as violating obscenity, child pornography, and harmful-to-minors statutes or permitting user activities that create a hostile work environment. Libraries can face potential liability for installing content-based filtering software or for failing to install it. When librarians specifically select and point to Internet resources, they apply the appropriate criteria for quality, authenticity, and so forth. "Open" Internet access is, however, a much more complex issue.[88] As the Internet expands and the number of public and school libraries with Internet access increases, this issue will continue to trouble librarians and their user communities.

Responding to Complaints and Challenges to Materials

The best defense against challenges to a library collection is prior preparation. This begins with a written collection development policy. Many libraries post the Library Bill of Rights in a public place and use additional methods to promote their commitment to intellectual freedom. ALA's Office for Intellectual Freedom (www.ala.org/oif/) and many organizations provide advice and assistance in case of attempted censorship. These include the National Council of Teachers of English Anti-Censorship Center (www.ncte.org/about/issues/censorship/), state educational and library associations, and the American Civil Liberties Union (www.aclu.org). Notifying the material's publisher may be helpful because the publisher may have assembled information in response to previous challenges.

The library should have a process for handling complaints, and staff members should be familiar with it. ALA's *Intellectual Freedom Manual* contains guidelines for developing a local process. Many libraries provide a template or form that can be used to request that an item be removed from the collection. The form provides space for individual's name and contact information, title and bibliographic information about the item, and what the concerns are. It also may ask if the individual is representing him- or herself or an organization. Some forms ask if the individual can suggest alternative resources that provide additional information or other viewpoints.

Gail Dickinson makes a careful distinction between "questioned" and "challenged" materials.[89] A library item is questioned when a parent, citizen, administrator, teacher, or staff person expresses concern. This is often an emotional stage and requires a calm response by the librarian. He or she should notify the school principal or library director. Sometimes an informal complaint can be resolved by referring to the collection development policy or selection criteria, or by suggesting alternative materials. Only when the proper form (sometimes called a "Request for Reconsideration Form") is completed and submitted is an item considered formally challenged. Ideally, a challenge initiates a formal review process by a committee, which may be at the school level or the school district level, or in the case of a public library at the library level or the library system level. Following the authorized and board-approved process for reviewing challenges is critically necessary to treat all challenges fairly and to avoid legal consequences. The librarian's role at this point is to present the facts for the committee's deliberation, including criteria for selecting the item, how it meets these criteria, and (when pertinent) quotations from reviews—and let the committee complete its work.

Summary

Collection building is about making choices within parameters defined by the community being served and the funds available. Selection begins with knowing the types of materials for which one is responsible. Responsibility may be assigned according to format, genre, subject, language, geographic coverage, and reader or user group. In a small library, a librarian may be responsible for selection decisions across all these areas and types. Collection building consists of four steps: identifying the relevant items, assessing the item to decide if it is appropriate for the collection and evaluating its quality, deciding to purchase, and preparing an order. Identifying materials requires factual information about authors, titles, publishers, and topics. Many tools and resources help identify possible acquisitions. Items are appropriate if they meet the needs of current and future users, are consistent with collection development policies, and are fiscally responsible.

Evaluative criteria can be extensive, ranging from literary merit to comprehensiveness and breadth to ease of access and use. Some types of materials have supplemental criteria that address particular aspects of the format, genre, or audience. The selection of e-resources is complex because of supplemental criteria, the legally binding contracts that license their access, and the implicit continuing financial commitment.

Collection building is intimately involved with the acquisition process. In some libraries, the individuals who select items also place the orders. Title-by-title selecting is selection at the micro level. In macro selection, many items are added to the library without being selected individually. The most common approach to macro selection is the approval plan, through which vendors select items for a library based on a profile defined by that library. Other forms of macro selection are standing orders, blanket orders, exchange agreements, and government document depository agreements. Libraries also add collections of materials that are donated. Gifts must be reviewed carefully, and they have legal, financial, and political implications. Retrospective selection is the process through which older materials are selected either to fill gaps or to develop new collection areas.

As society and libraries' specific user communities become more diverse, librarians have an obligation to develop collections that reflect the interests and meet the needs of various user groups. Numerous resources and tools are available to help identify titles that reflect ethnic, racial, political, religious, social, and cultural diversity. Selectors must take care to avoid self-censorship, that is, make sure that their personal experiences, perspectives, and biases do not consciously or unconsciously influence the materials they select or exclude.

Censorship, whether self-imposed or external, restricts free access to ideas and intellectual freedom, rights embodied in the First Amendment. Librarians are encouraged to prevent censorship and ensure freedom to read and to access diverse viewpoints within their collections. Most attempts to remove or limit availability of materials are made on the grounds of immoral, obscene, or pornographic content. Other reasons to exclude materials are that they are inappropriate to some age groups, politically subversive, or socially offensive. Most challenges against materials are lodged in schools and school libraries. Many are the result of different viewpoints about what is dangerous, offensive, inappropriate, or illegal. Although librarians support the idea of freedom to read, they frequently moderate selection (self-censor) to avoid possible confrontations. Many attempts to censor materials are successful, but more than half are not. Librarians who have a written collection development policy and formal procedures to handle calls for censoring materials are best positioned to handle them effectively.

CASE STUDY

Ida Public Library is located in Ida, Ohio, and serves a population of 23,200, 12,000 of whom live in the town of Ida. Ida Public Library has an annual acquisitions budget of $186,000 for books, periodicals, and audiovisual materials and $45,000 for access to e-resources. The e-resource access is provided as part of agreements managed through consortial library partners. The library has 75,000 print volumes, 180 active periodical subscriptions, 4,863 videos, and 3,450 audio-format materials, including downloadable audiobooks. The library celebrated it one-hundredth anniversary in 2006 and is housed in an expanded and remodeled Carnegie building. Families, children, and teens use the library extensively. Ida Public Library loaned 300,000 items in the previous year; 77,500 of these were loans to children and teens. More than two thousand children attended weekly story hour programs. The Ida public schools have comprehensive media centers, which support curriculum and most of the study and research needs of students. The Ida Public Library has a staff of sixteen. Casey has just joined the staff as the new children and young adult librarian and is a new MLIS graduate. She is responsible for the collection, programming, and that portion of the library's website that support services to children and teens.

Activity

What sources should Casey use to locate new materials to add to the collection? Compile a selected, annotated bibliography of sources that provide reviews of new publications and are useful for selecting materials for children and teens who visit the Ida Public Library. Although available funds are always a consideration in the selection process, this activity focuses on the first two steps in selection: identification, and evaluation and assessment. Remember to consider all formats, genres, and age groups being served. Annotations should include a full citation for the source, the number of issues per year, the scope and coverage of the source, the average number of reviews per issue or volume, types of review (descriptive? evaluative? both?), the types of materials excluded from coverage, and how the source can best be used.

Note: This book's first edition also provided a case study and activity that was related to electronic resources. It can be viewed at www.ala.org/editions/extras/Johnson09720 as a supplementary resource.

Notes

1. Dennis P. Carrigan, "Librarians and the 'Dismal Science,'" *Library Journal* 113 (June 15, 1988): 22.

2. *UNESCO Statistical Yearbook* (Paris: UNESCO, 1999).

3. Brian F. Lavoie and Roger C. Schonfeld, "Books without Boundaries: A Brief Tour of the System-wide Print Book Collection," *Journal of Electronic Publishing* 9, no. 2 (2006), http://quod.lib.umich.edu/cgi/t/text/text-idx?c=jep;view=text;rgn=main;idno=3336451 .0009.208.

4. Bowker, "Bowker Reports U.S. Book Production Flat in 2007" (May 28, 2008), www .bowker.com/index.php/press-releases/526?task+view.

5. Janet Belanger Morrow, "Prices of U.S. and Foreign Published Materials," in *The Bowker Annual: Library and Book Trade Almanac*, 52nd ed., ed. Dave Bogart (Providence, N.J.: Bowker, 2007): 467.

6. *Film and Video Finder* (Medford, N.J.: National Information Center for Educational Media, 1987–).

7. *Index to Social Sciences and Humanities Proceedings* (Philadelphia: Thomson Scientific, 1979–); Matthew D. Zbaracki, *Best Books for Boys: A Resource for Educators* (Westport, Conn.: Libraries Unlimited, 2008); *Public Library Core Collection: Fiction, a Selection Guide* [formerly *Fiction Catalog*] (New York: Wilson, 2008–).

8. Sheila S. Intner, "Recruiting Non-Bibliocentric Collection Builders," in *Recruiting, Educating, and Training Librarians for Collection Development*, ed. Peggy Johnson and Sheila S. Intner, 69–84 (Westport, Conn.: Greenwood, 1994).

9. Stephen Abram, "Social Libraries: The Librarian 2.0 Phenomenon," *Library Resources and Technical Services* 52, no. 2 (2008): 21.

10. Audio Publishers Association, "Americans Are Tuning in to Audio: Audiobook Sales on the Rise Nationally" (Aug. 24, 2007), www.audiopub.org/PDFs/2007SalesSurveyrelease.pdf.

11. Association of College and Research Libraries, Media Resources in Academic Libraries Review Task Force, "Guidelines for Media Resources in Academic Libraries (2006)," www.ala.org/ala/acrl/acrlstandards/mediaresources.cfm.

12. Arnie Cardillo et al., "Tuning in to Audiobooks; Why Should Kids Listen?" *Children and Libraries* 5, no. 3 (2007): 42–46.

13. John A. Lent, "Introduction," in John A. Lent, ed., *Illustrating Asia: Comics, Humor Magazines, and Picture Books*, 3–4 (Honolulu: University of Hawai'i Press, 2001).

14. Philip Charles Crawford, *Graphic Novels 101: Selecting and Using Graphic Novels to Promote Literacy for Children and Young Adults: A Resource Guide for School Libraries and Educators* (Salt Lake City, Utah: Hi Willow Research and Publishing, 2003), 17.

15. Art Spiegelman, *Maus: A Survivor's Tale* (New York: Pantheon Books, 1986).

16. Charles McGrath, "Not Funnies," *New York Times Magazine*, July 11, 2004, http://query.nytimes.com/gst/fullpage.html?res=9F07E3D6143BF932A25754C0A9629C8B63.

17. Young Adult Library Services Association, Great Graphic Novels for Teens, www.ala.org/ala/yalsa/booklistsawards/greatgraphicnovelsforteens/gn.cfm.

18. Barbara Blummer, "E-Books Revisited: The Adoption of Electronic Books by Special, Academic, and Public Libraries," *Internet Reference Services Quarterly* 11, no. 2 (2006): 1–13.

19. Association of American Publishers, "Book Sales Continue Upward Swing for November" (Jan. 24, 2008), www.publishers.org/main/PressCenter/NovStatsRelease.htm.

20. John Rutledge and Luke Swindler, "The Selection Decision: Defining Criteria and Establishing Priorities," *College and Research Libraries* 48, no. 2 (1987): 128.

21. Lynn B. Williams, "Subject Knowledge for Subject Specialists: What the Novice Bibliographer Needs to Know," *Collection Management* 14, nos. 3/4 (1991): 39.

22. Brian Quinn, "Cognitive and Affective Processes in Collection Development," *Library Resources and Technical Services* 51, no. 1 (2007): 5–15.

23. Francis K. W. Drury, *Book Selection* (Chicago: American Library Association, 1930), 1.

24. S. R. Ranganathan, *The Five Laws of Library Science* (Madras, India: Madras Library Association; London: Edward Goldston, 1931).

25. Rose Zertuche Treviño, *The Pura Belpré Awards: Celebrating Latino Authors and Illustrators* (Chicago: American Library Association, 2006); Association for Library Service to Children, *Newbery and Caldecott Medal Books: A Comprehensive Guide to the Winners* (Chicago: American Library Association, 2007), which is updated annually.

26. Henrietta M. Smith, Coretta Scott King Book Awards Committee, and Ethnic and Multicultural Information Exchange Round Table, eds., *The Coretta Scott King Awards Book: 1970–2004*, 3rd ed. (Chicago: American Library Association, 2004).

27. *Graphics Novels Core Collection* (New York: Wilson, 2007–).

28. *Index to Social Sciences and Humanities Proceedings.*

29. Juris Dilevko and Lisa Gottlieb, "The Politics of Standard Selection Guides: The Case of the *Public Library Catalog*," *Library Quarterly* 73, no. 3 (2003): 289–337.

30. *Encyclopedia of Associations: National Organizations of the U.S.* (Detroit: Gale, 1961–); *Yearbook of International Organizations* (Munich: K. G. Saur, 1967–).

31. *College and Research Libraries News* (Chicago: Association of College and Research Libraries); C&RL NewsNet, Internet Reviews Archive, www.bowdoin.edu/~samato/IRA/.

32. Camille Livingston and Antje Mays, "Using Interlibrary Loan Data as a Selection Tool: ILL Trails Provide Collection Clues," *Against the Grain* 16, no. 2 (2004): 22, 24, 26, 28; Suzanne M. Ward, Tanner Wray, and Karl E. Debus-López, "Collection Development Based on Patron Requests: Collaboration between Interlibrary Loan and Acquisitions," *Library Collection, Acquisitions, and Technical Services* 27, no. 2 (2003): 203–13.

33. Lisa A. Ennis, *Government Documents Librarianship: A Guide for the Neo-Depository Era* (Medford, N.J.: Information Today, 2007), 67.

34. U.S. Government Printing Office, "Digital Distribution" (April 10, 2007), handout from the Annual Spring Depository Library Council Meeting, April 15–18, 2007, Denver, Colorado.

35. Government Printing Office, *Catalog of U.S. Government Publications*, http://catalog.gpo .gov/F; Basic Collection, www.access.gpo.gov/su_docs/fdlp/coll-dev/basic-01.html; Core Documents of U.S. Democracy, www.gpoaccess.gov/coredocs.html.

36. *Statistical Reference Index: A Selective Guide to American Statistical Publications from Sources Other than the U.S. Government* (Washington, D.C.: Congressional Information Service, 1981–); LexisNexis Statistical [online resource] (Dayton, Ohio: LexisNexis); *Index to Current Urban Documents* (Westport, Conn.: Greenwood, 1972–).

37. Phyllis J. Van Orden and Sunny Strong, *Children's Books: A Practical Guide to Selection* (New York: Neal-Schuman, 2007).

38. Peggy Johnson, "Selecting Electronic Resources: Developing a Local Decision-Making Matrix," in *Electronic Resources: Selection and Bibliographic Control*, ed. Ling-yuh W. Pattie and Bonnie Jean Cox, 9–24 (New York: Haworth, 1996).

39. Association for Library Collections and Technical Services, Serials Section, Acquisitions Committee, "Serials Acquisitions Glossary," 3rd ed. rev. (2005), www.ala.org/ala/ alctscontent/pubsbucket/webpublications/alctsserials/serialsacquisiti/05_serials_glossary .pdf.

40. Joint Steering Committee for the Development of RDA, Draft of Part I of RDA, 5JSC/RDA/Part 1 (Dec. 5, 2005), 1–3, http://collectionscanada.gc.ca/jsc/docs/5rda-part1.pdf.

41. *Readers' Guide to Periodical Literature* (New York: Wilson).

42. Lotsee P. Smith, "The Curriculum and Materials Selection: Requisite for Collection Development," *Collection Management* 7, nos. 3/4 (1985–86): 39.

43. Sandra Hughes-Hassell and Jacqueline C. Mancall, *Collection Management for Youth: Responding to the Needs of Learners* (Chicago: American Library Association, 2005).

44. Primary Research Group, *The Survey of Library Database Licensing Practices* (New York: Primary Research Group, 2007).

45. Ibid.

46. Yale University Library, Liblicense: Licensing Digital Information: A Resource for Librarians, CLIR/DLF Model License, www.library.yale.edu/~llicense/modlic.shtml; Licensingmodels.com: Model Standard Licenses for Use by Publishers, Librarians and Subscription Agents for Electronic Resources, www.licensingmodels.com.

47. International Federation of Library Associations and Institutions, Committee on Copyright and Other Legal Matters, "Licensing Principles (2001)," www.ifla.org/V/ebpb/copy.htm; University of California Libraries, Collection Development Committee, "Principles for Acquiring and Licensing Information in Digital Formats" (July 2006), http://libraries.universityofcalifornia.edu/cdc/principlesforacquiring.html.

48. Stephen Bosch, Patricia A. Promis, and Chris Sugnet, with contributions by Trisha Davis, *Guide to Licensing and Acquiring Electronic Information*, ALCTS Acquisitions Guides no. 2 and Collection Management and Development Guides no. 13 (Lanham, Md.: Association for Library Collections and Technical Services with Scarecrow, 2005).

49. National Information Standards Organization, "SERU: A Shared Electronic Resource Understanding" (Jan. 2008), NISO RP-7-2008, www.niso.org/publications/rp/RP-7-2008.pdf.

50. Ross Atkinson, "Access, Ownership, and the Future of Collection Development," in *Collection Management and Development: Issues in an Electronic Era*, ed. Peggy Johnson and Bonnie MacEwan, 92–109 (Chicago: American Library Association, 1994), 97.

51. Hendrik Edelman and Robert P. Holley, eds., *Marketing to Libraries for the New Millennium: Librarians, Vendors, and Publishers Review the Landmark Third Industry-wide Survey of the Library Marketing Practices and Trends* (Lanham, Md.: Association for Collections and Technical Services with Scarecrow, 2002).

52. Byron Anderson, *Alternative Publishers of Books in North America*, 6th ed. (Duluth, Minn.: Library Juice, 2006) and Len Fulton, ed., *The Directory of Small Press and Magazine Editors and Publishers* (Paradise, Calif.: Dustbooks) are two sources for identifying small press and alternative publishers.

53. Wanda V. Dole, "The Feasibility of Approval Plans for Small College Libraries," in *Collection Development in College Libraries*, ed. Joanne Schneider Hill, William E. Hannaford Jr., and Ronald H. Epp, 154–62 (Chicago: American Library Association, 1991); Susan Mueller, "Approval Plans and Faculty Selection: Are They Compatible?" *Library Collections, Acquisitions, and Technical Services* 29, no. 1 (2005): 61–70; Clare Appavoo, "Size Doesn't Matter: Book Approval Plans Can Be Catered to Tight Budgets," *Feliciter* 53, no. 5 (2007): 238–40.

54. Tina Feick, Gary Ives, and Jo McClamroch, "The Big E-Package Deals: Smoothing the Way through Subscription Agents," *Serials Librarian* 50, nos. 3/4 (2006): 267–70; Kenneth Frazier, "What's the Big Deal?" *Serials Librarian* 48, nos. 1/2 (2005): 49–59; Jeffrey N. Gatten and Tom Sanville, "An Orderly Retreat from the Big Deal: Is It Possible for Consortia?" *D-Lib Magazine* 10, no. 10 (2004), www.dlib.org/dlib/october04/gatten/10gatten.html; David Ball, "What's the 'Big Deal,' and Why Is It a Bad Deal for Universities?" *Interlending and Document Supply* 32, no. 2 (2004): 117–25; Kenneth Frazier, "The Librarians' Dilemma: Contemplating the Costs of the 'Big Deal,'" *D-Lib Magazine* 7, no. 3 (2001), www.dlib.org/dlib/march01/frazier/03frazier.html.

55. Cecilia Botero, Steven Carrico, and Michele Tennant, "Using Comparative Online Journal Usage Studies to Assess the Big Deal," *Library Resources and Technical Service* 52, no. 2 (2008): 61–68.

56. EBSCOhost, Academic Search Premier Database Coverage List, www.ebscohost.com/titleLists/ap-complete.htm.

57. Ann L. O'Neill, "How the Richard Abel Co., Inc. Changed the Way We Work," *Library Acquisitions: Practice and Theory* 17 (1993): 41–46.

58. Michael Sullivan, *Fundamentals of Children's Services* (Chicago: American Library Association, 2005), 55.

59. See Carol Reid, "Down and Outsourced in Hawaii," *American Libraries* 28 (June/July 1997): 56–58; Rebecca Knuth and Donna G. Bair-Mundy, "Revolt over Outsourcing: Hawaii's Librarians Speak Out about Contracted Selection," *Collection Management* 23, nos. 1/2 (1998): 81–112.

60. Knuth and Bair-Mundy, "Revolt over Outsourcing," 109.

61. Kristi Ekonen, Päivi Paloposki, and Pentti Vattulainen, *Handbook on the International Exchange of Publications*, 5th ed. (Munich: K. G. Saur, 2006).

62. Louis A. Pitschmann, *Building Sustainable Collections of Free Third-Party Web Resources* (Washington, D.C.: Digital Library Federation and Council on Library and Information Resources, 2001), 6.

63. *American Book Trade Directory* (New Providence, R.I.: Bowker).

64. U.S. Census Bureau, United States Population and Housing Narrative Profile: 2006, "The Foreign-Born Population: 2000," Census Brief, Current Population Survey CENBR/01-1 (2003), www.census.gov/prod/2003pubs/c2kbr-34.pdf.

65. U.S. Census Bureau, "School Enrollment—Social and Economic Characteristics of Students: October 2003," Current Population Reports P20-554 (2005), www.census.gov/prod/2005pubs/p20-554.pdf.

66. U.S. Census Bureau, Population Projections Program, "(NP-D1-A) Annual Projections of the Resident Population by Age, Sex, Race, and Hispanic Origin: Lowest, Middle, Highest Series and Zero International Migration Series, 1999 to 2100" (Washington, D.C.: U.S. Census Bureau, Jan. 13, 2000), www.census.gov/population/www/projections/natdet-D1A.html and www.census.gov/population/projections/nation/detail/d2001_10.pdf.

67. American Library Association, "Diversity in Collection Development: An Interpretation of the Library Bill of Rights" (adopted July 14, 1982, by the ALA Council; amended Jan. 10, 1990), www.ala.org/Template.cfm?Section=interpretations&Template=/ContentManagement/ContentDisplay.cfm&ContentID=8530.

68. Denise E. Agosto, "Building a Multicultural School Library: Issues and Challenges," *Teacher Librarian* 34, no. 3 (2007): 27–31.

69. Crystal E. Kaiser, "Is Your Early Childhood Literature Collection Disability-Inclusive and Current?" *Children and Libraries* 5, no. 3 (2007): 5–14.

70. Chris Atton, "The Subjects of Alternative Literature: A General Guide," in *Alternative Literature: A Practical Guide for Librarians*, 39–64 (Aldershot, Hampshire, England: Gower, 1996).

71. American Library Association, Office for Intellectual Freedom, *Intellectual Freedom Manual*, 7th ed. (Chicago: American Library Association, 2006).

72. Barbara A. Jones, *Libraries, Access, and Intellectual Freedom: Developing Policies for Public and Academic Libraries* (Chicago: American Library Association, 1999).

73. American Library Association, "Access to Electronic Information, Services, and Networks: An Interpretation of the Library Bill of Rights" (adopted by the ALA Council Jan. 24, 1996, amended Jan. 19, 2005), www.ala.org/ala/oif/statementspols/statementsif/interpretations/accesselectronic.cfm.

74. Association of College and Research Libraries, "Intellectual Freedom Principles for Academic Libraries" (approved by ACRL Board of Directors June 29, 1999, adopted July 12, 2000, by the ALA Council), www.ala.org/Template.cfm?Section=interpretations&Template=/ContentManagement/ContentDisplay.cfm&ContentID=8551; American Association of School Librarians, "Access to Resources and Services in the School Library Media Program: An Interpretation of the Library Bill of Rights" (adopted July 2, 1986 by the ALA Council; amended Jan. 10, 1990; July 12, 2000; January 19, 2005), www.ala.org/ala/oif/statementspols/statementsif/interpretations/accessschoollibrarymediaprogram.pdf.

75. American Library Association, "Freedom to Read Statement" (adopted June 25, 1953, by the ALA Council and the AAP Freedom to Read Committee; amended January 28, 1972; January 16, 1991; July 12, 2000; June 30, 2004), www.ala.org/ala/oif/statementspols/ftrstatement/freedomreadstatement.cfm.

76. Robert Hauptman, *Ethical Challenges in Librarianship* (Phoenix, Ariz.: Oryx, 1988), 66.

77. Herbert N. Foerstel, *Banned in the Media: A Reference Guide to Censorship in the Press, Motion Pictures, Broadcasting, and the Internet* (Westport, Conn.: Greenwood, 1998), 2.

78. American Library Association, Office of Intellectual Freedom, Top Ten Challenged Authors 1990–2004, www.ala.org/ala/oif/bannedbooksweek/bbwlinks/authors19902004.cfm.

79. American Library Association, Office of Intellectual Freedom, "Children's Book on Male Penguins Raising Chick Tops ALA's 2008 List of Most Challenged Books" (May 7, 2008), www.ala.org/ala/pressreleases2008/May2008/penguin.cfm.

80. *United States v. One Book Called "Ulysses,"* 5 F. Supp. 182 (S.D.N.Y. 1933), affirmed 72 F.2d 705 (2d Cir. 1934); *Roth v. United States*, 354 U.S. 476 (1957); *Miller v. California*, 413 U.S. 15 (1973).

81. People for the American Way, "Censors Succeed in 41% of School Cases," *Library Hotline* 22 (Sept. 27, 1993): 2.

82. Kevin W. Saunders, "The Government Should Help Parents Shield Children from Obscene and Violent Materials," in *Censorship*, ed. Julia Bauder, 164–87 (Detroit: Deephaven Press, 2007).

83. See Frances B. MacDonald, *Censorship and Intellectual Freedom: A Survey of School Librarians, Attitudes, and Moral Reasoning* (Metuchen, N.J.: Scarecrow, 1993); Andrea E. Niosi, "An Investigation of Censorship and Selection in Southern California Public Libraries," *Public Libraries* 37, no. 5 (1998): 310–15; Ken P. Coley, "Moving toward a Method to Test for Self-Censorship by School Library Media Specialists," *School Library Media Research* 5 (2002), www.ala.org/ala/aasl/aaslpubsandjournals/slmrb/slmrcontents/volume52002/coley.cfm.

84. Lester E. Asheim, "The Librarian's Responsibility: Not Censorship, but Selection," in *Freedom of Book Selection: Proceedings of the Second Conference on Intellectual Freedom, Whittier, California, June 20–21, 1953*, ed. Fredric J. Mosher, 90–99 (Chicago: American Library Association, 1954).

85. *Reno v. American Civil Liberties Union*, 521 U.S. 844 (1997).

86. *American Civil Liberties Union v. Reno*, 31 F. Supp. 2d 473 (E. D. Pa. 1999).

87. Opinions on CIPA can be found at the ALA Washington Office website devoted to the Children's Internet Protection Act, www.ala.org/ala/washoff/woissues/civilliberties/cipaweb/cipa.cfm, and the American Association of School Librarians, Children's Internet Protection Act and School Libraries, www.ala.org/ala/aasl/aaslissues/cipaandschoollib/cipaschoollibraries.cfm.

88. For in-depth analyses of censorship and Internet access, see Marjorie Heins and Christina Cho, for the National Coalition against Censorship, "Internet Filters: A Public Policy Report" (Fall 2001), www.ncac.org/internet/20010901~USA~Internet_Filters.cfm; American Library Association, Office of Intellectual Freedom, Filters and Filtering, www.ala.org/ala/oif/ifissues/filtersfiltering.cfm.

89. Gail Dickinson, "The Challenges of Challenges: Understanding and Being Prepared?" *School Library Media Activities Monthly* 23, no. 5 (2007): 26–28; and Dickinson, "The Challenges of Challenges: What to Do?" *School Library Media Activities Monthly* 23, no. 6 (2007): 21–24.

Suggested Readings

General

Alabaster, Carol. *Developing an Outstanding Core Collection: A Guide for Libraries.* Chicago: American Library Association, 2002.

Algenio, Emilie, and Alexia Thompson-Young. "Licensing E-Books: The Good, the Bad, and the Ugly." *Journal of Library Administration* 42, nos. 3/4 (2005): 113–28.

Allison, Dee Ann, Beth McNeil, and Signe Swanson. "Database Selection: One Size Does Not Fit All." *College and Research Libraries* 61, no. 1 (2000): 56–63.

Armstrong, Chris, and Ray Lonsdate. *E-books in Libraries.* London: Facet, 2006.

Auger, Charles P. *Information Sources in Grey Literature.* 4th ed. London: Bowker-Saur, 1998.

Baird, Brian J. *Library Collection Assessment through Statistical Sampling.* Lanham, Md.: Scarecrow, 2004.

Baker, Sharon L., and Karen L. Wallace. *The Responsive Public Library: How to Develop and Market a Winning Collection.* 2nd ed. Englewood, Colo.: Libraries Unlimited, 2002.

Ballestro, John, and Philip C. Howze. "When a Gift Is Not a Gift: Collection Assessment Using Cost-Benefit Analysis." *Collection Management* 30, no. 3 (2005): 49–66.

Barreau, Deborah. "Information Systems and Collection Development in Public Libraries." *Library Collections, Acquisitions, and Technical Services* 25, no. 3 (2001): 263–79.

Bertot, John Carlo, and Denise M. Davis. *Planning and Evaluating Library Networked Services and Resources.* Westport, Conn.: Libraries Unlimited, 2004.

Black, Steven. *Serials in Libraries: Issues and Practices.* Westport, Conn.: Libraries Unlimited, 2006.

Bluh, Pamela, and Cindy Hepfer, eds. *Managing Electronic Resources: Contemporary Problems and Emerging Issues.* Chicago: Association for Collections and Technical Services, 2006.

Blummer, Barbara. "E-Books Revisited: The Adoption of Electronic Books by Special, Academic, and Public libraries." *Internet Reference Services Quarterly* 11, no. 2 (2006): 1–13.

Brenner, Robin E., *Understanding Manga and Anime.* Westport, Conn.: Libraries Unlimited, 2007.

Chapman, Liz. *Managing Acquisitions in Library and Information Services.* 3rd ed. London: Facet, 2004.

Christianson, Marilyn. "Patterns of Use of Electronic Books." *Library Collections, Acquisitions, and Technical Services* 29, no. 4 (2005): 351–63.

Collections, Content, and the Web. Washington, D.C.: Council on Library and Information Resources, 2000. www.clir.org/pubs/reports/pub88/contents.html.

Conger, Joan E. *Collaborative Electronic Resource Management: From Acquisitions to Assessment.* Westport, Conn.: Libraries Unlimited, 2004.

Connaway, Lynn Silipigni, and Heather L. Wicht. "What Happened to the E-Book Revolution? The Gradual Integration of E-Books into Academic Libraries." *Journal of Electronic Publishing* 10, no. 3 (2007), http://hdl.handle.net/2027/spo.3336451.0010.302.

Curtis, Donnelyn, with contributions by Virginia M. Scheschy. *E-Journals: A How-to-Do-It Manual for Building, Managing, and Supporting Electronic Journal Collections.* How-to-Do-It Manuals for Libraries no. 134. New York: Neal-Schuman, 2005.

Edlin, Aaron S., and Daniel L. Rubinfeld. "Exclusion or Efficient Pricing? The 'Big Deal' Bundling of Academic Journals." *Antitrust Law Journal* 72, no. 1 (2004): 119–57.

Farmer, Lesley S. J. "Collection Development in Partnership with Youth: Uncovering Best Practices." *Collection Management* 26, no. 2 (2001): 67–78.

Fenner, Audrey. "The Approval Plan: Selection Aid, Selection Substitute." *Acquisitions Librarian,* nos. 31/32 (2004): 227–40.

Flood, Susan, ed. *Guide to Managing Approval Plans.* Acquisitions Guidelines no. 11. Chicago: Association for Library Collections and Technical Services, 1998.

Flowers, Janet L. "Standing Orders: Considerations for Acquisitions Method." *Library Collections, Acquisitions, and Technical Services* 25, no. 3 (2001): 323–28.

Goldsmith, Francisca. *Graphic Novels Now: Building, Managing, and Marketing a Dynamic Collection.* Chicago: American Library Association, 2005.

Gregory, Vicki L., and Ardis Hanson. *Selecting and Managing Electronic Resources: A How-to-Do-It Manual for Librarians.* Rev. ed. How-to-Do-It Manuals for Librarians no. 146. New York: Neal-Schuman, 2006.

Guide to Performance Evaluation of Serials Vendors [prepared for the Association for Library Collections and Technical Services]. Acquisitions Guidelines no. 10. Chicago: American Library Association, 1997.

Hahn, Karla L. "SERU (Shared Electronic Resources Understanding): Opening Up New Possibilities for Electronic Resources Transactions." *D-Lib Magazine* 13, nos. 11/12 (2007), www.dlib.org/dlib/november07/hahn/11hahn.html.

———. "The State of the Large Publisher Bundle: Findings from an ARL Member Survey." *ARL: A Bimonthly Report,* no. 245 (April 2006): 1–6, www.arl.org/bm~doc/arlbr245bundle.pdf.

———. "Tiered Pricing: Implications for Library Collections." *portal: Libraries and the Academy* 5, no. 2 (2005): 151–63.

Handman, Gary, ed. *Video Collection Development in Multi-Type Libraries: A Handbook,* 2nd ed. Westport, Conn.: Greenwood, 2002.

Hillesund, Terje. "Reading *Books in the Digital Age* Subsequent to Amazon, Google, and the Long Tail." *First Monday* 12, no. 9 (2007), http://firstmonday.org/issues/issue12_9/hillesund/index.html.

Intner, Sheila S. "Impact of the Internet on Collection Development: Where Are We Now? Where Are We Headed? An Informal Study." *Library Collections, Acquisitions, and Technical Services* 25, no. 3 (2001): 307–22.

Jacoby, Beth E. "Status of Approval Plans in College Libraries." *College and Research Libraries* 69, no. 3 (2008): 227–40.

Jewell, Timothy D. *Selection and Presentation of Commercially Available Electronic Resources: Issues and Practices.* Washington, D.C.: Digital Library Federation and Council on Library and Information Resources, 2001. www.clir.org/pubs/reports/pub99/contents.html.

Keller, Cynthia A. "Collection Development: Electronic or Print Subscription Resources?" *School Library Media Activities Monthly* 22, no. 9 (2006): 56–59.

Kovacs, Diane. *Building Electronic Library Collections: The Essential Guide to Selection Criteria and Core Subject Collections.* New York: Neal-Schuman, 2000.

Kranich, Nancy. "A Question of Balance: The Role of Libraries in Providing Alternatives to Mainstream Media." *Collection Building* 19, no. 3 (2000): 85–90.

Kulp, Christina, and Karen Rupp-Serrano. "Organizational Approaches to Electronic Resource Acquisition: Decision-Making Models for Libraries." *Collection Management* 30, no. 4 (2005): 3–29.

Laskowski, Mary S. "Stop the Technology, I Want to Get Off: Tips and Tricks for Media Selection and Acquisition." *Acquisitions Librarian,* nos. 31/32 (2004): 217–25.

Lee, Stuart D., and Frances Boyle. *Building an Electronic Resource Collection: A Practical Guide*. 2nd ed. London: Facet, 2004.

Leonhardt, Thomas W. *Handbook of Electronic and Digital Acquisitions*. Binghamton, N.Y.: Haworth, 2006.

Lightman, Harriet, and John P. Blosser, eds. *Perspectives on Serials in the Hybrid Environment*. ACLTS Papers on Library Technical Services and Collections no. 15. Chicago: American Library Association, 2007.

Lukenbill, W. Bernard. *Collection Development for a New Century in the School Library Media Center*. Westport, Conn.: Greenwood, 2002.

Lukenbill, W. Bernard, and James K. Lukenbill. "Censorship: What Do School Library Specialists Really Know? A Consideration of Students' Rights, the Law and Implications for a New Education Paradigm." *School Library Media Research Journal* 10 (2007). www.ala.org/ala/aasl/aaslpubsandjournals/slmrb/slmrcontents/volume10/lukenbill_censorship.cfm.

Mederios, Norm, et al. "White Paper on Interoperability between Acquisitions Modules of Integrated Library Systems and Electronic Resources Management Systems." Prepared by a Subcommittee of the Digital Library Federation's Electronic Resource Management Initiative, Phase II (Jan. 2008). www.diglib.org/standards/ERMI_Interop_Report_20080108.pdf.

Metz, Paul. "Principles of Selection for Electronic Resources." *Library Trends* 48, no. 4 (2000): 711–28.

Miller, Steve. *Developing and Promoting Graphic Novel Collections*. New York: Neal-Schuman, 2005.

Mortimore, Jeffrey M. "Access-Informed Collection Development and the Academic Library: Using Holdings, Circulation, and ILL Data to Develop Prescient Collections." *Collection Management* 30, no. 3 (2007): 21–37.

Myers, Nan. "Documents Data Miner: Creating a Paradigm Shift in Government Documents Collection Development and Management." *Reference Librarian* no. 94 (2006): 163–90.

Nebraska Educational Media Association. *Guide for Developing and Evaluating School Library Media Programs*. Englewood, Colo.: Libraries Unlimited, 2000.

Nisonger, Thomas E. "The Internet and Collection Management in Academic Libraries: Opportunities and Challenges." In *The Role and Impact of the Internet on Library and Information Services*, ed. Lewis-Guodo Lui, 59–83. Contributions in Librarianship and Information Science no. 96. Westport, Conn.: Greenwood, 2001.

Pawuk, Michael G. *Graphic Novels: A Genre Guide to Comic Books, Manga, and More*. Westport, Conn.: Libraries Unlimited, 2007.

Primary Research Group. *Prevailing and Best Practices in Electronic and Print Serials Management*. New York: Primary Research Group, 2006.

———. *The Survey of Library Database Licensing Practices*. New York: Primary Research Group. 2007

Rao, Siriginidi Subba. "Electronic Books: Their Integration into Libraries and Information Centers." *Electronic Library* 22, no. 1 (2005): 116–40.

Rowlands, Ian, et al. "What Do Faculty and Students Really Think about E-Books?" *Aslib Proceedings: New Information Perspective* 59, no. 6 (2007): 489–511.

Safley, Ellen. "Demand for E-Books in an Academic Library." *Journal of Library Administration* 45, nos. 3/4 (2006): 445–57.

Sandler, Mark, Kim Armstrong, and Bob Nardini. "Market Formation for E-Books: Diffusion, Confusion or Delusion?" *Journal of Electronic Publishing* 10, no. 3 (2007). http://hdl.handle.net/2027/spo.3336451.0010.310.

Schmidt, Karen A., ed. *Understanding the Business of Acquisitions.* 2nd ed. Chicago: American Library Association, 1999.

Schmidt, William D., Donald Arthur Rieck, and Charles W. Vlcek. *Managing Media Services: Theory and Practice.* 2nd ed. Englewood, Colo.: Libraries Unlimited, 2000.

Schweinsburg, Jane D. "Professional Awareness of the Ethics of Selection." In *Encyclopedia of Library and Information Science,* edited by Allen Kent, vol. 63, supp. 26, 247–59. New York: Marcel Dekker, 1998.

Staley, Robert A. "Electronic Government Information Dissemination: Changes for Programs, Users, Libraries, and Government Documents Libraries." *Collection Management* 32, no. 2 (1007): 305–26.

Su, Di, ed. *Collection Development Issues in the Online Environment.* Binghamton, N.Y.: Haworth, 2007.

Tafuri, Narda, Anna Seaberg, and Gary Handman. *Guide to Out-of-Print Materials.* Acquisitions Guidelines no. 12. Lanham, Md.: Scarecrow; Chicago: Association for Library Collections and Technical Services, 2004.

Van Orden, Phyllis J. *Selecting Books for the Elementary School Library Media Center: A Complete Guide.* New York: Neal-Schuman, 2000.

Van Orden, Phyllis J., and Kay Bishop. *The Collection Program in Schools: Concepts, Practices, and Information Sources.* 4th ed. Westport, Conn.: Libraries Unlimited, 2007.

Wilkinson, Frances C., and Linda K. Lewis. *Writing RFPs for Acquisitions: A Guide to the Request for Proposal.* ALCTS Acquisitions Guides no. 14. Chicago: American Library Association, 2008.

Young, Robyn. "Graphically Speaking: The Importance of Graphic Books in a School Library Collection." *Library Media Connect* 25, no. 4 (2007): 26–28.

Diverse and Alternative Literatures and Communities

Agosta, Denise E. "Building a Multicultural School Library: Issues and Challenges." *Teacher Librarian* 34, no. 3 (2007): 27–31.

Alexander, Linda B., and Sarah D. Miselis. "Barriers to GLBTQ Collection Development and Strategies for Overcoming Them" *Young Adult Library Services* 5, no. 3 (2007): 43–49.

Albright, Meagan. "The Public Library's Responsibilities to LGBT Communities: Recognizing, Representing, and Serving." *Public Libraries* 45, no. 5 (2006): 52–56.

Alire, Camila A., and Jacqueline Ayala. *Serving Latino Communities: A How-to-Do-It Manual for Librarians.* 2nd ed. How-to-Do-It Manuals for Librarians no. 158. New York: Neal-Schuman, 2007.

Circle of Inclusion Project. "Nine Ways to Evaluate Children's Books That Address Disability as Part of Diversity" (2002). www.circleofinclusion.org/english/books/section1/a.html.

Clyde, Laurel A., and Marjorie Lobban. "A Door Half Open: Young People's Access to Fiction Related to Homosexuality." *School Libraries Worldwide* 7, no. 2 (2001): 17–39.

Cuban, Sondra. *Serving New Immigrant Communities in the Library.* Westport, Conn.: Libraries Unlimited, 2007.

Darby, Mary Ann, and Miki Pryne. *Hearing All the Voices: Multicultural Books for Adolescents.* Lanham, Md.: Scarecrow, 2002.

East, Kathy, and Rebecca L Thomas. *Across Cultures: A Guide to Multicultural Literature for Children.* Westport, Conn.: Libraries Unlimited, 2007.

Gilton, Donna L. *Multicultural and Ethnic Children's Literature in the United States.* Lanham, MD.: Scarecrow, 2007.

Gough, Cal, and Ellen Greenblatt. "Gay and Lesbian Library Materials: A Book Selector's Toolkit." In *Public Library Collection Development in the Information Age,* ed. Annabel K. Stephens, 151–70. New York: Haworth, 1998.

Helbig, Alethea K., and Agnes Regan Perkins. *Many Peoples, One Land: A Guide to New Multicultural Literature for Children and Young Adults.* Westport, Conn.: Greenwood, 2001.

Hill, Nanci Milone. "Out and About: Serving the GLBT Population @ Your Library." *Public Libraries* 46, no. 4 (2007): 18–24.

Kranich, Nancy. "A Question of Balance: The Role of Libraries in Providing Alternatives to Mainstream Media." *Collection Building* 19, no. 3 (2000): 85–90.

Simpson, Stacy H. "Why Have a Comprehensive and Representative Collection? GLBT Material Selection and Service in the Public Library." *Progressive Librarian,* no. 27 (Summer 2006): 44–51.

Wadham, Tim. *Libros Esenciales: Building, Marketing, and Programming a Core Collection of Spanish Language Children's Materials.* New York: Neal-Schuman, 2007.

Warner, Jody Nyasha. "Moving beyond Whiteness in North American Academic Libraries." *Libri* 51, no. 3 (2001): 167–72.

Wesson, Caren, and Margaret J. Keefe, eds. *Serving Special Needs Students in the School Library Media Center.* Westport, Conn.: Greenwood, 1995.

Wood, Irene, ed. *Culturally Diverse Videos, Audios, and CD-ROMs for Children and Young Adults.* New York: Neal-Schuman, 1999.

Censorship and Intellectual Freedom

Association for Library Service to Children. *Intellectual Freedom for Children: The Censor Is Coming.* Chicago: American Library Association, 2000.

Bukoff, Ronald N. "Censorship and the American College Library." *College and Research Libraries* 56, no. 5 (1995): 395–407.

Cline, Edward. "Censorship." In *Encyclopedia of Library and Information Science,* edited by Allen Kent, vol. 62, supp. 25, 65–82. New York: Marcel Dekker, 1998.

Doyle, Tony. "Selection versus Censorship in Libraries." *Collection Management* 27, no. 1 (2002): 15–25.

Foerstel, Herbert N. *Free Expression and Censorship in America: An Encyclopedia.* Westport, Conn.: Greenwood, 1997.

Gibson, Jeffrey. "Championing Intellectual Freedom: A School Administrator's Guide." *Knowledge Quest* 36, no. 2 (2007): 46–48.

Higgins, Susan E. "Information, Technology, and Diversity: Censorship in the Twenty-first Century." In *Collection Management*, edited by G. E. Gorman, 99–117. International Yearbook of Library and Information Management, 2000–2001. London: Library Association Publishing, 2000.

Intner, Sheila S. "Dollars and Sense: Censorship versus Selection, One More Time." *Technicalities* 24, no. 3 (2004): 1, 7–10.

Karolides, Nicholas J. *Censored Books II: Critical Viewpoints, 1985–2000.* Lanham, Md.: Scarecrow, 2002.

Karolides, Nicholas J., Lee Burress, and John M. Kean. *Censored Books: Critical Viewpoints.* Metuchen, N.J.: Scarecrow, 1993.

Kelsey, Marie. "Are We Lucky for the First Amendment? A Brief History of Students' Right to Read." *Knowledge Quest* 36, no. 2 (2007): 26–29.

Kravitz, Nancy. *Censorship and the School Library Media Center.* Westport, Conn.: Libraries Unlimited, 2002.

LaRue, James. *New Inquisition: Understanding and Managing Intellectual Freedom Challenges.* Westport, Conn.: Libraries Unlimited, 2007

Martin, Ann M. "Preparing for a Challenge." *Knowledge Quest* 36, no. 2 (2007): 54–56.

Osif, Bonnie. "Selection and Censorship." *Library Administration and Management* 19, no. 1 (2005): 42–46.

Peck, Robert S. *Libraries, the First Amendment, and Cyberspace: What You Need to Know.* Chicago: American Library Association, 2000.

Reichman, Henry. *Censorship and Selection: Issues and Answers for Schools.* 3rd ed. Chicago: American Library Association; Arlington, Va.: American Association of School Administrators, 2001.

Managing Collections

Much of the education and training for collection development focuses on building collections, which can seem the most stimulating and satisfying part of the work. An equally important and challenging responsibility is collection management or collection maintenance.

Collection management is an umbrella term covering all the decisions made after an item is part of the collection. These decisions often become critical tasks because of condition, budget or space limitations, or shifts in the library's user community and parent organization priorities. Collection management often is more politically charged than collection development. User communities, administrative agencies, and funding bodies may be suspicious about the disposition of materials for which "good money" has been spent. They may have an emotional investment in the library's collections. Some preservation reformatting products are less comfortable to use. Moving materials to remote storage sites usually delays access. Canceling journals distresses at least part of the user group. Moving from print to an electronic-only version raises anxiety about continuing access.

This chapter explores making decisions that constitute collection management—withdrawal, transfer to storage, preservation, serial cancellation, transition to electronic-only—and concludes with a section on protecting collections from theft, mutilation, and natural disasters.

Weeding

Weeding is the process of removing materials from the active collection for withdrawal or transfer. Alternately, this activity is referred to as pruning, thinning, culling, deselection, deaccession, relegation, deacquisition, retirement, reverse selection, negative selection, and book stock control. The extensive list of euphemisms suggests the degree to which librarians are uncomfortable getting rid of materials. As Will Manley notes, "Next to emptying the outdoor bookdrop on cold and snowy days, weeding is the most undesirable job in the library. It is also one of the most important."[1] Some authors make distinctions between these terms; others use them synonymously. *Withdrawal* is the physical process of pulling materials from the collection and removing the descriptive records from the catalog. In school media centers and public libraries, weeding is often synonymous with withdrawal. Donna J. Baumbach and Linda L. Miller offer a succinct description of weeding in school library media centers:

> Simply put, weeding is selection in reverse. It is deselection. Weeding is the act of reevaluating items in the collection and removing any that are inaccurate, out of date, misleading, inappropriate, unused, in poor condition, or otherwise harmful to students. It is something all librarians and library media specialists must do regularly if they want to maintain the best possible collections for their school communities. It is a professional responsibility that cannot be taken lightly.[2]

Items withdrawn from the active collection may be discarded, offered for sale, or given to other organizations. Transferred items may be moved to another location within the library or library system, or to storage.

Libraries have run into political problems when their communities have discovered withdrawn materials in dumpsters and landfills. Nicholson Baker attracted national attention with his 1996 *New Yorker* article on massive withdrawal and discard projects at the San Francisco Public Library.[3] The University of New Mexico Library made the news in 2001 when faculty members protested withdrawing back runs of several hundred math journals. The library faced severe space constraints and was, at the time of the withdrawal, providing online access to the titles through JSTOR. As a result of the protest, the library reacquired or replaced all withdrawn volumes.[4] In 2004, East St. Louis citizens discovered ten thousand deselected books and albums in a decommissioned library building. The items had been withdrawn and left behind when the library moved to a new, smaller building in 2001. The intention had been to sell the materials, but a new library director knew nothing about the collection or the intent to sell it. The discovery resulted in an imbroglio and bad publicity for the library and East St. Louis.[5]

Libraries did not give much attention to withdrawals until late in the 1800s. Library materials were so scarce and valuable that the emphasis was on building collections, not culling them. But as the number of books in libraries increased and space grew more limited, withdrawing and discarding items in public and school libraries became more common. One early report from the Lunn Public Library in Massachusetts noted that five hundred books were withdrawn in 1883 because they were superseded or no longer useful.[6] A weeding plan proposed to address the overflowing Quincy Public Library (also in Massachusetts) caused a major flap at the ALA 1893 annual meeting.[7] William Frederick Poole, a leading figure in librarianship of the time, railed against weeding and said the solution was to build bigger libraries. Large academic and research libraries, which value comprehensiveness and quantity, have been less likely to discard materials, looking instead to transfer volumes to remote storage. In 1893, in one of the earliest documented examples, Harvard librarian Justin Winsor oversaw moving 15,000 volumes to storage because of space constraints.[8]

Reasons for Withdrawal

Reasons for withdrawal are usually related to saving money or improving services and collections. More effective use of the library's space and staff required to maintain the collection represents one justification for withdrawal. Libraries dispose of materials that are no longer useful, current, or appropriate. Little-used materials can be sent to a site less expensive to maintain or put into compact storage in a less accessible area of the main library building. These tactics can alleviate space problems and make servicing the active collection easier. Another important reason is to assure continued quality in the collection. When weeding is justified on the grounds of improved user service, the rational is that borrowers can more easily find up-to-date materials; sexist, racist, out-of-date, and possibly inaccurate materials are no longer available; the general appearance of the library is improved; and browsing capability is enhanced.

A library should have established criteria, documented in a written policy, guiding weeding decisions. The library then has a measure of protection in pointing to a systematic plan for not only building but also managing its collection. Criteria vary from library to library, depending on the library's mission, priorities, users, physical facilities, staffing, and age and type of collection. A study of forty public libraries conducted by Juris Dilevko and Lisa Gottlieb in 2000 reported that the three most common criteria for weeding were circulation, physical condition, and accuracy of information.[9]

Successful Weeding

The important elements in successful weeding are a clear purpose (improving the collection, making materials more accessible, freeing space, etc.), sound planning, good communication, sufficient time to do it well, careful consideration, and appropriate communication with administrators and constituents. The process should be conscientious, consistent with policy and institutional goals, attentive to consortial commitments, and sensitive to users.

Robert D. Stueart describes the process of selecting to acquire and selecting to weed as linear:

> On the one hand, one must evaluate materials before purchasing them, and on the other hand, one must re-evaluate their usefulness to the collection and then remove them, if they have lost their value. This removal requires judgment just as selection does, and involves added pressures that the initial purchase did not.[10]

Weeding is not simple. It is time consuming, involves many library units, and can be "the most politically charged responsibility any librarian will assume."[11]

Ideally, libraries review materials for weeding with the same regularity that they add them. One technique is the use of periodic collection inventories or reviews. An example of this approach is the CREW method developed by Joseph P. Segal and updated by Belinda Boon.[12] The CREW manual recommends establishing guidelines for weeding each part of the collection according to the classification into which it falls, building weeding into the year's work calendar, and combining inventory review with careful consideration of each item in the collection for discarding, binding, weeding, or replacement.

More frequently, a withdrawal project is a discrete project, forced upon the library by circumstances. The motivation may be a critical demand for more space, the need to review a portion of the collection prior to compacting, an inventory or collection analysis project, a project to reclassify materials, or a physical disaster. Such a crash project can put pressure on several library units—circulation, cataloging, stack maintenance—as well as the collections librarians reviewing items. Planning a project should include comparing the costs of the effort with the costs of doing nothing. Costs associated with weeding include staff time to review materials, revise associated records, move materials, shift remaining materials within the space, educate users, and retrieve materials or obtain them from elsewhere if later requested. Costs resulting from doing nothing include ongoing collection maintenance (reshelving, shifting collections, maintaining catalog records, etc.), unavailable shelf space, and provision of dated and possibly inaccurate information.

Weeding Criteria

Most weeding processes combine mechanical, objective approaches (e.g., analysis of circulation data and citation frequency) with more judgmental, subjective considerations (e.g., local program needs and knowledge of the subject literature). Reviewing en masse depends more on objective data because each item is not considered individually. Criteria for weeding are similar to those used in selecting items, remembering that all libraries are different and criteria are more or less relevant depending on the subject area, format, and user community. The three most frequently asked questions are Has it been used? Is it worn, soiled, or damaged? Is it outdated? Although these are valid, the following questions also should be considered.

Is the content still pertinent?

Is it in a language that current and future users can read?

Is it duplicated in the collection, either in another copy or a comparable item on the same topic?

Is it available elsewhere?

Is it rare or valuable or both?

Has it been superseded by a new edition?

Was it originally selected in error?

Is it cited in standard abstracting or indexing tools?

Is it listed in a standard bibliography of important works?

Does it have local relevance?

Does it fill a consortial commitment or regional need?

If available in electronic format, is continued access to retrospective files ensured?

School library media centers often have guidelines to keep a collection fresh and current. Some guiding principles apply to the length of time the content remains up to date and the frequency with which materials should be withdrawn and replaced. Figure 5-1 offers possible replacement guidelines for a school media center.

Stanley J. Slote recommends an objective, scientific approach to collection weeding in which the amount and time of use are the principal criteria for deciding what items to remove.[13] Slote proposes a macro methodology in which library materials are divided into two groups, a core collection that serves 90–95 percent of current use and a "weedable" collection consisting of a larger group of materials that provides the remaining 5–10 percent of use. Much of the literature on collection review has considered use as a primary criterion. A famous study by Allen Kent and colleagues at the University of Pittsburgh indicated that 40

Type of material	Replace after
Geography	5 to 7 years
Career	5 years
Pure science (except botany and natural history)	5 years
Technology and applied science	5 to 10 years
Computer science	3 years
General encyclopedias	5 years
Atlases	5 years
Almanacs, yearbooks, statistical compilations	1 year or when new edition issued
Dictionaries	5 to 10 years
Journals	Keep only one year if not indexed

FIGURE 5-1 Guidelines for replacing materials in a school media center. These guidelines are available from www.ala.org/editions/extras/Johnson09720.

percent of materials purchased never circulated.[14] A Richard W. Trueswell study conducted in the 1960s determined that 20 percent of a collection accounted for 80 percent of the circulation and that one-half of the collection met 99 percent of its users' needs.[15] He noted that "the last circulation date may be an ideal statistic to define and measure circulation requirements and patterns."[16]

Relying on past use data as a predictor of future use does, however, have its problems. Programs, interests, and priorities change. The energy crisis produced interest in peat and wind as sources of energy and sent researchers after publications that had not been requested in seventy years. Additionally, most circulation data do not reflect in-house use. Librarians have not been able to predict accurately the use of materials before purchase and cannot be confident of their ability to do much better after the item is in the collection. Predicted future use is seldom applied as the single criterion for withdrawing items.

CREW (Continuous Review, Evaluation, and Weeding) is one of most popular methods for weeding. The CREW method applies objective and subjective criteria in the evaluation of materials. The two main objective factors are the age of the materials and circulation or use. The CREW method uses another acronym, MUSTIE, to describe the subjective criteria: Misleading (factually inaccurate), Ugly (worn beyond mending or rebinding), Superseded (by a new edition or by a better book on the same subject), Trivial (of no discernible literary or scientific merit), Irrelevant (unrelated to the needs and interests of the library's community), and Elsewhere (it is easily obtainable from another library). A variation is MUSTY, in which the Y stands for "Your collection has no use for this book." Another easily remembered acronym for weeding criteria is WORST: Worn out, Out of date, Rarely used, System (e.g., in-library equipment) cannot support, and Trivial (faddish).

A frequently applied technique for weeding is shelf scanning, which involves direct examination of volumes. Title-by-title review provides information about the size, scope, depth, and currency of materials. It can, however, become a slow and tedious process if the selector seeks to answer all possible questions. Although success depends on the experience and knowledge of the selector, he or she must balance available time against the desired outcomes. Sometimes the selector works in consultation with other librarians, teachers, or faculty members. The selector may make a preliminary identification of items to weed, then teachers or faculty members review the decisions in a two-step process. Even title-by-title review requires knowledge of the collection and subject area, circulation activity, user community, curricular and research needs—and the library's collection development policy.

A straightforward process to weeding is to work through the physical collection and place materials on a book truck, separating into categories those to be withdrawn (sold, donated, disposed), repaired, transferred, and so on. Another technique is to insert decision forms in the items. Decision forms can be brief, providing one or two treatment options, or quite detailed. The simple form specifies the treatment the item is to receive. A more detailed form can be designed to record answers to questions that may be asked when reviewing items, such as when and how often the item circulates and whether the item is a duplicate copy. It can include sections for a second person to approve the decisions and for dates that track the item's routing through the library units that process it. The detailed form offers the opportunity to compile data about the collection at large. For example, when a representative sample is in hand, several forms can be tallied to learn what percentage of the collection is in poor condition. The level of detail collected on a treatment decision form varies according to the purpose of the project, level of staff involved, and time available. Figure 5-2 offers a sample abbreviated treatment decision form.

Another approach to the process of identifying materials for weeding is to begin with collection analysis tools—circulation reports and date of publication reports, usually sorted by classification. This can generate a pick list of likely candidates for weeding, and the actual pulling from the shelves can be done by other staff, student workers, or, perhaps, volunteers. If materials are being

Title: _____

Call number: _____

    ❏ Rebind

    ❏ Repair

    ❏ Transfer to storage

    ❏ Withdraw

    ❏ Replace with print, microform, digital resource

    ❏ Replace with new edition

    ❏ Sell

    ❏ Donate to _____

    ❏ Destroy

Reviewer name: _____

Date: _____

FIGURE 5-2 Simple treatment decision form. A detailed treatment decision form is available at www.ala.org/editions/extras/Johnson09720. Either version can be modified to meet the needs of the library.

transferred to a storage facility, additional review by the librarian may not be needed. If the materials are to be withdrawn, good practice suggests that the librarian review the materials to confirm the initial decision. A critical step in weeding is to ensure that the bibliographic records are updated to reflect the disposition of the item.

Some libraries do massive weeding projects every few years, some weed as materials cross the circulation desk or are reshelved, and some weed by collection segments; for example, a public library might weed picture books in the spring and young adult fiction in the fall. Other techniques are to divide the collection into equal parts and work through the entire collection in a year, month by month, or to develop a multiyear schedule in which portions of the collection are reviewed cyclically.

Because of the potential political consequences of disposing of materials, libraries should have a disposition policy that states the options and processes for disposing of materials and is consistent with the policies of the parent agency and legal considerations. Most libraries stamp the item "Discard" and deface ownership marks. Although the San Francisco Public Library (mentioned above) acted within the governing laws in its massive weeding project, city auditors have cited libraries for illegally disposing of city property.[17] Some best practices should be followed when disposing of materials. Items that are outdated, inaccurate, offensive, or in very poor condition should not be sold, donated, or traded. Do not pass withdrawn materials that are no longer appropriate for the school media center on to classroom teachers. Do not store withdrawn materials to avoid disposing of them properly. Be careful about piling large amounts of discarded materials in dumpsters, where they are easily seen and questioned. Consider paper recycling for materials that are being disposed. When donating materials, librarians should check the gift criteria of the potential recipient.

The public relations aspects of weeding should not be overlooked. Issues most often arise and controversy develops as the result of large projects, but even small projects that are not handled effectively can cause a commotion. Without a context, many people are affronted that libraries do not keep everything forever. The librarian provides the context—the need for space, availability of electronic versions of the same materials, new materials replacing outdated materials, unacceptable condition (e.g., damaged, moldy), and so on. Reflecting on a project at the Virginia Tech Libraries in which 160,000 volumes were withdrawn and 270,000 volumes moved to storage over a seven-year period, Paul Metz and Caryl Gray recommend advance and continuous information to describe the project, the reasons for it, the criteria guiding decisions, and speedy response to questions raised.[18] Many libraries can provide opportunities for consultation with faculty and teachers. For example, an academic library moving extensive back runs of serials to a storage facility might ask faculty members to review the list of titles to ensure that no critical titles are relocated. Often the opportunity for consultation can diffuse anxiety yet result in few titles needing to be retained on site. Other library staff members or units should be informed so that they can plan for the work—record updating, disposal, transport, shifting, repair, and so on. The library director, principal, or other internal administrator should be part of the project planning and aware of ongoing weeding activities. He or she can make the decision about how or if the information should be shared more widely.

Variations in Library Types

School, public, and smaller academic libraries are more likely than large research libraries to withdraw and dispose of items. They need current nonfiction, attractive new items, and popular fiction and often have severe space limitations. Out-of-date information disadvantages students and citizens, who should have the most recent and relevant information.

Public libraries often have space limitations. Much of the recreational reading material and popular reference material (e.g., travel books) becomes dated within a few years. Multiple copies of no longer popular novels do not need to be retained. Small and branch public libraries usually concentrate on high-demand materials and can rely on a central library or state or regional interlibrary loan system to supply items that have little demand. Small public libraries should routinely review popular fiction, children's and young adult books, and reference collections.

College libraries may be weeded regularly and carefully because of limited stack and storage space. Focusing on a working collection for undergraduates reduces the need to maintain a constantly growing collection of all materials acquired. Increased access to retrospective files of journals online, along with improved bibliographic and physical access to collections elsewhere, has reduced the pressures on small academic libraries to retain everything.

Reference collections in all types of libraries usually are weeded more regularly than other portions of collections. Some libraries have a policy that a title must be removed from the reference collection whenever a new volume is added. They may have a schedule for replacing reference books. Bibliographies and encyclopedias are of little use after ten years, with a few exceptions such as the famous *Britannica* eleventh edition. Almanacs and yearbooks should be withdrawn when they are superseded and a new edition is received.

Special libraries serve many different clientele groups, from hospitals to law firms to corporations. Weeding and withdrawal policies must pay special attention to the particular user community being served. Many special libraries are expected to provide up-to-date technical information and to withdraw obsolete materials. The emphasis tends to be on an efficient core collection, providing materials "just in time" instead of "just in case." Weeding is regular and constant.

Weeding with the intent to dispose of materials has not been as common in large academic and research libraries. Items considered outdated or less relevant are usually placed in storage instead of being removed from the collection. A few circumstances, such as unneeded duplicates or materials in very poor condition, which are replaced or reformatted, do prompt removal. The availability of archival back files of e-journals is changing how large libraries view the need to retain large retrospective runs of print journals. Weeding a collection is more likely to be for the purpose of transferring materials—from a reference collection to the general collection, from the general collection to storage, or from the general collection to a special collection. The Rare Books and Manuscripts Section of the Association of College and Research Libraries has developed guidelines to inform transfer of materials to special collections.[19]

Most of the literature on withdrawals focuses on print items, but all formats deserve consideration. Computer software becomes obsolete as new versions are released and new equipment is required for its use. Multimedia should be reviewed using the same criteria applied to print materials. Special attention should be given to visual and audio quality and physical condition. School library media specialists consult with teachers to ensure that media continue to satisfy instructional needs. E-books are easy to ignore because they do not take up physical space and their use does not appear in standard circulation activity reports. Nevertheless, the same criteria should be applied (e.g., currency, scope of coverage, usage), and these materials should be reviewed along with the rest of the collection.

Storage

Storing library materials has been called "a necessary evil for which there are no obvious alternatives."[20] It splits collections, limits browsability, and inconveniences users. Nevertheless, use of library storage facilities has a long history. It has been traced to the ancient library in Alexandria, which is reported to have placed duplicate scrolls in a separate location.[21] When libraries run out of room, librarians face the choice of withdrawal or storage. Larger American research libraries were coping with this problem by the end of the nineteenth century. Charles W. Eliot, president of Harvard in 1891, wrote, "What then can keep the shelves from encumbrance? Only constant elimination, convenient storage, frequent rearrangement. The books less wanted must be stacked away . . . and the books most valued must be brought forward."[22]

Despite a common perception that collections have stopped growing because "everything is electronic," academic and research libraries continue to build physical collections. The number of books printed increases annually. For many parts of the world, publications are available only in print-on-paper formats.

Large academic and research libraries hold large collections of rare and unique materials that are retained even if digital surrogates are available. For less rare and unique materials, mass commercial scanning projects hold promise. Google Books Library Project (http://books.google.com/googlebooks/library.html) makes freely available online the digital content of volumes that are in the public domain or out of copyright. Lizanne Payne suggests that

> digitization projects are likely to drive additional volumes to storage, even from libraries not directly participating as contributors to the digitization efforts. . . . Some libraries may be willing to discard the print versions in favor of an online or print-on-demand version, but many more are likely to save and store a print copy in a local or shared storage facility.[23]

Whether libraries move to withdrawing large numbers of volumes in the future remains an open question. In the short term, the need for collections storage continues to grow. According to a 2005 Heritage Health Index, 60 percent of the more than five thousand responding libraries reported a need for new or additional off-site storage.[24]

Libraries have explored various models for determining which materials are appropriate candidates for storage.[25] Storage in this context means a location where less used library materials are gathered or deposited; it may be remote or on site with standard, high-density, or compact shelving and is generally not open for public browsing or retrieval.[26] Materials in a storage facility are usually paged upon request for users and delivered to a library site or perhaps campus office. Some facilities provide an on-site reading room to which materials are brought upon user request.

Off-Site Storage

By the middle of the twentieth century, several academic and research libraries were coping with limited space by building off-site storage facilities.[27] Many were shared by several institutions to gain further economies. The New England Depository opened in 1942 as a cooperative storage facility for seven academic libraries and four nonacademic libraries. The Midwest Inter-Library Center (now the Center for Research Libraries) opened in 1951 to provide storage for member academic libraries as part of several cooperative programs. In the early 1980s, the University of California system opened the Northern and Southern Regional Library Facilities. The Minnesota Library Access Center, opened in 2000 and located on the University of Minnesota campus in Minneapolis, provides a below-ground storage cavern that is shared by libraries of all types in Minnesota. Most cooperative facilities have policies that address costs, criteria for placing materials in storage, retrieval procedures, whether on-site use is permitted, and requirements for condition of items and associated bibliographic records.

Several institutions, including Cornell University, Penn State University, and Harvard University, have their own storage facilities. Most academic storage facilities provide high-density shelving on which items are arranged by size to maximize capacity.[28] Items are frequently stored in trays or bins. Item bar codes are linked to tray bar codes, and the trays are linked to shelf and stack range numbers. Shelving areas are normally closed to users. Some storage facilities provide a reading room; others have no on-site user services.

Libraries place materials in storage because they do not have enough room in their main facility yet wish to retain the items. Lesser- or little-used materials, as well as materials that need special protection, are moved to storage. Many libraries face an economic necessity to find financially reasonable ways to retain materials. Yale has calculated off-site storage to be one-tenth as expensive as on-campus, open-stack libraries.[29] The type of storage used depends on funds the library has to invest in storage facilities, the probable costs of moving materials back and forth, the difficulty of changing library records to show location of materials, and estimates of how much users will be inconvenienced by remote materials. Criteria for storing materials may be influenced by the provision of a reading room at the storage facility and the speed with which items are delivered to users at the main library. Placing materials in storage can serve as a conservation treatment if the storage facility has optimum temperature and humidity conditions. The reduction in handling that is a consequence of storage can benefit collections. An additional benefit of placing materials in storage is an often increased ability to locate materials; the likelihood of misshelved materials is much lower because of controlled access.[30]

Selecting and processing materials for storage are labor intensive. Staff members throughout the library are involved. Collection management librarians define the criteria and review materials. Even with the most logical and defensible criteria, informed judgment is necessary. Technical services staff change the location on bibliographic records and mark items for storage. Materials are pulled from stacks and transported to the new location. Physical control at the storage site requires a finding and retrieval system. This may involve creating a parallel catalog and putting additional markings on the items.

Either a separate policy or a section in the library's general collection management policy should address criteria and rationale for storing items. A policy should define the process through which materials are reviewed and evaluated, by whom, and how. Making clear the operating principles under which these decisions are made protects the library from charges of bias and irresponsible behavior. Academic librarians who have a policy that references institutional priorities and to which they can direct constituents find it easier to explain that eliminating a degree program has led to transferring supporting materials to remote storage. By identifying the library's participation in cooperative collection building, resource sharing, and regional storage programs, the policy explains the library's obligations to its partners.

Criteria for Storage

The primary criterion for moving materials to storage has been use.[31] More recently, an additional consideration has been added to the decision process: can the material be accessed electronically? JSTOR (www.jstor.org) is intended to ease the problems faced by academic and research libraries seeking to provide stack space for long back files of scholarly journals and to address preservation issues by providing a trusted digital archive. JSTOR titles are selected for digitization on the basis of the number of institutional subscribers a journal has, citation analysis, recommendations from experts in the field, and how long the journal has been published. JSTOR aims to digitize selected titles from volume 1 forward. JSTOR's agreements with publishers include an updating provision known as a "moving wall." The moving wall is a fixed period of time, usually ranging from two to five years, that defines the gap between the most recently published issue and the date of the most recent issues available in JSTOR.

The simplest approach may be moving to storage all materials that have not circulated after a specified date or that have circulated fewer than a certain number of times within a specified period. This approach ignores in-library use and variations across different disciplines' use of their literatures. Projected use is a variation of historical use criteria and is, obviously, more subjective. This approach presupposes a clear understanding of institutional priorities and detailed knowledge of the collection. Because it is based on perceptions of future utility and cannot be documented, justification is difficult.

One approach is to move all inactive serials or all bound serial volumes published before a specified date. This has the advantage of freeing up the most space with the smallest number of bibliographic record changes. Again, variations across disciplines are ignored. Splitting serial runs can cause user confusion and frustration. Another straightforward approach is to apply the date-of-publication criterion to all formats. An advantage is that the "pain" of remote storage is spread across subjects. On the other hand, this method ignores variations in literature use across discipline. Date-of-publication criteria can serve a preservation function. All older materials are moved to a facility where they have significantly less handling and usually benefit from environmental controls. Identifying blocks of materials for storage simplifies the review process and makes possible "global" changes to bibliographic records. This approach assumes knowledge of how the block of material is used—or not used. It also runs the risk of antagonizing an entire segment of users.

Refinements are added as required by users and as time and staffing permit. Typical additional criteria address superseded reference volumes, duplicates, print materials duplicated by microforms or in digital format, condition, and value. Criteria can be modified within subjects or disciplines. For example, date of publication may be considered inappropriate in the humanities but appropriate in the sciences. Exceptions are, however, persistent. Older materials in botany are heavily used resources, for example. Each exception requires a staff member to intervene and apply judgment. Review for transfer to storage typically follows procedures similar to those used for other collection review decisions, such as use of decision forms, consultation with other units in the library, and—as appropriate—consultation with teachers and faculty members.

Meeting the needs of collection users is a critical aspect of effective storage programs. Careful selection and good bibliographic control are meaningless without speedy and effective delivery of materials to users. A willingness to reverse storage decisions, sometimes called derelegation, can be desirable. Moving such items back to the main collection saves the library money and reduces user dissatisfaction. All criteria are scrutinized and questioned by collection users, and communicating with users is a critical part of any storage initiative. Well-informed and well-prepared librarians can help defuse user anxieties and misconceptions.

Preservation

Preservation encompasses activities intended to prevent, retard, or stop deterioration of materials or to retain the intellectual content of materials no longer physically intact. Michael Gorman describes preservation as part of librarians' stewardship responsibilities: "the preservation of the human record to ensure that future generations know what we know."[32] The ALA has identified preservation as a core value of librarianship and issued a policy affirming this.[33] Preservation includes selecting replacement copies, moving items to a protected area, and selecting materials for reformatting. Binding, rebinding, repairing, using protective enclosures, controlling use, monitoring environmental conditions, and conserving are preservation activities intended to prolong the useful life of materials. An alternative to preservation is planned deterioration, in which an item is retained until it has deteriorated beyond use and then is withdrawn or replaced. Preservation challenges all types of libraries. Federal funding, through the National Endowment for the Arts and, more recently, the Institute of Museum and Library Services, has provided millions of dollars for preservation activities across the country. Grants have funded conservation projects, reformatting projects, research, and education.

Heavy use may result in wear on even the newest materials, but many libraries face the added burden of an aging collection. The greatest source of deterioration in large academic and research collections is the acidic paper manufactured after 1840 and the binding, glues, and other components of printed objects. Before 1840, most paper was made from linen and cotton rags and is much more stable than the paper made from wood pulp that replaced it. Chemicals used during the papermaking process result in chemical processes that cause embrittlement.[34] Brittle paper breaks when page corners are folded one or two times. Books have been known to crumble when moved on shelves, leaving debris reminiscent of corn flakes. Deterioration is compounded by poor housing conditions in which temperature, excess light, and humidity extremes accelerate deterioration. Research conducted by Robert M. Hayes in the mid-1980s determined that 25 percent of the volumes held in ARL member libraries were embrittled, and the percentage was increasing annually.[35]

Librarians and publishers became increasingly aware of the problem of brittle books in the 1970s and 1980s and began calling it the "slow fires" eating away at library collections.[36] Many scholarly publishers, government agencies, professional associations, and trade publishers now use alkaline papers and comply with the national standard for permanent paper, first issued in 1985.[37] Standards are concerned both with performance (how long paper's shelf life is) and durability (how paper stands up to use). Several methods of deacidification have been developed, including processes that treat large numbers of items and techniques that can be applied individually.[38] During deacidification an alkaline agent is deposited in the paper to neutralize the acid, but this does not restore paper strength. Several commercial deacidification techniques are on the market. Most treatments are done in special plants, requiring that libraries send books off-site. BookKeeper, the only mass-deacidification process widely used in the United States, is available through Preservation Technologies, L.P. The CSC BookSaver is available through Conservación de Sustratos Celulósicos S.L. (Barcelona, Spain). Papersave was developed by Battelle Ingenieurtechnik GmbH and is, therefore, often called the Battelle process. Unlike BookKeeper, it can be installed at libraries for on-site use. The Wei T'o process, developed by Richard Smith, is usually used for single-item treatment and less commonly for mass deacidification. BookKeeper, CSC BookSaver, Papersave, and Wei T'o are also available as handheld sprays; all require special care in their use because of health and environmental concerns.

Before 1900, most techniques used to repair materials drew on traditional bookbinding practices and materials. As collections began to age and become worn, numerous detrimental treatments became common. Using Scotch brand cellophane tape, household glues and pastes, and flimsy, acidic pamphlet binders accelerated deterioration. Benign neglect has been more effective in preserving library materials. Librarians have become more conscious of the consequences of poor repair techniques and materials. Commercial suppliers now offer a variety of archivally sound and reversible materials for cleaning, repairing, and storing materials. Government and private agencies and organizations provide information, advice, and services.[39]

Preservation microfilming increased in popularity as a reformatting approach in the 1980s, though it has a long history. In the 1930s, the New York Public Library and Columbia University began microfilming fragile materials. As the library world became aware of the pervasive problem of embrittled paper and disintegrating collections, reformatting on a large scale became an attractive option. Many materials fell apart when handled, and reliable surrogates became desirable. Patricia Battin, president of the Commission on Preservation and Access, wrote,

> We faced very painful and wrenching choices—we had to accept the fact that we couldn't save it all, that we had to accept the inevitability of triage, that we had to change our focus from single-item salvation to a mass production process, and we had to create a comprehensive cooperative strategy. We had to move from the cottage industries in our individual library back rooms to a coordinated nationwide mass production effort.[40]

Several developments fostered cooperative preservation microfilming projects, which were seen as the best option for dealing with a critical situation. National standards for microfilm durability and permanence were developed, and 35 mm silver halide film was accepted as a reliable medium. National bibliographic utilities provided access to holdings and helped libraries avoid duplication of effort. The federal government began funding preservation microfilming projects. The Commission on Preservation and Access was created in 1986 to instigate and coordinate collaborative efforts, publicize the problem of brittle books, and provide national leadership; the Commission merged with the Council on Library Resources to form the Council on Library and Information Resources in 1997. Cooperative microfilming projects through consortia and the United States Newspaper Program have coordinated national efforts to identify, describe, and preserve fragile resources.

Nicholson Baker focused the nation's attention on preservation microfilming.[41] He lamented the destruction and disposal of items that were microfilmed. Baker's book has been called a "journalistic jeremiad" because of his relentless attack on libraries, librarians, and preservation microfilming.[42] His critics maintain that the practices he described were in place for a limited period and that he misrepresented much of the history of library preservation.[43] Some statements he made regarding the durability of acidic paper remain under question. The routine disbinding and discarding of materials as part of microfilming is no longer done. In some cases, however, reformatting is the only option to preserve the content.

Preservation combines evaluating materials and selecting the appropriate action. Micro decisions often are made when an item in poor condition is discovered during circulation or when a staff member is working with materials on the shelves. Macro decisions treat large portions of a collection. The collections librarian reselects materials by selecting them for preservation. The questions to be answered are, Is treatment desirable? Suitable? Available? Affordable?

Nonprint collections also need preservation. Libraries holding rare non-print materials (audio recordings, photographs, etc.) may face special challenges. Several sources offer guidelines and best practices for preserving such items.[44] Libraries with commercially produced media often replace the item, if it is still available. Born-digital resources and digitized files present different problems because of various formats and the speed with which standards, software, and hardware change. Libraries with digital collections plan for refreshing and migrating the data or emulating obsolete software and hardware if they wish to retain the content beyond the life of the medium.

Several initiatives are seeking to address on a larger scale the preservation of digital content. The Research Libraries Group and OCLC explored the concept of trusted digital repositories to "provide reliable, long-term access to managed digital resources to its designated community, now and in the future" in a 2002 report that defines digital preservation as "the managed activities necessary for ensuring both the long-term maintenance of a bitstream and continued accessibility of content."[45] The notion of a trusted digital repository implies an ethical obligation as well as the technical and organizational infrastructure to sustain it. Digital repositories also may be called digital archives and institutional repositories. Institutional repositories were defined in a SPARC position paper as "digital collections capturing and preserving the intellectual output of a single or multi-university community."[46] In this model, faculty and researchers at universities deposit digital copies of their articles, conference papers, research data sets, working papers, and course materials into a centrally managed electronic archive. Some institutional repositories limit access to affiliated users; others provide open access to all to promote the free exchange of scholarship.

One of the first institutional repositories was the Massachusetts Institute of Technology DSpace (http://libraries.mit.edu/dspace-mit/). Other repositories are discipline based, such as the e-Print archive (http://arxiv.org) established by Paul Ginsparg and now hosted at Cornell University. Serving as an online preprint archive and distribution server for research papers, this service has become a major forum for speedy dissemination of results in physics and related disciplines, mathematics, nonlinear sciences, computational linguistics, and neuroscience. The success of digital repositories depends on individuals depositing content, tools that harvest content, and effective dissemination. The Open Archives Initiative (www.openarchives.org) develops and promotes protocols and standards for interoperability to facilitate the efficient dissemination of content.

The mutability of the Internet has led some scholars and librarians to ponder how to preserve a medium that is constantly changing in content, location, and organization. The Internet Archive (www.archive.org) is building an Internet library to offer free and permanent access to historical collections that exist in digital format. Founded in 1996 by Brewster Kahle and John Gage, the Internet Archive is collaborating with institutions such as the Library of Congress and the Smithsonian Institution to collect and store web pages, texts, audio, moving images, and software and to prevent Internet content and other born-digital materials from disappearing. Part of this initiative is the Internet Wayback Machine, which allows people to surf nearly two petabytes (growing at a rate of twenty terabytes per month) of data collected from websites from 1996 to the present.

Repair and Conservation

School library media centers, small and medium-sized public libraries, and special libraries commonly focus on treatments that extend the physical life of items. They are unlikely to have full-time preservation staff. These libraries do not have a primary responsibility to retain materials or their intellectual content in perpetuity. They do have an obligation to extend the life of the items in their collections, to protect the investment reflected in their holdings, and to keep their collections as attractive as possible.[47] Many activities contribute to extending the useful life of materials. At the top of the list is good housekeeping—keeping materials dusted and the library free of food or other wastes that attract insects. Controlling temperature, humidity, pollution, and exposure to light protects collections. Educating staff members and users in proper handling of materials is important. Shelves should be the proper height for the items placed on them and should not be packed too tightly. Storage containers and protective enclosures should be archivally sound. Book drops should be padded and emptied frequently.

Library supply companies sell products that can be used for in-house cleaning and simple mending. Materials, procedures, and techniques should meet the latest standards and be acid-free, nondamaging, and safe for workers. Cleaning supplies can remove ballpoint pen ink and crayon marks from book pages, residue from compact disks, and mold and mildew. Assorted types of tape can mend pages or reinforce book spines. Libraries can reglue end papers, headbands, and spines. Many of these supplies are appropriate for extending the life of the item but are not true conservation techniques. If, however, the library plans to retain the item in perpetuity, specialized cleaning and repair should be done by a trained conservator. Individual items may be encapsulated between sheets of polyester film. Deacidification can neutralize the acidity and stabilize paper but cannot restore lost physical properties or reverse the damage done.

Some materials may be appropriate for reconstructive binding, such as reference titles or other heavily used materials. Recasing can reattach the existing covers. Rebinding can be cost effective if the volume has adequate margins and is not brittle and if the original binding is not of value as an artifact. Libraries may have some softcover items bound on receipt if they expect heavy use. Most research libraries bind all the periodical titles they retain. Libraries rely on commercial binderies. Binding should follow the library binding standard developed by the National Information Standards Organization and the Library Binding Institute.[48] Other options are to retain unbound periodical issues, to replace some or all periodicals with commercial microform, or to rely on centrally archived collections in digital format or those held in larger libraries.

Any library may have some materials that require conservation. If the physical entity or artifact is of value, the library may choose to conserve it. Conservation is the effort to save an item in its original condition. The first step is to take good care of materials. This usually means storing in special containers, not circulating valuable items, and permitting use only under supervision. Effective conservation treatment is costly, requiring specialized training and expensive supplies and equipment. In such cases, relying on professional conservators and regional conservation centers is the best option.

Replacement and Reformatting

If an item is worn beyond repair or the cost of repair is too high, a library may replace it. Options are a commercial paper reprint or microform copy, a used copy through an out-of-print dealer, an electronic equivalent, or local reformatting. Commercial publishers reprint paper facsimiles, provide microforms, and offer digital surrogates of high-demand titles and packages of specialized titles. A library may decide to photocopy the original when it expects moderate use and cannot locate a reprint. Microfilm and microfiche are less appealing to users but withstand more use. Reformatting on an item-by-item basis is expensive. The collections librarian must decide if the intellectual content of an item has sufficient enduring value to justify reformatting or replacing, and if the format selected will capture the content and support current and future use. If the librarian opts to replace or reproduce an item, he or she should select a company that follows accepted guidelines and standards for permanence, durability, and fidelity—or ensure that appropriate standards are met if the work is done in-house. Whenever librarians identify an item that is to be reformatted, they should be aware of the copyright law and its amendments.

Copyright law has been described as "complicated, arcane, and counterintuitive."[49] The intended purpose of copyright is to balance the rights of the public for access to information and creative expression with the rights of its creator, and to provide incentives for the advancement of knowledge and creativity. Copyright law gives authors and the owners of copyrighted materials several broad rights and also subjects these rights to expectations, such as "first sale doctrine" (the copyright owner has no right to control the distribution of a copy of a work after that copy has been sold), "fair use" (the legal privilege to make unauthorized use of a copyrighted work for good reason), and the right to make copies for archival and preservation, for patrons, and for interlibrary loan.

Section 108 of Title 17, United States Code, grants libraries and archives the right to create reproductions of their own holdings during the last twenty years of any term of copyright for purposes of preservation and replacing deteriorated materials if the item cannot be obtained at a reasonable price. Works are protected by copyright in the United States if created after 1923 and registered before 1978, or created after 1978. If a work is protected within its term of copyright but the author, creator, or copyright holder cannot be located by someone (a library, another author, etc.) who wishes to use the work and is seeking permission to do so, that work is called an "orphan work." A 2006 report prepared for the U.S. Office of Copyright recommended legislation to provide a meaningful solution to the problem of orphan works.[50] Several bills seeking to limit the compensation in cases where the owner of the orphan work cannot be identified or located have been introduced but have failed to pass. The ALA monitors legislation regarding copyright,[51] and all librarians should do likewise.

Digitizing as a preservation treatment is becoming increasingly accepted in libraries.[52] A digitized surrogate can add value through enhanced description and search capabilities. Digitization has the advantage of reducing handling of the original artifact and making it accessible to more people as a surrogate. The Digital Library Federation has developed a "Benchmark for Faithful Digital Reproductions of Monographs and Serials," which provides standards for optimally formatted digital content that address quality, persistence, and interoperability.[53] Digitization is often combined with conservation of the original or with microfilm reformatting. Libraries that undertake local digitization as a mode of preservation must have a robust hardware and software infrastructure and the resources to carry out the project and provide continuing access. Libraries should strive not to duplicate work done at other libraries. One initiative to aid in locating digitized works is the Registry of Digital Masters, a collaborative project of the Digital Library Foundation and OCLC.[54] This registry includes both digitally reformatted and born-digital objects and seeks to foster the communication, coordination, and discovery of information about digital masters, their production, and the availability of copies for use.

The Council on Library and Information Resources (using data provided by the Library of Congress Preservation Directorate) compared the costs of various preservation treatments for a single 300-page book in 2001.[55] The estimated costs are binding or boxing, $10; mass deacidification, $15; preservation facsimile, $65; microfilming, $185; conservation, $430; base level digitization, $1,600; and enhanced digitization, $2,500. Each of these costs includes the various steps (selection, book checkout, packing, transport, quality control, reshelving, etc.) required to prepare the materials for use. The Library of Congress's base level digitization includes machine-readable, minimally encoded text generated by fully automated processes of optical character recognition and text markup and basic bibliographic description. Enhanced digitization offers improved access through the addition of enhancements such as essays and finding aids.

Mass commercial digitization projects have created controversy since the arrival of the Google Print project (now the Google Books Library Project) in 2004, in which Google announced partnerships with libraries at the University of Michigan, Harvard, and Stanford, the Bodleian Library at Oxford, and the New York Public Library to digitize all or large portions of their print collections. The number of partners continues to grow. In most agreements, Google digitally scans and makes searchable both public domain and copyrighted materials. For books protected by copyright, a search yields basic information (book title, author name, etc.) and a few lines of text (called "snippets" by Google) related to the search along with information about purchasing or borrowing the volume from a library. Public domain materials can be viewed, searched, or downloaded in their entirety from the Google site. Google provides partner libraries with a digital copy of their public domain materials scanned in the project.

Much of the discussion has been around three topics: intellectual property and copyright, technical aspects, and the social impact of these projects. The copyright issues are made more complex by the variety of agreements Google has reached with the partnering university and research libraries. In some cases Google scans only volumes that are out of copyright and in the public domain. In others the library's complete holdings are being scanned regardless of copyright status, though Google does not make these titles available in their entirety.

Contention between publishers and Google has led to legal challenges.[56] The Authors Guild of America, the Association of American Publishers, and publishers' groups have criticized the project's inclusion of snippets of copyrighted works as willful infringement of copyright. Google claims its project represents a fair use because it is providing only bibliographic information (the equivalent of a card catalog) and snippets. Of note is the fact that many publishers (including those who are challenging the mass scanning projects) already partner with Google and provide digital versions of their publications, with the understanding that searchers will be directed to sites where they can purchase the books.

Criticisms of the Google project have focused on quality control (inadvertent pictures of the fingers of scanning equipment operators, lost text from books positioned incorrectly, etc.), insufficient description (metadata), and the difficulties presented in a project that is digitizing millions of books—thousands of books every day. Paul Duguid raises these concerns in "Inheritance and Loss: A Brief Survey of Google Books."[57] Others, for example, Barbara Quint, Anthony Grafton, and Lorcan Dempsey, see more opportunities than problems.[58] Dempsey suggests that the Google initiative is part of the "changing dynamic of discovery and delivery in a network environment."[59] He goes on to suggest that, through Google's assembled resources and indexing and linking capabilities, new relationships between items and content can be discovered. Further, the growth in digitized content creates new opportunities for more collective approaches to collection development and management. The mass digitization of printed cultural heritage has the potential to contribute to the public good in unprecedented ways.[60]

The Open Content Alliance (www.opencontentalliance.org), a nonprofit established in 2005, has sought to avoid many of the legal challenges directed at Google by digitizing only material that is in the public domain or has the copyright holders' authorization. One feature of the Open Content Alliance is the storage and maintenance of data in multiple repositories. Without the financial resources of Google and dependent on content contributors and donors, the Alliance is moving slowly to build a mass of scanned data. The limitations of such projects are not just financial—the percentage of titles not covered by copyright is extremely modest. Denise Troll Covey estimates that 95 percent of books ever printed are still in copyright, yet fewer than 3 percent are still in print.[61]

Many of the mass digitization projects are partnerships between libraries and commercial entities and involve complex contractual agreements. Peter B. Kaufman and Jeff Ubois recommend that libraries negotiate intensively with their commercial partners.[62] They also recommend seeking limited confidentiality so that libraries can offer advice to peers; more complete deliverables; more open access that can support innovative research and allow development of new applications; less restricted distribution; and responsible treatment of usage data to protect users' privacy.

Preservation Plans

Many libraries prepare a systematic preservation plan.[63] Plans vary in scale and complexity depending on the size and nature of the library. A comprehensive preservation plan prepares the library to deal with complex preservation challenges on an ongoing basis. Initially, it increases knowledge among library staff members of existing conditions and use issues, possible approaches, existing capabilities, and the financial and technical resources currently available. A preservation plan is also a political instrument. It can serve to raise awareness in the library and the parent organization about preservation problems and help develop a consensus on how to address them.

The first element of a preservation plan is a survey of the collection condition. This involves determining the extent to which all parts of the collection are at risk from acidic paper; embrittlement; loose or incomplete text blocks; deterioration of the text, image, or medium; damaged bindings; or lack of protective enclosures. A second component of a plan is a gathering of data on environmental conditions: temperature, relative humidity, cleanliness, potential exposure to pollution, excessive light, and pests; disaster preparedness; and staff and user education. It includes information about fire prevention, detection, and suppression systems and security measures. Identifying the protective measures in place allows the library to assess the degree to which collections are exposed to future deterioration and sudden damage.

Once librarians have an understanding of collection and environmental conditions, they can begin establishing preservation priorities. Priorities balance the importance of materials with treatment capacities within the context of available and potential funds and staffing. Strategies for selecting materials for preservation may include treating those materials at greatest risk, those that can be treated quickly and inexpensively, those that need a particular type of treatment, or those materials most important to the library.

A library looks at available and potential resources for preservation activities. This means reviewing available staff time, staff competencies, and on-site equipment and funding sources. Technical expertise and resources available locally and regionally are inventoried. Information about the condition of the collections, their environment, and potential risk is weighed against the resources and technical capabilities available to address the needs identified. The result is a systematic plan to meet preservation needs now and in the future.

Serial Cancellation and the Transition to Electronic-Only Access

Not too many years ago, serial cancellation meant canceling a subscription and relying on interlibrary loan for individual articles. This decision is still an important one facing many libraries as they cope with price increases. To this has been added an alternative, one that can be equally politically charged—canceling a print journal subscription and initiating access to the electronic version, or retaining the e-version only if the library had both formats.

The process of serial cancellation begins with a review that parallels that for other collection maintenance functions. Ideally, active serial subscriptions are reviewed regularly as part of ensuring that the collection continues to meet user needs and library goals and objectives. In reality, identifying serials to cancel has become an annual activity in many—perhaps most—libraries for at least the past fifteen years because of constant and rapid increases in serial prices in excess of budget increases. Although academic and research libraries have been hit hardest because of their heavy concentration of expensive scholarly journals, all libraries have experienced serial cost increases in excess of national inflation rates.

Other reasons lead libraries to cancel serials. A library may aim for a constant ratio between expenditures for serials and for monographs. Libraries may cancel titles because they seek to maintain expenditure ratios between disciplines or between user groups. For example, journals in the children's and young adult room do not cost as much or increase in price as rapidly as titles provided in the business section. Therefore, the library may opt to cancel more titles and set a higher dollar target when reviewing the business serials. The focus of the curriculum or the user community may make some titles less relevant. The library may have access to an online version and not perceive a need for a paper copy. A compelling reason to cancel a journal is declining quality or content that is no longer appropriate.

Librarians use many techniques to make the cancellation process as logical and defensible as possible. Every library needs policies and procedures to guide cancellations and to keep user communities informed and involved to the extent that is reasonable and practical. The same criteria (quality and appropriateness) that guide the selection of a journal or standing order are applied when considering it for cancellation. Use is a leading criterion. Use data may be available from circulation statistics, interlibrary loan requests, user surveys, and in-house use.[64] The difficulty with use studies is that many libraries do not circulate serials, and in-house use data are notoriously unreliable.

Use data often are combined with cost of the title to determine a cost-per-use figure. Very expensive titles that get little use do not provide the benefits to the library and its users that cheaper titles with heavy use do. Journals in some disciplines, typically in the humanities and social sciences, may be more cost effective. They are so low in price that subscribing to them may be cheaper than requesting them through interlibrary loan or document delivery.[65] Combining cost data with the number of pages or frequency of a publication is another way of looking at cost and benefit. Cost may be the first criterion considered when a library faces a budget-driven cancellation project.

Availability of serial titles within a consortium and through interlibrary loan can influence decisions. Libraries need to honor commitments made to partner libraries to retain titles and protect specific disciplines. Libraries first may cancel titles to which convenient access is available regionally or through an established cooperative delivery service. In many cases, commercial document delivery services and full-text online pay-per-use services have proven a viable and cost-effective alternative to local subscriptions in libraries.[66] Access via an electronic format, when canceling the paper subscription does not increase the cost of the electronic version, may be an option.

Librarians in academic libraries usually work closely with faculty when canceling serials. Canceling journals, like placing materials in storage and withdrawing items, has significant political implications. Many journal users in academic libraries remain oblivious to the extreme price increases that have haunted librarians for years; librarians need to bring this problem before their user communities repeatedly. Consultation can prevent serious cancellation mistakes, though it can open heated debates in academic libraries as faculty members defend the importance of serial titles in their particular specialty. Nevertheless, surveying constituents is important because it both solicits their input and informs them of the continuing need for cancellations to operate within available budgets.[67]

Librarians have been seeking an ideal way to combine data assembled during the review and consultation process. Several approaches, including using weighted formulas, have been described in the literature.[68] Use data often are the most heavily weighted element. Paul Metz and John Cosgriff recommend creating a serials decision database to track information collected.[69] An important benefit of having data readily at hand is being able to explain and justify cancellations to disgruntled users.

Canceling print subscriptions and moving to electronic-only may be an option. Richard K. Johnson and Judy Luther report that 60 percent of active peer-reviewed journals were available in electronic form in 2007.[70] Chandra Prabha reports that (on average) ARL member libraries had converted 36 percent of their journal subscriptions to electronic-only format by 2006, and this ratio continues to increase.[71] A contractual guarantee to access to subscribed issues if the e-journal subscription is canceled, if the journal ceases, or if the publisher goes out of existence is often the deciding factor in whether to cancel print and move to electronic-only. Without these contractual guarantees to archival or perpetual access, many libraries do not cancel print subscriptions, even if the savings gained in moving to electronic-only are substantial (e.g., reduced subscription cost, savings in shelf space, elimination of expenses for receipting, claiming, stack maintenance, and binding paper issues). Access via a journal aggregator service alone would not satisfy the requirement for perpetual access, since the aggregator as a third party usually does not hold permanent access to its constituent publisher's titles, and titles come and go with little or no notice.

Other typical criteria for retaining print subscriptions instead of moving to electronic-only may include these:

- user preference (e.g., print needed for particular research practices or methodologies, especially high-profile titles, or those that are heavily used in print format)
- content (e.g., content of print differs from that of e-versions; print has significant artifactual or aesthetic value; print journal functions better as a browsing journal or current awareness source; images and graphics unavailable or of poorer quality in e-journal)
- subscription model (e.g., online access based on continued print subscription)
- current availability (e.g., provider of e-journal technically unreliable or does not provide prompt technical support; electronic issue not made available promptly)
- cooperative resource sharing (e.g., contract does not permit interlibrary lending or document delivery services using e-format)
- consortial commitment (e.g., library agrees to retain print format as part of larger collaborative preservation effort)

The criteria that guide selection decisions for all materials and for e-content specifically are also considered.

Several options exist for perpetual access.[72] A publisher may guarantee access on its own website, though libraries have been reluctant to place their confidence in publishers, who do not have the same commitment to long-term preservation as libraries and are subject to the shifts in the changing marketplace. Some publishers have reached agreements with national libraries to preserve content. For example, Elsevier is partnering with the Koninklijke Bibliotheek, the national library of the Netherlands, through which the library is the official digital archive for Elsevier Science journals. If Elsevier ceases to make these journals available on a commercial basis, the Koninklijke Bibliotheek will provide remote access to the entire archive.

A library either individually or as part of a consortium may negotiate keeping and mounting content locally, but it faces the challenge of migrating and refreshing the data over time. The OhioLINK Electronic Journal Center contains more than 6,900 scholarly journal titles and is an optional service of OhioLINK for libraries in Ohio. OhioLINK intends to maintain this journal content as a permanent archive and has perpetual archival rights through the consortial licenses from all publishers except the American Chemical Society. The LOCKSS (Lots of Copies Keep Stuff Safe) program, originated at Stanford University, offers an open-source software appliance that allows libraries to collect, store, preserve, and provide access to their own, local copies of purchased content. Libraries manage their LOCKSS boxes and capture content from participating publishers. LOCKSS is a light archive, meaning that content is currently accessible, under the terms of applicable publisher agreements. CLOCKSS (Controlled LOCKS) is a membership organization that holds digital assets on behalf of the larger community. CLOCKSS is a dark archive, meaning that content is available only in the event of a "trigger event" (the publisher stops operations, ceases to publish a title, or no longer offers back issues, or the publisher's delivery platform suffers catastrophic and sustained failure).

Some publishers are establishing perpetual preservation agreements with Portico (www.portico.org).[73] The mission of Portico, a nonprofit service with library and publisher partners, is to preserve scholarly literature published in electronic form and to ensure that these materials remain accessible to future scholars, researchers, and students. In keeping with this mission, Portico established an agreement with the Koninklijke Bibliotheek in 2008 through which the library placed a copy of the Portico archive in a secure access- and climate-controlled facility, in essence a dark archive. Library partners pay Portico an annual archive support payment. Publisher partners provide Portico with the original source files of e-journals, and Portico normalizes the original source files to an archival format and assumes responsibility for future content migrations. When a title becomes unavailable from the publisher or any other source through a trigger event, Portico makes the content available to member libraries. The first trigger event was announced in late 2007, when the journal *Graft:*

Organ and Cell Transplantation, published by Sage, was removed from Sage's online offering and made accessible through Portico.

Project MUSE (http://muse.jhu.edu), a nonprofit collaboration between libraries, publishers, and the Milton S. Eisenhower Library at Johns Hopkins University, provides access to current and retrospective issues of scholarly journals in the humanities and social sciences. At the conclusion of each year during which a library subscribes to Project MUSE, it may request an archival digital file copy containing all the articles published online during the previous subscription year. Libraries, therefore, own the material from the electronic files to which they subscribe. Project MUSE has made a commitment to provide permanent maintenance and preservation of all the digital files in the MUSE database. All MUSE partner publishers are contractually bound to allow journal content published in MUSE to remain permanently in the database, even if they should discontinue their relationship with MUSE.

Collection Protection and Security

Collection protection is another collection management responsibility. This includes proper handling of items by staff members and users, appropriate environmental conditions, security against theft and mutilation, protection of electronic resources, and planning for and responding to disasters. Some libraries hold regular training for staff members, covering such topics as how to remove volumes from shelves, the importance of not shelving volumes too tightly, and the need to use approved supplies for simple mending. Libraries often run publicity campaigns to educate users in the proper care of library materials and to protect against food and drink near collections and computers.

A proper environment protects collections. Sound shelving and storage containers, moderate temperature and humidity with minimal fluctuations in each, cleanliness including pest control, and the avoidance of excessive light and ultraviolet radiation all support preservation. Ideal temperatures are 65–70° for general collections and 55–65° degrees for special collections and archives. Libraries generally make accommodations for personal comfort and increase temperatures slightly for areas in which users and collections share space. Optimum relative humidity is between 25 and 50 percent.

Protection against theft is the issue that comes most frequently to mind when considering collection security. The most famous book thief is Stephen Carrie Blumberg, who, when apprehended in 1990, had amassed nearly 25,000 volumes stolen during more than twenty years from 327 libraries across the United States.[74] People steal for different reasons—to build their own collections, to sell the items, because they are angry, to remove materials they find offensive. Both library patrons and staff members can be thieves. Theft and mutilation have legal implications under local and federal ordinances and laws. Libraries should work with their governing body and local law enforcement agencies when theft is suspected.

Several steps help protect libraries from theft. All holdings should be documented through a catalog or other means. All items should carry ownership markings, unless inappropriate to the items. The library should conduct regular inventories. The library should have limited entrances and exits with, ideally, some sort of monitoring. Book theft detection systems are common. Some libraries employ surveillance camera systems. Others hire security monitors. Some libraries require users to show identification and register when entering. Useful guidelines can be found in a document developed by the Association of College and Research Libraries and approved by the ALA.[75] Collections should be reviewed regularly to determine which materials should be transferred to special collections or to other more secure areas because of either value or vulnerability to mutilation. Rare book and special collections usually have more stringent security measures, such as excluding users from the stacks and prohibiting briefcases and bags in the reading room. The Rare Books and Manuscripts Section of the Association of College and Research Libraries has developed guidelines for the security of special collections.[76] These guidelines contain an appendix of organizations and electronic discussion lists to which thefts can be reported. Protecting against theft needs to be balanced with users' access to the collection and their privacy rights.

Mutilation is frequently not discovered until someone uses a damaged item. Mutilation can result when patrons remove pages because they do not want to make a photocopy, they want a high-quality illustration, they are censoring the collection, or they are making another type of personal statement. Protecting collections from mutilation involves many of the same procedures as protecting it against theft. Libraries have found that having good, convenient, inexpensive photocopy machines reduces collection damage. School library media centers and academic libraries may want to reach agreements with instructors regarding illustrative matter in submitted reports and papers; ideally, homework should not contain material cut from original books and journals. Only photocopies, digitally generated images, or illustrations created by the student should be acceptable.

Natural disasters—earthquakes, fires, floods, burst pipes and building leaks, hurricanes, tornados, volcanoes, vermin infestations, wind damage, chemical spills, and extended power failures—can be very costly. A 1997 flood at Colorado State University caused $100,000,000 in damages.[77] In the fall of 2005, Hurricane Katrina devastated libraries of all types in Louisiana and Mississippi.[78] Twenty-three public libraries in Louisiana were destroyed. Damage to the New Orleans Public Library system was estimated at $26–$30 million. Eight public and forty-three school libraries in Mississippi were destroyed or suffered catastrophic damage. University, college, and community college libraries were equally hard hit. Natural disaster cannot be prevented, but libraries are well served by knowing what to do when one strikes.

All libraries should have an up-to-date, comprehensive disaster preparedness plan.[79] This document, also called a disaster response plan, provides a policy and procedures for responding to emergencies and specifies priorities and techniques for salvaging different types of material if damaged by fire, flood, or other kinds of disasters. It lists who should be notified, what the chain of command is, who is responsible for which steps, where equipment and supplies (e.g., buckets, plastic sheeting, gloves, dust masks) are kept, and safety considerations. It provides contact information for services, which may include collection transport and rapid freezing, needed to respond to different conditions.

Ensuring security for electronic files and systems adds another dimension to collection protection. Issues of concern are protecting against unauthorized access, theft of resources, damage by hackers, viruses, unintentional damage, confidentiality of patron information, and ensuring availability of e-resources to legitimate users. Libraries may back up information resources and seek to negotiate replacement files from suppliers in the event of data destruction.

Several activities can help librarians protect their collections. A staff training program can address proper handling of library materials, monitoring security issues, and responding to emergencies. A security audit or risk assessment detects problem areas where the library and its collections are vulnerable. The library should have a clear reporting procedure and designated leader for each situation. An individualized disaster preparedness plan provides specific procedures for dealing with different crises. Although librarians can do much to minimize risk to collections, equally important is knowing how to react when problems develop.

Summary

Collection maintenance, or collection management, encompasses the decisions made about materials already selected by librarians. The criteria applied when initially selecting an item are revisited, and additional factors, primarily condition and use, are considered. Weeding is done to maximize space and to improve the library's collection and services. Titles may be weeded because of poor condition, decreased use, or lack of relevance to a changing user community. Items may be moved from one collection or location to another. They may be withdrawn and sold, donated to another library or agency, or destroyed. Storage is an option for materials that are still important though less frequently used, for those that must be retained for institutional reasons, and for those requiring protection from theft or excessive handling. Preservation decisions address how best to extend the useful life of materials as artifacts or to preserve their content for future users.

Reviewing materials for withdrawal, transfer, storage, preservation, and cancellation is an ongoing responsibility and best guided by library policies and specific criteria. Review can be conducted on macro and micro levels. Although some types of review are mandated by a crisis and must be handled rapidly and efficiently, continuous attention to collection maintenance is recommended. The CREW (continuous review, evaluation, and weeding) method speaks to the continuing nature of collection management. Decisions should be made within the context of cooperative agreements and local and regional resources. Consultation with other library units and staff members is important because the consequences of any decision affect others in the library. Consultation with user groups is equally important in order to make informed decisions sensitive to user priorities and to keep the user community informed. Collection maintenance decisions, like selection decisions, require a combination of objective data and sound subjective judgment.

Libraries preserve collections through careful handling, appropriate shelving, and clean and environmentally sound facilities. Simple mending and cleaning can be done in-house and can extend the life of items. Acidic paper and bindings are a major cause of deterioration in aging collections. Deacidification can neutralize the acidity but does not restore embrittled volumes. Conservation treatments preserve the item itself and should conform to best practices. Librarians turn to trained conservators to restore valuable, unique, and rare items. Replacement is an option if the item itself is not precious. Librarians can seek paper reprints and microfilm or digital surrogates from commercial publishers or look for a replacement on the out-of-print market. If the item cannot be replaced commercially, the librarian can choose to reformat the item as a photocopy, microfilm, or digital surrogate. All should conform to national standards for durability and permanence and comply with copyright law.

Cancellation of serials and standing orders has been a concern of librarians for more than twenty years. Rapid increases in prices that have been in excess of inflation and most library budgets have forced librarians to review and cancel subscriptions frequently and regularly. Academic and research libraries have faced the most difficulty because of their dependence on scholarly titles in scientific, technical, and medical fields. These areas have the most expensive titles and have seen the most extreme price increases, but all libraries are obligated to review subscriptions and standing orders within the context of priorities and available funds. Moving to electronic-only access to replace print journals and other print resources requires careful consideration of the criteria that guide all collection management decisions. Of particular concern are guarantees of perpetual access to the content if the contract for access is canceled or the publisher or vendor ceases to supply the title.

Protecting collections against theft and damage requires attention to library facilities and security measures. Monitoring users and the use they make of library materials should be continuous. Temperature, humidity, and light should be within recommended guidelines to preserve collections as long as possible. An important part of protecting collections is having a disaster response plan that outlines responsibilities and tasks in the event of a natural disaster.

Maintaining and managing a collection require personal attention, just as does building a collection. They are equally time consuming and integral to a high-quality collection. In a process similar to selecting materials to add to a collection, librarians consider materials and their continuing importance to the library's mission and user community. Collection management is expensive, both in staff time to make the decisions and implement them and in dollars spent to replace, repair, reformat, conserve, and store materials. It seeks to balance access to library resources with their protection. Collection management is a central part of the library's and its librarians' investment in the quality and responsiveness of its collections.

CASE STUDY

Beta College is located in a small midwestern town. Beta College Library contains more than 600,000 items including books, music scores, bound periodicals, sound recordings, videos, and electronic resources and offers access to many electronic journals through individual, consortial, and regional agreements, including titles in Project MUSE and JSTOR. The library has the option to store materials in a shared high-density facility. Materials can be paged from the facility and delivered within twenty-four hours. Beta College Library stacks are currently at 93 percent capacity, and more room is needed for growth. Michelle, the head of the library, has decided to either move 60,000 volumes to the shared storage facility or withdraw them from the collection to provide room for growth and to improve the appearance of the library. She has discussed this proposal with the college president, who supports it; the president is not willing to endorse expansion of the library and sees weeding the collection as a more attractive approach.

Michelle has asked Kevin, her collections coordinator, to develop a plan to move forward with removing approximately 60,000 volumes from the collection. She has told Kevin to develop the first phase of a plan, which will focus on bound serial volumes. After this first phase is completed, they will be able to estimate the number of monographic volumes that need to be weeded and determine how to move forward with that part of the collection.

Activity

Develop a plan for weeding bound volumes from the serials collection. The plan should have at least two components: (a) criteria to apply in decision making (remembering that you have two options—withdrawal or transfer to remote storage), and (b) communication and consultation with faculty. Criteria should explore the conditions and circumstances that will guide the decisions. The communication and consultation segment should identify how these activities will be handled, who will deliver the messages and engage in consultation, and what should be conveyed. Include a suggested time line. You are not expected to develop title lists because you do not have access to the library's catalog or the A-to-Z e-journal title list. You do not need to go into the details of how the processing is handled once decisions are made, although you should note the steps involved in general terms.

Note: The first edition's case study and associated activity that relate to the information provided in this chapter are reproduced as a supplementary resource at www.ala.org/editions/extras/Johnson09720.

Notes

1. Will Manley, "The Manley Arts: If I Called This Column 'Weeding,' You Wouldn't Read It," *Booklist* 92 (March 1, 1996), 1108.

2. Donna J. Baumbach and Linda L. Miller, *Less Is More: A Practical Guide to Weeding School Library Collections* (Chicago: American Library Association, 2006), 3.

3. Nicholson Baker, "The Author vs. the Library," *New Yorker* 72, no. 31 (Oct. 14, 1996): 50–62; and "A Couple of Codicils about San Francisco," *American Libraries* 30, no. 3 (1999): 35–36.

4. Michael Rogers and Norman Odor, "Spectre of Baker Hangs over UNM?" *Library Journal*, June 15, 2001, www.libraryjournal.com/article/CA85295.html.

5. Terrence C. Miltner and Gordon Flagg, "10,000 Books Found in Abandoned East St. Louis Library," *American Libraries* 35, no. 9 (2004): 13.

6. "Abstracts of and Extracts from Reports," *Library Journal* 8 (1883): 257.

7. Loriene Roy, "Weeding," in Allen Kent, ed., *Encyclopedia of Library and Information Science*, vol. 54, suppl. 15, 352–98 (New York: Dekker, 1994).

8. Kenneth J. Brough, *Scholar's Workshop: Evolving Conceptions of Library Service*, Illinois Contributions to Librarianship no. 5 (Urbana: University of Illinois, 1953).

9. Juris Dilevko and Lisa Gottlieb, "Weed to Achieve: A Fundamental Part of the Public Library Mission?" *Library Collections, Acquisitions, and Technical Services* 27, no. 1 (2003): 73–96.

10. Robert D. Stueart, "Weeding of Library Materials—Politics and Policies," *Collection Management* 7, no. 2 (1985): 49.

11. Osburn, "Collection Management," 41.

12. Joseph P. Segal, *Evaluating and Weeding Collections in Small and Medium-Sized Public Libraries: The CREW Method* (Chicago: American Library Association, 1980); Belinda Boon, *The CREW Method: Expanded Guidelines for Collection Evaluation and Weeding for Small and Medium-Sized Public Libraries* (Austin: Texas State Library, 1995).

13. Stanley J. Slote, *Weeding Library Collections: Library Weeding Methods*, 4th ed. (Littleton, Colo.: Libraries Unlimited, 1997).

14. Allen Kent et al., *Use of Library Materials: The University of Pittsburgh Study* (New York: Marcel Dekker, 1979).

15. Ferdinand F. Leimkuhler, "The Bradford Distribution," *Journal of Documentation* 23 (Sept. 1967): 199; Richard W. Trueswell, "A Quantitative Measure of User Circulation Requirements and Its Possible Effect on Stack Thinning and Multiple Copy Determination," *American Documentation* 16 (Jan. 1965): 20–25; and "Some Behavioral Patterns of Library Users: The 80/20 Rule," *Wilson Library Bulletin* 43 (1969): 458–61.

16. Richard W. Trueswell, "Determining the Optimal Number of Volumes for a Library's Core Collection," *Libri* 16 (1966): 58–59.

17. Evan St. Lifer and Michael Rogers, "City Rebukes Philadelphia Library on Weeding Practices," *Library Journal* 122 (May 15, 1997): 12.

18. Paul Metz and Caryl Gray, "Public Relations and Library Weeding," *Journal of Academic Librarianship* 31, no. 3 (2005): 273–79.

19. Association of College and Research Libraries, Rare Books and Manuscripts Section, "Guidelines on the Selection and Transfer of Materials from General Collections to Special Collections" (Feb. 2007, Draft Revision), www.ala.org/ala/acrl/acrlstandards/selectransfer.cfm.

20. Dan C. Hazen, "Selecting for Storage: Local Problems, Local Responses, and an Emerging Common Challenge," *Library Resources and Technical Services* 44, no. 4 (2000): 176.

21. David Block, "'Remote Storage in Research Libraries: A Microhistory," *Library Resources and Technical Services* 44, no. 4 (2000): 184–89.

22. Quoted by Kenneth I. Brough, *Scholars Workshop: Evolving Conceptions of Libraries Services*, Illinois Contributions to Librarianship no. 5 (Urbana: University of Illinois, 1953), 125.

23. Lizanne Payne, "Library Storage Facilities and the Future of Print Collections in North America" (Dublin, Ohio: OCLC, 2007), www.oclc.org/programs/publications/reports/2007-01.pdf, 22.

24. Heritage Preservation, "Collections Storage," in *A Public Trust at Risk: The Heritage Health Index Report on the State of American's Collections*, 57–60 (Washington, D.C.: Heritage Preservation), www.heritagepreservation.org/HHI/HHIchp6.pdf.

25. Evaristo Jiménez-Contreras et al., "A Bibliometric Model for Journal Discarding Policy at Academic Libraries," *Journal of the American Society for Information Science and Technology* 57, no 2 (2006): 198–207. Despite the title, this article proposes a bibliometric model for the removal of journal volumes to off-site storage.

26. Danuta A. Nitecki and Curtis Kendrick, eds. *Library Off-Site Shelving: Guide for High-Density Facilities* (Englewood, Colo.: Libraries Unlimited, 2001); Payne, *Library Storage Facilities*; Bernard F. Reilly Jr., *Developing Print Repositories: Models for Shared Preservation and Access* (Washington, D.C.: Council on Library and Information Resources, 2003).

27. Willis E. Bridegam, *A Collaborative Approach to Collection Storage: The Five-College Library Depository* (Washington, D.C.: Council on Library and Information Resources, 2001); Scott Seaman, "Collaborative Collection Management in a High-Density Storage Facility," *College and Research Libraries* 66, no. 1 (2005) p. 20–27; David Weeks and Ron Chepesiuk, "The Harvard Model and the Rise of Shared Storage Facilities," *Resource Sharing and Information Networks* 16, no. 2 (2002): 159–68.

28. Payne, *Library Storage Facilities.*

29. Yale University, Library Shelving Facility, "Final Report of the Working Group" (Oct. 1996), www.library.yale.edu/Administration/Shelving/historical1.html.

30. Stephanie S. Atkins and Cherié L. Weible, "Lost Is Found: The Impact of a High-Density Shelving Facility on a Library's Collection," *Collection Management* 31, no. 3 (2006): 15–32.

31. See Robert M. Hayes, "Making Access Allocation Decisions," in *Strategic Management for Academic Libraries: A Handbook* (Westport, Conn.: Greenwood, 1993), 169–87; Hur-Li Lee, "The Library Space Problem: Future Demand, and Collection Control," *Library Resources and Technical Services* 37, no. 2 (1993): 147–66; Wendy P. Lougee, "Remote Shelving Comes of Age: Storage Collection Management at the University of Michigan," *Collection Management* 16, no. 2 (1992): 93–107.

32. Michael Gorman, *Our Enduring Values: Librarianship in the Twenty-first Century* (Chicago: American Library Association, 2000), 58.

33. American Library Association, "American Library Association Preservation Policy" (2001), www.ala.org/ala/alctscontent/pubsbucket/webpublications/alctspreservation/alapreservationp/alapreservation.cfm.

34. Chandru J. Shahani and William K. Wilson, "Preservation of Libraries and Archives," *American Scientist* 75 (May/June 1987): 240–51.

35. Robert M. Hayes, "Analysis of the Magnitude, Costs, and Benefits of the Preservation of Research Library Books," working paper (Washington, D.C.: Council on Library Resources, 1985).

36. Terry Sanders, *Slow Fires: On the Preservation of the Human Record* [video recording] (Santa Monica, Calif.: American Film Foundation, 1987).

37. *American National Standard for Information Sciences—Permanence of Paper for Printed Publications and Documents in Libraries and Archives*, ANSI Z39.48-1992 (Gaithersburg, Md.: National Institute of Standards and Technology, 1992).

38. Michele V. Cloonan, "Mass Deacidification in the 1990s," *Rare Books and Manuscripts Librarianship* 5, no. 2 (1990): 95–103.

39. Among these are American Institute for Conservation of Historic and Artistic Works (http://aic.stanford.edu); Preservation and Reformatting Section of the Association for Library Collections and Technical Services (www.ala.org/ala/alcts/sections/preservation/default.cfm); and several regional conservation centers, such as the Northeast Document Conservation Center in Massachusetts (www.nedecc.org).

40. Patricia Battin, "Substitution: The American Experience," typescript, lecture in Oxford Library Seminars, "Preserving Our Library Heritage," February 25, 1992, 9.

41. Nicholson Baker, "Deadline: The Author's Desperate Bid to Save America's Past," *New Yorker* 76, no. 29 (July 24, 2000): 42–61; and his *Double Fold: Libraries and the Assault on Paper* (New York: Random House, 2001).

42. Robert Darnton, "The Great Book Massacre," review of *Double Fold: Libraries and the Assault on Paper*, by Nicholson Baker, *New York Review of Books* 48 (April 26, 2001): 16–19.

43. Richard J. Cox, *Vandals in the Stacks? A Response to Nicholson Baker's Assault on Libraries*, Contributions in Librarianship and Information Science no. 98 (Westport, Conn.: Greenwood, 2002), offers one of many thoughtful responses to Baker.

44. Mike Casey and Bruce Gordon, *Sound Directions: Best Practices for Audio Preservation* (Bloomington, Ind.: Trustees of Indiana University; Boston: President and Fellows of Harvard University, 2007), www.dlib.indiana.edu/projects/sounddirections/papersPresent/index.shtml. The Northeast Document Conservation Center offers several leaflets addressing specific formats; see www.nedcc.org/resources/leaflets.list.php.

45. RLG/OCLC Working Group on Digital Archive Attributes, *Trusted Digital Repositories: Attributes and Responsibilities* (Mountain View, Calif.: RLG, 2002), www.oclc.org/programs/ourwork/past/trustedrep/repositories.pdf.

46. Raym Crow, "The Case for Institutional Repositories: A SPARC Position Paper" (Washington, D.C.: Scholarly Publishing and Academic Resources Coalition, 2002), www.arl.org/sparc/bm%7Edoc/ir_final_release_102.pdf.

47. Susan L. Tolbert, "Preservation in American Public Libraries: A Contradiction in Terms?" *Public Libraries* 36 (July/Aug. 1997): 236–45.

48. National Information Standards Organization, "Library Binding: An American National Standard," ANSI/NISO/LBI Z39.78-2000 (Bethesda, Md.: NISO, 2000), www.niso.org/kst/reports/standards?step=2&gid=None&project_key=20b6444f170a5a8ced24d9a69d8f65151f9087ce.

49. Jessica Litman, *Digital Copyright* (Amherst, N.Y.: Prometheus, 2001), 112.

50. Library of Congress, U.S. Copyright Office, *Report on Orphan Works: A Report to the Register of Copyrights* (Jan. 2006), www.copyright.gov/orphan/orphan-report.pdf.

51. See American Library Association, Washington Office, Issues, Copyright, www.ala.org/ala/washoff/woissues/copyrightb/copyright.cfm.

52. Daniel Greenstein and Suzanne E. Thorin, *The Digital Library: A Biography* (Washington, D.C.: Council on Library and Information Resources, 2002), www.clir.org/pubs/abstract/pub109abst.html.

53. Digital Library Federation, "Benchmark for Faithful Digital Reproductions of Monographs and Serials, Version 1 (Dec. 2002)," www.diglib.org/standards/bmarkfin.htm.

54. Registry of Digital Masters, http://purl.oclc.org/DLF/collections/reg/OCLCservice.

55. Stephen G. Nichols and Abby Smith, *The Evidence in Hand: The Report of the Task Force on the Artifact in Library Collections* (Washington, D.C.: Council on Library and Information Resources, 2001), www.clir.org/pubs/abstract/pub103abst.html.

56. The full complaint—*The McGraw-Hill Companies, Inc., Pearson Education, Inc., Penguin Group (USA) Inc., Simon and Schuster, Inc., and John Wiley and Sons, Inc., Plaintiffs, v. Google, Inc., Defendant*, filed in October 2005—is available at http://publishers.org/main/Copyright/attachments/40_McGraw-Hill_v_Google.pdf; see also Jeffrey Toobin, "Google's Moon Shot: The Quest for the University Library," *New Yorker* 82, no. 48 (Feb. 2, 2005): 30–35, and Johnathan Band, "The Google Library Project: Both Sides of the Story," *Plagiary: Cross-Disciplinary Studies in Plagiarism, Fabrication, and Falsification* 2, no. 2 (2006): 1–17.

57. Paul Duguid, "Inheritance and Loss? A Brief Survey of Google Books," *First Monday* 12, no. 8 (2007), www.uic.edu/htbin/cgiwrap/bin/ojs/index.php/fm/article/view/1972/1847.

58. Barbara Quint, "Who the Heck Is Tristram Shandy? Or What's Not Wrong with Google Book Search?" *Information Today* 24, no. 9 (2007): 7–8; Anthony Grafton, "Future Reading: Digitization and Its Discontents," *New Yorker* 83, no. 34 (Nov. 5, 2007): 50–54; Lorcan Dempsey, "Systemic Change: CIC and Google," *Lorcan Dempsey's Weblog*, June 6, 2007, http://orweblog.oclc.org/archives/001366.html.

59. Dempsey, "Systemic Change."

60. See Richard K. Johnson, "In Google's Broad Wake: Taking Responsibility for Shaping the Global Digital Library," *ARL: A Bimonthly Report*, no. 250 (Feb. 2007): 1–15, for an exploration of what libraries can and should do in shaping mass digitization initiatives; see also Oya Y. Rieger, *Preservation in the Age of Large-Scale Digitization: A White Paper* (Washington, D.C.: Council on Library and Information Resources, 2008), www.clir.org/pubs/abstract/pub141abst.html.

61. Denise Troll Covey, *Acquiring Copyright Permission to Digitize and Provide Open Access to Books* (Washington, D.C.: Digital Library Federation and Council on Library and Information Resources, 2005), www.clir.org/pubs/reports/pub134/pub134grey.pdf.

62. Peter B. Kaufman and Jeff Ubois, "Good Terms—Improving Commercial-Noncommercial Partnerships for Mass Digitization: A Report Prepared by Intelligent Television for RLG Programs, OCLC Programs and Research," *D-Lib Magazine* 13. nos. 11/12 (2007), www.dlib.org/dlib/november07/kaufman/11kaufman.html.

63. The following manual is a useful planning tool: *Preservation Planning Program: An Assisted Self-Study Manual for Libraries*, developed by Pamela W. Darling, with Duane E. Webster; revised by Jan Merrill-Oldham and Jutta Reed-Scott (Washington, D.C.: Association of Research Libraries, 1993).

64. Carol French and Eleanor Pollard, "Serials Usage Study in a Public Library," *Public Library Quarterly* 16, no. 4 (1997): 45–53; John Gallagher, Kathleen Bauer, and Daniel M. Dollar, "Evidence-Based Librarianship: Utilizing Data from All Available Sources to Make Judicious Print Cancellation Decisions," *Library Collections, Acquisitions, and Technical Services* 29, no. 2 (2005): 169–79; Halcyon R. Enssle and Michelle L. Wilde, "So You Have to Cancel Journals? Statistics That Help," *Library Collections, Acquisitions, and Technical Services* 26, no. 3 (2002): 259–81.

65. Dorothy Milne and Bill Tiffany, "A Survey of the Cost-Effectiveness of Serials: A Cost-Per-Use Method and Its Results," *Serials Librarian* 19, nos. 3/4 (1991): 137–49; Brinley Franklin, "Managing the Electronic Collection with Cost per Use Data," *IFLA Journal* 31, no. 3 (2005): 241–48.

66. Richard P. Widdicombe, "Eliminating All Journal Subscriptions Has Freed Our Customers to Seek the Information They Really Want and Need: The Result—More Access, not Less," *Science and Technology Libraries* 14, no. 1 (1993): 3–13.

67. Paul Metz, "Thirteen Steps to Avoiding Bad Luck in a Serials Cancellation Project," *Journal of Academic Librarianship* 18, no. 2 (1992): 76–82.

68. Betty E. Tucker, "The Journal Deselection Project: The LSUMC-S Experience," *Library Acquisitions: Practice and Theory* 19, no. 3 (1995): 313–20; Paul Metz and John Cosgriff, "Building a Comprehensive Serials Decision Database at Virginia Tech," *College and Research Libraries* 61, no. 4 (2000): 324–34.

69. Metz and Cosgriff, "Building a Comprehensive Serials Decision Database."

70. Richard K. Johnson and Judy Luther, "The E-Only Tipping Point for Journals: What's Ahead in the Print-to-Electronic Transition Zone" (Washington, D.C.: Association of Research Libraries, 2007), www.arl.org/bm~doc/Electronic_Transition.pdf.

71. Chandra Prabha, "Shifting from Print to Electronic Journals in ARL University Libraries," *Serials Review* 33, no. 1 (2007): 4–13.

72. Anne R. Kenney et al., *E-Journal Archiving Metes and Bounds: A Survey of the Landscape* (Washington, D.C.: Council on Library and Information Resources, 2006), www .clir.org/pubs/reports/pub138/pub138.pdf; Eun G. Park, "Perspectives on Access to Electronic Journals for Long-Term Preservation," *Serials Review* 33, no. 1 (2007): 22–25.

73. Eileen Gifford Fenton, "An Overview of Portico: An Electronic Archiving Service," *Serials Review* 32, no. 2 (2006): 81–86.

74. Susan M. Allen, "The Blumberg Case: A Costly Lesson for Librarians," *AB Bookman's Weekly* 88 (Sept. 2, 1991): 769–73; Philip Weiss, "The Book Thief: A True Tale of Bibliomania," *Harper's Magazine* 288, no. 1724 (1994): 37–56.

75. Association of College and Research Libraries, "Guidelines Regarding Thefts in Libraries" (approved by ACRL and ALA, Jan. 2003), www.ala.org/ala/acrl/acrlstandards/ guidelinesregardingthefts.cfm.

76. Association of College and Research Libraries, Rare Books and Manuscripts Section, "Guidelines for the Security of Rare Books, Manuscripts, and Other Special Collections," *College and Research Libraries News* 67, no. 7 (2006): 426–33.

77. "Flood Toll at Colorado State Could Reach $100 Million," *American Libraries* 28, no. 8 (1997): 16.

78. Tom Clareson and Jane S. Long, "Libraries in the Eye of the Storm: Lessons Learned from Hurricane Katrina," *American Libraries* 37, no. 7 (2006): 38–41; Jamie Ellis, "Lessons Learned: The Recovery of a Research Collection after Hurricane Katrina," *Collection Building* 26, no. 4 (2007): 108–11; "Hurricane Katrina Damage: A Summary," *Mississippi Libraries* 69, no. 4 (2005): 93–95.

79. A simple template for developing an emergency response plan, prepared by Karen E. Brown, is available through the Northeast Document Conservation Center. See "Worksheet for Outlining a Disaster Plan" (2007), www.nedcc.org/resources/ leaflets/3Emergency_Management/04DisasterPlanWorksheet.php.

Suggested Readings

Ackerson, Linda G. "Is Age an Appropriate Criterion for Moving Journals to Storage?" *Collection Management* 26, no. 3 (2001): 63–76.

Alire, Camila, ed. *Library Disaster Planning and Recovery Handbook.* New York: Neal-Schuman, 2000.

Baird, Brian J. *Preservation Strategies for Small Academic and Public Libraries.* Lanham, Md.: Scarecrow, 2003.

Baker, Nicholson. *Double Fold: Libraries and the Assault on Paper.* New York: Random, 2001.

Balloffet, Nelly, and Jenny Hille. *Preservation and Conservation for Libraries and Archives.* Chicago: American Library Association, 2005.

Banks, Julie. "Weeding Book Collections in the Age of the Internet." *Collection Building* 21, no. 3 (2002): 113–19.

Banks, Paul, and Roberta Pilette, eds. *Preservation: Issues and Planning.* Chicago: American Library Association, 2000.

Baumbach, Donna J., and Linda L. Miller. *Less Is More: A Practical Guide to Weeding School Library Collections.* Chicago: American Library Association, 2006.

Bluh, Pamela. *Managing Electronic Serials.* ALCTS Papers on Library Technical Services and Collections no. 9. Chicago: American Library Association, 2001.

Boon, Belinda. *The CREW Method: Expanded Guidelines for Collection Evaluation and Weeding for Small and Medium-Sized Public Libraries.* Austin: Texas State Library, 1995.

Borghoff, Uwe, et al. *Long-Term Preservation of Digital Documents: Principles and Practices.* Berlin: New York Springer, 2006.

Bracke, Marianne Stowell, and Jim Martin. "Developing Criteria for the Withdrawal of Print Content Available Online." *Collection Building* 24, no. 2 (2005): 61–64.

Bradford, Jane T. "What's Coming Off the Shelves? A Reference Use Study Analyzing Print Reference Sources Used in a University Library." *Journal of Academic Librarianship* 31, no. 6 (2005): 546–58.

Building a National Strategy for Digital Preservation: Issues in Digital Media Archiving. Washington, D.C.: Council on Library and Information Resources and Library of Congress, 2002. www.clir.org/pubs/reports/pub106/contents.html.

Bushing, Mary, and Elaine Peterson. "Weeding Academic Libraries: Theory into Practice." *Advances in Collection Development and Resource Management* 1 (1995): 61–78.

Calvi, Elise, et al. *The Preservation Manager's Guide to Cost Analysis.* Chicago: Association for Library Collections and Technical Services, 2006.

Caplan, Priscilla, ed. "The Preservation of Digital Materials." [special issue] *Library Technology Reports* 44, no. 2 (2008).

Carey, Ronadin, Stephen Elfstrand, and Renee Hijleh. "An Evidenced-Based Approach for Gaining Faculty Acceptance in a Serials Cancellation Project." *Collection Management* 30, no. 2 (2005): 59–72.

Center, Clark, and Donnelly Lancaster. *Security in Special Collections.* SPEC Kit 284. Washington, D.C.: Association of Research Libraries, 2004.

Colson, Jeannie. "Determining Use of an Academic Library Reference Collection: Report of a Study." *Reference and User Services Quarterly* 47, no. 2 (2007): 168–75.

Cravey, Pamela J. *Protecting Library Staff, Users, Collections, and Facilities: A How-to-Do-It Manual for Librarians.* How-to-Do-It Manuals for Librarians no. 103. New York: Neal-Schuman, 2001.

Curry, Ann, Susanna Flodin, and Kelly Matheson. "Theft and Mutilation of Library Materials: Coping with Biblio-Bandits." *Library and Archival Security* 15, no. 2 (2000): 9–26.

Davis, Vivian R. "Weeding the Library Media Center Collection." *School Library Media Activities Monthly* 17, no. 7 (2001): 26–28.

Deardorff, Thomas C., and Gordon J. Aamot. *Remote Shelving Services.* SPEC Kit 295. Washington, D.C.: Association of Research Libraries, 2006.

Deegan, Marilyn, and Simon Tanner, eds. *Digital Preservation.* London: Facet, 2006.

Dillon, Ken. "Maintaining Collection Viability." In *Collection Management for School Libraries,* edited by Joy McGregor, Ken Dillon, and James Henri, 225–44. Lanham, Md.: Scarecrow, 2003.

Drewes, Jeanne, and Julie A. Page, eds. *Promoting Preservation Awareness in Libraries: A Sourcebook for Academic, Public, School, and Special Collections.* Westport, Conn.: Greenwood, 1997.

Eells, Linda. "Born-Digital Agricultural Resources: Archives and Issue." *IAALD Quarterly Bulletin* 52, nos. 3/4 (2007): 67–82.

Fenner, Audrey. "Library Book Sales: A Cost-Benefit Analysis." *Library Collections, Acquisitions, and Technical Services* 29, no. 2 (2005): 149–68.

Franklin, Brinley. "Managing the Electronic Collection with Cost per Use Data." *IFLA Journal* 31, no. 3 (2005): 241–48.

Frase, Rose M., and Barbara Salit-Mischel. "Right-Sizing the Reference Collection." *Public Libraries* 46, no. 1 (2007): 40–44.

Gallagher, John, Kathleen Bauer, and Daniel M. Dollar. "Evidenced-Based Librarianship: Utilizing Data from All Available Sources to Make Judicious Print Cancellation Decisions." *Library Collections, Acquisitions, and Technical Services* 29, no. 2 (2005): 169–79.

Gorman, G. E., and Sydney J. Shep. *Preservation Management for Libraries, Archives and Museums.* London: Facet, 2006.

Gwinnett County Public Library. *Weeding Manual.* 2nd ed. Chicago: American Library Association, 2002.

Heritage Preservation. *Emergency Response and Salvage Wheel.* Washington, D.C.: American Heritage, 2005.

———. *Field Guide to Emergency Response.* Washington, D.C.: American Heritage, 2006.

Hickey, C. David. "Serials 'Derelegation' from Remote Storage." *Collection Building* 18, no. 4 (1999): 153–60.

Higginbotham, Barbra Buckner, and Judith W. Wild. *The Preservation Program Blueprint.* Frontiers of Access to Library Materials no. 6. Chicago: American Library Association, 2001.

Intner, Sheila S. "Weeding, Collection Development, and Preservation." *Technicalities* 26, no. 3 (2006): 1, 14–18.

Jaguszewski, Janice M., and Laura K. Probst. "The Impact of Electronic Resources on Serial Cancellations and Remote Storage Decision in Academic Research Libraries." *Library Trends* 48, no. 4 (2000): 799–820.

Johnson, Richard K., and Judy Luther. "The E-Only Tipping Point for Journals: What's Ahead in the Print-to-Electronic Transition Zone." Washington, D.C.: Association for Research Libraries, 2007. www.arl.org/bm~doc/Electronic_Transition.pdf.

Jones, Maggie, and Neil Beagrie. *Preservation Management of Digital Materials: A Handbook.* London: British Library for Resource, Council for Museums, Archives and Libraries, 2001. The online version of the handbook is being maintained and updated by the Digital Preservation Coalition and is freely available. www .dpconline.org/graphics/handbook/index.html.

Kahn, Miriam B. *Disaster Response and Planning for Libraries.* Chicago: American Library Association, 2002.

———. *The Library Security and Safety Guide to Prevention, Planning, and Response.* Chicago: American Library Association, 2008.

Kerby, Romana. "Weeding Your Collection." *School Library Media Activities Monthly* 18, no. 6 (2004): 22–24.

Lambert, Dennis K., et al. *Guide to Review of Library Collections: Preservation, Storage, and Withdrawal.* 2nd ed. Collection Management and Development Guides no. 9. Lanham, Md.: Scarecrow, for the Association for Library Collections and Technical Services, 2002.

Lavoie, Brian F. "The Fifth Blackbird: Some Thoughts on Economically Sustainable Digital Preservation." *D-Lib Magazine* 14, nos. 3/4 (2008), www.dlib.org/dlib/march08/lavoie/03lavoie.html.

———. "The Incentives to Preserve Digital Materials: Roles, Scenarios, and Economic Decision-Making." Dublin, Ohio: OCLC, 2003. www.oclc.org/research/projects/digipres/incentives-dp.pdf.

Library of Congress. "The Deterioration and Preservation of Paper: Some Essential Facts" (Oct. 18, 2006). www.loc.gov/preserv/deterioratebrochure.html.

Long, Jane S. *Field Guide to Emergency Response: A Vital Tool for Cultural Institutions.* Washington, D.C.: Heritage Preservation, 2006.

Merrill-Oldham, Jan, and Paul Parisi. *Guide to the ANSI/NISO/LBI Standard for Library Binding.* [rev. ed.] Chicago: American Library Association, 2008.

Miller-Francisco, Emily. "Managing Electronic Resources in a Time of Shrinking Budgets." *Library Collections, Acquisitions, and Technical Services* 27, no. 4 (2003): 507–12.

Mugridge, Rebecca. *Managing Digitization Activities.* SPEC Kit 294. Washington, D.C.: Association of Research Libraries, 2006.

Ogden, Sherelyn, ed. *Preservation of Library and Archival Materials: A Manual.* 3rd ed. Andover, Mass.: Northeast Document Conservation Center, 1999.

Park, Eun G. "Perspectives on Access to Electronic Journals for Long-Term Preservation." *Serials Review* 33, no. 1 (2007): 22–25.

Reiger, Oya Y. *Preservation in the Age of Large-Scale Digitization: A White Paper.* Washington, D.C.: Council on Library and Information Resources, 2008. www.clir.org/pubs/abstract/pub141abst.html.

Rupp-Serrano, Karen, Sarah Robbins, and Danielle Cain. "Canceling Print Serials in Favor of Electronic: Criteria for Decision Making." *Library Collections, Acquisitions, and Technical Services* 26, no. 4 (2002): 369–78.

Schonfeld, Roger C. "Getting from Here to There, Safely: Library Strategic Planning for the Transition Away from Print Journals." *Serials Librarian* 52, nos. 1/2 (2007): 183–89.

Sitts, Maxine K, ed. *Handbook for Digital Projects: A Management Tool for Preservation and Access.* Andover, Mass.: Northeast Document Conservation Center, 2000.

The State of Digital Preservation: An International Perspective. Washington, D.C.: Council on Library and Information Resources, 2002. www.clir.org/pubs/reports/pub107/contents.html.

Thomas, Charles F. "Preservation Management: Something Old, Something New." In *Collection Management*, edited by G. E. Gorman, 365–80. International Yearbook of Library and Information Management, 2000–2001. London: Library Association Publishing, 2000.

Tyler, David C., and Brian L. Pytlik Zillig. "Caveat Relocator: A Practical Relocation Proposal to Save Space and Promote Electronic Resources." *Technical Services Quarterly* 21, no. 1 (2003): 17–29.

Wellheiser, Johanna G., and Nancy E. Gwinn, eds. *Preparing for the Worst, Planning for the Best: Protecting Our Cultural Heritage from Disaster: Proceedings of a Special IFLA Conference Held in Berlin in July 2003.* IFLA Publications no. 111. Munich: K. G. Saur, 2005.

Wellheiser, Johanna G., and Jude Scott. *An Ounce of Prevention: Integrated Disaster Planning for Archives, Libraries, and Record Centres.* 2nd ed. Lanham, Md.: Scarecrow, and Canadian Archives Foundation, 2002.

Williams, Roy. "Weeding Library Collections: Conundrums and Contradictions." In *Collection Management,* edited by G. E. Gorman, 339–61. International Yearbook of Library and Information Management, 2000–2001. London: Library Association Publishing, 2000.

Wilson, A. Paula. "Weeding the E-Book Collection." *Public Libraries* 43, no. 3 (2004): 158–59.

CHAPTER SIX

Marketing, Liaison, and Outreach Activities

Every library that serves a constituency seeks to build collections and develop services to match its service or user community, within the constraints of its financial resources and consistent with its mission. The challenge facing collection development librarians is learning about and keeping current with users' changing needs, wants, and demands in order to develop collections and services in response. To be truly effective, collection development must consider future needs, not simply the needs of today's most frequent or vocal users. This chapter defines marketing concepts, explores them in the library context, and introduces suggested best practices for marketing, liaison, and outreach.

What Is Marketing?

Marketing is the process of determining the user communities' wants and need, developing the products and services in response, and encouraging users (i.e., consumers) and potential users to make use of the products and services. Regular communication with clientele is essential for gathering the information needed both to perform routine collection development and management activities and to plan for the future. Regular communication, formal and informal, is equally fundamental for sharing information about the library—new acquisitions, new programs and services, successes, problems, and constraints. Sharon L. Baker and Karen L. Wallace write, "In essence, marketing library collections involves using strategic planning techniques to both anticipate and respond to the short- and long-term collection-related needs and desires of the individuals and groups whom the library serves."[1] Regardless of library type, understanding the library's users, governing and funding bodies, community leaders, and administrators and consulting with these groups are essential responsibilities of librarians.

Liaison and *outreach* are terms that describe aspects of the same activity—communication or linkages with the library's community to share and gain information. Communication is a two-way enterprise. Librarians need to learn about and listen to their constituents' concerns and ideas as well as share information. Academic libraries tend to use *liaison* to refer to communication with their constituents. Liaison is communication for establishing and maintaining mutual understanding and cooperation. The "Guidelines for Liaison Work in Managing Collections and Services" developed by the ALA Reference and User Services Association explains liaison work as "the process by which librarians involve the library's clientele in the assessment and satisfaction of collection needs," which "enables the library to communicate its collection policies, services, and needs to its clientele and to enhance the library's public relations."[2]

Public and school librarians more commonly use the term *outreach* to describe the act of reaching out or extending services beyond current or usual limits. Part of outreach is informing constituents about the library's collections and services, especially those for special groups. Such targeted groups may be people who are homebound or visually impaired, preschool children, older adults, small business owners, and so forth. The ALA Office for Literacy and Outreach Services offers a website (www.ala.org/ala/olos/literacyoutreach.cfm) that provides resources to help reach various targeted, traditionally underserved populations. As librarians come in contact with users through the promotion and delivery of collections and services, they gain information that can translate user needs and suggestions into responsive collections and services.

Marketing as a term and a concept is significant in libraries of all types, as is reflected in the number of publications on marketing, outreach, liaison activities, public relations, and advocacy that have appeared in the past few years. Much of the attention focuses on how to reach users and potential users effectively and how to make clear what the library has to offer—its value. Helping user communities, stakeholders, and funders understand libraries as both a common good (shared and beneficial for members of a community) and a public good (one that is not diminished by use) is of increasing importance. Doing this well depends on understanding the community and determining the products and services to develop and then promote. Much of the outreach and liaison work librarians do includes tasks traditionally associated with marketing, and all librarians can benefit from knowing basic marketing concepts.

The American Marketing Association adopted a new definition of marketing in the fall of 2007: "Marketing is the activity, set of institutions, and processes for creating, communicating, delivering, and exchanging offerings that have value for customers, clients, partners, and society at large."[3] In a library context, the aim of marketing is to satisfy the library user and achieve a set of articulated goals, which may be increased use, community support, more patrons, a larger budget, or increased donations. For the collection development librarian, marketing means understanding the library's public (users, potential users, supporters, funding and administrative bodies) in order to develop a product (the collection) and related services. The success of that product and those services is then measured or evaluated to ensure that performance is responsive to the public and gains support. Library marketing should always take place within the context of the library's mission, goals, and objectives. Successful marketing helps position the library to plan for that future.

Marketing as part of collection development in libraries is not a completely new idea. In 1969, Martin Lopez wrote that marketing is one of the seven selector responsibilities constituting collection development, along with fiscal management, planning, evaluation, review, quality control, and resource sharing.[4] The *Guide for Training Collection Development Librarians* contains a section on "Marketing, Outreach, and Communications with Constituencies," documenting the increasingly widespread acceptance of marketing as a core competency for selectors.[5] Marketing, in the narrower sense of promotion, in libraries has an even longer history. Walter Alwyn Briscoe's *Library Advertising*, published in 1921, suggested techniques like publishing library newsletters aimed at different groups and promoting books that related to popular movies.[6]

A common misconception is that marketing is the same as advertising or promotion. Although marketing does include promotion, this is only one aspect. The aims of marketing in collection development are to understand the library's present and future users; to develop a collection that satisfies their needs, wants, and demands; to inform users about the resources available; and to monitor success or failure in conveying its message. Once the library understands its potential market, it formulates marketing strategies. These include developing overall plans to maximize impact on the market in both the short and long terms, deciding which information resources and services to offer, and establishing standards and measures for performance. In other words, marketing is *market research, planning, implementation,* and *control.* These activities are increasingly important in the nonprofit sector. Social agencies, educational institutions, charities, and libraries employ marketing to learn the needs and wants of their target markets and to deliver the desired satisfaction more effectively and efficiently than their competitors.

Marketing can challenge libraries because, without profit-and-loss figures such as found in the commercial sector, measuring the success of marketing efforts is often difficult. Yet performance measurement is an essential component of effective collection development and management, and various methodologies for evaluation and assessment have been developed over time. Librarians evaluate collections to determine how well they support the needs of users and the goals of the parent organization. They survey users to learn their level of satisfaction. They assess collections by examining a collection in its own terms or relative to other collections and checklists.

The library's community—consisting of users, potential users, and its funding and governing bodies—is its market. Marketing is implicit in Charles B. Osburn's analysis of the relationship between libraries and their communities:

> Since . . . libraries depend upon their communities for support, the future of libraries does hinge very definitely on the priority and importance assigned to

them by their respective communities. . . . For this reason alone, each library will be better off for defining its community, trying to understand it, and demonstrating to it the value that can be expected of the library.[7]

Marketing Concepts in a Library Context

In *Strategic Marketing for Nonprofit Organizations,* Philip Kotler and Alan R. Andreasen define marketing as the effective management by an organization of its exchange relations with various markets and publics.[8] Kotler and Gary Armstrong stress that marketing should be understood in the new sense of satisfying customer needs, not in the old sense of making a sale.[9] Marketing begins with research—understanding who the market is and that market's needs, wants, and demands. A *need* is a state of felt deprivation of some basic satisfaction. Needs require solution. *Wants* are desires for specific satisfiers of these deeper needs. *Demands* are wants for specific products or services. Marketers can influence wants. For example, I need information. I want the library to help me find this information, by either giving it to me or directing me to a resource that will provide it. I demand, in the marketing sense of this word, to use an online resource. I have been influenced by marketing, either by the library or the commercial sector, to prefer electronic information resources over traditional printed information tools. Most people who enter the library or access it online seek information or entertainment. The individual may want a mystery novel. He or she may demand the newest John Grisham novel.

Selectors should be cautious about seeking to meet all their users' perceived needs and wants, which is usually too narrow an objective. Most libraries have long-range goals and objectives, articulated in a mission statement and mandated by a parent authority or agency. Kotler and Karen F. A. Fox refer to keeping the bigger picture in mind as a "societal marketing orientation."[10] The selector's task is developing and managing collections to enhance the current users' level of satisfaction and to increase user support while preserving society's or the library's well-being and long-term interests.

Products and *services* are anything that can be offered to satisfy a need or want. Libraries provide products in the form of information, books, journals, multimedia, online resources, customized bibliographies, handouts, library web pages, and so on. Library services are reference, interlibrary loan, reader counseling, training, story hours, class visits, and any personal staff contact with a patron. Collection development librarians can see the collections they build and manage as the product. Every contact they make with their constituents is a service.

In addition to gathering information to understand needs better, the selector works with users to identify and solve problems they have experienced with the library. These include both inadequacies with the collection and problems with library services. Often selectors discover that a user's assessment of the collection is based on incomplete or inaccurate knowledge of resources held locally and of the means available to access online resources or to request materials through interlibrary loan. The librarian gains information that helps develop outreach activities that more clearly and completely convey to users what the library has and does.

When a user's dissatisfaction is based on real problems, not misunderstanding, the selector takes on the role of advocate in trying to solve these problems within the context of available library and institutional resources. The selector solicits advice from constituents regarding specific collection issues. This form of consultation is more common in academic and school libraries, in which faculty members and teachers make recommendations about purchasing items, adding and canceling journal titles, replacing specific titles and materials in particular subject areas, placing materials in storage, and needing multiple copies of individual titles.

Value and *satisfaction* define how consumers choose between the products and services that might satisfy a given need. Value is a complicated concept with a long history in economic thought. Karl Marx thought that the value of an object depended on how much labor went into its production. Contemporary thought defines value as subjective and suggests that value depends on its capacity to satisfy wants. I value the library and its services to the extent that they meet my wants. Do I get the information I need? Does the library have the book I want? Did the selector order the book I recommended? How long do I have to wait? Even if I am satisfied, I may not value the library much. Recent research indicates that satisfaction does not necessarily translate into customer loyalty.[11]

Citizens may value the library, be satisfied with its collections and service, but be unwilling to approve a tax increase to support it. Faculty members may proclaim the library as essential for teaching and research but fail to protect its budget allocation. Parents and school boards value their school media centers but may reduce the number of media specialists before they cut back on coaching staff.

The terms *exchange* and *transaction* denote the act of obtaining a desired product or service by offering something in return. The concept of exchange is central to marketing because it implies that—by agreeing to the exchange—the participating parties see themselves as better off after the exchange. Transactions consist of a trade of values between two parties. The commodity exchanged for the product or service may not be financial, though it often is. Academic libraries, frequently glibly called the heart of the university, are seldom funded to the financial level this "value" might suggest. Time and effort may be equally valuable commodities. The faculty member or teacher, valuing students who use the library, may give time in his or her classroom to the librarian, who provides an orientation to library resources and services. Many public libraries are finding that citizens are willing to pay for specialized reference service and document delivery if it is speedier and easier than doing the research and retrieval themselves. Academic libraries may offer document delivery services to affiliated users on a cost-recovery basis, gaining in goodwill and satisfying the user that the time savings is worth the usually modest fee.

The *market* consists of all the potential customers who share a particular need or want and who might be willing and able to engage in exchange, which may be money, time, effort, or all three, to satisfy that need or want. A *marketer* is one who engages in marketing—who analyzes and understands the market, develops a valued product or service for that market, communicates the offering, and monitors satisfaction. Libraries typically deal with a complex community or potential customer base over which they have no authority and only indirect influence yet to which they must respond effectively in an anticipatory mode. Even when they do not seek direct cost recovery, libraries seek support and loyalty in exchange for user satisfaction.

Neil H. Borden introduced the phrase *marketing mix* in the late 1940s to describe the creative mix of *product, price, place,* and *promotion* that informs marketing.[12] Philip Kotler has explored these "Four Ps" of marketing extensively in his many books. In the library context, *product* refers to both library collections (on-site and online) and services. Consumers make choices about products based on perceived functionality, utility, and reliability. The library examines the needs, demands, and wants of all segments of its public and the long-term requirements of the communities it serves and designs a product—library services and resources—to meet those needs. Does the public library's community want more electronic resources, more copies of popular novels, more large-print materials, or fewer books and more journals? What services and types of contact do faculty members want from selectors? Can the library or the librarian modify current practices to satisfy the public better? Libraries face challenges building collections that balance formats, monographs and serials, and immediate needs and long-term mission. Developing and modifying the collections and services the library provides are what librarians do constantly, though they seldom think of these as marketing activities. The contact between librarian and community is an important product. The librarian should develop, monitor, and modify these liaison or outreach activities so that they become a valued service, for which the user community member is willing to exchange time, effort, and support.

Modifying either *price* or *place* modifies the product and influences demand. Librarians should understand these components and can adjust them, when appropriate, to increase the likelihood that a patron will use and be satisfied with the library's collections and services. Price is what it costs the library user to acquire and access the library's products and services. Price can be measured in financial cost or in the time or effort needed to obtain the product, that is, its convenience. Price is determined by a variety of factors, including competition, input costs, product identity, and the customer's perceived value of the product or services. The librarian's goal is to set the price of using the collection and services as low as is feasible, given the constraints placed on the library by its budget and staffing. Generally, traditional or routine services have no direct financial cost for primary constituents. Fees are seldom charged to borrow books and audio recordings, read journals, consult reference materials and staff members, or use the library's electronic resources. Some libraries charge users fees for receiving interlibrary loans, borrowing videos and best-sellers, requesting recalls, being placed on a waiting list, and using reference services extending beyond a certain length of time. Most libraries charge for photocopy services, printing, and retrieval and delivery to a home or office, though special libraries may be budgeted to absorb or subsidize these costs.

Collection development librarians have more influence on the cost of time and effort to users than they do on price. Librarians aim to lower users' perception of cost by saving their time and effort, and they assume that this increases user satisfaction. The user's perception of the ideal library is one in which everything a user seeks is not only owned by the library but easy to locate and ready to use. Libraries' decreasing ability to develop collections that meet most local user expectations directly affects the cost to users in time and effort. Waiting to use a computer workstation to access a single CD-ROM, waiting to access an online electronic resource because the library must limit its simultaneous users, initiating an interlibrary loan request and waiting for the item, and waiting on a list for a popular title all can decrease user satisfaction. Selectors are always seeking to satisfy users within the library's mission, priorities, and budget. Being unable to locate a resource results in user frustration and perceived cost of using the library.

Place is the point at which the exchange of value for product and service occurs and may be referred to as the *distribution channel.* It can be in the library, media center, or a bookmobile; via a website; or in the user's office, home, or classroom. The librarian's goal is to design a place, point of contact, or distribution system that allows patrons to find and get what they want—which may be information, an item, or the collection development librarian's attention—as quickly and conveniently as possible. The academic library may offer free or minimal cost delivery of locally owned materials to on-campus offices. The special librarian may deliver items directly to the executive or researcher who requested them. The selector, regardless of library type, may provide users with mechanisms to recommend materials for purchase. Academic and special librarians may schedule office hours within the departments and divisions to facilitate contact with users. The goal is to make it as convenient as possible for selectors to provide services to their constituents. Selecting between print and electronic resources when making collection decisions has obvious "place" implications. Users value the time saved when they can access electronic resources from home or office.

All liaison and outreach activities—all of the library's and librarian's communication activities and formats—are *promotion*. Many users have very little idea of what librarians do or what they and the libraries in which they work offer. Liaison and outreach are the librarian's chance to inform and educate. The librarian should take every opportunity to promote the library's collections and services along with his or her availability. Information about the library should not focus only on collections and information resources. The selector keeps constituents aware of all relevant library services, programs, and policies. Some services may be offered by selectors. Others may be the responsibility of various library units. These might include current awareness services, routing of journals, document delivery services, preparation of library handouts tailored to specific class needs, workshops offered by the library, guest lectures and book talks by librarians, and library tours and demonstrations. Relevant policies may address collection development and management, gifts, Internet use, user privacy, course reserves, copyright, authorized access to electronic information resources, and borrowing privileges. Keeping constituents informed about all aspects of the library is an important part of outreach.

Promotional activities are both formal and informal. Formal activities are structured and planned interactions, such as scheduled presentations and meetings and the preparation of print and digital informational materials. Informal promotion can occur every time a librarian comes in contact with a member of the library's community. Advances in telecommunication options are expanding opportunities for library outreach and liaison activities. These include sending e-mail messages to individuals and groups and creating library web pages, with online opportunities for comments and questions and forms for suggesting materials for purchase.

The concept of the marketing mix (product, price, plan, and promotion) has a long history. It is not without critics, who have seen it as too inward-looking without sufficient customer focus. In response, a more customer-centered approach to marketing, called *customer relationship management*, has developed. The basic idea is that building relationships with customers is more effective than mass marketing. On the for-profit side, customer relationship management has evolved into automated systems that manage and coordinate information and activities within the business to provide a consistent and coherent image to the customer. On a more theoretical level, customer relationship management is a coordinated strategy to use the information gathered about customers (or library users) to attract and keep them—to build confidence, trust, and loyalty. Kotler and Nancy Lee have described this customer-centered focus as assuming that the target audience is constantly asking the question, What's in it for me?[13] This "WIFM phenomenon," they argue, motivates marketers to understand the wants and needs of target customers better than competitors do. Customer relationship management is pertinent in libraries because it looks out to the user community rather than inward at what librarians think about the library's offering, to develop what Terry Kendrick calls a "mutually beneficial relationship" that can be sustained over time and leads to advocacy and support as well as user satisfaction.[14] In other words, marketing is more effective if it begins with what the community sees and thinks about libraries. Understanding the community's perspective provides a better foundation for library marketing.

One important aspect of marketing is knowing the *competition*. Understanding the library's competition can come through market research—learning where users and potential users seek the products and services to satisfy their needs, wants, and desires, and why. Competition can be direct or indirect. Direct competition is when products or services that perform the same function compete against each other. For example, airlines are direct competitors. Indirect competition is when products or services are close substitutes for each other. Buses and trains are indirect competitors with airlines. Companies use several approaches to come out ahead of the competition, including adjusting the marketing mix (e.g., lowering prices, improving the product or services, or increasing promotion), differentiating the product or services from that offered by competitors, fostering customer loyalty through brand recognition, and maintaining a customer-centered focus.

Even without intentional market research, libraries are aware that they face competition from bookstores and direct online information sources and search engines, particularly Google. More in-depth research seeks to determine why these competitors are perceived as more appealing, attractive, efficient, or convenient. Librarians have determined that coffee shops and comfortable seating can make bookstores more appealing and so have been adding both to libraries. In response to user perceptions that Google makes finding information easier, libraries are experimenting with new types of catalogs such as Endeca and ExLibris's Primo. These approaches seek to improve the library's competitive edge and to improve its position in the market. Many librarian activities have been directed to positioning the library, its collections, and its services in the user community's awareness. Librarians do not want users to think only of books when they think of libraries and seek to promote the benefits the library offers through its collections and services and to differentiate themselves from competitors.

Another approach to improving the library's position in the information and entertainment marketplace is what Lorcan Dempsey calls getting "in the flow."[15] He suggests that the library needs to coevolve with user behaviors—which can be monitored through market research. As information and entertainment resources are increasingly integrated (e.g., Google, Netflix online delivery of rented movies, courseware management systems), librarians need to think more about getting into that flow of the user environment and think less about getting users into the library either physically or virtually. For example, public librarians are exploring getting into the flow in an iPod world by offering audiobooks that can be downloaded from the library's website. Special collections librarians are creating description and access tools that lead users directly from discovery through Google to the local collection. Other librarians are aiming to put libraries in the flow by podcasting and using social networking sites.[16] The challenge is to do these things authentically. Dempsey concludes his blog posting by stating that "integration of library resources should not be seen as an end in itself but as a means to better integration with the user environment."[17] Intentional positioning is essential.

Market Research

Marketing begins with *market research*. The American Marketing Association defines it as "the function that links the consumer, customer, and public to the marketer through information—information used to identify and define marketing opportunities and problems; generate, refine, and evaluate marketing actions; monitor marketing performance; and improve understanding of marketing as a process."[18] Market research specifies the information required to address these issues, designs the method for collecting information, manages and implements the data collection process, analyzes the results, and communicates the findings and their implications.

A library must undertake research to define and understand its user community—its market. Market research establishes the overall size and structure of the community, identifies user characteristics, assesses needs of the users, and interprets trends. The terms *community analysis*, *needs assessment*, and *needs analysis* may be more familiar to librarians.[19] All are research or studies through which librarians seek as much information as possible about their community or constituencies—users, potential users, supporters, and funding bodies.

Market Segmentation

Market segmentation—dividing the market into categories in order to understand each one better—is one common strategy in market research. The library's user community can be understood in terms of its components or segments. Librarians can gather secondary and primary data about each market segment and then develop collections that respond to these various user groups. The community can be segmented in many ways. Common approaches consider demographic characteristics (e.g., age, gender, income level, ethnic background, occupation, educational level), geographic characteristics (e.g., ability to travel to library, distance that must be traveled, resident/nonresident status of potential patron), behavioral characteristics (extent and type of a patron's use/nonuse of the library in general or of specific collections and services within it), and sociological characteristics (e.g., socioeconomic class, lifestyle, personality, interests, opinions). All types of libraries can segment their user community for market research.

George D'Elia divided public library users into six target markets: people who only borrow books, people who only use materials in the library, people who use the library lightly, heavy users, hard-core nonusers, and potential users.[20] His 1981 analysis predated online access to libraries and resources. Another way to categorize public library users is suggested in the working draft of RASD/RUSA's "Guidelines for Liaison Work."[21] The categories or segments proposed (and not intended to be inclusive) are

- recreational users
- new adult readers
- businesspersons
- civic groups, including neighborhood improvement associations, fraternal organizations, women's organizations, and business and professional organizations
- local, state, and regional departments and agencies
- teachers and students from preschools, primary and secondary schools, and vocational and post-secondary institutions
- senior citizens
- new immigrants and populations having English as a second language
- people with disabilities
- institutionalized populations, including those in nursing and retirement homes, residential treatment centers, residential facilities for children, and jails and prisons
- independent and lifelong learners

Samantha Chmelik stresses the importance of detailed information about the various market segments and their characteristics in the development and promotion of collections and services in special libraries.[22] A corporate library might segment its users into researchers, marketers, sales people, legal staff, and management, with the aim of satisfying the information needs of each. Chmelik, a corporate librarian, determined that her most active user group consisted of individuals in middle to upper management, who needed timely, concise responses to questions and had greater information needs at the beginning and end of each quarter. With this information in hand, she could look for the best matches with available resources and identify possible additions—and develop a marketing plan that would reach her target audience most effectively.

The academic library's community is often analyzed along the categories of faculty members, students, institutional staff members, administrators, and external users. The first four groups are usually considered primary or affiliated users. External users, who might be segmented into categories such as alumni, citizens, and corporate researchers, are often called secondary or unaffiliated users. In many academic libraries, the same categories are employed when developing outreach and liaison activities. Responsibilities for faculty liaison are usually divided among various selectors along subject or discipline lines. Outreach to students may be aligned according to subject focus or directed to undergraduate, graduate professional school student groups, on-campus and distance education students, honors program students, and so on. How the market is segmented can determine how responsibilities are assigned. In addition, librarians may have liaison responsibilities with student government bodies and student organizations (ethnic, social, service, etc.). Each targeted group can provide information that aids the selector in developing collections to meet that group's needs and interests.

School librarians usually think of their user community in terms of students, teachers, and—in some libraries—students' families. Students can be further segmented into, for example, age or grade groups, native English speakers and students for whom English is not their first language, or those with special needs or special abilities. Teachers can be categorized along similar lines, depending on their teaching responsibilities. School librarians might consider parent advisory groups and site counsels, parent-teacher associations, school boards, and school administrators as part of the community for which their libraries are responsible and to whom they are accountable.

Data Gathering

After a librarian decides how he or she will define the components of the library's community, data are gathered. Market research is conducted by analyzing secondary (existing) data and gathering and analyzing primary data. Many public sources provide useful data. Census data can be a valuable resource. For example, the U.S. Census Bureau Population and Household Economic Topics website (www.census.gov/population/www/) provides information on ethnicity, income, education level, and so on when one types in a city, town, county, state, or ZIP code. Many states have state department of education websites that allow drilling down to specific schools, where one can find data about test scores, reading levels, percentage of students participating in free and reduced-cost lunch programs, and more. Such data are often available in the school itself or from the central office of school systems. The school media librarian should seek current information on special needs students, including nonnative English speakers, attending the school.

Many secondary sources are available to help librarians understand academic user communities. Academic institutions normally provide data on number of students by program and level, international students and scholars, faculty and researchers (by discipline, department, college), and staff. Many departments, research centers, and individual faculty members have web pages which, along with course catalogs, can be a rich resource for secondary information. Other sources are departmental promotional materials; newsletters and reports, which may list new hires; faculty publications; and research grants.

Other information can be gained only through contact with faculty members. This may be by meeting with individual faculty members and attending departmental meetings. The lucky selector has an established vehicle for communication—a departmental library committee or a designated departmental liaison—through whom information and requests for advice on general issues can be funneled. Less formal meetings, such as getting together with one or two faculty members over coffee or lunch, foster communication as well. The following list identifies information that is helpful in understanding academic user communities:

- faculty research interests and areas of concentration
- faculty language abilities
- grants and research centers
- number of faculty members and their ranks
- number of students and research assistants
- courses being taught and being planned
- special collection and resource needs
- requests for particular library services
- areas of crossover with other disciplines
- plans for future programs and degrees
- national standing of the department or program
- department's or program's priority in the institution

The academic library selector can begin by creating a list of faculty members in the subject areas for which he or she has collection management responsibilities. This list can be enhanced through the creation of faculty profiles and by soliciting faculty vitae. Many selectors regularly survey their constituents to learn their interest, needs, problems, and perceptions about library collections and services. Several examples of survey instruments and questionnaires are available.[23]

Figure 6-1 provides one example of a simple faculty questionnaire. This instrument collects information for the selector's file on faculty members' interests.

Faculty Profile

Name: _____

Office address: _____

E-mail address: _____

Phone: _____

Field(s) and geographical area(s) of interest:

_____

_____

Current research projects:

_____

_____

Course(s) you are currently teaching or have under development:

_____

_____

FIGURE 6-1 Simple faculty profile form. An example of an extended faculty questionnaire is provided at www.ala.org/editions/extras/Johnson09720.

This information can be gathered through personal interaction instead of by asking the individual to respond to a form. A selector could expand the survey to ask questions about perceptions of collections and services, both existing and desired, or ask these questions in a subsequent survey. A single survey is never sufficient. Faculty members and their interests change, and selectors need to resurvey their constituents periodically. A subject specialist should be cautious about using the detailed form to collect data in an initial meeting. Faculty members may be more receptive to the survey questions that expand on the simple form after they have developed rapport with the librarian.

The selector's success in making and maintaining good user community contacts depends on both enthusiasm and initiative. Only through constant attention can a selector gain and supply the information needed to make liaison work meaningful. The approaches selectors use to learn about their constituents and their needs and interests vary with the situation. Even the most aggressive selector may run into a brick wall with some departments and some faculty members, who fail to respond to any library initiative. A common challenge reported in an ARL study on liaison activities was "establishing and maintaining contact with faculty, especially when they seem time-pressured, uninterested, or unresponsive to outreach."[24] In these situations, the selector should continue promotional activities, even if the communication remains one-directional.

Using some form of user profile is beneficial in all types of libraries. In special libraries, profiles can help identify the needs and interests of specific library and information center users by tracking the research and development activities of individuals. School librarians may maintain profiles for each teacher and his or her curriculum support needs. Philip M. Turner and Ann Marlow Riedling propose creating what they call "Instructional Consultation Assessment Charts" to track past interaction with teachers.[25] The school library media specialist records the degree of a teacher's involvement in several areas, including discussion of instructional objectives and materials selection. Curriculum mapping can also provide data to inform the development of teacher profiles. Another approach, suggested by Mary Jo Langhorne, is to enter data into a spreadsheet that tracks monthly media center use by teachers, their classes, activities, level of instructional support, and dates.[26] Not only does this help to develop a teacher profile, it can be correlated with the curriculum map and local educational standards.

Primary data are obtained through observational research, qualitative research (individual interviews and focus groups), and formal research through surveys and experimental research. Some libraries collect data through their websites via one- or two-sentence surveys that simply ask "How are we doing?" and provide a text box for comments. Surveys range from the very simple to the very complex. An extensive market research project that collected primary data from 4,438 respondents resulted in the 2005 publication *Perceptions of Libraries and Information Resources: A Report to the OCLC Membership.*[27] This research determined that, for most of those surveyed, books come first to mind when they think of libraries. In other words, books are, in essence, the library's brand. Though few libraries hire consulting firms to undertake research this extensive, the primary data collected are of interest to all.

When selectors gather and analyze primary data through observation, interviews, and surveys, they seek specific answers that help guide collection development. Questions may address why an individual does or does not use a library resource, if a resource is easy to use or not, what the individual needed or wanted and was unable to obtain, how long he or she is willing to wait for the resource, and preferences for formats. Information gathered on these topics, in addition to guiding collection development, is useful in collection assessment. Information collected in these ways must be analyzed cautiously, however, because both user and researcher biases can skew results. User perceptions, memories, and understanding of collections and services may not always reflect reality. Researchers may have framed the questions in such a way that ambiguous responses result.

Focus groups or group interviews are another way to gather data about users' perceptions, values, and opinions. They are effective in creating an opportunity to collect data from small numbers of people in an informal and relaxed setting. Focus groups are led by a moderator and range in size from six to twelve. A focus group session is usually approximately two hours and may be shorter, depending on the age of participants, the area of interest, and the time participants have available. Focus groups are a form of qualitative research. They are appropriate for all types of libraries and often prove more informative than surveys when working with children and young people.[28]

The library itself can provide data on the ability of the existing collection to meet current needs; such information can be found in interlibrary loan requests, circulation activity, reference questions, and purchase suggestions from users. Library automation has the potential to produce a wealth of constituent user data that can guide collection development; however, not all systems live up to this promise, nor do selectors always make use of the available information. Dennis P. Carrigan suggests that data generated through automated library systems can be used to guide decisions at the individual title level or at the subject or call number range level.[29] If the library system can correlate use by various user categories (e.g., activity by adult and juvenile users in a public library or by student, staff, faculty, or unaffiliated users in an academic library), the selector obtains hard data on market needs and wants that can help develop a responsive collection. Use statistics should be weighed against categories of materials for which such data are not collected, such as noncirculating materials and those used on site.

Planning and Implementation

After a library has conducted market research, the next steps are planning the products (collections) and services that will meet the needs and expectations of its user community and then implementing these decisions. Terry Kendrick defines an effective marketing plan as a strategy that

> will identify what drives users and build products and services around their needs; enable a highly differentiated service, not "one size fits all"; create value and inspiration to use the library; and do all this with as little cost as possible. It will provide a process to ensure maximum use of the public libraries by the pubic, attract non-users and develop loyalty behaviours in existing users, and will clearly influence attitudes towards the library—our "offer" as the best, the winning offer (in terms of use of time) in the scramble for their attention.[30]

This description applies to all types of libraries in their goal of understanding and serving their communities.

The marketing plan is sometimes called the *marketing strategy*. In this planning process, the library develops its market mix of product (collections and services), price, place, and promotion, sets goals, and determines how to reach them. A collections librarian cannot determine the marketing mix in isolation from the library's mission and goals but usually has primary responsibility for setting collection goals (through the collection development policy, addressed in chapter 3) and developing a portion of the promotional plan.

Once a marketing plan is developed, it is implemented. The collections librarian implements the collection plan through selecting the appropriate materials and properly managing the collection. The promotional component is implemented through outreach and liaison activities.

Liaison and Outreach

Public Libraries

The need for and value of public library promotion has been the topic of numerous recent books, particularly as a means of fostering advocates.[31] The goal is to get public libraries back into the lives of their users and potential users, identifying market segments and targeting the message to these various segments on the basis of their needs, wants, and desires. Kendrick stresses the need first to identify the factors that influence users and competitors, then to develop or identify existing products and services that are appropriate for user segments, and only then to develop the appropriate means to reach these segments. Some forms of communication are targeted and some are appropriate for general promotional activities. The following are some options:

- Prepare bookmarks and handouts that promote specific collections, information resources, and services.
- Publish library newsletters or new acquisitions lists, which can be targeted to specific user groups.
- Provide public service announcements.
- Issue press releases.
- Prepare displays that promote new acquisitions and resources on a particular topic.
- Give book talks in classes, in the library, to citizen's groups, and elsewhere.
- Create a library website (or subject- and age-specific sites) that promotes collections and services.
- Make book and journal request forms easily available online and at service desks.
- Participate in library Friends group meetings.
- Attend meetings of citizens' interest groups (e.g., League of Women Voters, Chamber of Congress, Urban League).

Special Libraries

Jim Harrington suggests that librarians in special libraries need to supplement more familiar approaches with different techniques to reach their constituents.[32] He emphasizes personal contact and recommends hand-delivering the book, article, or research report to the individual who has requested it. Marketing the special library is about fostering personal relationships. Janet Peros calls this person-to-person marketing and stresses the value of getting out of the library and "walking the halls," where every encounter with an individual builds and strengthens the relationship between librarian and user.[33] Special librarians should participate in company, business, and agency departmental meetings and attend company social events. They can involve others when making decisions about the collection and services. This does not need to be a standing committee but can consist of people who are interested in the issue being discussed. Keeping track of who is interested in which topics can prepare the special librarian to alert individuals about research or industry news that may be of significance in their work. Some methods, such as a weekly e-mail list of new materials added, are equally valuable promotional vehicles for special librarians.

Jane Bridges developed a list of suggestions for a hospital library, many of which are appropriate for other types of libraries:[34]

- Develop a brand (logo or slogan or both) and use it on all communications from the library—all forms, coversheets on articles, and so forth.
- Develop a flyer that explains library services and provides contact information.
- Attend informational meetings and ask how the librarian can support projects.
- Deliver items in person.
- Host brown-bag discussions and coffee hours on focused topics.
- Make presentations at regular meetings of various groups.
- Form partnerships, for example, with the information technology department.
- Host a vendor fair and invite companies to demonstrate new technologies.
- Ensure that the library in included in new employee orientation.
- Celebrate accomplishments and successes of others.

School Media Centers

School librarians can promote school media centers with many of the same approaches already suggested. Amy Burkman identifies target groups for media center librarians' promotional activities as administrators, teachers, students, parents, and the general community and notes that each audience requires a different strategy.[35] She suggests that school librarians share data about circulation, numbers of students and classes using the library, and collaborative projects twice a year with school administrators. Wendy Worley proposes assembling a portfolio that documents and can serve to promote the activities and contributions the library makes to the curriculum and to school life more broadly.[36] Helping administrators understand the value of school library media centers and of trained librarians can be an important way of marketing. Providing school administrators with local data on use and information drawn from research can encourage their advocacy of adequate media center budgets and professional staffing. For example, research by Keith Curry Lance and David V. Loertscher has consistently demonstrated that the quality of the school library media center strongly correlates with student achievement and higher test scores, regardless of socioeconomic factors, teacher-pupil ratios, or amount spent per pupil.[37] The Library Research Service (www.lrs.org/impact.php) provides links to numerous school library impact studies.

As appropriate, school librarians can try the following activities to promote collections and services:

- Participate in teachers' meetings.
- Be in the library during school open houses and parent-teacher meetings.
- Become involved in the PTA.
- Hold book fairs a few times a year for parents and students.
- Celebrate National Book Week or Library Week.
- Create reading contests for students.
- Schedule regular classroom visits and collaborate with teachers in other ways.
- Prepare bookmarks and handouts promoting specific collections, information resources, and services.
- Prepare library newsletters or new acquisitions lists and distribute them electronically or in print to teachers.
- Prepare displays that promote new acquisitions and resources on a particular topic.
- Give book talks in classes.
- Create a library website that promotes collections and services.
- Make book and journal request forms easily available.

Academic Libraries

Liaison activities in academic libraries are typically the official and assigned contacts between selectors and designated individuals, departments, units, committees, or organizations outside the library. Successful liaison provides a local context in which to apply all other collection development and management skills. Liaison activities can serve to promote the library's collections and services and create improved visibility for the library. They provide a forum to gather data about the user community and enhance a selector's ability to build responsive collections. The Association of College and Research Libraries has published *The Power of Personal Persuasion*, which speaks to the important role individual librarians can take in reaching out to user communities.[38]

Traditionally, most liaison activities in academic libraries have involved contact with faculty members. A 2007 ARL survey reported that all but one of the sixty-six responding libraries provided liaison services to academic departments in their universities and that most provided outreach to faculty of all types, graduate assistants and other graduate students, administrative staff, and undergraduates.[39] The specialist selector in an academic library cannot develop and manage a collection without knowing his or her user community. Faculty members are an important target or market segment because they depend on the library for research, give course assignments that use library resources, and can be important campus supporters of the library. Knowing and being known by faculty are important for success.

Each selector typically interacts with one or more groups of professors, usually defined by their affiliation with specific teaching departments or programs that parallel the subjects or disciplines for which the selector is responsible. Selectors assigned interdisciplinary responsibilities, including area studies, face a greater challenge in identifying their constituents and reaching them. No matter what their subject assignment, selectors cannot depend solely on the knowledge they bring to the job. They must seek out their faculty user community and learn about it. By learning as much as possible about the specialties, needs, and interests of their assigned faculties, academic library selectors increase their ability to develop a collection that serves these specialties, needs, and interests. Besides following individual faculty member's requirements and expectations, the selector needs a collective understanding of the department's needs in order to balance collection development activities within this larger view.

Some academic libraries view outreach to faculty members as so important that they create a separate position charged with developing systematic programs to reach all faculty and target university administrators as a special user group.[40] The outreach librarian position created at the Virginia Tech University Libraries is paired with a marketing team, which is charged "(1) to determine what products and services should be offered, (2) to whom these products and services should be targeted, and (3) the best methods of informing potential customers of the offering and convincing them to use the product or service."[41] Other libraries develop liaison toolkits that combine information for selector liaisons and, in the case of the library at the State University of New York at New Paltz, a series of workshops on effective liaison activities for librarians.[42]

Selectors in academic libraries can assemble an informational packet of materials to give to each faculty member, ideally in person. This might include a collection development policy, information about services, relevant guides and bibliographies, and an information sheet about the selector. E-mail is frequently used for sharing information. In addition, academic librarians can try some of the following faculty liaison activities:

- Attend academic departmental meetings and special events and let people know they are representing the library.
- Seek opportunities for collaborative teaching projects, research, and grants.
- Participate in university orientation programs for new faculty, students, teaching assistants, research assistants, and international and graduate students.
- Send notes of recognition when faculty members get grants and awards.
- Audit classes.
- Meet with new faculty members within their first academic term and tell them about the library collections and services.
- Meet regularly with department chairs and library-faculty liaison groups.
- Develop a mailing list and send regular announcements of library activities, acquisitions, and events of interest.
- Post news and information on the library's web pages or in the library's newsletter, or both.[43]
- Creating electronic discussion lists, blogs, and RSS feeds to share pertinent information—about new resources, recent acquisitions, programs, and the like.

Reaching out to and building relationships with college and university students can present different challenges. Possible market segments might be type of student (undergraduates, graduate students, distance education students, students living in campus housing, commuter students, older students returning to school), program of study, affiliation with social and service organizations, and more. Age is seen as a powerful way to segment the student population in higher education. John Wesley Lowery writes that the millennial generation (those born in and after 1979) has significant implications for student programs and services.[44] An important research project at the University of Rochester examined undergraduate students and their use of information.[45] Described as an anthropological study using ethnographic tools, this is, at heart, consumer research, and it provided the library at University of Rochester with a wealth of information to use in redesigning its website and developing new forms of outreach and promotion. Lara Ursin Cummings suggests partnering with campus organizations and services (e.g., residency service, freshmen orientation, athletic department) to target messages to various market segments.[46] Other libraries, such the University of Minnesota Libraries in its Virtual Undergraduate Library (www.lib.umn.edu/undergrad/), have created websites customized to specific student groups. This site offers the Assignment Calculator, which walks a student through the steps of researching and writing a research paper and provides suggested completion dates for each phase. Another feature of the site is the Research Quick Start, with links to subject-based pages prepared by the University of Minnesota Libraries' departmental liaisons. These tools aim to match the needs and behaviors of millennial undergraduates.

Liaison activities and community outreach are not just essential to successful collection development and management, they are also satisfying and fun. This part of collection development work places the selector at the heart of the community. The selector has the chance to satisfy needs, respond to requests, answer questions, and solve problems. Leading users, potential users, funding agencies, and governing bodies to an understanding of the library, its collections, services, and constraints in which it operates benefits both the faculty and the library.

Control

Control is measuring performance—monitoring and analyzing ongoing results—and taking corrective actions where necessary. Developing a marketing plan for the library or for an individual selector's services is pointless if the resulting performance is not measured. Collections are evaluated to determine how well they support the needs of users and the goals of the parent organization. Collection assessment (addressed in chapter 7) seeks to examine or describe collections in their own terms or relative to other collections and checklists. Measuring the community's response to collections and associated services is essential. Feedback should inform change. Performance measurement should occur as an integral part of working with the library's public. The selector seeks to learn not only the users' needs, wants, demands, and interests but also the extent to which collection resources and services are meeting these requirements.

Control determines whether the needs of the various library market segments have been identified correctly and met, and whether the promotional activities aimed at them have succeeded. This phase seeks to answer many questions.

Are library users satisfied with the collection and information resources? Do teachers feel the school library media center is meeting their curriculum needs? Are faculty members happy with how they interact with selectors? Do users feel the library is responsive? Do they know what the library offers? The library or the selector needs to develop performance measures that are meaningful. Besides survey instruments and focus groups, selectors might track how frequently users contact them directly. Libraries and collections librarians develop their own performance measures. Possibilities include visits to the physical library; library website hits; questions by phone, in person, and through the website; and circulation transactions. The ultimate goal is to use these performance measurements to improve and enhance collections and services and increase community satisfaction.

Successful marketing is continuous, with each component interacting with and driving the others (see figure 6-2). The selector researches his or her user groups (public) to track their needs, wants, and demands. This information is supplemented by information from secondary sources—demographic data, topics of research, curriculum standards, emerging programs, and so forth. Part of the research is development of a marketing plan, based on the determined marketing mix of product, price, place, and promotion. The library collections and associated services (the products) are configured to meet needs, wants, and demands within the terms and limits of the library's mission and financial resources.

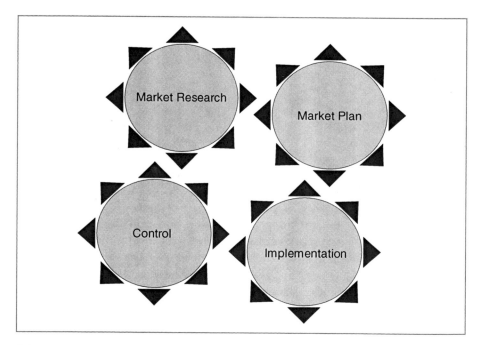

FIGURE 6-2 Interrelated aspects of marketing

The selector implements the plan, which involves promoting the product and associated services to the library's user community and also gathering information that continues to inform the marketing mix. Control is monitoring users' perceptions of and response to the marketing mix. The collection is also evaluated through external performance indicators. Through successful marketing (the four related aspects represented as cogs in figure 6-2), the library's collection and services develop in response to its users, potential users, supporters, funding agencies, and governing bodies—always in the context of collection development policies, library mission, and available funding.

Benefits and Hazards of Liaison and Outreach Activities

The foremost benefit a selector gains through liaison work is the information necessary to develop a collection that meets the needs of constituents. Other benefits accrue over time. When an academic library selector has detailed knowledge about a department's programs, the research interests of faculty members, and the directions in which they are moving, he or she can make a case for appropriate support when library materials budgets are allocated. Developing public library collections and services that respond to and satisfy users builds community advocacy. Knowing the particular focuses of special library users positions the selector to respond appropriately and plan for the future. The selector has information at hand to explain needs and justify the resources required to meet them.

Effective liaison work saves time. Knowledge about individuals' interests prepares the selector to contact the appropriate person for advice on particular topics. Knowing who specializes in decorative arts in the art department means that neither the librarian's nor other faculty members' time is wasted getting opinions on the value of a possible acquisition. Knowing the specific information needs of special library users means the librarian can anticipate and be proactive in providing resources. Developing teacher profiles and tracking student demographics help the school library media specialist develop responsive collections.

Ongoing liaison and outreach work give the selector the opportunity to establish credibility and trust. He or she demonstrates subject knowledge, understanding of the literature, and expertise in library activities through consistent, frequent contact. Individuals come to trust the selector's judgment and to value his or her opinion. Good relationships with individual users and user groups are indispensable when undertaking serial cancellations. If the selector has kept the library's community informed about pricing trends and library budgets, the library's need to cancel serials or access to online resources will not come as a surprise. A productive relationship means that the selector is not seen simply as the bearer of bad news but as someone who understands user needs and will continue to work, despite constraints, to meet them. Decisions about canceling resources become just another part of the ongoing dialogue between the selector and the library's public.

Over time, the selector may come to personify the library to his or her constituents. Effectively handled, this relationship between selector and users can enhance the library's image and reputation. Public librarians become a felt presence in their communities because they attend community meetings, sponsor exhibits and programs, provide reading lists, and serve on the boards of community and government organizations. Library professionals are seen as peers and colleagues by faculty members throughout the academic institution. Departments call on the selector to represent the library on departmental committees, contribute to accreditation studies, and in some cases participate in developing new courses, programs, and grant proposals. Teachers ask the selector to speak to their classes and help them with reference and curriculum needs. Schools and community groups invite public librarians to give book talks. Users may begin to contact the selector for help in solving any problems they perceive with the library, its collections, and services.

Strong personal relationships between librarians and constituents can also lead to a troubling pitfall—being perceived as one's personal librarian. Academic selectors must be cautious not to become connected more to academic departments than to the library, placing themselves in a position in which departmental concerns take precedence over library priorities. Librarians should treat all members of the user community equally. A too-personal relationship between the school library media specialist and one or two teachers can be off-putting for other teachers. Perceptions of preferential treatment have negative consequences in fostering broad-based communication and outreach.

A parallel hazard is unreasonable or inappropriate requests by users for services or information the selector cannot or should not provide. Some individuals and constituent groups can become extremely demanding, pressuring the selector for personal services, special treatment, and purchase of out-of-scope materials. The selector becomes a personal or private librarian, caught between personal demands and library obligations. A fine line exists in liaison work between supporting user needs and demands and allegiance to the library.

At the heart of successful liaison work are good interpersonal and communication skills. Selectors need to work at building good working relationships with all members of their community. They must be skilled in dealing with demanding and unreasonable constituents as well as those who understand the selector's responsibilities to the library. Selectors need to make these responsibilities clear while emphasizing their role in supporting users' needs and interests.

Summary

Marketing, outreach, and liaison activities are critical for libraries and for collection development librarians in particular. In a climate in which explicit community support for libraries is increasingly important, effective techniques for understanding and reaching that community are essential. Marketing techniques equip the library and librarians to monitor changing needs, wants, and demands and to adjust services and collection development practices as needs and wants evolve. A societal marketing orientation ensures that current needs and wants are balanced against the library's mission and long-term goals.

Market research is how librarians come to understand various segments of their market—that is, their user community, stakeholders, or public. The library's public includes many types of users, potential and inactive users, library supporters, governing bodies, and funding agencies. Information about the market comes from existing published information and information collected and generated by the library over the course of routine activities. Information is also collected through primary research, which may involve individual interviews, surveys, and focus groups. The selector's goal in market research is to learn as much as possible about the library's public in order to develop responsive collections and associated services.

A marketing mix consists of product, price, place, and promotion. The product the selector develops is the library's collection, which includes on-site and online resources, and the services he or she provides the users. Part of developing the collection is understanding what it costs the user in time and effort to use the collection and what the user is willing to expend to do so. These data inform selectors' decisions about what to acquire for on-site use and for online access and which items can be borrowed from other collections. Equally important is an understanding of place—what location of information resources means to the user and how the user wishes to interact with the selector.

Promotion is an important part of marketing. The intent is to bring a thorough understanding of the collections and allied services to the user and to provide the user with information about how to influence future collection development. Effective promotion involves two-way communication. The selector both shares and gains information. Many vehicles exist for fostering formal and informal information sharing. Some techniques are tailored to specific types of libraries and some are universally applicable. At their core, all aim to communicate effectively with users, stakeholders, and potential users. The information gained through outreach and liaison activities becomes part of market research and informs the marketing mix. Librarians need to take care to listen to their users and potential users and to avoid developing and adjusting collections and services that reflect only the library's perspective on what is "good."

Control, or performance measurement, completes the marketing cycle, leading the selector back to responding to the public and modifying the collection to better meet their needs, wants, demands, and interests. Control is the phase that checks the librarian's success in understanding the community and developing a market mix that satisfies them.

CASE STUDY

Kimberly has been reassigned to Dewey Public School, a K–6 school in large urban school district. She has an MLIS with school library media certification and has been a school library media specialist for fifteen years, assigned to various schools in the school district. Dewey has 866 students, nearly all of whom take a bus to and from school. Many students are the children of immigrant parents. Their countries of origin are varied; 21 percent of them are considered to have limited English proficiency. The school meets the federal criteria for high poverty, with 83 percent of the students eligible for free or reduced-price lunches. Eleven percent of the students participate in special education programs. The most recent data show that students are not making "Adequate Yearly Progress" (a means of measuring, through standards and assessments, the achievement of the No Child Left Behind goal). Dewey benefits from having a dedicated staff of fifty-eight teachers, nine other licensed professionals, twenty-five paraprofessionals, and three administrators—66 percent of which have master's degrees. The Dewey staff meets the federal requirement for "highly qualified." The school district offers a fairly extensive package of age-appropriate online resources. Collection development and management are decentralized. Kimberly has a $5,000 budget to select new and replacement materials for the collection and to purchase supplemental curriculum materials for teachers. She is able to use the school's modest supplies and printing budget. She begins her new position at Dewey the first of August, the same day as teachers. School starts the day after Labor Day, so she has a month before students arrive.

Activity

Develop an outreach plan for Kimberly. Consider how she will segment her market (user community and stakeholders), gather primary and secondary data, understand the needs and desires of the various market segments, build relationships, promote the library media center collection and services, and evaluate her outreach success. Identify the activities that will go into Kimberly's plan and assign a time line for their execution over the school year.

Note: The case study and associated activity related to the marketing topics in the first edition are available at www.ala.org/editions/extras/Johnson09720 as a supplemental resource.

Notes

1. Sharon L. Baker and Karen L. Wallace, *The Responsive Public Library: How to Develop and Market a Winning Collection*, 2nd ed. (Englewood, Colo.: Libraries Unlimited, 2002), 3.

2. ALA Reference and User Services Association, Liaison with Users Committee, "Guidelines for Liaison Work in Managing Collections and Services," *Reference and User Services Quarterly* 41, no. 2 (2001): 107, www.ala.org/ala/rusa/protools/referenceguide/guidelinesliaison.cfm.

3. American Marketing Association, Marketing Definitions (Oct. 1007), www.marketingpower.com/AboutAMA/Pages/DefinitionofMarketing.aspx.

4. Martin Lopez, "A Guide for Beginning Bibliographers," *Library Resources and Technical Services* 13 (Fall 1969): 462–70.

5. Susan L. Fales, ed., *Guide for Training Collection Development Librarians*, Collection Management and Development Guides no. 8 (Chicago: American Library Association, 1996).

6. Walter Alwyn Briscoe, *Library Advertising: "Publicity" Methods for Public Libraries, Library-Work with Children, Rural Library Schemes, &c., with a Chapter on the Cinema and Library* (London: Grafton; New York: H. W. Wilson, 1921).

7. Charles B. Osburn, "Toward a Reconceptualization of Collection Development," *Advances in Library Administration and Organization* 2 (1983): 188.

8. Philip Kotler and Alan R. Andreasen, *Strategic Marketing for Nonprofit Organizations*, 8th ed. (Upper Saddle River, N.J.: Prentice-Hall, 2008).

9. Philip Kotler and Gary Armstrong, *Principles of Marketing*, 11th ed. (Upper Saddle River, N.J.: Prentice-Hall, 2006).

10. Philip Kotler and Karen F. A. Fox, *Strategic Marketing for Educational Institutions*, 2nd ed. (Englewood Cliffs, N.J.: Prentice-Hall, 1995).

11. Svein Ottar Olsen, "Comparative Evaluation and the Relationship between Quality, Satisfaction, and Repurchase Loyalty," *Journal of the Academy of Marketing Science* 30, no. 3 (2002): 240–49; Anders Gustafsson, Michael D. Johnson, and Inger Roos, "The Effects of Customer Satisfaction, Relationship Commitment Dimensions, and Triggers on Customer Retention," *Journal of Marketing* 69, no. 4 (2005): 210–18.

12. Neil H. Borden, "The Concept of the Marketing Mix," in *Science in Marketing*, ed. George Schwartz, 386–97 (New York: Wiley, 1965).

13. Philip Kotler and Nancy Lee, *Marketing in the Public Sector: A Roadmap for Improved Performance* (Upper Saddle River, N.J.: Wharton School Publishing, 2007).

14. Terry Kendrick, *Developing Strategic Marketing Plans That Really Work: A Toolkit for Public Libraries* (London: Facet, 2006), 121.

15. Lorcan Dempsey, "In the Flow," *Lorcan Dempsey's Weblog*, June 24, 2005, http://orweblog.oclc.org/archives/000688.html.

16. Vincci Kwong, "Reach Out to Your Students Using MySpace and Facebook," *Indiana Libraries* 26, no. 3 (2007): 53–57; Deborah Lee, "iPod, You-Pod, We-Pod: Podcasting and Marketing Library Services," *Library Administration and Management* 20, no. 4 (Fall 2006): 206–8.

17. Dempsey, "In the Flow."

18. American Marketing Association, Marketing Definitions.

19. David Nicholas, *Assessing Information Needs: Tools, Techniques, and Concepts for the Information Age* (London: Aslib Information Management, 2000), provides a concise introduction to data collection methods for user studies.

20. George D'Elia, "A Descriptive Market Segmentation Model of the Adult Members of the Public Library's Community," in *Beyond PR: Marketing for Libraries; LJ Special Report 18*, ed. Joseph Eisner, 37–42 (New York: Library Journal, 1981).

21. Reference and User Services Association, Liaison with Users Committee, Liaison with Users guidelines working document, www.ala.org/ala/rusa/rusaourassoc/rusasections/codes/codessection/codescomm/liaisonwithusers/liaisonusers.cfm.

22. Samantha Chmelik, "Market Research for Libraries," *Information Outlook* 10, no. 2 (2006): 23–25.

23. Roger E. Stelk, Paul Metz, and Lane Rasmussen, "Departmental Profiles: A Collection Development Aid," *College and Research Libraries News* 54, no. 4 (1993): 196–99; Doreen Kopycinski and Kimberley Sando, *User Surveys in College Libraries*, CLIP Note no. 38 (Chicago: Association of College and Research Libraries, 2007); Catherine E. Pasterczyk, "Checklist for the New Selector," *College and Research Libraries News* 49, no. 7 (1988): 434–35.

24. Susan Logue et al., comps., *Liaison Services*, SPEC Kit no. 301 (Washington, D.C.: Association of Research Libraries, 2007), 14.

25. Philip M. Turner and Ann Marlow Riedling, *Helping Teachers Teach: A School Library Media Specialist's Role*, 3rd ed. (Westport, Conn.: Libraries Unlimited, 2003).

26. Mary Jo Langhorne, "Using Data in the School Library," in *Toward a 21st-Century School Library Media Program*, ed. Esther Rosenfeld and David V. Loertscher, 367–72 (Lanham, Md.: Scarecrow, 2007).

27. Cathy De Rosa et al., *Perceptions of Libraries and Information Resources: A Report to the OCLC Membership* (Dublin, Ohio: OCLC, 2005), www.oclc.org/reports/pdfs/Percept_all.pdf.

28. Melissa L. Becher and Janice L. Flug, "Using Student Focus Groups to Inform Library Planning and Marketing," *College and Undergraduate Libraries* 12, nos. 1/2 (2005): 1–18; Nancy Everhart and Kay Bishop, "Using Focus Groups with Young People," *Knowledge Quest* 30, no. 3 (2002): 36–37; Pam Harris and Pamela J. McKenzie, "What It Means to Be 'In-Between': A Focus Group Analysis of Barriers Faced by Children Aged 7 to 11 Using Public Libraries," *Canadian Journal of Information and Library Science* 28, no. 4 (2004): 3–24; Sandra Hughes-Hassell and Kay Bishop, "Using Focus Group Interviews to Improve Library Services for Youth," *Teacher Librarian* 32, no. 1 (2004): 8–12; Deborah Lee, "Can You Hear Me Now? Using Focus Groups to Enhance Marketing Research," *Library Administration and Management* 19, no. 2 (2005): 100–101; Christine Olson, "Making Marketing Materialize: 10 Pointers for Better Focus Groups," *Business and Finance Division Bulletin* no. 132 (Spring 2006): 14–15; Michael A. Weber and Robert Flatley, "What Do Faculty Want? A Focus Group Study of Faculty at a Mid-Sized Public University," *Library Philosophy and Practice* 9, no. 1 (2006): 1–8; Deborah K. Wilson-Matusky, "Implications of Using Focus Groups to Improve Library Services," *School Libraries Worldwide* 12, no. 2 (2006): 52–73.

29. Dennis P. Carrigan, "Data-Guided Collection Development: A Promise Unfilled," *College and Research Libraries* 57, no. 5 (1996): 429–37.

30. Kendrick, *Developing Strategic Marketing Plans*, 9.

31. Ibid.; Susan Webreck Alman, *Crash Course in Marketing for Libraries* (Englewood, Colo.: Libraries Unlimited, 2007); Sharon L. Baker and Karen L. Wallace, *The Responsive Public Library: How to Develop and Market a Winning Collection*, 2nd ed. (Englewood, Colo.: Libraries Unlimited, 2002); Public Library Association, *Libraries Prosper with Passion, Purpose, and Persuasion! A PLA Toolkit for Success* (Chicago: American Library Association, 2007); Lisa A. Wolfe, *Library Public Relations, Promotions, and Communications: A How-to-Do-It Manual*, 2nd ed. How-to-Do-It Manuals for Librarians no. 126 (New York: Neal-Schuman, 2005); Jeannette Woodward, *Creating the Customer-Driven Library: Building on the Bookstore Model* (Chicago: American Library Association, 2005).

32. Jim Harrington, "Get Out of Your Office and Practice In-Your-Face Marketing," *Information Outlook* 9, no. 2 (2005): 19–20.

33. Janet Peros, "Face Time: The Power of Person-to-Person Marketing," *Information Outlook* 9, no. 12 (2005): 25–27.

34. Jane Bridges, "Marketing the Hospital Library," *Medical Reference Services Quarterly* 24, no. 3 (2004): 81–92.

35. Amy Burkman, "A Practical Approach to Marketing the School Library," *Library Media Connections* 23, no. 3 (2004): 42–43.

36. Wendy Worley, "Promoting the School Library: A Portfolio Is a Visual Record of Achievement," *School Librarian* 54, no. 4 (2006): 178–79.

37. Keith Curry Lance and David V. Loertscher, *Powering Achievement: School Library Media Programs Make a Difference: The Evidence Mounts* (Salt Lake City, Utah: Hi Willow Research and Publishing, 2005).

38. Julie Beth Todaro, *The Power of Personal Persuasion: Advancing the Academic Library Agenda from the Front Lines: Toolkit* (Chicago: Association of College and Research Libraries, 2006).

39. Susan Logue et al., comps., *Liaison Services*.

40. Scott Stebelman et al., "Improving Library Relations with the Faculty and University Administrators: The Role of the Faculty Outreach Librarian," *College and Research Libraries* 60, no. 2 (1999): 121–30; Luke Vielle, "The Best Is Yet to Come: Laying a Foundation for Marketing," *Technical Services Quarterly* 24, no. 2 (2006): 9–26.

41. Vielle, "Best Is Yet to Come," 23.

42. Stephan J. Macaluso and Barbara Whitney Petruzzelli, "The Library Liaison Toolkit: Learning to Bridge the Communication Gap," *Reference Librarian*, nos. 89/90 (2005): 163–77.

43. Karla L. Hahn and Kari Schmidt, "Web Communications and Collections Outreach to Faculty," *College and Research Libraries* 66, no. 1 (2005): 28–40; Jeanie M. Welch, "The Electronic Welcome Mat: The Academic Library Web Site as a Marketing and Public Relations Tool," *Journal of Academic Librarianship* 31, no. 3 (2005): 225–28.

44. John Wesley Lowery, "Student Affairs for a New Generation," in *Serving the Millennial Generation*, ed. Michael D. Coomes and Robert DeBard, 87–99 (San Francisco: Jossey-Bass, 2004).

45. Nancy Fried Foster and Susan Gibbons, eds., *Studying Students: The Undergraduate Research Project at the University of Rochester* (Chicago: Association of College and Research Libraries, 2007).

46. Lara Ursin Cummings, "Bursting Out of the Box: Outreach to the Millennial Generation through Student Services Programs," *Reference Services Review* 35, no. 2 (2007): 285–95.

Suggested Readings

Adams, Kate E., and Mary E. Cassner. "Marketing Library Resources and Services to Distance Faculty." *Journal of Library Administration* 31, nos. 3/4 (2001): 5–22.

Block, Marylaine. "The Secret of Library Marketing: Make Yourself Indispensable." *American Libraries* 32, no. 8 (2001): 48–50.

Borsche, Judith K. "Marketing the School Library." *PNLA Quarterly* 69, no. 3 (2005): 6, 26–28.

Bush, Gail, and Merrilee Andersen Kwielford. "Marketing Reflections: Advocacy in Action." In *Toward a 21st-Century School Library Media Program*, edited by Esther Rosenfeld and David V. Loertscher, 380–85. Lanham, Md.: Scarecrow, 2007.

Byrd, Susannah Mississippi. *¡Bienvenidos! ¡Welcome! A Handy Resource Guide for Marketing Your Library to Latinos*. Chicago: American Library Association, 2005.

Callison, Daniel. "Student-Talk." *School Library Media Activities Monthly* 14, no. 10 (1998): 38–41.

Campbell, Jennifer, and Sally Gibson. "Implementing an Action Plan: Strategies for Marketing Libraries Services." *College and Undergraduate Libraries* 12, nos. 1/2 (2005): 153–64.

Chu, Felix Tse-Hsiu. "Librarian-Faculty Relations in Collection Development." *Journal of Academic Librarianship* 23 (Jan. 1997): 15–20.

Coffman, Steve. "What If You Ran Your Library Like a Bookstore?" *American Libraries* 29 (March 1998): 40–46.

De Sáez, Eileen Elliott. *Marketing Concepts for Libraries and Information Services*. 2nd ed. London: Facet, 2002.

Duke, Lynda M., and Toni Tucker. "How to Develop a Marketing Plan for an Academic Library." *Technical Services Quarterly* 25, no. 1 (2007): 51–68.

Fabian, Carole Ann, et al. "Multiple Models for Library Outreach Initiatives." *Reference Librarian* no. 82 (2003): 39–55.

Fisher, Patricia H., and Marseille M. Pride, with Ellen G. Miller. *Blueprint for Your Library Marketing Plan: A Guide to Help You Survive and Thrive*. Chicago: American Library Association, 2006.

Flaten, Trine Kolderup, ed. *Management, Marketing and Promotion of Library Services Based on Statistics, Analyses and Evaluation*. IFLA Publications no. 120/121. Munich: K. G. Saur, 2006.

Freda, Cecilia. "Promoting Your Library Program: Getting the Message Out." *Knowledge Quest* 36, no. 1 (2007): 48–51.

Glynn, Tom, and Connie Wu. "New Roles and Opportunities for Academic Library Liaisons: A Survey and Recommendations." *Reference Services Review* 31, no. 2 (2003): 122–28.

Gupta, Dinesh K. *Marketing Library and Information Services: International Perspectives.* Munich: K. G. Saur, 2006.

Hallmark, Elizabeth Kennedy, Laura Schwartz, and Loriene Roy. "Developing a Long-Range and Outreach Plan for Your Academic Library: The Need for a Marketing Outreach Plan." *College and Research Libraries News* 68, no. 2 (2007): 92–95.

Harrington, Jim. "Get Out of Your Office and Practice: In-Your-Face Marketing" *Information Outlook* 9, no. 2 (2005): 19–20.

Karp, Rashelle S. *Powerful Public Relations: A How-to Guide for Libraries.* Chicago: American Library Association, 2002.

Lindsay, Anita Rothwell. *Marketing and Public Relations Practices in College Libraries.* CLIP Note no. 34. Chicago: American Library Association, 2004.

Livingston, Jill. "The Benefits of Library Liaison Programs for Small Libraries: An Overview." *Medical Reference Services Quarterly* 22, no. 1 (2003): 21–30.

Marshall, Nancy J. "Public Relations in Academic Libraries: A Descriptive Analysis." *Journal of Academic Librarianship* 27, no. 2 (2001): 116–21.

Mozenter, Frada L., Bridgette T. Sanders, and Jeanie M. Welch. "Restructuring a Liaison Program in an Academic Library." *College and Research Libraries* 61, no. 5 (2000): 432–40.

Nelson, James A. "Marketing and Advocacy: Collaboration in Principle and Practice." In *Current Practices in Public Libraries,* edited by William Miller and Rita M. Pellen, 117–35. Binghamton, N.Y.: Haworth, 2006.

Norris, Melissa Cox. "Marketing: A New Way of Doing Business in Academic Libraries." *Advances in Library Administration and Organization* 22 (2005): 275–95.

Osif, Bonnie A. "Branding, Marketing, and Fund-Raising." *Library Administration and Management* 20, no. 1 (2006): 39–43.

Owens, Irene, ed. *Strategic Marketing in Library and Information Science.* Binghamton, N.Y.: Haworth, 2002

Petruzelli, Barbara Whitney, ed. *Real-Life Marketing and Promotion Strategies in College Libraries: Connecting with Campus and Community.* Binghamton, N.Y.: Haworth, 2005.

Pfeil, Angela B. *Going Places with Youth Outreach: Smart Marketing Strategies for Your Library.* Chicago: American Library Association, 2005.

Reed, Sally Gardner. *Making the Case for Your Library: A How-to-Do-It Manual.* How-to-Do-It Manuals for Librarians no. 104. New York: Neal-Schuman, 2001.

Reeves, Linda, et al. "Faculty Outreach: A Win-Win Proposition." *Reference Librarian,* no. 82 (2003): 57–68.

Robertson, Deborah A. *Cultural Programming for Libraries: Linking Libraries, Communities, and Culture.* Chicago: American Library Association, 2005.

Rossiter, Nancy Ellen. *Marketing a Library: Promoting the Best Deal in Town.* Oxford, England: Chandos, 2008.

Sanacore, Joseph. "Teacher-Librarians, Teachers, and Children As Cobuilders of School Library Collections." *Teacher Librarian* 33, no. 5 (June 2006): 24–29.

Schneider, Tina. "Outreach: Why, How, and Who? Academic Libraries and Their Involvement in the Community." *Reference Librarian,* no. 82 (2003): 199–213.

Siess, Judith A. *The Visible Librarian: Asserting Your Value with Marketing and Advocacy.* Chicago: American Library Association, 2003.

Silva, Jesse, and Sherry DeDecker. "Beyond the Library: Uncovering Users' Needs and Marketing Your Expertise." *DttP: Documents to the People* 35, no. 2 (2007): 46–48.

Soules, Aline. "The Principles of Marketing and Relationship Management." *portal: Libraries and the Academy* 1, no. 3 (2001): 339–50.

Speas, Bonnie. "Direct and Indirect Promotion of the School Library." *PNLA Quarterly* 71, no. 2 (2007): 10–13.

Sullivan, Michael. "Public Relations, Promotion, and Marketing." In *Fundamentals of Children's Services*, 203–12. Chicago: American library Association, 2005.

Sympson, Penny S. "How I Made a Library Indispensable and Saved It from Outsourcing." *Information Outlook* 9, no. 3 (2005): 29–30.

Tennant, Michele R., et al. "Customizing for Clients: Developing a Library Liaison Program from Need to Plan." *Bulletin of the Medical Library Association* 89, no. 1 (2001): 8–20.

Verostek, Jane M. "Affordable, Effective, and Realistic Marketing." *College and Undergraduate Libraries* 12, nos. 1/2 (2005): 119–38.

Wakeham, Maurice. "Marketing and Health Libraries." *Health Information and Libraries Journal* 21, no. 4 (2004): 237–44.

Wallace, Linda K. *Libraries, Mission, and Marketing: Writing Mission Statements That Work.* Chicago: American Library Association, 2004.

Walters, Suzanne. *Library Marketing That Works!* New York: Neal-Schuman, 2004.

Weingand, Darlene E. *Future-Driven Library Marketing.* Chicago: American Library Association, 1998.

Wilson, Kerry, and Briony Train. "Marketing Library Services to Children and Young People: The Role of Schools' Library Services." *New Review of Children's Literature and Librarianship* 12, no. 2 (2006): 147–61.

Yeo, Geoffrey. "Understanding Users and Use: A Market Segmentation Approach." *Journal of the Society of Archivists* 26, no. 1 (2005): 25–53.

CHAPTER SEVEN

Collection Analysis: Evaluation and Assessment

Collection analysis is more than analyzing the collection per se. It encompasses analysis of the library's collection, its use, and ultimately its impact. Analysis provides information on various aspects of the collection, for example, the number of pieces and titles in a particular subject; formats represented; age and condition of materials; breadth and depth of coverage; language in which the resources are available; patron use and nonuse of the collection; and impact the collection has on its user community. Although librarians may think of collection analysis as measuring the collection's quality (an amorphous concept, at best), the real objective is to measure the collection's utility—how effective the collection is in satisfying the purpose for which it is intended. This chapter explores the purposes and methods of collection analysis and offers advice on conducting analyses.

Collection Analysis as a Management Tool

Collection analysis is part of the effective and efficient management of resources. Mary C. Bushing, writing about collection mapping (collection analysis using the Conspectus collecting level definitions), defines it as "the ability to understand the specific strengths and weaknesses of information resources with statistical data as well as impressionistic judgments based on experience and knowledge of the discipline area under consideration."[1] Amy Hart writes, more succinctly, "The most basic question in a collection analysis is 'Where is my collection weak, and where is it strong?'"[2] Collection analysis can document how fiscal resources are being used and how investments are being maintained. *Learning for the Future* suggests that collection review be used to determine (1) the effectiveness of the available information resources in meeting the curricular and extracurricular needs of the school and in contributing to improvement in student outcomes, and (2) the effectiveness of the school's collection development strategies in attaining the policy priorities within budget targets.[3] Being accountable requires evidence that libraries are delivering the collections and services expected on investments. In addition, collection analysis can serve as an internal control mechanism to measure individual performance. Decisions about other areas such as cooperative agreements, space limitations and needs, and ownership and access are informed through collection analysis.

Paul Mosher traces the formal evaluation of American library collections to a 1849 report by Charles C. Jewett to the Smithsonian Institution. Jewett investigated the capabilities of U.S. libraries to provide the literature for two extensive scholarly histories and found the nation's libraries deficient.[4] According to Mosher, examining the adequacy of U.S. libraries characterized evaluation into the 1930s and 1940s, then attention turned toward the assessment of individual collections in terms of given needs in the 1950s and 1960s.[5]

Librarians often use the terms *assessment* and *evaluation* interchangeably. They can, however, be distinguished according to the intent of the analysis. The aim of *assessment* is to determine how well the collection supports the goals, needs, and mission of the library or parent organization. The collection (both locally held and remotely accessed materials) is assessed in the local context. The library's goals and purpose, therefore, must be stated clearly before any meaningful evaluation of a library's collection can take place. Once collecting goals (ideally, in a collection development policy statement) have been assigned to subject areas, the library can assess whether it has been collecting at the desired level.

Evaluation seeks to examine or describe collections either in their own terms or in relation to other collections and checking mechanisms, such as lists. Both evaluation and assessment provide a better understanding of the collection and the user community. A librarian gains information that helps him or her decide if a collection is meeting its objectives, how well it is serving its users, in which ways or areas it is deficient, and what remains to be done to develop it. As librarians learn more about the collection and its utility, they are able to manage the collection—its growth, preservation and conservation, storage, withdrawal, and cancellation of periodicals—in relation to users' needs and the library's and parent institution's mission.

Assessment has received increasing attention in libraries since the late 1990s, paralleling increasing emphasis on performance measurement to demonstrate accountability through positive outcomes, quality from the user's perspective, cost efficiencies and effectiveness, and responsible stewardship of resources. Creating a culture of assessment has been promoted as an important component in engaging everyone in a library in this critical activity.[6] Amos Lakos and Shelley Phipps define a culture of assessment as "an organizational environment in which decisions are based on facts, research, and analysis, and where services are planned and delivered in ways that maximize positive outcomes and impacts for customers and stakeholders."[7] One can broaden this definition to state that effective assessment results in services *and collections* that create positive outcomes for library users and stakeholders.

Inputs are the resources available in a library and have been measured for a long time. These include staffing, allocations and expenditures, and collection size and growth. *Output* measures are those activities that the library provides, based on inputs. These include hours of service, availability and use of collections, reference transactions, and instructional sessions. *Outcomes* are the benefits to the user or user community as a result of a library's inputs and outputs. The Institute of Museum and Library Services offers this definition:

> Outcomes—Benefits or changes for individuals or populations during or after participating in program activities, including new knowledge, increased skills, changed attitudes or values, modified behavior, improved condition, or altered status (e.g., number of children who learned a finger play during story time, number of parents who indicated that they gained new knowledge or skills as a result of parent education classes, number of students whose grades improved after homework clinics, number of children who maintained reading skills over the summer as a result of the summer reading program, number of people who report being better able to access and use networked information after attending information literacy classes).[8]

Peter Hernon and Robert E. Dugan are more concise: outcomes assessment seeks to answer the question "How are users of our library changed as a direct result of their contact with our collections and services?"[9] Developing outcome measures is more challenging than developing input and output measures, and several have explored this topic. Eliza T. Dresang, Melissa Gross, and Leslie Edmonds Holt address outcome measures for youth services, and Peter Brophy looks more broadly at how to measure the library's impact on its users and society.[10] The ARL undertook an "e-metrics" project to define and collect data on the use and value of electronic resources, with an emphasis on how academic libraries might specify, produce, and assess institutional outcomes.[11] The challenges are, first, developing clear and meaningful definitions of desired outcomes so that the correct questions can be asked and the appropriate data collected and analyzed and, second, combining outcomes assessment with multiple approaches to analysis in order to have a complete understanding of the collection, its use, and its users.

Knowing the Collection

Knowing the collection is a selector's responsibility. Collection analysis leads to this knowledge. Collection analysis is not, therefore, a one-time project. Collection analysis is an ongoing process informed by both individual analysis projects and constant attention to collection quality and its responsiveness to the user community. Assessment and evaluation provide, through specific methods of analysis and continuous monitoring, information about the current collection and about progress toward collection goals. Each analysis project provides a snapshot of or baseline information about the existing collection.

A common misconception is that collection assessment and evaluation determine how "good" a collection is. Earlier chapters in this book explore the debate over what defines a good book or other library resources. Contemporary theory advances the idea that a collection is considered good and appropriate to the extent that it matches the goals of the library and its parent institution. The collection developed to serve an elementary school is not an appropriate or good collection for a high school, a collection serving a two-year technical college is not a good collection for a university with many graduate programs and professional schools, and a collection developed to meet the needs of an electrical engineering firm is not a good collection for a teaching hospital. Even when evaluation techniques examine the collection in relation to an external measure, that measure must relate to the goals of the collection being considered. Deciding what not to collect is as important as deciding what to collect. Although analyses do identify collection areas that should be developed as well as strengths, intentional nonstrengths are equally valid.

Techniques of Collection Analysis

Methods and techniques of collection analysis range from impressionistic, descriptive assessments to complex statistical investigations. All seek to provide organized, pertinent, specific, and accurate information about the collection. Two topologies are used in discussing the various approaches to analysis. Techniques are either collection-based or use- and user-based and either quantitative or qualitative. Figure 7-1 represents these topologies as a matrix within which various techniques are organized; the commercial products listed are representative and not intended to be exhaustive.

Collection-based techniques examine the size, growth, depth, breadth, variety, balance, and coverage of library materials—often against an external standard or the holdings of one or more libraries known to be comprehensive in the relevant subject area. Techniques include checking lists, catalogs, and bibliographies; looking at materials on the shelf; and compiling statistics. Collection-based techniques provide information that can guide selector decisions about preservation and conservation treatments, withdrawals, serial cancellations, duplication, and storage.

Use- and user-based approaches look at who is using the materials, how often, and what their expectations are. Emphasis may be on the use or on the user. A use study focuses on the materials and examines individual titles or groups of titles or subject areas to determine user success in identifying and locating what is needed and in using these items. User studies focus on the individuals or

	Use- and user-based	**Collection-based**
Quantitative	Interlibrary loan statistics	Collection size and growth
	Circulation statistics	Materials budget size and growth
	In-house use statistics	Collection size standards and formulas
	Document delivery statistics	Citation analysis/studies
	ILL transactions	Ratio measures (e.g., monographs expenditures to serials expenditures; expenditures compared to citizens)
	"Hits" and downloads (e.g., transaction logs, vendor-supplied data, COUNTER)	Content overlap studies
	Cost per use	
Qualitative	User opinion surveys (e.g., LibQual+, Web-based, e-mail)	List checking (e.g., catalogs, bibliographies)
	User observation	Verification studies
	Focus groups	Citation analysis
	Usability testing	Direct collection checking
		Collection mapping (assigning Conspectus levels)
		Brief tests of collection strength
		Commercial products (e.g., WorldCat Collection Analysis, Bowker's Book Analysis System, Ulrich's Serials Analysis System, Follett Library Resources' TitleWise, Sagebrush BenchMARC)

FIGURE 7-1 Methods of collection analysis

groups using the collection and how they are using its various components. Use- and user-based studies include research into users' failure to locate and obtain materials locally and how alternatives, such as interlibrary loan, are used. Use and user studies collect information about user expectations, how users approach the collections, and the materials users select from those available.

Quantitative analysis counts things. It measures titles, circulation transactions, interlibrary loan requests, access and download transactions with electronic resources, and dollars spent. Quantitative analysis compares measurements over time within a library and with other libraries. It considers ratios such as expenditures for serials in relation to expenditures for monographs and expenditures for print resources in relation to those for e-resources. An academic library may analyze total collection expenditures in relation to number of students, faculty members, and degree programs. A public library may consider annual expenditures or circulation transactions per user group or branch library.

Quantitative methods demonstrate growth and use of collections by looking at collection and circulation statistics, e-resource use, interlibrary loan requests, and budget information. Once a baseline is established, the size, growth, and use of a collection over time can be measured.

Automated systems have made the collection of use data much easier. Librarians can extract data directly from a local system using various reports provided by the system or from specially written reports. Some services, such as Follett Library Resources' TitleWise Online Collection Analysis, Bowker's Book Analysis System, and Ulrich's Serials Analysis System, can generate reports on the basis of a copy of the library's bibliographic data provided to them. TitleWise and many others are free to current customers. These reports can analyze a collection from a single school or a school district, compare the collection to other grade-appropriate collections, and identify areas that are strong or need weeding or further development. OCLC's WorldCat Collection Analysis, another vendor tool, relies on the library's holdings as recorded in the WorldCat database. Regardless of how generated, these reports can provide counts and percentages of titles held by classification ranges, average date of publication for classification ranges, growth by classification range, and so on. Several of these services can evaluate a library's circulation activity (when a file of the library's circulation activity data is uploaded to the service provider) to help identify collection areas that need attention. A vendor service can also compare local holdings against peer libraries and against various authoritative title lists, such as *Choice Magazine*'s Outstanding Academic Titles or grade-appropriate recommended school library collections. WorldCat Collection Analysis can also identify the uniqueness of a library's holdings.

Qualitative analysis is more subjective than quantitative analysis because it depends on perception, opinion, and the context in which the data are gathered. G. E. Gorman and Peter Crayton offer this definition:

> Qualitative research is a process of inquiry that draws data from the context in which events occur, in an attempt to describe these occurrences, as a means of determining the process in which events are imbedded and the perspectives of those participating in the events, using induction to derive possible explanations based on observed phenomena.[12]

The goal of qualitative analysis is to determine collection strengths, weaknesses, and nonstrengths (which reflect conscious decisions not to collect). Qualitative analysis depends on the opinion of selectors and external experts and the perceptions of users. Even when collections are checked against external lists, these lists are themselves the result of informed opinion about what constitutes a good collection or what characterizes a collection designated at a specific collecting level or appropriate for a specific user group.

All collection analysis, whether qualitative or quantitative, should employ sound research practices. These require a clear understanding of what is being measured, how to measure it, and how to interpret the results. Collection analysis begins with a clear question to be answered. Competent research projects produce information that is both reliable (likely to yield the same results if repeated) and statistically valid (the observed result can be relied upon and not attributed to random error in sampling, measurement, or testing). In other words, the findings are repeatable, and the conclusions are true. Several sources provide guidance for conducting research in libraries.[13] In addition to understanding and practicing sound research, librarians who plan to use survey instruments should consult with experts in their development and application.

Purposes of Collection Analysis

A primary goal of collection analysis is to increase selector knowledge about the collection and its use so he or she can measure its success and develop and manage it effectively. Collection analysis also provides information that may be used for many other purposes. Analysis can be used to demonstrate accountability by marking progress toward performance goals and showing that investments are being used effectively.[14] A collection analysis provides a detailed subject profile that can inform new library staff members and users about the nature of the collection. It can assist in the writing or revision of a collection development policy and provide a measure of an existing policy's effectiveness. Collection analysis can help explain decisions and expenditures; for example, documented high use of e-resources during hours the library building is closed might be used to explain allocating an increased percentage of the total acquisitions budget for this format.

Information (e.g., areas that need strengthening, weeding, updating) collected through collection analysis can be used in the planning process, including justifications for budget requests and funding referendums. It can guide and inform decisions and policymaking throughout the library, including budget and staffing allocations. Analyses that focus on the condition of materials and their availability can be used for disaster preparedness, inventory purposes, and space planning.

Reports from collection analyses can be used in accreditation reports and for other external purposes. Some academic libraries are involved in institutional planning for new degree programs. A specific and detailed collection analysis can demonstrate the degree to which a library can or cannot support a new program or major. Information about collection strengths can be used to recruit new faculty members and students. Corporate libraries can gain the information to document their ability to support new research and development programs. School media centers can document the age of collections by subject area and compare circulation activity against titles held by subject, thus showing areas that may need strengthening. Information may be gathered through collection analysis that can be used in press releases, library reports and newsletters, and grant proposals. Collection analysis positions a library to share information with other libraries with which it is involved through existing or proposed partnerships.

Historical Overview of Collection Analysis

Until the end of the nineteenth century, collection analysis focused on description rather than assessment and evaluation. This was, in large part, a function of the manner in which collections were developed—through donations and what was available for acquisition rather than by intentional collection building to meet specific needs and goals. Around 1900, librarians began using selected bibliographies or lists against which individual library holdings were checked. These lists were prepared by the ALA and its divisions, authoritative librarians, and subject specialists. Another form of list checking involved collecting reviews and then determining if the library held those titles that received favorable reviews. Libraries also checked references and bibliographies in scholarly works against library holdings. List checking was the primary method of collection analysis until the middle of the twentieth century.

Quantitative Studies

In the 1960s, librarians began to promote more diverse and scientific methods of collection analysis. These included studying citation patterns, collection overlap and uniqueness, comparative statistics, and classification and curriculum relationships; developing formulas for collection size and acquisitions budgets; and employing sociological tools in the design and application of use and user studies. Much of the emphasis in this period was on the objectivity of analysis results. College and university librarians, particularly, sought quantitative measures that were both easy to apply and objective. Many studies focused on collecting and comparing collection size and expenditure statistics, both seen as measures of excellence.

Since the 1970s, both quantitative and qualitative methods of collection analysis have been developed and promoted. Much of the impetus has been a desire to facilitate cooperative collection development in consortia and large library systems. Academic and research libraries have initiated several cooperative projects. The ARL's Collection Analysis Project was begun in the 1970s to analyze collections within institutional contexts with hopes for increasing cooperative collection development among large research libraries.[15]

Collection size formulas that use local variables to calculate the number of volumes required to meet local needs have been developed. The use of formulas depends on the notion of a minimum size for collections or budgets relative to the size of a library's user community or level of parent institution's programs. The Clapp-Jordan formula, which uses an acceptable core collection count plus volumes per student, per faculty, per undergraduate field, and per graduate field, is one model for this approach.[16] Others have been proposed over the years. Existing collections can be compared to the ideal specified by the formula. Some library standards provide formulas for deciding optimum collection size. Formulas have become less popular as libraries have moved away from relying solely on numbers (e.g., collection counts, dollars expended) as measures of quality and begun to consider impact as well.

Collection analysis by studying collection use produced one of the more controversial statistical studies—that conducted by Allen Kent and others at the University of Pittsburgh in the 1970s.[17] This study found that 26.8 percent of the monographs held in the University of Pittsburgh Library's collection accounted for 82.2 percent of the use, and only 60.1 percent of the collection circulated at all, leading researchers to suggest implications for past and future collection management practices. This finding confirmed earlier research on the circulation of materials in public, special, and university libraries conducted by Richard W. Trueswell, who suggested that the "80/20 Rule" (previously applied to business inventories in which 80 percent of business transactions involve only 20 percent of stocked items) also applied to libraries' holdings.[18] The 80/20 ratio is a reference to the phenomenon that 20 percent of the collection accounts for 80 percent of circulation. Questions remain about whether frequency of book and journal circulation is an appropriate measure of academic library effectiveness, but circulation studies can provide guidance about which parts of a collection can be put in storage or withdrawn as well as which areas need to be developed.

Other quantitative use studies examine a collection by collection profile, in-library use, shelf availability, document delivery, downloads from remote resources, or interlibrary lending and borrowing statistics. Budget-based quantitative studies—which, for example, measure growth of the materials budget, track changes in the ratio of expenditures for serials to those for monographs, and compare allocations between subject areas—are additional techniques for considering the relation of a library's operations to its goals and long-term mission.

Quantitative measures must be approached with some caution. Thomas E. Nisonger lists several weaknesses in such data.[19] For example, all uses are counted equally, with no indications of value or benefit from the use. The data reflect success in locating an item but ignore failure. They measure what was used, not what should have been used. Use data do not take into account nonusers. Numbers can be skewed to emphasize a particular point or perspective.

Qualitative Studies

Qualitative studies seek to evaluate the intrinsic worth of the collection and are, by nature, subjective. They depend on the perceptions of librarians and library users. Qualitative studies for libraries were hampered initially by a lack of standard terminology. One of the first steps toward developing a shared vocabulary to describe collection strength or levels appeared in the 1979 *Guidelines for Collection Development*, which designated five collecting levels, which were applied to existing collections ("collection density") and current collecting activity ("collection intensity").[20] The levels were (A) Comprehensive, (B) Research, (C) Study, (D) Basic, and (E) Minimal. This stratified view sought to analyze each collection according to its intended use.

These levels (with one additional level—Out of Scope) were inverted to form the basis of the Research Libraries Group's Conspectus, initiated in 1980. Though no longer maintained by its originators, the Conspectus has become one of the most frequently used qualitative methods and is used worldwide in all types of libraries.[21] A *conspectus* is a brief survey or summary of a subject. The Conspectus is a comprehensive collection analysis tool intended to provide a summary of collecting intensities arranged by subjects, classification scheme, or a combination of both. The Conspectus method is also called *collection mapping* and *inventory profiling*. Ideally, the Conspectus provides a standardized procedure and terminology for sharing detailed descriptions of collections among libraries. Librarians apply numeric codes to identify five levels of existing collection strengths; 0 is used for areas in which no collection exists. Each level builds on the previous level. The WLN Conspectus definitions include subdivisions for levels 1, 2, and 3 to meet the needs of smaller and medium-size libraries, as follows:[22]

0. Out of Scope: Library intentionally does not collect materials in any format in this area.

1. Minimal: Library collects resources that support minimal inquiries about this subject and include a very limited collection of general resources.

    1a. Uneven

    1b. Focused

2. Basic Information: Library collects resources that introduce and define a subject and can support the needs of general library users through the first two years of college instruction.

    2a. Introductory

    2b. Advanced

3. Study or Instructional Support: Library collects resources that provide knowledge about a subject in a systematic way, but at a level of less than research intensity, and support the needs of general library users through college and beginning graduate instruction.

    3a. Basic study

    3b. Intermediate

    3c. Advanced

4. Research: Library collects the major published source materials required for doctoral study and independent research and is very extensive.

5. Comprehensive: Library strives to collect as exhaustively as is reasonably possible in all pertinent formats, in all applicable languages, in both published materials and manuscripts.

Libraries may also apply language coverage indicators:

P   primary language predominates

S   selected other-language materials

W wide selection of languages represented

X   material mainly in one language other than primary national language

D   dual languages or two primary languages

Finally, libraries have the option of indicating collecting activity and collection goal levels:

CL current collection level

AC acquisition commitment

CG collection goal

PC preservation commitment

The Conspectus grew out of the Research Libraries Group's interests in mapping the collection depths of its members. Other groups around the world have adapted the Conspectus for their own use, both for individual library collection analysis and to provide a synopsis of a consortium's or network's coordinated collection development. Versions of the Conspectus permit use of the Library of Congress, Dewey Decimal, and National Library of Medicine classification systems and can be adapted for use in all types of libraries. The Conspectus approach to collection analysis has become accepted as a tool that is both easily adapted to local needs and widely applicable. Its greatest strength is a shared vocabulary to describe collection levels.

Conspectus level definitions were revised in the mid-1990s to reflect the emerging role of electronic resources.[23] E-resources, both locally held and remotely accessed, are considered equivalent to print materials as long as the policies and procedures for their use permit at least an equivalent information-gathering experience. The revised definitions use the term *defined access* to refer to menu options on a library's web interface that link the user to owned or remotely accessed e-resources selected by the library, but it means more than simply providing patrons with access to the Internet and one or more Internet browsers.

The Conspectus has been criticized as being too subjective because it depends on the subject expertise and personal perceptions of the librarians using it. In rebuttal, Mary H. Munroe and Jennie E. Ver Steeg suggest that the question of external validity is moot, because the Conspectus offers descriptive analysis, which by definition cannot have external validity, and seeks to assess the collection in relation to local needs, not in relation to an external measure of quality.[24] According to Charles B. Osburn, subjectivity is the key to effective evaluation because a "collection is of value only as it relates in subjective, cognitive ways to the community" it is intended to serve.[25]

The Conspectus also has been condemned because of its complexity. It offers from twenty-four to thirty-two divisions (broad disciplines), approximately five hundred categories (topics within disciplines), and as many as seven thousand subjects (the most detailed identification with a category). Applying all possible indicator levels to all possible subjects would be an impossible task. Most librarians choose a subset and select only the divisions, categories, and subjects that are relevant to the particular library and collection being analyzed.

"Brief tests of collection strength" is a technique developed by Howard D. White to verify the Conspectus levels that have been assigned to a collection.[26] Conducting a brief test of collection strength requires access to the OCLC WorldCat database. This method consists of five steps:

1. Choose a subject or area of the collection to evaluate.
2. Without reference to the collection being evaluated, create a list of ten or more titles that a library should have if it were collecting at the minimal level and create additional lists for the basic, instructional, and research levels. All lists should be of equal length.
3. Search each title in OCLC WorldCat and list the number of holdings.
4. Arrange the master list of all titles according to the WorldCat holdings from minimal level (the most holding libraries) to research level (the fewest holding libraries). Divide the list into four equal parts, which correspond to the Conspectus levels. Thus, the group of titles (one-fourth of the total list) with the most holdings indicates a minimal level collection, and so on.
5. Search the titles in the local collection to determine which titles are held.

A collection is then evaluated at the level in which half of more of the titles are held locally. For example, a library might hold all ten titles on the minimal list, nine of the ten titles on the basic list, eight of the ten titles on the instructional list, and three of the titles on the research list. This brief test would indicate that the library has an instructional level collection (in Conspectus terms) because it holds more than half the titles on the instructional list but not more than half on the research list.

Collection mapping is used more commonly than the Conspectus as a qualitative approach to collection analysis in school media centers, though the latter is also used.[27] This approach begins with a curriculum map. The school library media specialist creates a chart that lists key topics divided by subject and grade level. Five to eight topics are selected for each subject and grade level, reflecting the school and district curriculum (and state curriculum, where appropriate). The media specialist should review the curriculum map with teachers to ensure that it reports what is actually being taught in the classroom. The library's collection is then mapped against the curriculum map to visually show areas of concentration and gaps. The collection map is also shared with teachers to help set collection goals that match the curriculum and encourage teachers to be participants in collection development plans.

Electronic Resources and Collection Analysis

The increasing use of e-resources in all types and sizes of libraries presents different challenges for analysis. The cost of these materials and the increasing percentage of library budgets going toward their acquisition and access mandate careful consideration of their value to users and role within a library collection. Although e-resources always should be considered part of the collection being analyzed, many of the types of analyses described in detail in this chapter cannot be applied to these formats easily. Many e-resources do not circulate, nor are they available through interlibrary loan. E-books may circulate in the sense that the library has licensed a book with limitations to the number of users who may simultaneously view it. The circulation of these materials is not reflected in the library's circulation system; those use data must be collected via the e-book supplier's reports. Not all e-resources are classified and represented in a shelf list. Direct collection checking and document delivery studies do not apply to most e-resources. The lists developed for checking holdings are only now beginning to include e-resources. Citation analysis studies have been equally sparse in representing e-resources. Comparative collection statistics have focused on traditional formats.

Use statistics for e-resources are receiving more attention. ICOLC has been a leader in identifying both the statistics that are desirable and the obligations of remote resource providers to supply these statistics. ICOLC's "Revised Guidelines for Statistical Measures of Usage of Web-Based Information Resources" defines and creates a common set of basic use information requirements that all electronic products should provide.[28] These metrics permit libraries to analyze use within the individual library and in comparison with others. The data elements to be provided are

- number of sessions (log-ins)
- number of queries (searches)
- number of menu selections
- number of full-content units examined, downloaded, or otherwise supplied to user
- number of turn-aways, peak simultaneous users, and any other indicator relevant to the pricing model applied to the library or consortium

Tracing usage patterns across large and active populations of users is increasingly important as more funds are devoted to e-resources. Feeding data directly into reports designed to compare user behaviors by discipline, status, time of day and year, preferred path to resources, turn-aways, failed searches, and other indicators of preference and satisfaction are important metrics for collection analysis.

ICOLC took the lead in identifying desired data elements, but vendors and their software have defined and counted elements differently. Project COUNTER (Counting Online Usage of NeTworked Electronic Resources; www .projectcounter.org) emerged to standardize how elements are defined and counted. COUNTER is an international initiative of librarians and publishers and their professional organizations established to develop and maintain international codes to govern the recording and exchange of online usage data. COUNTER has released two documents, "COUNTER code of Practice for Journals and Databases" and "COUNTER Code of Practice for Books and Reference Works." The COUNTER Code of Practice for Journals and Databases was updated in 2008 to include consortial usage reports.[29] With COUNTER developing guidelines for counting and reporting usage and usage statistics now available from online content providers, a remaining problem has been providing these statistics to libraries in a consistent data container. Libraries have had to download data individually provider-by-provider and manipulate it locally or contract with a third party, such as SerialsSolutions and Scholarly Stats. The National Information Standards Organization (NISO) has stepped forward to work with interested parties in SUSHI (Standardized Usage Statistics Harvesting Initiative). SUSHI is developing an XML schema for COUNTER usage reports and a standard protocol for machine-to-machine automation of statistics harvesting that can be used by electronic resources management (ERM) and other systems.[30]

Peter T. Shepherd assessed the feasibility of developing and implementing a new journal usage factor based on COUNTER data that would provide an alternative to citation-based measures of journal performance. He suggests that this metric could be based on the data contained in COUNTER Journal Report 1—the number of successful full-text article requests by month and journal. The resulting equation for an individual journal would be[31]

$$\text{Usage Factor} = \frac{\text{Total usage (COUNTER Journal Report 1 data for a specified period)}}{\text{Total number of articles published online (during a specified period)}}$$

As the nature of collections changes, libraries must seek new techniques for assessing them.

Lisa M. Covi and Melissa H. Cragin explore the need for a new framework to assess all electronic collections, which encompass e-journals, e-books, e-reference materials, databases, and indexing and abstracting tools.[32] They point to a problem with what they call unintentionally masked information, which is electronic content that is available but not readily accessible through the user interface or metadata. An item simply may not be accessible because of difficulties with interface use, typographical errors, or screening. In print collections, missing materials are relatively easy to notice—the book is missing from the shelf. When electronic materials are missing, the circumstances are less obvious to the user. Print materials disappear because of circulation control failure, human error, or both. E-resources disappear, in part, because of the multilayering of the information delivery system. Evaluating nonuse of electronic collections must account for resources that are hidden, omitted, or gone.

One form of e-resource use statistics that can be collected locally is a transaction log, which measures use of information held locally and delivered via a local server. Transaction logs can determine the type of user actions, percentage of users accessing the site from a specific domain, number of hits the server gets during specific hours, number of hits every page receives within a site, and path by which a user navigates through the site. Transaction log analysis can assist the study of user behavior and is an efficient technique for collecting longitudinal usage data. Local transaction logs track hits but do not necessarily distinguish between hits and full-text downloads. Repeated hits on a site may indicate failure to locate a desired or pertinent resource. In addition, extracting data, interpreting the data, and detecting trends and patterns can be difficult.[33]

Because users increasingly access e-resources from outside the library, librarians often lack qualitative information about the resource. Determining who is using which e-resource and the degree to which it meets the users' needs can be difficult. Effectiveness, impact factors, and data about outcomes can be lacking. Questions remain about how to determine which resources are of the greatest value to users and, for that matter, what makes a resource of greater or lesser value. Availability and accessibility are one area of study.[34] Usability testing is a technique employed by librarians to assess the effectiveness and efficiency of an e-resource and user satisfaction with it.[35] In usability testing, representatives of the user community perform predetermined tasks while being observed by researchers; the results are used to evaluate the degree to which the e-resource meets usability criteria.[36]

One approach to assessing e-resources is to consider their cost-effectiveness and success in meeting user needs.[37] Cost-effectiveness means that the cost of providing resources is justified by the value they provide to the user. E-resources are assessed to learn how well they are satisfying the library's objectives and meeting the demands placed on them. Another aspect is an examination of how efficiently objectives are being satisfied. Libraries look at congruity between e-resources and local collecting priorities. Comparing the cost of providing full-text articles online to either print subscriptions or delivery via interlibrary loan or commercial document delivery service is one means of assessing the cost-effectiveness of e-resources.[38]

Interdisciplinary Fields

Interdisciplinary fields can present unique problems for collection analysis.[39] Such areas as ecology and the environment, bioethics, women's studies, biotechnology and genetic engineering, and diversity and multiculturalism are highly fluid and evolving fields of study. The nature of interdisciplinary study, teaching, and research requires the collection analyst to cross traditional discipline divisions, although these divisions are reflected in the library's classification schemes and subject headings. Interdisciplinary fields may have a core of materials but expand out to broader, related areas. Analyses based on call numbers present difficulties because of the extensive range of classifications used in interdisciplinary research. Citation studies and user surveys can offer viable alternatives for analyzing interdisciplinary fields.

Methods of Collection-Based Analysis

Some collection-based analyses are quantitative, some are qualitative, and some have aspects of both approaches. If all e-resources (whether classified or not) are represented in the library's catalog, many of these methods are applicable to them.

Collection Profiling

The term *collection profile* is sometimes used synonymously with *collection development statement*. In addition, a profile is used to describe the set of criteria a library prepares to guide the provision of materials by an approval plan vendor. When the term is used in collection analysis, *collection profiling* is the process of assembling a numerical picture of the collection at one point in time—a statistical description. A collection profile may be as modest as a count of titles held within a specified set of classification ranges, or by broad categories such as picture books, young adult books, and adult books. A collection profile can report the distribution of titles by imprint years, perhaps arranged by decade—and this can be combined with title counts.

Creating a collection profile became much easier with automated library systems, which can be mined for desired data. The data can be manipulated in various ways to answer different questions and serve different purposes. Anna H. Perrault and colleagues report on an analysis project that extracted data from a shared catalog and created a profile of the collective holdings of Florida community colleges.[40] This project provided counts of titles held by imprint date in twenty-nine broad LC classification ranges, cumulated percentages held by decade of publication, and provided individual collection-specific data. The collection profile revealed, for example, that more than 55 percent of the collective holdings were published in the 1960s and 1970s.

Collection profiles can provide baseline data for future collection analysis, provide information for cooperative collection development and management, present a statistical description of the collection to stakeholders and funders, and identify areas that need improvement and, perhaps, warrant additional funding.

List Checking

In *list checking*, the selector compares lists of titles appropriate to the subject area being analyzed against the library's holdings. The list may be another library's catalog, general list, specialized list or bibliography, publisher's or dealer's catalog, annual subject compilation, list prepared by a professional association or government authority, course syllabus or required or recommended reading list, list of frequently cited journals, list of journals covered by an abstracting and indexing service, recent acquisitions list from a specialized library, or list prepared for a specific library, type of library, user group, or specific objective. One example is *Best Books for Young Adults*, now in its third edition.[41] The commercial tools for collection analysis are a form of list checking; they compare a library's holdings to the universe of titles and the holdings of peer libraries. A collection is studied by finding the percentage of the titles on the list that are owned by the library. List checking can be a more qualitative, less number-based evaluation method.

Verification studies are a variation on list checking in which libraries check their collections against a specially prepared list of titles designed to encompass the most important works within a specific area. These lists are designed to verify that the libraries understand their collections' strengths and that they have correctly and consistently reported on an analytical instrument, often the Conspectus. The brief tests of collection strength described earlier in this chapter are a form of list checking. Any list selected for checking should match the library's programs and goals and be appropriate to the subjects collected.

List checking is often used because it is easy to apply and lists are available that meet many different libraries' needs. Librarians usually can find a list that has credibility because of the authority and competence of those who compiled it. All or parts of the list can be checked. Many published lists are updated frequently and can be used to check the collection at regular intervals. List checking not only increases knowledge of the collection being analyzed but also increases the selector's knowledge of the subject's or discipline's literature. A selector can also use a list as a purchase guide to identify missing titles that should be acquired.

List checking combines both qualitative and quantitative techniques. The selection by the librarian of the list to be checked is a subjective decision, as was the development of the list, but the result is a statistical report of the number of titles on the list that the library owns. When analyzing the report, the librarian usually converts this percentage to a quality judgment about the collection. List checking also can identify gaps—titles not held and areas with low coverage.

List checking has disadvantages as well as advantages.[42] The library may have used the list as a selection tool in the past. Any list prepared by an individual or group reflects the biases and opinions of the compiler(s). Its validity rests on the assumption that those titles in the resource list are worthy and that the library needs them to satisfy patrons and support programs. A selector may have difficulty finding a list that matches the focus of the collection being analyzed and the mission of the library. Finding an up-to-date list may also present problems. Some items on a list may be out of print. Carol A. Doll cautions against relying too heavily on standard bibliographies when evaluating school library media collections because such lists are often seriously out of date.[43] Many lists cover materials for all ages and may not be useful when compared to a collection developed to serve a specific age group. The selector should recognize that a supplemental tool may be necessary to analyze the collection for materials published since the list was compiled.

Direct Collection Analysis

In *direct collection analysis*, sometimes called *shelf scanning*, someone with knowledge of the literature being analyzed physically examines the collection. That person then draws conclusions about the size, scope, depth or type of materials (textbooks, documents, paperbacks, beginning level, advanced level, professional level), and significance of the collection; the range and distribution of publishing dates; and the physical condition of the materials. The need for preservation, conservation, restoration, or replacement of materials may also be evaluated during this process. This method is most practical when the collection is small or the subject treated is narrowly defined. The evaluator's reputation must be sufficient to give credibility to the evaluation results. Physical analysis depends on labor, the time to do it, and personal judgment.

One advantage of this approach is its appropriateness to any discipline or library collection. Assuming that the collection being reviewed is of a manageable size, its strengths, weaknesses, and condition can be evaluated rapidly. This method is appropriate for a large collection if time is not a major consideration and the selector is interested in working through the collection one segment at a time. Direct collection checking can serve several objectives simultaneously, because the items are physically handled. It is particularly useful as a learning tool for new selectors, who can gain an intimate knowledge of the collection in the process.

The problems with direct collection checking stem from its dependency on individuals and personal perspective and its reliance on physical items. Local selectors may be less than objective as they review the collections they have built. External evaluators who know the subject and its literature, have time to devote to the project, and are affordable may be difficult to recruit. External evaluators also lack the local context and, even if provided the library's collection development policy, may be less effective than someone who knows the user community and local context. The subjective and impressionistic nature of this method does not provide comparable information. Only careful recording of findings provides a quantitative report, and its accuracy may be suspect. Because this approach examines the materials on the shelves, those items not on the shelf cannot be examined, thus excluding most e-resources as well as materials available through resource-sharing arrangements. The evaluator also should consult a shelf list, subject headings in the local catalog, and circulation records. Filling in information from these sources does not provide information on condition. Collection checking is most appropriate for small and focused collections or when the librarian has no time constraints.

A variation on direct collection analysis involves working from the shelf list, which may be a paper or electronic file rather than the physical items on the shelf. Although physical items are not handled in this approach, it does have the advantage of making all other information about the items immediately available. Detailed information about imprints—age, language of publication, percentage of duplication, and subject coverage—can be collected easily. Reports can calculate the distribution of a collection by determining the percentage of holdings by call number range and then by copyright date within these call number ranges. These reports can be combined with circulation data. Such reports can be useful in identifying subject areas that need to be updated, weeded, or expanded. Qualitative information can be used to supplement the quantitative information collected in a shelf list title count. The primary drawback of this method is the potential absence of many items and formats from the classified shelf list. Portions of the collection, such as e-resources and microforms, may not be classified, or the collection may be split between two or more classification schedules.

Comparative Statistics

Libraries have used *comparative statistics* on collection size and materials expenditures to determine relative strengths for many years—often under the assumption that bigger is better. Although depth and breadth of a collection are partly a function of collection size, numerical counts do not measure quality. The ARL member libraries submit comparative statistics in many areas, including several collection measures; these are maintained on the ARL statistics website (www .arl.org/stats/). The ARL annually calculates a weighted index formula and index for its university library members. In 2007 it moved to an expenditures-focused index (total library expenditures, salaries and wages for professional staff, expenditures for total library materials, and number of professional plus support staff). Although member libraries frequently reference their annual ranking in this index, the ARL states explicitly that the index does not measure a library's services, quality of collections, or success in meeting the needs of users. The ARL also developed its New Measures Initiative (www.arl.org/stats/initiatives/), which emphasizes outcomes, impacts, and quality based on user satisfaction, and is working to develop a service-based index that combines three factors: collections, services, and collaborative relationships.

When libraries collect and compare a specific group of statistics, they must agree on the definition of each statistical component and implement identical measurement methods. Comparisons are meaningless without consistency. Libraries typically measure size of collections in volumes and titles and by format, rate of net growth, and expenditures for library materials by format and by total budget. Additional collection comparisons may include number of bound volumes and expenditures on preservation and conservation treatments. Another frequently used comparison is the degree of collection overlap and extent of unique holdings. The OCLC WorldCat Collection Analysis tool is a commercial product that measures overlap and unique holdings. Libraries seek to determine how many titles are held in common and what percentage are unique among two or more libraries.

Statistics to be used for comparison can be gathered in various ways. Libraries' automated systems may generate counts based on cumulative transactions or through specially prepared programs run periodically. These reports count totals as well as activity (titles added and withdrawn, dollars expended, etc.) within a specified period. Various sources offer data with which to compare local findings. The National Center for Education Statistics offers two web tools, Compare Academic Libraries and Compare Public Libraries, which allow libraries to compare their collections with those of a peer institution or peer group of their choice.[44]

If the various measures are clearly defined, the statistics can be compared and have meaning to a wide audience. If the statistics are accurate, they can provide objective, quantifiable data. But statistical compilations are not without problems. If portions of a library's collection are not cataloged and not reflected in either online records or paper files, the statistics will not be accurate. Additionally, manual collection of statistics can be labor intensive and data may not be recorded accurately if their collection is manual or if the definitions of categories are not consistently understood or applied. This can lead to results that are not comparable between libraries. Finally, statistics cannot measure collection quality or, on their own, verify collection levels.

Application of Standards

Collection and resource standards, which have been developed by professional associations, accrediting agencies, funding agencies, and library boards, may be used by those types of libraries for which the standards have been developed. These standards have moved away from prescribing volume counts and budget sizes and applying formulas and now emphasize addressing adequacy, access, and availability. The ALA and its divisions have been leaders in developing standards and output measures for various types of libraries.

Information Power: Building Partnerships for Learning, issued by the American Association of School Librarians and the Association for Educational Communications and Technology, established qualitative standards for student information literacy learning outcomes but offered no quantitative recommendations.[45] Some states have developed standards that supplement national standards. For example, the Minnesota Educational Media Organization developed "Minnesota Standards for Effective School Library Media Programs," which contains quantitative as well as qualitative standards.[46] These standards recommend numbers of current (i.e., average age not greater than ten years) print resources and e-resources per student at minimum, standard, and exemplary levels. The Texas State Library and Archives Commission prepared "School Library Programs: Standards and Guidelines for Texas," which recommends tracking data points, including average number of print, Internet, and online resources utilized per student per week and number of resources checked out by students and staff.[47]

The 2004 Association of College and Research Libraries standards apply to all types of libraries in higher education and "focus on documenting the library's contribution to institutional effectiveness and student learning outcomes."[48] They are no longer prescriptive. Instead of suggesting appropriate size, as earlier Association standards did, the 2004 standards suggest points of comparison with peers and for internal longitudinal analysis. Possible input measures for comparison are ratio of volumes to combined student and faculty FTE and ratio of volumes added per year to combined total student and faculty FTE. Suggested outcome measures that can be compared with peers and longitudinally include ratio of circulation to combined student and faculty FTE and ratio of interlibrary loan requests to combined student and faculty FTE. Outcomes assessment is always more challenging—in both formulating the question and determining the answer.

Standards developed by the ALA and other professional associations and agencies are usually considered authoritative and widely accepted. Their credibility often means that they can be effective in securing library support. If a standard exists for the library type being studied, it generally relates closely to the library's goals. Standards provide a framework for comparing libraries of similar types. Still, the application of externally developed standards can present problems. Some standards are very general and difficult to apply to specific collections. As with any externally developed measure, standards are the product of opinion, and not everyone will agree with the standard. In addition, individuals may not agree with or accept the results reported. Some standards may set a minimum level of volumes, expenditures, or collection level, and the tendency is to view this minimum as the goal. If, for example, a college library reports its volume count as slightly above the minimum standard, some may believe that the library collection is acceptable because it is interpreted as exceeding the target.

Methods of Use- and User-Centered Analysis

The methods of *use- and user-centered analysis* may be quantitative, qualitative, or a combination of the two. Collecting and analyzing use and user data must be handled in a manner that protects and respects users' privacy. User opinion surveys, user observation, and focus groups can be designed to gather perceptions of the breadth, scope, and depth of coverage of e-resources and the ease of access and use. A cardinal principle of librarianship is to protect the privacy of library users with respect to their information seeking. Most academic institutions have specific policies that must be followed when data are gathered from human subjects, ensuring that the privacy as well as the well-being of individuals is not at risk. Many states have statutes that protect the privacy of citizens. The electronic environment makes it much easier to collect information about individuals. In July 2002, the International Coalition of Library Consortia endorsed and released "Privacy Guidelines for Electronic Resources Vendors," which includes this statement: "Publisher respects the privacy of the users of its products. Accordingly, Publisher will not disclose information about any individual user of its products . . . to a third party without the permission of that individual user, except as required by law."[49] Librarians conducting user and usage studies must protect the privacy of individuals while collecting data.

Citation Studies

Citation studies are a type of bibliometrics—the quantitative treatment of the properties that describe and predict the nature of scholarly literature use. Source publications are searched for bibliographic references, and these citations are used to analyze the collection. Citation studies assume that the more frequently cited publications are the more valuable, will continue to be used heavily, and, consequently, are more important to have in the library collections. Citation analysis is closely related to list checking and consists of counting or ranking (or both) the number of times sources are cited—for example, in footnote references, bibliographies, or indexing and abstracting tools—and comparing those figures to the collection.

The two basic approaches employed in citation studies are (1) using published citation studies based on use of the literature by many scholars, and (2) conducting studies in a specific library to determine the literature cited by the library's patrons. The first approach often uses data compiled by Thomson Scientific (formerly ISI) and available through Thomson Scientific's *Journal Citation Reports*. Thomson Scientific evaluates leading journals and, through frequency of citation, their impact factor and influence in the research community. The validity of the data has been questioned by some.[50] In the latter, in-house approach, sources cited in research papers, theses, and dissertations written by the library's users are tracked. The emphasis for establishing relative importance is on how many times an item is cited. Citation studies are particularly useful in collections where journals are important. They are most frequently used to determine the extent to which the collection responds to users' research needs, to develop core lists of primary journals, and to identify candidates for cancellation or storage. A 2008 research project by Thomas E. Nisonger examined use of citation data as a technique for evaluating database content.[51]

School library media centers can use students' bibliographies to check citations and learn about the information needs of the local user. However, if the students use only the collection being evaluated, the value of such citation studies is questionable. In addition, such bibliographies are limited to the subjects on which students write papers, the number of students who write papers, and the number of teachers who require bibliographies.

Data collected in citation studies can be arranged easily into categories for analysis. Citation studies can identify trends in the literature. Online databases can make assembling a citation list efficient and rapid, and several published citation indexes exist. Externally prepared citation lists may not, however, match the bibliographic formats of the library, and developing a list of source items that reflect the subject studied or user needs can be challenging. Subareas of one discipline may have different citation patterns from the general subject. Citation studies are not appropriate to all disciplines. The time lag inherent in citations means that such studies do not reflect recent changes of emphasis in disciplines or the emergence of new journals. Citation analysis is time consuming and labor intensive. Important materials for consultation or background work may not be cited frequently. Finally, a citation to a work is not an inherent guarantee of quality of that work.

Circulation Studies

Circulation studies analyze local circulation transactions. Information can be collected for all or part of the circulating collection by user group, location, date of publication, subject classification, and type of transaction, such as loans, recalls, reserves, or renewals. Circulation studies can identify those portions of the collections that are little used, and these materials can then be weeded, transferred, or placed in storage. Information that indicates lesser-used subject areas may suggest curtailing future acquisitions in these areas. The librarian may decide to duplicate titles that are heavily used or to select additional materials in the same subject area. Circulation statistics can be used to compare use patterns in selected subject areas or by types of materials against their representation in the total collection. This information may be used to modify collection development practices or fund allocations. Journal use statistics, if they combine circulation and in-house use, can be used to calculate cost per use and provide guidance for journal cancellation decisions.

The circulation data can be arranged easily into categories for analysis, and these categories can be correlated in various ways. For example, a public library system can compare circulation of various categories of fiction in each of several branch libraries, leading to decisions about where to place larger mystery, romance, and science fiction collections. A school library media center might use the automated system to provide statistics about the age of the collection broken down by classification number and include circulation data. If the system cannot provide this information or one is not available, the library media specialist can pick random parts of the collection and average the publication dates of the books. Circulation data can determine how many items are checked out each month, what areas are most heavily used, and what areas get little or no use. For example, consider these findings from a school library that uses the Dewey Decimal Classification system: if 23 percent of the titles circulated are from the 500s, and only 10 percent of the budget is designated for titles in the 500s, one might want to readjust that spending—remembering to consider areas emphasized by the curriculum when making these comparison. Circulation data can usually be collected easily, and they are objective. Automated circulation systems make data collection extremely efficient.

The major problem with circulation studies is that they record circulation and exclude in-house use (unless a mechanism is in place to capture in-house use) and use of e-resources. Circulation statistics for materials that are heavily used do not always reflect the true demand for these items, because circulation studies reflect only user successes in identifying, locating, and borrowing items. They provide no information on user failure to find or the collection's failure to provide materials.

In-House Use Studies

Several techniques are available for recording the use of materials consulted by users in the library and reshelved by library staff. *In-house use studies* can focus on either materials used or the users of materials. It can focus on the entire collection or a part of the collection or on all users or a sample of users. In-house use studies are most often used for noncirculating periodical collections or to measure book usage in noncirculating collections. They can be used to correlate type of user with type of material used. Combined with a circulation study, an in-house use study gives more accurate information on use of the collection.

Use studies of noncirculating materials depend on users' willingness to refrain from reshelving materials after use. Materials must be set aside so use can be tracked either manually or by scanning bar codes directly into an automated system. Because in-house use studies rely on users' cooperation, they may be less accurate. Most libraries use direct observation to correct for uncooperative users. If the study is conducted over a limited time, care must be taken to time the study appropriately so data do not reflect use in peak or slow periods. Studies of in-house use report only users' success in locating materials; user failures are not reported.

User Surveys and Focus Groups

User surveys seek to determine how well the library's collections meet users' needs and expectations and to identify those that are unmet. Surveys may be administered in various ways: verbally in person or on the phone, by e-mail, through pop-up screens on the library's catalog or web page, via web-based surveys, or as written questionnaires handed to users in the library either as they enter or exit or mailed to them at offices and homes. Information from user surveys can be used to assess quantitatively and qualitatively the effectiveness of the collections in meeting users' needs, help solve specific problems, define the makeup of the actual community of library users, identify user groups that need to be better served, provide feedback on successes as well as deficiencies, improve public relations and assist in the education of the user community, and identify changing trends and interests.

User surveys can improve the library's relations with its community and help educate users and nonusers. User surveys are not limited to existing data, such as circulation statistics, but permit the library to study new areas. They solicit direct responses from users and can collect opinions not normally shared with the library. The survey can range from short and simple to lengthy and complex.

LibQUAL+ (www.libqual.org), offered by the ARL since 2000, is an online survey instrument within a suite of services that all types of libraries can use to solicit, track, understand, and act upon users' perceptions of library service quality.[52] In 2006, 212 libraries in thirteen countries used the survey; more than five hundred libraries have used it since its inception. The LibQUAL+ survey instrument is a derivation of the SERVQUAL tool created to measure service quality in the private sector.[53] LibQUAL+ calculates gap scores between minimum and perceived expectations and desired and perceived expectations. Sections of the survey measure perceived quality in provision of physical collections and access to collections. Libraries can identify areas that users say are below their minimum expectation (e.g., access to e-resources) and begin to address problems of both library quality and user perception. A library that uses the LibQUAL+ instrument can collect longitudinal data and compare local findings with peer libraries.

The DigiQUAL (www.digiqual.org/digiqual/index.cfm) project is modifying and repurposing the existing LibQUAL+ protocol to assess the services provided by digital libraries. The ARL "MINES (Measuring the Impact of Networked Electronic Services for Libraries) for Libraries" is another new initiative that uses an online transaction-based survey to collect data on the purposes of use and demographics of e-resource users.[54] It is proving useful for gathering collection information from users who no longer need to enter the library physically to access resources.

Focus groups are a research tool in which a small representative group of people (usually eight to ten) selected from the user community engages in a guided discussion in an informal setting. The discussion is directed by a moderator who guides the discussion to obtain the group's opinions about or reactions to specific services or resources. Focus groups can provide in-depth information through facilitated conversation that explores topics and issues that cannot be covered in surveys, which do not provide an opportunity to engage in conversation and explore topics in depth. One difficulty is in measuring the results objectively. Nevertheless, focus groups can provide detailed comments, identification of issues, suggestions, and concerns. Other challenges include selecting participants and getting them to come, deciding how many focus groups are sufficient, facilitating a session effectively, taking good notes, and then analyzing and presenting findings.

Designing even the shortest survey instrument can be difficult. Crafting questions that yield the results sought often requires the help of an experienced questionnaire designer. The parent agency of some libraries may require prior approval for any research that involves human subjects, even a brief library user survey. Crafting surveys for young children can be difficult. Analyzing and interpreting data from an opinion survey are challenging. Users are often passive about collections and so must be surveyed personally, increasing survey costs. Even with individual attention, some users may not cooperate in the survey, resulting in skewed results. Many users are uninformed or unaware of actual and possible library collections. They have difficulty judging what is adequate or appropriate. User surveys may record perceptions, intentions, and recollections that do not reflect actual experiences or patterns of user behavior. Perceptions and opinions are not always quantifiable. By definition, surveys of user opinions miss valuable statements from and about the nonuser.

Interlibrary Loan Analysis

Items requested through interlibrary loan represent a use of the collection because the requester has checked the collection, found the item lacking (either not owned or missing), and decided that he or she still needs it. *Interlibrary loan analysis* can identify areas in which the collection is not satisfying patron needs and can monitor resource-sharing agreements. This is also a way to identify specific current or retrospective journal titles to add to the collection. Statistical results are often readily available and can be analyzed by title, classification, date of imprint, or language. Analyses of subject classifications are best interpreted in conjunction with corresponding acquisitions and circulation data. Results must be interpreted in relation to the collection development policy and in relation to existing resource-sharing agreements that rely on interlibrary loan. Requests can serve as an indicator to the library of new research staff, new program needs, changes in the community, or a long-standing deficiency and can inform budget allocation and reallocation decisions. One approach is to look at interlibrary loan activity within a specific subject area and compare this to the level of collecting reported in the library's collection development policy. For example, a library might report a Conspectus level 4 (research) collection but be borrowing extensively in this area. The implication would be that the collection needs to be developed in this area to be a true level 4. One problem with the use of interlibrary loan statistics is that their significance may be difficult to interpret. Also, this type of study does not reflect users who go elsewhere instead of requesting resources through interlibrary loan.

Document Delivery Test

A *document delivery test* checks the library's ability to provide users with items at the time they are needed. Searching is done by library staff, who simulate users. Document delivery tests build on citation studies by determining first if the library owns a certain item and then if the item can be located and how long it takes to do so. The most frequent approach is to compile a list of citations that reflect the library users' information needs. Externally developed lists can also be used. The test determines both the number of items owned by the library and the time required to locate a specific item. Document delivery testing can provide objective measurements of a collection's capacity to satisfy user needs. If identical lists are used by two or more libraries, data can be compared. This type of testing may identify service problems that can then be corrected. Benchmark data are gathered, and changes can be measured through subsequent testing. Compiling a list of representative citations can, however, be challenging. Because the testing is done by library staff members, it can underestimate the problems encountered by users, such as user error in locating materials. To be meaningful, results require repeated tests or comparisons with studies conducted in other libraries.

Each method described above has advantages and unique benefits for analyzing collections. Each also has disadvantages. No single method of gathering data provides a complete understanding of a collection. Effective collection analysis requires a combination of techniques to gain a complete understanding of a collection and its users. Most methods provide data that can be compared against data collected in subsequent studies. Repeating studies at regular intervals permits the library to show progress toward meeting goals and areas that need attention.

Planning and Conducting a Collection Analysis Project

Although collection analysis should be an ongoing endeavor, it tends to be defined by discrete projects. Ideally, the projects can be repeated and are part of a long-range analysis plan. Each project should be planned carefully to ensure efficiency and effectiveness. An analysis plan can be developed by the individual selector or by a working group. The first step is to define the purposes of the study and the hypotheses to be tested. What are the objectives of this project, why is the information being collected, and how will it be used? A plan identifies specific questions to be answered.

The next step is to determine the data to be gathered and the methods to be used to collect and analyze the data. Each measurement technique collects specific information, and each has drawbacks and advantages. Because each approach has strengths and weakness, using more than one approach is usually beneficial. Consider the format in which the results will be presented, to whom the report is directed, and the tables to be generated from these data. Subject the choice of data to the same rigorous standards used in defining purposes, because each data element adds to the expense and complexity of the study.

The librarian should decide the intended audience of the resulting report. This may be the chief collection development officer, library director, school principal, or funding agency or board. An analysis project may generate information that can be used for more than one audience or purpose. The librarian decides which part of the collection or representative sample to study. This will depend, among other things, on the size of the collection and the time and resources available to conduct the analysis. All steps in an analysis project should be documented so that it can be repeated easily. The librarian should consider whether comparability of results with those of other libraries is desirable and what commonly used classification divisions, statistical categories, terminology, output measures, or survey questions may facilitate comparisons. Before undertaking an analysis project, the librarian should estimate the resources in staff time and funding needed to conduct the analysis. Many methods are time consuming or require external experts. The librarian should consult existing collection information, which may include a collection development policy, library mission or goal statement, and previously conducted analysis projects.

After the data are collected and analyzed, the report is prepared and disseminated. The report should follow generally accepted practices for reports. It should explain the purposes of the study, method(s) used, and problems encountered. It provides general comments on the collection analyzed and the purposes it is intended to serve. As part of the findings, the report summarizes specific strengths, nonstrengths, and weaknesses. A good report provides both written and graphic representations of findings. Visualizations (charts and graphs) can provide

> useful insights about how the collection compares to other collections, how it is developing over time, unintended gaps in the collection, strengths, and weaknesses in the support of interdisciplinary studies, the extent to which [the] collection contributes to the whole of the consortia in which you participate, the scatter of material needed for one discipline across the full subject scope of the library, and so on.[55]

An effective report both shares and interprets the data. It draws relevant conclusions and suggests a plan to improve collection in areas of undesirable weakness along with listing specific items or types of materials needed and cost estimates.

Summary

Collection assessment measures the extent to which the collection, both on-site and accessed remotely, meets the goals, needs, and mission of the library and its parent organization. Collection evaluation examines the collection in relation to other collections and comparative tools or considers the collection on its own terms. Techniques of analysis may be quantitative or qualitative. They may focus on the collection or on the collection's use and users. Each technique has disadvantages and advantages. Using two or more approaches provides a more complete understanding of the collection and serves to validate findings. Some analyses, such as the Conspectus and various commercial products, facilitate comparisons and cooperation between libraries through the use of standardized definitions or classification ranges. Collection mapping compares the library's collection against a school's curriculum map to show areas of concentration and gaps. To be effective, collection analysis projects should be repeatable and comparable.

Collection analysis serves many purposes. Through increased knowledge of the collection and its use, the selector can better understand the extent to which the collection meets the goals and mission of the library and can adjust collecting and managing activities to increase congruence between collection and mission. Measuring performance demonstrates financial and professional accountability through positive outcomes, quality from the user's perspective, cost efficiencies and effectiveness, and responsible stewardship of resources.

Electronic resources present different challenges in analysis. Many traditional methods of analysis cannot be applied to these formats easily. E-resources often do not circulate, nor are they available through interlibrary loan. Direct collection checking and document delivery studies are not applicable to most e-resources. Determining who is using which e-resource and the degree to which it meets the users' needs can also be difficult. Effectiveness, impact factors, and data about outcomes can be lacking. Analyzing use data, provided by publishers and vendors, is becoming more standard and provides one measure of effectiveness.

Collection analysis should be continuous and systematic. When specific analysis projects are undertaken, they should be planned carefully. Librarians conducting the research should have a clear understanding of the uses for which the resulting report is intended. Collection analysis is now an important part of collection development and management responsibilities, and every librarian should understand it, how to perform it, and the purposes it serves.

CASE STUDY

Brigit has recently been hired by Mega State University Library as the librarian responsible for liaison activities and collections to support the departments of astronomy, astrophysics, geology, geophysics, and physics. Combined, these programs serve nearly three thousand students, one-third of whom are graduate students. The faculty members for all five departments total 110, plus several adjunct faculty. The departments are heavily engaged in research, with numerous large, multiyear research grants. More than sixty researchers are involved in the departments' research initiatives along with members of the faculty. The library licenses for access to all the major indexes and abstracting tools and has subscriptions to more than three hundred relevant e-journals. In recent years, the library has also acquired access to the complete online back files for most of these journals. Unlike many libraries, Mega State University Library has not been forced to cancel journals, though it has cancelled most print subscriptions in favor of the electronic versions. The students, faculty, and researchers have made it clear that they value and appreciate the extensive e-resources available. The total acquisitions budget for the five subject areas is $658,000, with $547,000 allocated for continuing resources (print and e-journals, indexes and abstracts, and licensed reference sources). Recently, some faculty have been complaining that the collection lacks current books of interest and value to undergraduates. Brigit wants to learn more about what these faculty members mean by this and what the problems are—perceived or real.

Activity

Identify two or more collection-based and use- or user-based methods of analysis that Brigit can employ to understand these concerns about the book collection. Develop a plan for applying each method, including an explanation of why each approach is being used, what information will be collected, how the information will be used, who the audience is, and a schedule for the projects. Consider focusing on one subject area as a first step, with the idea that the methods can later be applied to other areas. Explain how the proposed approaches complement each other.

Note: This book's first edition also provided a case study and activity related to the information in this chapter. It can be viewed at www.ala.org/editions/extras/Johnson09720 as a supplementary resource.

Notes

1. Mary C. Bushing, "Collection Mapping: An Evolving Tool for Better Resources and Better Access," *Signum 2006*, no. 3 (2006): 9, http://pro.tsv.fi/STKS/signum/200603.htm.
2. Amy Hart, "Collection Analysis: Powerful Ways to Collect, Analyze, and Present Your Data," *Library Media Connection* 21, no. 5 (2006): 36.
3. Australian School Association, *Learning for the Future: Developing Information Services in Australian Schools*, 2nd ed. (Melbourne, Australia: Curriculum Corporation, 2001).
4. Charles C. Jewett, *Appendix to the Report of Regents of the Smithsonian Institution Containing a Report on the Public Libraries of the United States of America. January 1, 1850* (Washington, D.C.: Smithsonian Institution, 1850).
5. Paul H. Mosher, "Quality and Library Collections: New Directions in Research and Practice in Collection Evaluation," *Advances in Librarianship* 13 (1984): 212–13.
6. See, e.g., Amos Lakos, "The Missing Ingredient—Culture of Assessment in Libraries: Opinion Piece," *Performance Measurement and Metrics*, sample issue (Aug. 1999): 3–7; Amos Lakos and Shelley Phipps, "Creating a Culture of Assessment: A Catalyst for Organizational Change," *portal: Libraries and the Academy* 4, no. 3 (2004): 345–61.

7. Lakos and Phipps, "Creating a Culture of Assessment," 352.

8. Institute of Museum and Library Services, "Perspectives on Outcome Based Evaluation for Libraries and Museums" (Washington, D.C.: IMLS, [n.d.]), 20, www.imls.gov/pdf/pubobe.pdf.

9. Peter Hernon and Robert E. Dugan, *An Action Plan for Outcomes Assessment in Your Library* (Chicago: American Library Association, 2002), x.

10. Eliza T. Dresang, Melissa Gross, and Leslie Edmonds Holt, *Dynamic Youth Services through Outcome-Based Planning and Evaluation* (Chicago: American Library Association, 2006); Peter Brophy, *Measuring Library Performance: Principles and Techniques* (London: Facet, 2006).

11. Association of Research Libraries, Statistics and Measurement, New Measures, E-Metrics: Measures for Electronic Resources, www.arl.org/stats/initiatives/emetrics/index.shtml.

12. G. E. Gorman and Peter Crayton, *Qualitative Research for the Information Professional: A Practical Handbook*, 2nd ed. (London: Library Association Publishing, 2005), 3.

13. See ibid.; Ronald R. Powell and Lynn Silipigni Connaway, *Basic Research Methods for Librarians*, 4th ed. (Westport, Conn.: Libraries Unlimited, 2004); and F. W. Lancaster, *If You Want to Evaluate Your Library*, 2nd ed. (Champaign: University of Illinois, Graduate School of Library and Information Science, 1993).

14. Sheila S. Intner and Elizabeth Futas, "Evaluating Public Library Collections: Why Do It, and How to Use the Results," *American Libraries* 25, no. 5 (1994): 410–12.

15. Jeffrey G. Gardner and Duane Webster, *The Collection Analysis Project: An Assisted Self-Study Manual* (Washington, D.C.: Association of Research Libraries, 1980).

16. Verner W. Clapp and Robert T. Jordan, "Quantitative Criteria for Adequacy of Academic Library Collections," *College and Research Libraries* 50, no. 3 (1989): 153–63 (originally published in 1965).

17. Allen Kent et al., *Use of Library Materials: The University of Pittsburgh Study* (New York: Marcel Dekker, 1979).

18. Richard W. Trueswell, "Some Behavioral Patterns of Library Users: The 80/20 Rule," Wilson *Library Bulletin* 43 (Jan. 1969): 458–61.

19. Thomas E. Nisonger, *Management of Serials in Libraries* (Englewood, Colo.: Libraries Unlimited, 1998).

20. David L. Perkins, ed., *Guidelines for Collection Development* (Chicago: Collection Development Committee, Resources and Technical Services Division, American Library Association, 1979).

21. The Conspectus has been the subject of debate and numerous papers. The following are a representative sample: Richard J. Wood, "The Conspectus: A Collection Analysis and Development Success," *Library Acquisitions: Practice and Theory* 20, no. 4 (1996): 429–53; Virgil L. P. Blake and Renee Tjoumas, "The Conspectus Approach to Collection Evaluation: Panacea or False Prophet?" *Collection Management* 18, nos. 3/4 (1994): 1–31; and Frederick J. Stielow and Helen R. Tibbo, "Collection Analysis in Modern Librarianship: A Stratified, Multidimensional Model," *Collection Management* 11, nos. 3/4 (1989): 73–91.

22. Mary Bushing, Burns Davis, and Nancy Powell, *Using the Conspectus Method: A Collection Assessment Handbook* (Lacey, Wash.: WLN, 1997).

23. International Federation of Library Associations and Institutions, Section on Acquisition and Collection Development, "Guidelines for a Collection Development Policy Using the Conspectus Model" (2001), www.ifla.org/VII/s14/nd1/gcdp-e.pdf.

24. Mary H. Munroe and Jennie E. Ver Steeg, "The Decision-Making Process in Conspectus Evaluation of Collections: The Quest for Certainty," *Library Quarterly* 74, no. 2 (2004): 181–205.

25. Charles B. Osburn, "Collection Evaluation: A Reconsideration," *Advances in Library Administration and Organization* 22 (2005): 10.

26. Howard D. White, *Brief Tests of Collection Strength: A Methodology for All Types of Libraries*, Contributions in Library and Information Science no. 88 (Westport, Conn.: Greenwood, 1995); see also Jennifer Benedetto Beals and Ron Gilmour, "Assessing Collections Using Brief Tests and WorldCat Collection Analysis," *Collection Building* 26, no. 4 (2007): 104–7; Jennifer Benedetto Beal, "Assessing Library Collections Using Brief Test Methodology," *Electronic Journal of Academic and Special Librarianship* 7, no. 3 (Winter 2006), http://southernlibrarianship.icaap.org/content/v07n03/beals_j01.htm; and David Lesniaski, "Evaluating Collections: A Discussion and Extension of Brief Test of Collection Strength," *College and Undergraduate Libraries* 11, no. 1 (2004): 11–24.

27. David V. Loertscher, *Collection Mapping in the LMC: Building Access in a World of Technology*, Excellence in School Media Programs no. 3 (San Jose, Calif.: Hi Willow Research and Publishing, 1996). Debra E. Kachel applied the Conspectus approach to school libraries in her *Collection Assessment and Management for School Libraries: Preparing for Cooperative Collection Development* (Westport, Conn.: Greenwood, 1997).

28. International Coalition of Library Consortia, "Revised Guidelines for Statistical Measures of Usage of Web-Based Information Resources" (Oct. 4, 2006), www.library .yale.edu/consortia/webstats06.htm.

29. Project COUNTER, Release 3 of the COUNTER Code of Practice for Journals and Databases (August 2008) and Release 1 of the COUNTER Code of Practice for Books and Reference Works (March 2006), www.projectcounter.org/code_practice.html.

30. National Information Standards Organization, NISO Standardized Usage Statistics Harvesting Initiative (SUSHI), www.niso.org/committees/SUSHI/SUSHI_comm.html.

31. Peter T. Shepherd, "Final Report on the Investigation into the Feasibility of Developing and Implementing Journal Usage Factors," sponsored by the United Kingdom Serials Group (May 2007), 4, www.uksg.org/sites/uksg.org/files/ FinalReportUsageFactorProject.pdf.

32. Lisa M. Covi and Melissa H. Cragin, "Reconfiguring Control in Library Collection Development: A Conceptual Framework for Assessing the Shift toward Electronic Collections," *Journal of the American Society for Information Science and Technology* 55, no. 4 (2004): 312–25.

33. An examination of transaction log analysis can be found in Denise Troll Covey, *Usage and Usability Assessment: Library Practices and Concerns* (Washington, D.C.: Digital Library Federation, Council on Library and Information Resources, 2002), www.clir.org/pubs/ reports/pub105/contents.html.

34. Steven L. MacCall, "Online Medical Books: Their Availability and an Assessment of How Health Sciences Libraries Provide Access on Their Public Websites," *Journal of the Medical Library Association* 94, no. 1 (2006): 75–80.

35. Heather L. Munger, "Testing the Database of International Rehabilitation Research: Using Rehabilitation Researchers to Determine the Usability of a Bibliographic Database," *Journal of the Medical Library Association* 91, no. 4 (2003): 478–83.

36. Jeffrey Rubin and Dana Chisnell, *Handbook of Usability Testing: How to Plan, Design, and Conduct Effective Tests*, 2nd ed. (New York: Wiley, 2008).

37. See Gary W. White and Gregory A. Crawford, "Cost-Benefit Analysis of Electronic Information: A Case Study," *College and Research Libraries* 59, no. 6 (1998): 503–10; A. Craig Hawbaker and Cynthia K. Wagner, "Periodical Ownership versus Fulltext Online Access: A Cost-Benefit Analysis," *Journal of Academic Librarianship* 22 (March 1996): 105–9; Mark Smith and Gerry Rowland, "To Boldly Go: Searching for Output Measures for Electronic Services," *Public Libraries* 36 (May/June 1997): 168–72; Carol Hansen Montgomery, "Measuring the Impact of an Electronic Journal Collection on Library Costs: A Framework and Preliminary Observations," *D-Lib Magazine* 6, no. 10 (2000), www.dlib.org/dlib/october00/montgomery/10montgomery.html; Steve Black, "Impact of Full Text on Print Journal Use at a Liberal Arts College," *Library Resources and Technical Services* 49, no. 1 (2005): 19–26.

38. Cecilia Botero, Steven Carrico, and Michele Tennant, "Using Comparative Online Journal Usage Studies to Assess the Big Deal," *Library Resources and Technical Services* 52, no. 2 (2008): 61–68.

39. Terese Heidenwolf, "Evaluating an Interdisciplinary Research Collection," *Collection Management* 18, nos. 3/4 (1994): 33–48; and Cynthia Dobson, Jeffrey D. Kushkowski, and Kristin H. Gerhard, "Collection Evaluation for Interdisciplinary Fields: A Comprehensive Approach," *Journal of Academic Librarianship* 22 (July 1996): 279–84.

40. Anna H. Perrault, "An Assessment of the Collective Resources Base of Florida Community College Library Collections: A Profile with Interpretative Analysis," *Resource Sharing and Information Networks* 14, no. 1 (1999): 3–20.

41. Holly Koelling, ed., *Best Books for Young Adults*, 3rd ed. (Chicago: American Library Association, 2007).

42. For studies on the utility of list checking, see Robert N. Bland, "The College Textbook as a Tool for Collection Evaluation, Analysis, and Retrospective Collection Development," *Library Acquisitions: Practice and Theory*, nos. 3/4 (1980): 193–97; and Anne H. Lundin, "List-Checking in Collection Development: An Imprecise Art," *Collection Management* 11, nos. 3/4 (1989): 103–12.

43. Carol A. Doll, "Quality and Elementary School Library Media Collections," *School Library Media Quarterly* 25 (Winter 1997): 95–102.

44. Institute of Education Sciences, U.S. Department of Education, National Center for Education Statistics, Library Statistics Program, Compare Academic Libraries (http://nces.ed.gov/surveys/libraries/compare/index.asp?LibraryType=Academic) and Compare Public Libraries (http://nces.ed.gov/surveys/libraries/compare/index.asp?LibraryType=Public).

45. American Association of School Librarians and Association for Educational Communications and Technology, *Information Power: Building Partnerships for Learning* (Chicago: American Library Association, 1998).

46. Minnesota Educational Media Organization, Minnesota Standards for Effective School Library Media Programs, www.memoweb.org/htmlfiles/linkseffectiveslmp.html.

47. Texas State Library and Archives Commission, "School Library Programs: Standards and Guidelines for Texas," www.tsl.state.tx.us/ld/schoollibs/sls/toc.html.

48. Association of College and Research Libraries, "Standards for Libraries in Higher Education" (June 2004), www.ala.org/ala/acrl/acrlstandards/standardslibraries.cfm.

49. International Coalition of Library Consortia, "Privacy Guidelines for Electronic Resources Vendors" (July 2002), www.library.yale.edu/consortia/2002privacyguidelines.html.

50. Mike Rossner, Heather Van Epps, and Emma Hill, "Show Me the Data," *Journal of Cell Biology* 179, no. 6 (2007): 1091–92.

51. Thomas E. Nisonger, "Use of the Checklist Method for Content Evaluation of Full-Text Databases: Investigation of Two Databases Based on Citations from Two Journals," *Library Resources and Technical Services* 52, no. 1 (2008): 4–17.

52. Yvonna S. Lincoln, "Insights into Library Services and Users from Qualitative Research: Designing the LibQUAL Survey Instrument," *Library and Information Science Research* 24, no. 1 (2002): 3–16.

53. A. Parasuraman, Valerie A. Zeitharnl, and Leonard L. Berry, "SERVQUAL: A Multiple-Item Scale for Measuring Consumer Perceptions of Service Quality," *Journal of Retailing* 64, no.1 (Spring 1988): 5–6.

54. Association for Research Libraries, Statistics and Measurement, New Measures, MINES for Libraries: Measuring the Impact of Networked Electronic Services, www.arl.org/stats/initiatives/mines/index.shtml; Brinley Franklin and Terry Plum, "Successful Web Survey Methodologies for Measuring the Impact of Networked Electronic Services (MINES for Libraries)," *IFLA Journal* 32, no. 1 (2006): 28–40.

55. Gary M. Shirk, "Towards a Topography of Library Collections," *Digital Information and Knowledge Management: New Opportunities for Research Libraries*, ed. Sul H. Lee, 99–111 (Binghamton, N.Y.: Haworth, 2007), 106.

Suggested Readings

Agee, Jim. "Collection Evaluation: A Foundation for Collection Development." *Collection Building* 24, no. 3 (2005): 92–95.

Armbruster, Chris. "Access, Usage and Citation Metrics: What Function for Digital Libraries and Repositories in Research Evaluation?" Working paper. Jan. 29, 2008. http://ssrn.com/abstract=1088453.

Bauer, Kathleen. "Indexes as Tools for Measuring Usage of Print and Electronic Resources." *College and Research Libraries* 62, no. 1 (2001): 36–42.

Beals, Jennifer Benedetto. "Assessing Library Collections Using Brief Test Methodology." *E-JASL: The Electronic Journal of Academic and Special Librarianship* 7, no. 3 (2006). http://southernlibrarianship.icaap.org/content/v07n03/beals_j01.htm.

Becher, Melissa L., and Janice L. Flug. "Using Student Focus Groups to Inform Library Planning and Marketing." *College and Undergraduate Libraries* 12, nos. 1/2 (2005): 1–18.

Bertot, John Carlo, and Denise M. Davis, eds. *Planning and Evaluating Library Networked Services and Resources.* Westport, Conn.: Libraries Unlimited, 2004.

Biblarz, Dora, Stephen Bosch, and Chris Sugnet. *Guide to Library User Needs Assessment for Integrated Information Resource Collection Management and Development.* Collection Management and Development Guides no. 11. Lanham, Md.: Scarecrow, and the Association for Library Collections and Technical Services, 2001.

Bishop, Kay. "Evaluation of the Collection." In *The Collection Program in Schools: Concepts, Practices, and Information Sources,* 141–59. 4th ed. Westport, Conn.: Libraries Unlimited, 2007.

Blake, Julie C., and Susan P. Schleper. "From Data to Decisions: Using Surveys and Statistics to Make Collection Management Decisions." *Library Collections and Technical Services* 28, no. 4 (2004): 460–64.

Blecic, Deborah D., Joan B. Fiscella, and Stephen E. Wiberley Jr. "Measurement of Use of Web-Electronic Resources: Advances in Use Statistics and Innovations in Resource Functionality." *College and Research Libraries* 68, no. 1 (2007): 26–44.

Bradford, Jane T. "What's Coming Off the Shelves? A Reference Use Study Analyzing Print Reference Sources Used in a University Library." *Journal of Academic Librarianship* 31, no. 6 (2005): 546–58.

Calvert, Philip J., Daniel Dorner, and G. E. Gorman. *Analysing What Your Users Need: A Guide for Librarians and Information Managers.* London: Facet, 2003.

Choudhury, Sayeed, et al. "A Framework for Evaluating Digital Library Services." *D-Lib Magazine* 8, nos. 7/8 (2002). www.dlib.org/dlib/july02/choudhury/07choudhury.html.

Clayton, Peter, and G. E. Gorman. "Updating Conspectus for a Digital Age." *Library Collections, Acquisitions, and Technical Services* 26 (2002): 253–58.

Colson, Jeannie. "Determining Use of an Academic Library Reference Collection: Report of a Study." *Reference and User Services Quarterly* 47, no. 2 (2007): 168–75.

Crawford, John. *The Culture of Evaluation in Library and Information Services.* Oxford: Chandos, 2005.

Dillon, Ken. "Collection Evaluation." In *Collection Management for School Libraries,* ed. Joy McGregor, Ken Dillon, and James Henri, 245–79. Lanham, Md.: Scarecrow, 2003.

Doll, Carol A., and Pamela Petrick Barron. *Managing and Analyzing Your Collection: A Practical Guide for Small Libraries and School Media Centers.* Chicago: American Library Association, 2002.

Durrance, Joan C., and Karen E. Fisher with Marian Bouch Hinton. *How Libraries and Librarians Help: A Guide to Identifying User-Centered Outcomes.* Chicago: American Library Association, 2005.

Duy, Joanna, and Liwen Vaughan. "Can Electronic Journal Usage Data Replace Citation Data as a Measure of Journal Use? An Empirical Examination." *Journal of Academic Librarianship* 32, no. 5 (2006): 512–17.

Elliott, Donald S., et al. *Measuring Your Library's Value: How to Do a Cost-Benefit Analysis for Your Public Library.* Chicago: American Library Association, 2007.

Fowler, David C., ed. *Usage Statistics of E-Serials.* Binghamton, N.Y.: Haworth, 2007.

Fraser Bruce T., Charles R, McClure, and Emily H. Leahy. "Toward a Framework for Assessing Library and Institutional Outcomes." *portal: Libraries and the Academy* 2, no. 4 (2002): 505–28.

Gorman, G. E., and Ruth H. Miller. "Changing Collections, Changing Evaluation." In *Collection Management*, edited by G. E. Gorman, 309–38. International Yearbook of Library and Information Management, 2000–2001. London: Library Association Publishing, 2000.

Greiner, Tony, and Bob Cooper. *Analyzing Library Collection Use with Excel.* Chicago: American Library Association, 2007.

Grover, Mark L. "Large Scale Collection Assessment." *Collection Building* 18, no. 2 (1999): 58–66.

Haycock, Laurel A. "Citation Analysis of Education Dissertations for Collection Development." *Library Resources and Technical Services* 48, no. 2 (2004): 102–6.

Hayslett, Michele M., and Barbara M. Wildemuth. "Pixels or Pencils? The Relative Effectiveness of Web-Based versus Paper Surveys." *Library and Information Science Research* 26, no. 1 (2004): 73–93.

Hiott, Judith. "Collecting and Using Networked Statistics: Current Status, Future Goals." *Library Quarterly* 74, no. 4 (2004): 441–54.

Intner, Sheila S. "Making Your Collections Work for You: Collection Evaluation Myths and Realities." *Library Collections, Acquisitions, and Technical Services* 27, no. 3 (2003): 339–50.

Knievel, Jennifer E., Heather Wicht, and Lynn Silipigni Connaway. "Use of Circulation Statistics and Interlibrary Loan Data in Collection Management." *College and Research Libraries* 67, no. 1 (2006): 35–49.

Kyrillidou, Martha. "From Input and Output Measures to Quality and Outcome Measures, or, From the User in the Life of the Library to the Library in the Life of the User." *Journal of Academic Librarianship* 28, nos. 1/2 (2002): 42–46.

Lakos, Amos, "Evidence-Based Library Management: The Leaderships Challenge." *portal: Libraries and the Academy* 7, no. 4 (2007): 431–50.

Lakos, Amos, and Shelley Phipps. "Creating a Culture of Assessment: A Catalyst for Organizational Change." *portal: Libraries and the Academy* 4, no. 3 (2004): 345–61.

Lee, Deborah. "Can You Hear Me Now? Using Focus Groups to Enhance Marketing Research." *Library Administration and Management* 19, no. 2 (2005): 100–101.

Leiding, Reba. "Using Citation Checking of Undergraduate Honors Thesis Bibliographies to Evaluate Library Collections." *College and Research Libraries* 66, no. 5 (2005): 417–29.

Lesniaski, David. "Evaluating Collections: A Discussion and Extension of 'Brief Tests of Collection Strength.'" *College and Undergraduate Libraries* 11, no. 1 (2004): 11–24.

Levitov, Deb, and Marilyn Sampson. *Guide for Developing and Evaluating School Library Media Programs.* Englewood, Colo.: Libraries Unlimited, 2000.

Lightman, Harriet. "The Challenge of Serials Collection Evaluation in a Changing Environment: Examples from Northwestern University Library." In *Perspectives on Serials in the Hybrid Environment*, ed. Harriet Lightman and John P. Blosser, 53–66. ALCTS Papers on Library Technical Services and Collections no. 15. Chicago: American Library Association, 2007.

Littman, Justin, and Lynn Silipigni Connaway. "A Circulation Analysis of Print Books and E-Books in an Academic Research Library." *Library Resources and Technical Services* 48, no. 4 (2004): 256–62.

Luther, Judy. *White Paper on Electronic Journal Usage Statistics*. Washington, D.C.: Council on Library and Information Resources, 2000. www.clir.org/pubs/reports/pub94/contents.html.

Lyons, Lucy E. "A Critical Examination of the Assessment Analysis Capabilities of OCLC ACAS." *Journal of Academic Librarianship* 31, no. 6 (2005): 506–16.

Marie, Kirsten I. "From Theory to Practice: A New Teacher-Librarian Tackles Library Assessment." *Teacher Librarian* 33, no. 2 (2005): 20–25.

Mathews, Joseph R. *The Evaluation and Measurement of Library Services*. Westport, Conn.: Libraries Unlimited, 2007.

———. *Library Assessment in Higher Education*. Westport, Conn.: Libraries Unlimited, 2007.

McGriff, Nancy, Carl A. Harvey, and Leslie B. Preddy. "Collecting the Data: Collection Development." *School Library Media Activities Monthly* 20, no. 9 (2004): 27–29.

Nelson, William Neal, and Robert Fernekes. *Standards and Assessment for Academic Libraries: A Workbook*. Chicago: American Library Association, 2002.

Ochola, John N. "Use of Circulation Statistics and Interlibrary Loan Data in Collection Management." *Collection Management* 27, no. 1 (2002): 1–13.

Poll, Roswitha, and Peter te Boekhorst, eds. *Measuring Quality: Performance Measurement in Libraries*. 2nd rev. ed. Munich: K. G. Saur, 2007.

Powell, Ronald R. "Measurement and Evaluation of Electronic Information Services." In *Information Services in an Electronic Environment*, edited by G. E. Gorman, 323–41. International Yearbook of Library and Information Management, 2001–2002. London: Library Association Publishing, 2001.

Rubin, Rhea Joyce, for the Public Library Association. *Demonstrating Results: Using Outcome Measurement in Your Library*. Chicago: American Library Association, 2006.

Samson, Sue, Sebastian Derry, and Holly Eggleston. "Networked Resources, Assessment, and Collection Development." *Journal of Academic Librarianship* 30, no. 6 (2004): 476–481.

Shepherd, Peter T., and Denise M. Davis. "Electronic Metrics, Performance Measures, and Statistics for Publishers and Libraries: Building Common Ground and Standards." *portal: Libraries and the Academy* 2, no. 4 (2002): 659–63.

Shim, Wonsik, and Charles R. McClure. "Data Needs and Use of Electronic Resources and Services of Academic Research Libraries." *portal: Libraries and the Academy* 2, no. 2 (2002): 217–36.

Shouse, Daniel L., and Linda Teel. "Inventory: Catalyst for Collection Development." *Collection Building* 25, no. 4 (2006): 129–33.

Smith, Alastair G. "Evaluating Digital Collections." In *The Digital Factor in Library and Information Services*, edited by G. E. Gorman, 261–81. International Yearbook of Library and Information Management, 2002–2003. London: Facet, 2002.

Tenopir, Carol. "Database and Online System Usage." *Library Journal* 126, no. 16 (2001): 41–45.

Troll Covey, Denise. *Usage and Usability Assessment: Library Practices and Concerns.* Washington, D.C.: Digital Library Federation, Council on Library and Information Resources, 2002. www.clir.org/pubs/reports/pub105/contents.html.

Twiss, Thomas M. "A Validation of Brief Tests of Collection Strength." *Collection Management* 25, no. 3 (2001): 23–37.

Walter, Virginia A. *Output Measures and More: Planning and Evaluating Public Library Services for Young Adults: Part of the Public Library Development Program.* Chicago: American Library Association, 1995.

———. *Output Measures for Public Library Service to Children: A Manual of Standardized Procedures.* Chicago: Association for Library Service to Children, Public Library Association, American Library Association, 1992.

Weiner, Sharon A. "Library Quality and Impact: Is There a Relationship between New Measures and Traditional Measures?" *Journal of Academic Librarianship* 31, no. 5 (2005): 432–37.

White, Andrew C., and Eric Djiva Kamal. *E-Metrics for Library and Information Professionals: How to Use Data for Managing and Evaluating Electronic Resource Collections.* New York: Neal-Schuman, 2006.

White, Howard D. "Better than Brief Tests: Coverage Power Tests of Collection Strength." *College and Research Libraries* 69, no. 2 (March 2008): 155–74.

Williams, Karen Carter, and Rickey Best. "E-Book Usage and the *Choice* Outstanding Academic Book List: Is There a Correlation?" *Journal of Academic Librarianship* 32, no. 5 (2006): 474–78.

Wright, Stephanie, and Lynda S. White. *Library Assessment.* SPEC Kit no. 303. Washington, D.C.: Association of Research Libraries, 2007.

CHAPTER EIGHT

Cooperative Collection Development and Management

Library cooperation takes many forms and is a part of many collection development and management activities. Cooperation in libraries takes much more than being good citizens and behaving altruistically. It is essential in today's environment of constrained budgets and limited space to house collections. The ability to leverage funds through cooperative purchasing and shared storage facilities and to offer library users access to the world's vast information resources are powerful forces toward cooperation. This chapter presents an overview of cooperative collection development and management and identifies types of cooperation and elements that contribute to their success.

Overview

David H. Stam provides one of the more elegant descriptions of library cooperation: "All libraries are linked in a great chain of access and what each has and does will have importance for the whole universe of libraries and their users."[1] He builds on the ancient concept of creation known as the Great Chain of Being—a theme that permeated science, literature, and philosophy from the time of Plato to its refinement in the eighteenth century by Gottfried Wilhelm Leibniz. This view held that all of existence is defined by plenitude, continuity, and gradation. These three elements can, as Stam implies, apply to libraries when *plenitude* is understood to mean abundance of the whole, *continuity* to mean uninterrupted connection, and *gradation* to mean variations between similar and related components.

Library cooperation is not a new idea. In 1886, Melvil Dewey listed one of the major needs of the modern library movement as "a practical means of bringing the enormous benefits of cooperation, which has been the watch word of the whole movement, into full play in the interests of the libraries."[2] Some have said that library cooperation is unnatural because of the difficulties it has presented libraries over the years, but most librarians believe, with Michael Gorman, that "cooperation is as essential to a library as is water to a fish or air to a mammal."[3]

A working definition of *cooperative collection development* is "the sharing of responsibilities among two or more libraries for the process of acquiring materials, developing collections, and managing the growth and maintenance of collections in a user-beneficial and cost-beneficial way."[4] The umbrella term used into the mid-1980s was *resource sharing* and applied broadly to cooperative cataloging, shared storage facilities, shared preservation activities, interlibrary loan (ILL), and coordinated or cooperative collection development.[5] Today, *resource sharing* is generally understood to be the sharing of materials, both returnables and nonreturnables (e.g., photocopies or digital versions of journal articles), through ILL.

Interlibrary loan, the reciprocal lending and borrowing of materials between libraries, has a long history. One of the earliest references dates from 200 BC, when the library in Alexandria is known to have lent materials to the Pergamum library.[6] Interlibrary lending did not become common in the United States until the last quarter of the nineteenth century. Ernest C. Richardson, librarian at Princeton University, promoted such cooperative exchanges and called for a national lending library in 1899. His rationale resonates in today's libraries:

> It is a matter of common observation that with the present limited facilities for our American libraries, students, whether dependent on college libraries or on general reference libraries, are constantly in lack of the books which they want. . . . We are duplicating, every year, a great many sets of periodicals, as we would not need to do under some system where all were free to borrow.[7]

Although the United States did not develop a national lending library, a formal process for managing lending and borrowing between libraries was in place in the United States early in the twentieth century. The Library of Congress issued its first policy governing ILL in 1917, and the American Library Association adopted an ILL code in 1919.[8] That code has been revised numerous times, the last in 2001. The 1993 National Interlibrary Code recognized the increased use and important role of ILL by changing the statement "Interlibrary loan is an adjunct to, not a substitute for, collection development" to "Interlibrary borrowing is an integral element of collection development for all libraries, not an ancillary option."[9]

Cooperative collection development is now understood to mean much more than resource sharing. Cooperative collection development and management involve an overarching planning strategy that libraries employ to work together and provide materials and information for their users—something that no single library can afford on its own. The goal of cooperative collection development and management is to improve access to information and resources by maximizing the use of those resources and leveraging available funding. Cooperative collection development and management have three interdependent components and can be thought of as a three-legged stool (see figure 8-1) that cannot

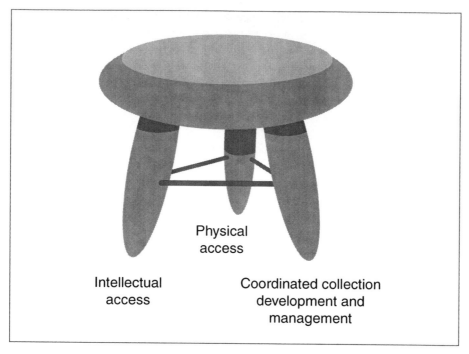

Physical
access

Intellectual
access

Coordinated collection
development and
management

FIGURE 8-1 Three components of cooperative collection development and management

stand without all three legs. The components are physical access through resource sharing, bibliographic access, and coordinated collection development and management.

The Research Libraries Group (RLG), one of the most ambitious and energetic efforts to create a national cooperative library initiative, was formed in 1973 by Harvard University, Yale University, Columbia University, and the New York Public Library. RLG's goal was to provide the three components of resource sharing: physical access through a good delivery system and reciprocal borrowing privileges (SHARES program), bibliographic access through a shared online catalog (RLIN, the Research Librarians Information Network) to facilitate coordinated acquisitions and resource sharing, and a program of coordinated collection development and management. RLG has been described as "a partnership to achieve planned, coordinated interdependence in response to the threat posed by a climate of increasing economic restraint and financial uncertainty."[10] Though Harvard withdrew from the partnership, RLG membership expanded to include many major academic and research libraries in the United States and abroad. In June 2006, RLG merged with OCLC. Its online catalog became part of OCLC's WorldCat and its programs joined OCLC Research to become part of OCLC Programs and Research.

Several RLG programs and projects had significant success and lasting impact. The Preservation Committee coordinated several cooperative microfilming projects. Cooperative collection development was the focus of RLG's Collection Management and Development Committee, which began with the realization that knowing the strengths, depth, and breadth of each library's collection was a first step toward coordination. To this end, the Committee developed the RLG Conspectus, a systematic analysis and assessment tool using the Library of Congress classification scheme and a common language to describe collections. The Conspectus has been modified by other groups and applied internationally to all types of libraries.

Resource Sharing

Resource sharing is a system for making requests and providing delivery of information, chiefly through the formal ILL process. Interlibrary loan handles both returnables (items that must be returned to the lender) and nonreturnables (photocopies or digital transmissions). It may be strengthened by agreements among members of a consortium to expedite service, charge members no ILL fees, or permit on-site use of collections by clientele of member libraries. Interlibrary loan encompasses a protocol for making requests and acceptable methods of delivery.

Interlibrary loan is the most pervasive form of library cooperation and links most libraries across the United States, Canada, and internationally as well. Academic library data collected by the National Center for Education Statistics for 2004 (the last year for which data are available) show increased activity over 1996. Loans provided to other academic libraries increased from 9,430,907 to 10,174,075, and loans received from libraries increased from 7,512,105 to 8,545,417.[11] The earlier data do not distinguish between returnables and nonreturnables; the 2004 data provide a breakdown, showing that returnables exceeded nonreturnables slightly in both categories.

Public library data for 2004 reveal the significant value resource sharing offers to citizens. In that year, the 9,207 libraries reporting data loaned 30,471,000 items and borrowed 30,158,000.[12] Data on returnables and nonreturnables was not provided. Regardless, these gross numbers indicate that public libraries across the United States shared more than sixty-five million items, a truly impressive number.

National Center for Education Statistics data on ILL activity for schools for 2002 indicate that 62 percent of school library media centers participated in some type of ILL program with other libraries.[13] These ranged from resource sharing with public libraries in the area (43 percent), with area high schools (42 percent), with colleges and universities (31 percent), with the state library (30 percent), or with other schools in the state (25 percent). Public schools and schools in the Northeast were more likely to participate in ILL programs than parochial schools, other private schools, or schools in the South and West.

Information Power, published by the American Association of School Librarians and the Association for Educational Communications and Technology, recommends that school library media specialists "participate in networks that enhance access to resources located outside the school."[14] Many school library media centers are creating and joining consortia or networks, developing resource-sharing agreements, and implementing mechanisms to request and deliver materials. George Bishop, librarian at Ovid-Elsie Area Schools in a small rural farming community, spoke to the world of resources available through OCLC membership when he said, "I announced to over 100 teachers and administrators that our school library would delivery 'everything they needed or wanted . . . period' . . . and then I did just that using OCLC."[15]

Effective and speedy delivery is central to the success of resource sharing. Ross Atkinson explains the quality of access—how well access is provided or achieved—in terms of time.[16] Users want speedy access to library resources because the user's time is a valuable commodity. Improvements in telecommunications have had a significant impact on physical access, in both the transmission of requests and the delivery of articles. The OCLC ILLiad Resource Sharing Management software automates routine ILL functions through a single Windows-based interface and supports an automated ILL subsystem that transmits requests to OCLC members and to others as well. Libraries can configure their ILLiad software so that users, who have created personal ILLiad accounts through the individual library, can request items directly from within OCLC's WorldCat or an OCLC FirstSearch database. VDX, another OCLC service, is specifically intended for use by groups of libraries (e.g., networks of libraries with multiple library systems) to manage ILL activities. Infotrieve's Ariel software is used worldwide with PCs, printers, and scanners to transmit documents in PDF files via the Internet, using either FTP or e-mail, to other Ariel-equipped workstations. The number of requests to borrow returnables continues to grow, and fast delivery is essential. Some regional networks and consortia, such as the CIC (Committee on Institutional Cooperation: the Big Ten universities plus the University of Chicago and Pennsylvania State University), have contracted with a single courier service to expedite delivery of returnables and other materials that are not suitable for electronic transmission.

The nature of resource sharing is changing as a result of evolving technologies. People can discover, identify, and retrieve many resources (articles, books, images, audio, video, and more) directly online and bypass the library. Unmediated ILL, through which a user directly requests the lending of an item from one library to his or her home library, is a growing trend. The increasing availability of e-journal articles through individual library subscriptions, consortial purchase agreements, and state and regional programs is reducing ILL requests for nonreturnables. Simultaneously, easy access to shared catalogs is increasing the requests for returnables. MINITEX, for example, reported a 254 percent increase in ILL requests in the first year the MnLINK Gateway to the statewide virtual catalog was available.[17]

Bibliographic Access

The second component of cooperative collection development and management is *bibliographic access*—knowing what is available from other sites through online catalogs, printed or microform catalogs, or bibliographic utilities. Bibliographic access to the holdings of other libraries is a critical component of cooperation. For many years, libraries depended on printed holdings information—records in the *National Union Catalog*, individual libraries' printed book catalogs, and union serials holdings lists. The first regional union catalog was developed at the California State Library in 1901, and the Library of Congress established the *National Union Catalog* in 1902. Checking such resources was tedious. The development of bibliographic utilities; multi-institutional, state, and regional online shared catalogs; and web-based access to online catalogs has been a tremendous step forward in bibliographic access for both library patrons and library staffs.

Some states have statewide catalogs that allow users to search holdings and enter unmediated ILL requests regardless of the holding library's location. MnLINK (www.minitex.umn.edu/mnlink/) is a virtual catalog linked to online catalogs from more than twenty Minnesota library systems representing some 480 libraries (public libraries and their branches, college and university libraries, and government libraries). Requests for ILL made within MnLINK are automatically sent to the owning library for attention. MINITEX, a regional network, provides the materials via daily deliveries.

Florida has a shared statewide catalog, SUNLINK (www.sunlink.ucf.edu), for K–12 public school library media centers. Member libraries agree to

- Participate in resource sharing within the guidelines of their local and district restrictions. Schools will always respect their local needs first, but the spirit of statewide resource sharing must be adopted by SUNLINK schools.

- Participate in the SUNLINK database maintenance procedure to ensure that the union database accurately reflects their changing local collection.

The last point above—agreeing to keep cataloging records current—is essential to effective resource sharing. Because bibliographic access is so essential, the OCLC Users Council adopted a resolution in 1999 that stresses the need for member libraries to contribute to OCLC promptly all current bibliographic and holdings information representing cataloged items in their collections and to create bibliographic records at the fullest possible level in order "to promote shared use of records and library resources."[18]

Coordinated Collection Development and Management

The third component, *coordinated collection development and management*, is, in its ideal manifestation, a coordinated scheme of purchasing and maintaining collections. Coordinated collection development and management aim to build complementary collections on which the cooperating libraries can draw. Joseph J. Branin identifies three elements to coordinated collection development: mutual notification of purchasing decisions, joint purchase, and assigned subject specialization in building collections.[19]

None of the three components in cooperative collection development and management (intellectual access, physical access, and coordinated collection management and development) works without some degree of success in the other two areas. Neither speedy delivery nor bibliographic access has meaning unless the resource the user wishes can be located—that is, is held by a library. If libraries have established partnerships to ensure coverage and collection gaps still exist, cooperation is not succeeding. A gap in one collection can be accommodated only if the same gap does not exist at a partner library. The ideal situation is equitable distribution of little-used titles. Collection overlaps (titles held by more than one library) are justified because these materials are used heavily in each library that owns them.

Coordinated collection development leverages available funds by increasing access to a wider collection of information resources. It enlarges the universe of titles available to library users and, when properly supported, speeds the delivery of materials through ILL systems. It also can be viewed as cost containment through purchase avoidance. The libraries that participate in coordinated collection development reduce duplication in order to provide a stronger collective collection and increased user satisfaction.

Despite a few isolated coordinated collection development successes, libraries do not have a notable history of altering traditional collection development behaviors. Libraries have not, in general, developed policies and practices that acknowledge or take advantage of being linked in a great chain of being. The extent to which meaningful and practical coordination has been implemented falls short of the enthusiasm with which it is proclaimed. Dan C. Hazen observed that the theory is compelling but the results thus far inconsequential.[20]

Types of Cooperative Collection Development

Several varieties of cooperative collection development have been tried with varying degrees of success. These include the status quo approach, the synergistic or coordinated approach, cooperative funding, coordinated weeding and retention, preservation initiatives, and shared storage.

Status Quo Approach

For many years, libraries have practiced what Paul H. Mosher and Marcia Pankake call the *status quo approach*.[21] This approach presumes that libraries' total collecting activities will build, on a national scale, reasonable depth in every area of interest. In other words, every title that anyone might want now and in the future will be held somewhere in the United States simply as a result of serendipitous collection development and management. This assumes that libraries select a certain number of titles that no other library is adding, though research shows that research libraries in the United States are acquiring fewer unique monographic titles.[22] The status quo approach, in which no intentional coordinated collecting activities are undertaken, is optimistic and increasingly unrealistic, given the financial constraints most libraries are experiencing.

Synergistic Approach

Ross Atkinson calls a second approach the *synergistic approach*, in which different libraries take responsibility for collecting different publications, according to some coordinated and collaborative plan.[23] This can be called *coordinated collection development* because it is intentional with distributed responsibility for collection development. Underlying all efforts at cooperation is, in the words of Edward Shreeves, a "widespread belief that cooperation in building collections can improve significantly the quality of library service by broadening and deepening the range of materials collectively available."[24] Formal coordinated and collaborative collection management programs are normally guided by written agreements, contracts, or other documents that outline the commitments and responsibilities of the participants.

The synergistic approach calls for dividing the information universe into core and peripheral materials and then dividing the periphery among the consortium members. An academic library has a responsibility to maintain a core collection on site that serves immediate needs, especially those of its undergraduates. A public library has a responsibility to meet the core information and recreational needs of its user community. Librarians use the term *core* for two kinds of collections: a collection representing the intellectual nucleus of a discipline (consisting of the classic, synoptic, and most influential texts), and a nucleus of materials that is determined by heaviest use or meets certain criteria.[25] H. W. Wilson Company uses "core collection" in the latter sense in the titles of its selection tools, such as *Public Library Core Collection: Nonfiction*, which aims to list a "well-rounded collection of the most highly recommended reference and non-fiction books for adults."[26] Core material, in this definition, is often considered the 20 percent of the collection that satisfies 80 percent of library users' needs. A library engaged in coordinated collection development develops collections of peripheral materials that respond to local needs and priorities but also serve consortial needs. This local collection, in turn, is backed up by the collections of consortial partners built through distributed responsibility for peripheral materials in complementary fields.

Defining *core* and *peripheral* in terms of collecting behavior has been a stumbling block to successful synergistic collection development projects in research libraries. Generally, materials in the periphery are considered to be research materials that are not in heavy demand and fall into Conspectus levels 4 (research collections) and 5 (comprehensive collections). One problem is that any research library's understanding of the core tends to shrink and expand in response to the funds available to that library during each budget cycle. Predicting what will constitute core materials is also a challenge. Ross Atkinson writes,

> Our effort to . . . distinguish core from non-core materials has been so far singularly unsuccessful, except through such retrospective methods as citation analysis or the use of circulation records. For purposes of planning, budgeting, or coordination, the concept of the core, for all its use, is practically useless.[27]

The only application of synergistic cooperation that is both logical and practical is one in which a library accepts responsibility for collecting in areas that also meet local needs and reflect local strengths. The history of cooperative initiatives has shown that libraries should not commit to developing and maintaining collections (or even subscribing to a single journal title) for which local need and usage are not present. The key to success is building on the local imperative. One example might be found in a public library cooperative with member libraries serving different immigrant populations. One library might assume primary responsibility for building a collection to serve its large Hispanic population and another library might assume responsibility for building a collection to serve a large group of Southeast Asian immigrants. Together, they have a coordinated collection which, through resource sharing, meets the needs of many. At the same time, a commitment by one library to a particular area does not obligate the other partners to give up supporting all needs in that area. Stam writes that "resource sharing does not remove in any way the obligation for any institution to fulfill its local mission."[28] Coordinated collection development cannot substitute for adequate local collections.

Two early examples of synergistic coordinated collection development are the agreement between the Research Triangle University Libraries in North Carolina and the Farmington Plan. The earliest is the Research Triangle, now consisting of Duke University, North Carolina State University, the University of North Carolina at Chapel Hill, and North Carolina Central University. In 1933, the University of North Carolina at Chapel Hill and Duke University formed the Joint Committee on Intellectual Cooperation in an effort to leverage limited financial resources during the Great Depression. Library cooperation began in 1934 with a plan for systematic division of responsibility for publications in major disciplines. This evolved into the area studies concept of dividing responsibilities by geographic coverage or language or both. The Research Triangle has an enviable record of success in leveraging financial resources and making unique materials available to its membership. Patricia Buck Dominguez and Luke Swindler reported in 1993 that 76 percent of the titles in the shared union catalog were found on only one campus, and only 7 percent were held by all universities. Much of the success of the Research Triangle can be attributed to upper-level institutional support; geographic proximity, which has meant easy and speedy access; bibliographic access to titles held in each of the member libraries; and a long history of realizing its goals.[29]

The Farmington Plan was less successful.[30] Launched in 1948 under the sponsorship of the ARL, it was a voluntary agreement on the part of approximately sixty academic, special, and research libraries. The goal of the Farmington Plan was to increase the nation's total resources for research. The participating libraries agreed to collect, for specified countries and subjects, one copy of each new foreign publication in which a U.S. researcher could be presumed to be interested. The Farmington Plan designed blanket order profiles that were placed with foreign dealers. Libraries were expected to accept all materials within the scope of their commitments.

The Farmington Plan was not concerned with the financial situations of its participants and expected each library to provide the budgetary support needed to accomplish the comprehensive plan goals. The Plan ceased in 1972 primarily because it failed to recognize the first condition of every successful cooperative plan—libraries always give priority to local needs and priorities. Ideally, each participating library should be able to combine self-interest with the overarching aims of the agreement. Each participant must be confident that it will receive benefits that outweigh its sacrifices. Successful cooperation depends on a high degree of altruism and a true sense of the common good. The tension between local needs and the needs of the consortium underlies all cooperative collection development and management ventures.

Coordinated collection development can benefit school library media centers, though coordination in selection may be more of a challenge for these libraries. School library media centers in the same region are less likely to have diverse collections than in the past. They have a tendency to develop very similar collections because all are aiming to collect resources that support equally similar curricula and graduation standards. Variations in collections may be appropriate in schools that have a special focus or specialized programs. For example, the media center in a Spanish immersion school may have many more resources in Spanish and can provide these materials to others; a magnet school that offers special, supplemental classes in science and math likely has more resources in these areas.

Debra E. Kachel suggests several steps to better prepare school library media centers to engage in coordinated collection development, including individual collection assessment, individual collection development policies, and regional resource mapping—a cooperative collection assessment to identify strengths and weaknesses across collections.[31] She writes, "The view of a library operating self sufficiently in isolation, with students and teachers having access only to what reside within the wall of the library, is outdated"[32] and recommends that school library media specialists start by developing coordinated collection activities with other media specialists in their own district. Success at this level can be a building block to expanded coordinated collection development.

One intentional approach to coordinated collection development is the use of a shared approval plan.[33] Such plans present challenges because of the political and administrative costs of designing and maintaining them and the need to balance expectations of the larger group against the requirements of the individual partnering libraries. Shared approval plans must be designed to complement any existing approval plans and work best when the partner libraries are already using the same approval plan vendor. Collections librarians at each library work together with the vendor to develop the shared profile. One benefit may be a deeper discount from the vendor because of the increased volume of books sold. These plans require each partner library to make a financial commitment at the beginning of the fiscal year to expend a set dollar amount. Sharing a single catalog is also an essential requirement, as is speedy delivery between the partner libraries.

Cooperative Funding

A third approach to cooperative collection development relies on *cooperative funding* for shared purchases with agreed locations. This approach, sometimes called *cooperative acquisition*, depends on a pool of shared monies used to acquire lesser-used, expensive items. The items purchased are placed either in a central site or in the library with the highest anticipated local use. A still successful program in the shared purchase mode is the Center for Research Libraries (CRL; www.crl .edu).[34] Part of each library's annual membership fee goes to purchase materials that the membership agrees are important. The CRL serves as a library's library—a complementary collection to extend the resources available to the membership.

The CRL is considered the nation's oldest cooperative research library. It was established in 1949 as the Midwest Inter-library Center. It had more than 230 U.S. and Canadian academic and research library members in 2008. The CRL facility in Chicago houses more than four million newspapers, journals, dissertations, archives, government publications, microform sets, and other traditional and digital resources for research and teaching, which are loaned to members. CRL members pay annual fees to support the CRL and provide pooled funds to acquire, store, and preserve materials that would otherwise be too costly for a single institution. Many materials (e.g., major microfilm sets) are purchased through a member nominating and voting process. The CRL has clear objectives and a long history of leveraging investments to provide a collection of resources that no one library can afford on its own.

California is the site of a long-term cooperative funding program agreement among libraries of the University of California (UC) system. The Shared Collections and Access Program (http://libraries.universityofcalifornia.edu/planning/shared_collections.html) began in 1976. The program has used a central pool of funds (to which member libraries contribute) to acquire resources and avoid duplication. Its goals are to

- broaden and deepen UC Library collections in the service of research, teaching, patient care, and public service
- offer economies not available through traditional models of collection development
- enhance access by the research community to important cultural assets by ensuring persistence over time
- enable UC Libraries to develop comprehensive research collections that would otherwise be impossible to build

More recently public libraries have started to use shared funding to provide access to downloadable audiobooks and videos for patrons' use on personal computers and MP3 players. The Oregon Digital Library Consortium, a group of public libraries and public library federations, offers its patrons Library2Go (http://library2go.lib.overdrive.com), a shared digital audiobook collection. Kansas State Library, through a statewide cooperative, offers Audiobooks, Music and More (http://kansas.lib.overdrive.com), which provides users access to digital videos, audiobooks, e-books, and music.

Collections librarians have a critical role in selecting cooperatively funded resources. Most of the cooperatives that engage in this activity rely on a group of librarians to propose and select the materials to be jointly acquired. For example, the University of California program has twelve system-wide groups of bibliographers in specific subject areas who meet to sponsor shared purchases and coordinate their collecting activities. The CRL accepts suggestions from its member libraries and provides ballots of possible additions for membership vote.

Coordinated Weeding and Retention

A fourth approach to cooperation is *coordinated weeding and retention*. These agreements seek to reduce the costs of maintaining collections by distributing responsibilities and sharing costs. Coordinated weeding and retention go hand in hand. They involve more than checking in a shared catalog to see that at least one other copy is held elsewhere before withdrawing the local copy. Just as coordinated collection development depends on identifying areas for which partner libraries have collecting responsibilities, coordinated weeding and retention rely on taking responsibility for retaining materials in certain areas or of certain types. Libraries that wish to withdraw materials because of condition issues or space limitations agree to check first to determine if the item is the last copy in the consortium or geographic area. This practice is often called *last-copy retention*, though a single last copy may not always be the best course of action. Although retention of unneeded duplicate materials is not desirable, a degree of redundancy is desirable to protect against catastrophic loss. The desirable number of copies held in a region or nationally is a frequently debated topic.

Coordinated Preservation Initiatives

Preservation microfilming projects have been some of the more successful approaches to *coordinated preservation* and have led to several cooperative projects over the years. Primarily funded through National Endowment for the Humanities (NEH) grants, these projects have sought to develop a national collection of preserved documents while meeting agreed-upon archival standards for quality and storage and avoiding duplication. For example, the CIC coordinated several cooperative projects in the 1980s and 1990s that filmed many thousands of volumes. The United States Agricultural Information Network and the National Agricultural Library coordinate a project that began in the early 1990s and, through a series of NEH grants, is microfilming important agricultural publications on a state-by-state basis. The Library of Congress and the NEH are directing the United States Newspaper Program (www.neh.gov/projects/usnp .html), a cooperative national effort started in the early 1980s to locate, catalog, preserve on microfilm, and make available to researchers newspapers published in the United States from the eighteenth century to the present.

The University of California libraries have had a collaborative and coordinated preservation program since the early 1980s. Its activities include repair and reformatting of materials, disaster planning, and providing disaster recovery supplies.

The shared mass digitization projects of recent years (e.g., Google Books Library Project and the Open Content Alliance) are cooperative projects primarily aimed to increase access to resources, but they have a preservation component as well. Many items that are scanned are in extremely poor condition, and digitization preserves their content for future generations of users.

Shared Storage

Efforts to achieve space economies through *shared storage* facilities have a long history. The New England Depository Library, founded in 1942, is the oldest shared storage facility in the United States and is used by libraries in the Northeast. The CRL opened in 1951 with the provision of a storage depository as one of its major goals. In addition to housing cooperative purchases, member libraries place lesser-used materials from their own collections in CRL's central storage building. Of the sixty-eight storage facilities in the United States and Canada, fourteen are shared by two or more libraries.[35]

Steve O'Conner, Andrew Wells, and Mel Collier distinguish between cooperative storage, "essentially the sharing of a space within a facility," and collaborative storage, "a shared approach to the collection in terms of growth, shape, management, and access."[36] Collaborative storage can be seen as coordinated storage because it is planned, and focused on maintaining a coordinated collection. Many libraries are implementing last-copy policies in their collaborative storage facilities as part of collaborative retention and preservation planning. The participating libraries do not deposit duplicate copies and guarantee permanent access to the stored materials. Several have developed formal shared print journal archiving agreements. According to Lizanne Payne, JSTOR titles are an easy starting point for shared journal holdings because the tiles are available online, and at least twelve university libraries have agreements to consolidate their holdings of JSTOR volumes in a shared storage facility.[37]

In the late 1990s, librarians began to talk about creating a formal, large-scale cooperative program for shared print management, including coordinating the use of shared storage facilities as last-copy repositories. The North American Storage Trust (www.oclc.org/programs/ourwork/collectivecoll/sharedprint/nast .htm) grew out of these discussions. This initiative aspires to provide a central registry for libraries to report which volumes they will retain and preserve either in storage facilities on in libraries, along with formal agreements that participating libraries may rely on access to the preserved copies if they withdraw their own. Payne compares this proposed voluntary distributed print retention and preservation system to LOCKSS (a voluntary distributed system to preserve electronic resources). She writes that, "by leveraging this collective capacity, and building on existing networks of trust within the library community, we can begin to manage our physical inventories in ways that reduce unnecessary redundancy while preserving the world's print heritage as a shared public good."[38]

A more recent approach to shared storage is the shared digital repository. Two examples are being developed by the CIC and the Colorado Digital Alliance. The CIC's shared digital repository (called the HathiTrust) is intended to archive and manage collectively the full content of public domain works digitized by Google that are held across the CIC libraries and, eventually, other digital content. The shared repository will give faculty and students access to a large and diverse online library previously housed in separate locations and connected only by online catalogs and ILL. The HathiTrust operates under the leadership of repository administrators Indiana University and the University of Michigan and is housed at the latter. Additional governance and financial support are provided by the charter participating libraries of the CIC and by other libraries and library consortia wishing to archive digital content.

The Alliance Digital Repository (http://adrresources.coalliance.org) is a preservation-oriented consortial digital repository service offered by the Colorado Alliance of Research Libraries to its member institutions and affiliates. Its stated purpose is to

- provide access to digital content by students, faculty, staff, patrons, researchers, and customers of Alliance institutions, as well as to the world
- host hardware and software infrastructure that supports digital repository services and functionalities for Alliance institutions and affiliated partners
- store digital assets created and collected by Alliance libraries, universities, and communities.

Additional Areas of Cooperation

Other cooperative initiatives directly related to cooperative collection development and management are library automation and cataloging. Many libraries, particularly smaller libraries, have joined in shared library automation projects to save money through the implementation of a single system and to provide easy bibliographic access to holdings in all participating libraries. Many state and regional initiatives implement statewide or regional shared automated systems. Some cooperative initiatives distribute responsibility for cataloging materials according to language or subject. This often goes along with distributed responsibility for acquiring those materials because intellectual access is an essential component of cooperative collection building. For example, a library that accepts an obligation to acquire Korean materials also agrees to provide the specialized cataloging necessary to add those materials in a timely manner to an accessible catalog. The bibliographic utilities are international cooperative cataloging projects.

Mechanisms for Cooperative Collection Development

Several mechanisms exist through which libraries manage cooperative activities. The terms *network* and *consortium* are often used interchangeably. Other terms are *cooperative, collaborative, council, federation,* and *alliance.* The *Guide to Cooperative Collection Development* provides the following definitions. A consortium is "a community of two or more libraries that have formally agreed to coordinate, cooperate in, or consolidate certain functions. Consortia may be formed on a geographic, function, type, format, or subject basis." A network is "the linking of libraries through shared bibliographic utilities or other formal arrangements."[39]

The National Information Standards Organization makes no similar distinction between networks and consortia, opting to define a *library cooperative* as

> an organization that has a formal arrangement whereby library and information services are supported for the mutual benefit of participating libraries. It must meet all of the following criteria:
>
> 1. Participants/members are primarily libraries.
> 2. The organization is a U.S. not-for-profit entity which has its own budget and its own paid staff.
> 3. The organization serves multiple institutions (e.g., libraries, school districts) that are not under the organization's administrative control.
> 4. The scope of the organization's activities includes support of library and information services by performing such functions as resource sharing, training, planning, and advocacy.[40]

The survey report of research conducted by the ALA Office for Research and Statistics covered all bases in its title—"Library Networks, Cooperatives and Consortia: A National Survey."[41]

Bibliographic utilities provide online access to the holdings of member libraries and additional services that may include shared cataloging, ILL, and group purchasing. James J. Kopp once called OCLC, the largest member-driven bibliographic utility, a "megaconsortium."[42] OCLC regional bibliographic utilities often include "network" as part of their name. Examples and the regions they serve are NELINET (New England), AMIGOS Services (Southwest), MINITEX (Minnesota and the Dakotas), and WILS (Wisconsin). These regional networks provide a variety of services that may include

- OCLC support
- consulting
- training
- contract cataloging

- reference service
- preservation support and disaster assistance
- discounted prices for library supplies through agreements with vendors
- regional document delivery
- cooperative purchase of online resources

Factors that affect organizational patterns include characteristics of individual members, administration of the program, kinds of cooperative activity, and sources of funding. Funding may be through membership fees or contributions, grants, external funds (e.g., via an annual allocation from state government), or a combination of these. Cooperating libraries, regardless of what they call their organization, may have a centralized or decentralized administrative structure. The source of funds often determines the kind of administrative structure. The common feature of the cooperative organization is the use of formal agreements that provide operating principles and, usually, define the goals of the organization. The AMICALnet Consortial Governance, Planning and Organization Documents site (www.amicalnet.org/resources/consortial-doc-examples/) lists examples of documents from consortia worldwide.

The precursors to consortia were library systems. Until the 1950s, most public libraries were independent, though a library might consist of a central library and branch libraries. Independent public libraries began to join together into library systems in order to use resources more efficiently and provide better services to users. This process began in the state of New York in the early 1950s and spread across the country; by 1969, 491 public library systems were in operation.[43] The number of library cooperatives has grown rapidly since the mid-1960s. A major impetus behind this growth has been the spread of library automation and the resulting development of shared bibliographic databases. Ninety-six academic library consortia were established just between 1966 and 1970.[44]

The 2007 *Bowker Annual Library and Book Trade Almanac* lists more than four hundred networks, consortia, and other cooperative library organizations in the United States and Canada.[45] These organizations have been merging to leverage their resources and collective power. For example, PALINET (a regional library network serving more than six hundred members in the mid-Atlantic region and beyond) and SOLINET (a library cooperative serving more than 2,500 library and other information organizations in the Southeast and Caribbean) merged in 2008. Formal cooperative collection management relationships with other libraries may be local, statewide, regional, national, or international. The membership may be focused on a particular type of library (e.g., academic, public), or the cooperative may serve several types of libraries. Many libraries belong to an OCLC regional network and a statewide or regional consortium. The latter is typically a cooperative organization, whose members have similar missions and serve similar constituencies.

The just-mentioned ALA survey compiled and analyzed responses from 225 library networks, cooperatives, and consortia (LNCCs) in 2006/7.[46] Among their findings are the following:

- More than four out of five LNCCs serve public libraries; three out of five serve academic libraries; half serve school libraries.

- California, Illinois, Massachusetts, Michigan, New York, Pennsylvania, Texas, and Wisconsin have the most LNCCs and the most LNCC members.

- Seven out of ten LNCCs are regional (i.e., multicounty or statewide), and three out of five serve multiple library types.

- LNCCs serving multiple library types are more likely to focus on resource sharing.

Funding models and organizational strategies for cooperatives vary from simple to complex. Some charge a flat membership fee. Others prorate the fee based on library operating budget or population served. Respondents to a Primary Research Group survey published in 2007 reported spending an average of $7,300 on annual dues and fees to consortiums.[47] Some are ad hoc and created primarily to serve as buying clubs, with no central office; Tim Bucknall calls these "virtual consortia."[48] Some statewide consortia are supported by the state government with members paying fees for additional services. Some cooperatives have central staffs of varying size; others rely on volunteers from the member libraries.

Several states have effective cooperative programs that provide a variety of services, including ILL, document delivery, and access to electronic resources. The programs are funded at the state level and do not require participating libraries to pay membership fees. They may be open to all citizens of the state or to individuals affiliated with member institutions and their libraries. A representative sampling is described here.

The Illinois Library and Information Network (ILLINET; www.cyberdrive illinois.com/departments/library/who_we_are/illinet.html) was formed in 1975 and is administered by the Illinois State Library.[49] More than five thousand academic, public, school, and special libraries are ILLINET members. A library becomes an ILLINET member when it is accepted for membership in one of the twelve state-funded regional library systems. ILLINET provides statewide ILL delivery service between libraries. It has an extensive program to provide access to e-resources through E-RICH, a tiered set of service offerings available to all ILLINET member libraries. Tier 1 e-resources are totally subsidized by the Illinois State Library and provided at no charge to all ILLINET member libraries. Tier 2 are e-resources partially subsidized by the Illinois State Library and available to all ILLINET member libraries; a portion of the cost must be paid by the subscribing library. Tier 3 e-resources are not subsidized, but the Illinois State Library negotiates for favorable pricing for purchasing libraries.

OhioLINK (http://ohiolink.edu) is a statewide, state-funded network of eighty-six Ohio college, university, and technical school libraries and the State Library of Ohio.[50] It provides access to more than 140 online research databases, more than seven thousand scholarly e-journals, approximately two thousand educational films, thousands of digital images (and more through its Digital Media Center), a growing collection of e-books, and approximately fourteen thousand electronic theses and dissertations from students at participating colleges and universities. Patrons at participating libraries use a single automated catalog that supports the submission of unmediated patron borrowing requests, and requested materials are delivered within forty-eight hours. Undergraduates are the heaviest users of the ILL service, representing nearly 40 percent of borrowing; the remaining 60 percent is split fairly evenly between graduate students and faculty/staff.[51] A parallel initiative is INFOhio (www.infohio.org), a virtual K–12 library, which, like OhioLINK, is funded by the state of Ohio. It provides free access to online resources for students, students' families, and educators.

The MINITEX Library Information Network (www.minitex.umn.edu) is a publicly supported network of academic, public, state government, and special libraries. MINITEX is funded by the Minnesota Legislature through the Minnesota Office of Higher Education; programs for Minnesota public libraries are funded through a contract with Minnesota State Library Services and School Technology, a unit of the Minnesota Department of Education. Libraries in North Dakota and South Dakota participate in MINITEX programs through contracts between the Minnesota Office of Higher Education and the North and South Dakota state libraries. MINITEX began as a document delivery service and continues to deliver materials in the tristate region. It serves as the regional OCLC network, and participating libraries pay fees for OCLC services. In addition to providing many typical services associated with cooperatives (e.g., training, contract cataloging, discounted prices for library supplies and e-resources), MINITEX provides statewide free access to Electronic Library for Minnesota, a suite of e-resources from the Gale Group, OCLC FirstSearch, ProQuest, and NetLibrary made available through state legislative funding. It also manages MnLINK and the MnLINK Gateway, Minnesota's statewide virtual online library catalog, and operates the Minnesota Library Access Center, a high-density storage facility for important but lesser-used items from libraries throughout Minnesota.

The Florida Electronic Library is a gateway to online resources for all ages—electronic magazines, newspapers, almanacs, encyclopedias, and books—and includes homework help for students and resources for teachers. Access requires entry of a Florida public library bar code number. Administered by the

Florida Division of Library and Information Services, this gateway also provides open access to FloridaCat, an online catalog of all of Florida's library holdings; Florida on Florida, a collection on Florida's history, culture, and environment from digital collections held by libraries, archives, museums, and historical societies throughout Florida; and the Florida Memory Project, information from the State Library and Archives of Florida.

Cooperatives and Acquisition of Electronic Resources

Collaboration in the acquisition of e-resources has expanded rapidly among all types of libraries. Sometimes called *consortial cost sharing* or *buying clubs*, this is one of the most successful areas of cooperation.[52] A Primary Research Group survey published in 2007 reported that consortium purchases accounted for a mean of 30 percent of the database licenses by the libraries in the sample.[53] Further, college and university libraries accounted for a mean of just over 41 percent of contracts, twice as much as for public or government and nonprofit libraries.

Libraries that have not previously engaged in formal cooperative agreements are joining multiple organizations to gain savings and greater power in contract negotiations with suppliers of electronic information resources. When assured of a certain number of purchasers, vendors frequently offer discount pricing. An added advantage for vendors is often reduced operational costs. A publisher or vendor need negotiate the license only with the consortium, not with individual libraries, and billing is often handled through a single statement sent to the consortium office.

Advantages for libraries are access to a greater domain of materials than they can normally afford, the ability to leverage their acquisitions budgets and acquire access to more resources than they can normally afford, reduced costs and time on the library side devoted to license negotiation since the consortium handles this, and increased likelihood that the collective clout of the consortium will be able to negotiate more favorable licensing terms. The OhioLINK Electronic Journal Center is one example of the expanded access to resources available to students, faculty, and staff at the eighty-six participating OhioLINK institutions. Even Ohio's major universities hold an average of only 25 percent of the available scholarly journals, but users at those institutions utilize 80 percent of the available Electronic Journal Center titles.[54]

Libraries are leveraging investments through reductions in resource costs. This can be seen as cost avoidance because the library spends more than if it acquired nothing but less than if it paid the full price charged individual libraries. Some cost reductions also may accrue if a library decides to cancel print and microform resources that duplicate the e-resource. As of March 2008, the CIC reported that its libraries realized more than $21.5 million in cost savings (paying less for resources they were already buying) and cost avoidance (mounting data at one site rather than at all member libraries).[55]

Allocation of costs for products acquired through consortial licenses varies from consortium to consortium. At the heart of cost allocation is the goal of being equitable to all participants. When member libraries are of similar size, the consortium may divide the total cost of the licensed product equally among those libraries that opt to acquire access. Another typical approach is differential pricing—that is, dividing costs proportionally among participants according to projected use or the size of the user population, based on either enrollment (or enrolled students plus staff and faculty/teachers) or number of citizens served by the library. Douglas Anderson notes that larger institutions may feel disadvantaged by this approach because vendors often discount their prices progressively according to the size of the user base.[56] Anderson explores several alternatives, including hybrid models that take into account the savings gained through the consortium compared to what the library would pay if it licensed the content independently.

Additional savings gained by working through a consortium to acquire e-resources can result from having a centralized staff to negotiate and administer the contracts. Individual libraries do not have to devote time to reviewing contracts and their negotiation. Another possible benefit is a multiyear contract that often guarantees reduced annual price increases.

Selection of resources is handled differently in each consortium and varies with the electronic content being considered. Sometimes a vendor approaches the consortium and puts a proposal forward. Sometimes collections librarians suggest a publisher or vendor whose package of e-resources is seen as attractive. In most cases, the proposal (regardless of its origin) is reviewed by collections librarians from the participating libraries, often through a committee of collection development officers that may include e-resource librarians (if different from the collections librarians). If a library already has access to the content, the collections librarian reviews the existing terms and pricing to see if the consortial proposal is more attractive. Most vendors require a certain number of consortial participants to move forward with the offer. In general, member libraries, though they can opt in or opt out, do not have the ability to customize their selection. They are offered the entire package and cannot select components according to their local, institutional preferences.

The role of consortia in acquiring e-resources and access continues to expand. A potent illustration is the International Coalition of Library Consortia (ICOLC; www.library.yale.edu/consortia/), organized in 1997. This informal group has a membership of more than 135 library consortia in several countries. Representatives from the various consortia, which primarily serve institutions of higher education, meet twice a year with e-resource providers and vendors to discuss new offerings, pricing practices, and contractual issues. Barbara McFadden Allen and Arnold Hirshon refer to ICOLC as "a reverse cartel because these independent consortia come together not to limit competition or fix prices, but to leverage their collection power to open up the market."[57] In 1998, ICOLC released its "Statement of Current Perspective and Preferred Practices for the Selection and Purchase of Electronic Information," which sought to establish an international perspective on consortial licensing and cooperative purchasing of electronic information by libraries; this was last updated in December 2004.[58]

Attributes of Successful Cooperative Collection Development

Libraries that make a commitment to build collections collaboratively need a clear understanding of what they hold locally and a common way to assess and compare collections with their partners. Two comparative assessment tools frequently used are collection profiles (or collection maps) and the Conspectus. Being able to assess and evaluate collections and to compare local collections with those held by partners is essential.

Effective coordinated collection development management requires finding an acceptable balance between local priorities and the priorities of the larger group seeking to cooperate. This tension has defined the history of library cooperation. The library's obligation to provide materials to meet local needs is a more powerful force than any external agreement to acquire materials to meet the needs of unknown, remote users. One source of this tension is the reality that every library serves a local community, which may be an institution of higher education, local citizens and governing body, school students, partners in a legal firm, hospital staff members, and so forth. Any cooperative program that requires a library to buy materials needed at another library at the expense of locally needed materials will fail. As entities accountable to their local communities and parent agencies and institutions, libraries must have a clear understanding of their institutional mission and be able to explain how resources are being used to meet the community's needs and desires along with the benefits gained through collaboration. The challenge of balancing local priorities and group commitments plagues every cooperative development initiative, but managing these counterpoints effectively is an attribute of successful cooperative initiatives.

Successful cooperative collection development in consortia requires a high level of trust between the institutions and the collections librarians and, in the case of formal consortia, effective governance. This means a clear governing structure, goals, and sufficient authority to make decisions. A competent, strong consortium leader or administrator is equally important. All formal agreements and commitments must be flexible and permit modification. Clarity and adequate understanding among partners of the shared goals and intentions of the consortium are important. The consortium must have a reliable communication system to share policy decisions and changes quickly and widely. E-mail, electronic discussion lists, and consortium websites have lessened many communication barriers, especially between individual selectors. Both the consortium staff and the library representatives should fulfill their obligations (responding to queries, evaluating resources, returning purchase agreements, etc.) in a timely manner.

Social and political pressure for parity of access to library materials, especially in rural areas, is leading government funding bodies to look favorably on cooperative initiatives. Cooperative ventures in several states, such as Ohio, Minnesota, and Georgia, are being funded at the state level—either through statewide academic initiatives or through projects that provide e-resources to libraries of all types. State legislatures are finding the appropriation of new funds for statewide access to e-resources through a central provider a more attractive option than funding several smaller agencies. Providing a common good continues to resonate with public funding agencies.

Enlightened self-interest of each institution in the consortium may be the most important element leading toward success. Inculcating cooperation as a core value within the library can foster a willingness to make sacrifices and a belief that benefits will accrue. Success depends on a high degree of altruism and respect for and recognition of the value of increased collaboration. One goal is to reach the stage at which the collections of cooperating libraries are no longer viewed as individual collections but as a single shared collection distributed in various locations linked by a shared catalog and delivery mechanism. Excitement can develop around the idea that library cooperation addresses inequities in service and produces significant cost savings and cost avoidance. Clear goals for cooperation, institutional and administrative commitment, recognition of the cooperative's value, and trust among the partners must be held by all. For cooperation to succeed, it must be considered a routine part of all work in the library.

Cynthia Shelton identifies these key aspects of successful cooperative collection development and management initiatives: effective communication and consultation, clear goals and focus for initiatives, willingness to be flexible and adapt to changes, and a viable technological infrastructure.[59] Debra Kachel stresses the need for a written consortium policy that spells out the commitments, responsibilities, goals, and objectives; the policy should be endorsed by signature of the appropriate administrators or perhaps (in the case of school library media centers) by the school board.[60]

Challenges to Cooperative Collection Development

Desire for Local Autonomy

Librarians, since the beginning of collection building, have seen their goal as meeting current and future community needs rapidly and effectively. This perspective has resulted in tremendous pride following on self-sufficiency. This tradition of a strong local collection of resources has been a defining characteristic of librarianship for centuries—fueled, suggests Martin Runkle, by "the major role of property in our social and legal system."[61] The dominant culture in the United States places tremendous value on ownership. In a material culture, the size of the local collection is a persistent measure of success. Many organizations, such as the ARL, are seeking supplemental and alternative measures of library success, yet the need for local ownership with its implications of control and independence remains a potent force against cooperation.

The desire for independence and local autonomy is as powerful a force as the value associated with holding large collections. Joseph Branin suggests that cooperative collection development has had problems in the United States because of a long and deep-rooted tradition of local autonomy. Librarians and their libraries have had difficulty overcoming their parochialism and thinking more broadly—at the consortial, network, or state level. Although cooperation and collaboration are considered good in the abstract, individual libraries' desire to be self-sufficient creates resistance to what is perceived as losing control. Consortia often stumble over the organizational and administrative aspects of establishing themselves. For Branin, "cooperative collection development is at its most basic level a political, not a technical issue."[62]

Professional Pride

The culture of collection development and the feeling that the role of every selector is to build the most complete collection possible also pulls against cooperation. This form of turf professionalism leads subject specialists in research libraries to see themselves as developing competing collections rather than cooperating to build a shared resource. A major challenge facing cooperative collection development is to change these selection virtues of the past. Pride among all types of librarians has a tendency to focus on the quality of the local collection rather than the quality of the consortial or regional collection. A spirit of interdependence and trust among collection development librarians is a key element in successful cooperative collection development.

Attitudes of faculty members at academic institutions are equally constrained by the belief that large local collections equal academic status and prestige. Faculty fear that reductions in local collection growth, regardless of the wealth of resources readily available, will reduce their own program's reputation and negatively affect decisions about accreditation, joining the department, and faculty retention, promotion, and tenure. Local ownership of extremely expensive, esoteric items is a point of pride and prestige—even when such items are used infrequently. Changing faculty perceptions and expectations about the benefits of cooperative collection development remains a challenge as long as extensive local collections continue to hold such symbolic status. Nevertheless, library users who appreciate and have confidence in the mutual benefits that can result from cooperation are essential for success.

Unequal Distribution of Commitment, Effort, and Money among Partners

Money remains a major barrier to successful cooperation. When funds are limited, priorities tend to be internal. The rapidly increasing costs of materials, resulting limitations on what can be acquired locally, and inevitability of depending on others have increased interest in formal cooperation even while making it difficult. Libraries participating in cooperative initiatives are concerned about financial parity. Financial commitments must be fair to all participants. This may be represented in a sliding scale of membership fees and equitable distribution of local financial commitments.

Another potential cause of the failure of cooperative initiatives lies within the library's own organization. Librarians often are unable to transcend organizational divisions and overcome communication barriers within their own libraries. If selection activities are too decentralized they occur in isolation, and efforts at cooperative policymaking do not succeed. If coordinating selection activities within a library is difficult, coordinating with external partners is more so. Technical services, reference services, preservation activities, and ILL operations all must be aware of and support cooperative commitments and endeavors. If the library does not have a supportive internal organizational structure and clear authority for collection development, cooperation with other libraries is nearly impossible.

Lack of support, commitment, and leadership from governing boards and administrators both within and external to the library can be a large problem. Strong leadership and constant support throughout the organization are important. The CIC is an example of a consortium that benefits from strong institutional support. The members of its governing committee are the chief academic officers from each of the twelve member universities. CIC programs and activities extend to all aspects of university activity except intercollegiate athletics. The Center for Library Initiatives is one of several cooperating ventures under the CIC umbrella, all of which are strongly supported by university administrators.

Dissatisfaction with the results of cooperation among library staff members and users creates difficulties. The absence of significant, observable accomplishments leads to self-defeating behaviors. Without some successes, momentum for progress is lacking. Thus, participants in cooperative collection development programs need a process for quantifying the cost benefits of cooperation and of regularly comparing the benefits of cooperation with those of independence.[63] Everyone must understand the consequences of ignoring consortial commitments. Documented evidence of the benefits of cooperation and the results of failing to cooperate is a powerful incentive.

Failures in Intellectual Access and Physical Access

Any difficulties in providing physical access to remote materials are a barrier to cooperative collection development. Users want speedy delivery of high-quality resources. To succeed, a consortium needs dependable mechanisms for affordable, timely, efficient, and effective delivery of resources.

Failure in the ability to identify and locate resources or to provide speedy physical access undermines cooperative collection development and management. Libraries have generally accepted that they cannot own everything and that access (bibliographic and physical) is the key to satisfying users' needs and desires. This view might be seen in terms of "just-in-time" compared to "just-in-case" collections. "Just-in-time" is a business phrase that describes a means of inventory control. The goal of just-in-time inventory management is to reduce the use of buffer inventories and to synchronize the movement of materials through the production process so that materials are delivered only just before they are needed. "Just-in-case" is the opposite approach and means that large inventories of production materials are held on site so they are always on hand whenever they are needed. Manufacturing businesses have found that reducing the size of inventories decreases costs by reducing the need for large warehouses and staff to manage the inventory and reducing the investment sunk into inventory waiting in warehouses until needed. To be successful, the just-in-case strategy depends on an infrastructure that accurately reports resources at hand and where additional resources are located, plus rapid delivery of the needed part. A library can be said to follow a just-in-time approach when it acquires either through purchase or loan materials its users need when they need them and does not invest all or large portions of its materials budget in acquiring collections just in case users need them at some future time.

Evaluating Cooperative Collection Development

Cost-Benefit Analysis

James Burgett, John Haar, and Linda L. Phillips observe that "illustrating the positive cost-benefit ratio of specific CCD [collaborative collection development] projects with concrete numbers has proven difficult and elusive."[64] This does not mean that libraries have not tried and should not continue to do cost-benefit analyses. Cost-benefit analysis compares the various costs associated with an expenditure against the benefits it proposes to return. Both tangible and intangible factors should be addressed and measured—to the extent possible. Cost-benefit analysis requires consistent measurements across the options compared; traditional forms of these analyses calculate both present and future costs and present and future benefits (i.e., value) in monetary terms, then measure the benefits per dollar spent. Such an analysis helps a library determine which decisions are fiscally responsible.

The 1990s saw cost-benefit analyses of resource sharing and commercial document delivery services compared to owning books and subscribing to print journals in academic libraries. In 1991 and 1992, Columbia University libraries compared costs of ownership with costs of borrowing from other libraries or using commercial document delivery.[65] The study found that the costs of owning a monograph used only once far exceeded the costs of accessing it through ILL, but the authors struggled with measuring and assigning values to intangibles, such as the importance to researchers of being able to browse new periodical issues. Louisiana State University, in a study reported in 1997, found that commercial document delivery was more economical for high-cost, low-use journals than local print subscriptions, and that users accepted the service when it met promised expectations, including twenty-four-hour turnaround.[66] Bruce R. Kingma's 1998 article applied cost-benefit analysis to access, ownership, and interlibrary loan.[67] He sought to assign a dollar value to all aspects of the analysis. Other researchers have investigated cost-benefit analysis of e-resources and various approaches to their acquisition. Donald W. King and colleagues observe that the complex decisions surrounding e-resources "require a sound economic underpinning as well as good judgment in applying economic information and metrics."[68] This complexity involves deciding if the library should

- rely exclusively on e-journals, or purchase both electronic and print subscriptions, and if so at what price
- subscribe to or rely on single article delivery for certain journals
- discard print issues, or rely on them as backup for archival purposes
- negotiate site licenses
- deal directly with publishers, or rely on intermediary services such as consortia, aggregators, gateways, and if so at what price

- depend, in some cases on information freely accessible on the Web as a substitute for costly e-resources.

Cost-benefit analysis can help inform these decisions. Determining the direct cost in dollars of a purchased book or print journal, e-book or e-journal licensed directly from the publisher, e-book or e-journal licensed through a consortium or as part of a bundled package, or provision through ILL or commercial document delivery is reasonably easy to do, but other aspects of the cost-benefit analysis are more challenging. A complete analysis calculates all costs in dollars on the library's side, including staffing costs associated with each task (selection, order placement, license negotiation and tracking, receipting physical items, invoice processing, cataloging, shelving, issue check-in, binding, reshelving, interlibrary loan processing, etc.) and benefits (money saved by reducing or eliminating tasks). Additional cost components, such as equipment and its depreciation and telecommunication charges, might logically be part of an analysis. Few libraries have the capacity to do this detailed and comprehensive a cost-benefit analysis.

Calculating costs and benefits from the user's perspective is even less straightforward. How does one measure user satisfaction in dollars? How does one measure user effort or the value of a user's time to locate and obtain an item? If the item is held locally in print format, the user must locate it, note the call number or shelving location, and then examine it in the library, check it out, or make a photocopy. If it is held electronically, the user still needs to find it but does not always need to visit the library. Regardless of remote or on-site access, the user may incur printing costs. If not available in the library or online through a library license, the library user may use an unmediated ILL option or complete a form—and then wait for delivery.

Patron satisfaction or utility cost is equally difficult to assess. Economists use *utility* as a measure or expression of an individual's expected or anticipated satisfaction. Ideally, one would contrast the utility of on-site or online patron access, in which the patron has speedy access and does the retrieval personally, with ILL (or commercial document delivery, if the library offers this), in which at least some of the work is transferred to staff, access takes longer, and fees may be charged. One could add the option that many publishers offer in which a customer orders an article directly and pays the publisher. Determining the opportunity cost (the true cost of choosing one alternative over another) from the user's perspective is difficult.

In the past few years, library valuation research has gained increasing importance and attention.[69] In particular, public library valuation researchers have adopted valuation methods from the field of economics that allow libraries to assign a dollar value to their programs and services. Much of this work has focused on demonstrating through cost-benefit analysis the value that tax dollars spent on libraries bring to a community. One approach, adopted from economists, uses stated-preference techniques to estimate how much consumers would pay for a good or service if it were available for purchase. This technique is explicitly designed to provide value equivalents in situations where no market price can exist. The intent is not to determine what people will pay but to gather data that can be used in combination with cost data to calculate a cost-benefit ratio. One stated-preference technique is contingent valuation, in which users and nonusers are surveyed about their value perceptions and asked to respond to hypothetical scenarios. In contingent-valuation surveys, individuals are asked how much they would be willing to pay for a good or service, or how much money they would accept in order to forgo the good or service—even though that good or service does not have a market price.[70] For example, library users and potential users could be asked to determine if they would assign a higher dollar value to having access to more materials combined with some delay in delivery (i.e., resource sharing and ILL) or a higher value to fewer materials with on-site access.

Not every librarian and every library is in a position to conduct a formal cost-benefit analysis when deciding to purchase a resource, to rely on resource sharing, or to purchase through a cooperative venture. Nevertheless, careful consideration is necessary and information can be gathered to make an informed decision. At its simplest, a cost-benefit analysis compares the pros and cons of alternatives. A librarian can supply direct costs where they are known and list staff tasks in general terms (without determining dollar costs) to compare costs and benefits on the library's side. Librarians can use existing library data where they are available, including circulation activity, ILL borrowing, and collection analyses about existing strengths and weaknesses. On the user side, the librarian can list any known fees or costs that the user is expected to pay and then list benefits and costs from the user's perspective in general terms (i.e., without trying to assign a dollar value). For example, one could confidently state that users assign proximity to physical collections a high value and twenty-four-hour access to online resources a higher value. King and colleagues suggest using these sorts of comparative terms—for example, lower cost, low cost, moderate cost, high cost, higher cost—and descriptive terms, such as "saves users time" and "less effort needed."[71] A fairly simple pro/con chart that lists costs and benefits from the library's perspective and from the user's perspective can be an effective tool to inform decision making.

Social Return on Investment and Balanced Scorecard

Concepts of *social return on investment* expand cost-benefit analysis to include explicitly the economic value of cultural and social impact. The method for calculating social return on investment (SROI) was pioneered by the Roberts Enterprise Development Fund (www.redf.org). SROI is intended to recognize the importance of metrics to manage and measure impacts that are not included in traditional profit-and-loss accounts and the need for these metrics to focus on outcomes over outputs.[72] In the library context, an SROI analysis is focused on the user community, aims to understand value (i.e., benefits) from their perspective, and, where possible, uses monetary values for these indicators.

One tool used in reporting SROI is the *balanced scorecard*, another technique borrowed from the for-profit sector. This tool continues to evolve. It is intended to provide a context for the measures chosen and permits expressing value in social as well as economic terms. It allows balancing successes across different types of measures and recognizes their interaction. In 2003, Stephen Bosch, Lucy Lyons, and Mary H. Munroe reported on work to develop a modified balanced scorecard that could measure the success of cooperative collection development activities.[73] They developed four groups of performance measures: resources or input data (numerical data like staff numbers and hours of work, items purchased, items in collections); financial data (library/group expenditures, unit costs, etc.); use data (use of electronic, print, or near print, documents delivered, etc.); and user satisfaction data. A library begins by identifying five or six key strategic objectives, maps causal links between them, and picks suitable measures for each objective. Unlike cost-benefit analysis, the intended result is not a formal comparison between cost dollars and benefit dollars (or value). The goal is to find an equilibrium in which outcomes are equally positive without significant gains (or losses) in one area to the detriment of others.

A library, for example, might select the following strategic objectives related to collaborative collection development and management as highest priorities:

a. access to more unique resources

b. expansion of digital collections through leveraged investment

c. increased availability in local shelf space through coordinated storage

d. reduced user effort and time

e. increased user satisfaction

f. reduced library personnel costs

Measures assigned to these objectives might be

a. title count of the shared universe of resources, or ILL activity

b. title count of e-resources or cost savings through consortial purchases

c. volumes withdrawn and local shelving space gained

d. improvement in user perceptions about effort and time required for different tasks

e. improvement in user satisfaction

f. declining library personnel costs

The balanced scorecard is prepared and then revisited as new data are gathered at periodic intervals to track changes in each key measure. The purpose is to have quantitative and qualitative measures that can help the library determine if a cooperative collection development program reduces costs, increases access to information resources, and results in increased use and user satisfaction—or if not, where it is failing.

Summary

Cooperative collection development needs three components to succeed: efficient resource sharing, easy bibliographic access to collections elsewhere, and coordinated collection development and management. Resource sharing was the first form of library cooperation. Escalating materials costs combined with budget constraints and increasing numbers of volumes published are leading libraries to depend more on other libraries and sources to meet user needs and expectations. Library automation and the resulting ease of searching local, state, and regional catalogs and bibliographic utilities have facilitated awareness of holdings elsewhere. Advances in the technologies that support interlibrary loan have improved, speeding the processes for libraries and offering patrons the functionality of unmediated request submission. Coordinated collection development and management remain the greatest stumbling block because of the tension between local priorities and those of the larger group with whom cooperation is sought.

Cooperative collection development and management can take several forms. The status quo approach assumes that coordination and comprehensive coverage will just happen. In the synergistic approach, different libraries take responsibility for collecting in different areas according to a coordinated and collaborative plan. Cooperative funding is used for shared purchases in agreed-upon locations. Coordinated weeding and retention mean that different libraries take responsibility for continuing to hold materials in different subjects or in different formats. Coordinated preservation initiatives have long history. Shared storage also has been in place for many years, but only recently have libraries begun to consider coordinating what they store to avoid duplication and preserve unique materials. Shared digital repositories are an emerging form of shared storage. Library cooperation is seen in shared automation and cataloging.

Library networks, consortia, and cooperatives are the primary vehicles for cooperation and range from two or three libraries with geographic proximity to multitype state ventures to national and international networks with hundreds of members. The most successful networks share bibliographic access, some mechanism to facilitate sharing of resources, and some degree of coordinated collection development and management. Many libraries are participating in cooperative ventures to secure acquisition of and access to e-resources at discounted group prices. Several forces foster a successful consortium, including a belief in and commitment to cooperation by local administrators and library staffs, equitable fees, clear understanding of local holdings and local needs, and effective consortial governance. Flexibility and responsiveness to local collection development needs are central to success.

Cooperative ventures have grown as the ability to build on-site collections has declined. Libraries struggle with making cost-effective decisions about their position on the continuum between access and ownership. Analyzing the costs and benefits for various approaches for providing materials remains a challenge. Various formal and less rigorous approaches to cost-benefit analysis are being explored, including social return on investment and balanced scorecard.

Most libraries have little choice but to cooperate. As libraries reduce acquisitions, they must rely on other libraries for critical materials that they do not have. They work with cooperative partners to secure the most cost-effective access to e-resources. Librarians coordinate local collection development and management with state, regional, and national cooperative programs to ensure that access to comprehensive national collections is maintained and users have timely access to the materials they seek.

CASE STUDY

Mathew is the collections and technical services coordinator for the Cochrane School District, which consists of twenty-five elementary schools, six middle and junior high schools, and five high schools. The elementary schools include a Spanish immersion school, French immersion school, Montessori school, and three magnet schools that emphasize humanities, music, and science and mathematics. The middle and junior high schools do not have specific focuses. One of the high schools is an open (alternative) school, one is devoted to the performing arts, and two offer international baccalaureate programs. The city of Cochrane has a reasonably well-funded public library with a large central facility and four geographically distributed branch libraries. Through state funding, all citizens have access to a comprehensive suite of e-resources. Of particular interest to the school system and its students are the Gale products InfoBits and InfoTrac Junior and Student Editions, MasterFILE Premier, and Academic Search Premier. Additional online reference sources are also provided. Librarians and school media specialists in each of the Cochrane schools manage their own acquisitions budgets, selecting materials for students and teachers in each location. Materials are receipted and cataloged centrally and sent to the schools on a twice-weekly basis. Journals and magazines are receipted centrally and also sent to the schools twice a week. The school system uses OCLC for cataloging and shares a single automated catalog; searching can be limited by location. Mathew manages the agreement with the system's monograph vendor and its serials agent and supervises the technical services department. The school library media centers only occasionally borrow materials from each other, and the librarians and school media specialists tell students to visit the public library for materials the school media center does not own.

Activity

Mathew believes that some type of coordinated selection would be valuable, enriching the print resources available to students and teachers in all the schools. He has a sense that within the school system are unrecognized and untapped resources. Are aspects of effective cooperative collection development and management already in place? If so, what are they? What steps should Mathew take to advance coordinated collection development, and why? Develop a sequenced list of activities for Mathew to follow as he moves the Cochrane School District libraries and school media centers toward cooperative collection development and management. What resources are needed?

Note: The first edition of this book also provided a case study and activity related to the information in this chapter. It can be viewed at www.ala.org/editions/extras/Johnson09720 as a supplementary resource.

Notes

1. David H. Stam, "Think Globally, Act Locally: Collection Development and Resource Sharing," *Collection Building* 5 (Spring 1983): 21.

2. Melvil Dewey, *Library Notes* 1 (June 1886): 5.

3. Michael Gorman, "Laying Siege to the 'Fortress Library,'" *American Libraries* 17, no. 5 (1986): 325.

4. Joseph J. Branin, "Cooperative Collection Development," in *Collection Management: A New Treatise*, ed. Charles B. Osburn and Ross Atkinson, 81–110 (Greenwich, Conn.: JAI Press, 1991), 82.

5. John R. Kaiser, "Resource Sharing in Collection Development," in *Collection Development in Libraries: A Treatise*, ed. Robert D. Stueart and George B. Miller Jr., 139–57. (Greenwich, Conn.: JAI Press, 1980).

6. John Fetterman, "Resource Sharing in Libraries: Why, How, When, Next Steps?" in *Resource Sharing in Libraries*, ed. Allen Kent, 1–31 (New York: Marcel Dekker, 1974), 3.

7. Ernest C. Richardson, "Co-operation in Lending among College and Reference Libraries," *Library Journal* 24, no. 7 (1899): 32–33.

8. Reference and User Services Association, RUSA Reference Guidelines, "Interlibrary Loan Code for the United States Explanatory Supplement: For Use with the Interlibrary Loan Code for the United States (January 2001)," www.ala.org/ala/rusa/protools/referenceguide/interlibraryloancode.cfm.

9. "National Interlibrary Loan Code, 1980" (adopted by the Reference and Adult Services Division Board of Directors, New York 1980), *RQ* 20 (1980): 29; "National Interlibrary Loan Code for the United States, 1993" (approved by the Reference and Adult Services Board of Directors, Feb. 8, 1994), *RQ* 33 (1994): 477.

10. Nancy E. Gwinn and Paul H. Mosher, "Coordinating Collection Development: The RLG Conspectus," *College and Research Libraries* 44, no. 2 (1983): 128; see also David H. Stam, "Collaborative Collection Development: Progress, Problems and Potential," *Collection Building* 7, no. 3 (1985): 3–9, for an analysis of the Conspectus role in cooperative collection development.

11. National Center for Education Statistics, Academic Libraries: 2004: First Look (Nov. 2006), table 1: "Total Circulation, Document Delivery, and Interlibrary Loan Transactions in Academic Libraries, by Control Level, Size, and Carnegie Classification of Institutions: Fiscal Year 2004," http://nces.ed.gov/pubs2007/2007301.pdf; National Center for Education Statistics, Academic Libraries: 1996 (Oct. 1999), table 1B: "Total Circulation and Interlibrary Loan Transactions in Academic Libraries by Control, Level, Size, and Carnegie Classification of Institution: 1996," http://nces.ed.gov/pubs2000/2000326.pdf.

12. National Center for Education Statistics, Public Libraries in the United States: Fiscal Year 2004; E.D. TAB (Aug. 2006), table 8: "Number of Public Library Services and Library Services per Capita or per 1,000 Population, by Type of Service and State: Fiscal Year 2004," http://nces.ed.gov/pubs2006/2006349.pdf.

13. "School Library Media Centers: Selected Results from the Education Longitudinal Study of 2002 (ELS:2002)," *Education Statistics Quarterly* (Jan. 2006), http://nces.ed.gov/programs/quarterly/vol_7/1_2/7_1.asp.

14. American Association of School Librarians and Association for Educational Communications and Technology, *Information Power: Guidelines for School Library Media Programs* (Chicago: American Library Association; Washington, D.C.: Association for Educational Communications and Technology, 1988), 1.

15. George Bishop, "Global Vision of Resource Sharing" (Feb. 2008), www.oclc.org/memberscouncil/meetings/2008/february/Bishop.ppt.

16. Ross Atkinson, "Access, Ownership, and the Future of Collection Development," in *Collection Management and Development: Issues in an Electronic Era*, ed. Peggy Johnson and Bonnie MacEwan, 92–109 (Chicago: American Library Association, 1993).

17. MINITEX, "Fiscal Year 2007 Overview: Facts and Figures," www.minitex.umn.edu/about/facts/overview.aspx.

18. OCLC Members Council, "WorldCat Principles of Cooperation" (May 21, 1996), www.oclc.org/us/en/worldcat/catalog/principles/default.htm.

19. Branin, "Cooperative Collection Development."

20. Dan C. Hazen, "Cooperative Collection Development: Compelling Theory, Inconsequential Results?" in *Collection Management for the Twenty-first Century: A Handbook for Librarians*, ed. G. E. Gorman and Ruth H. Miller, 263–83 (Westport, Conn.: Greenwood, 1997).

21. Paul H. Mosher and Marcia Pankake, "A Guide to Coordinated and Cooperative Collection Development," *Library Resources and Technical Services* 27, no. 4 (1983): 417–31.

22. Anna H. Perrault, "The Printed Book: Still in Need of CCD," *Collection Management* 24, nos. 1/2 (2000): 119–36; John Budd and Katharine K. Craven, "Academic Library Monographic Acquisitions: Selection of *Choice*'s Outstanding Academic Books," *Library Collections, Acquisitions and Technical Services* 23, no. 1 (1999): 15–17.

23. Ross Atkinson, "Crisis and Opportunity: Reevaluating Acquisitions Budgeting in an Age of Transition," *Journal of Library Administration* 19, no. 2 (1993): 33–55.

24. Edward Shreeves, "Is There a Future for Cooperative Collection Development in the Digital Age?" *Library Trends* 45, no. 3 (1997): 376.

25. Charles B. Osburn, "Collection Development and Management," in *Academic Libraries: Research Perspectives*, ed. Mary Jo Lynch, 1–37, ACRL Publications in Librarianship no. 47 (Chicago: American Library Association, 1990).

26. H. W. Wilson, Public Library Core Collection: Nonfiction (*Public Library Catalog*), www.hwwilson.com/print/publibcat.cfm.

27. Ross Atkinson, "Old Forms, New Forms: The Challenge of Collection Development," *College and Research Libraries* 50, no. 5 (1989): 508.

28. Stam, "Think Globally," 21.

29. Patricia Buck Dominguez and Luke Swindler, "Cooperative Collection Development at the Research Triangle University Libraries, a Model for the Nation," *College and Research Libraries* 54, no. 6 (1993): 470–96.

30. Hendrick Edelman, "The Death of the Farmington Plan," *Library Journal* 98, no. 9 (1973): 1251–53. See also Ralph D. Wagner, *A History of the Farmington Plan* (Lanham, Md.: Scarecrow, 2002).

31. Debra E. Kachel, "Look Inward before Looking Outward: Preparing the School Library Media Center for Cooperative Collection Development," *School Library Media Quarterly* 23 (Winter 1995): 101–13.

32. Debra E. Kachel, *Collection Assessment and Management for School Libraries: Preparing for Cooperative Collection Development* (Westport, Conn.: Greenwood, 1997), 77.

33. Margo Warner Curl and Michael Zeoli, "Developing a Consortial Shared Approval Plan for Monographs," *Collection Building* 23, no. 3 (2004): 122–28.

34. See Donald B. Simpson, "Economics of Cooperative Collection Development and Management: The United States' Experience with Rarely Held Research Materials," *IFLA Journal* 24, no. 3 (1998): 161–65; and Gay N. Dannelly, "The Center for Research Libraries and Cooperative Collection Development: Partnerships in Progress," in *Cooperative Collection Development: Significant Trends and Issues*, ed. Donald B. Simpson, 37–45 (New York: Haworth, 1998).

35. Lizanne Payne, *Library Storage Facilities and the Future of Print Collections in North America* (Dublin, Ohio: OCLC, 2007).

36. Steve O'Conner, Andrew Wells, and Mel Collier, "A Study of Collaborative Storage of Library Resources," *Library Hi Tech* 20, no. 3 (2002): 258.

37. Payne, *Library Storage Facilities*.

38. Ibid, 30.

39. Bart Harloe, ed., *Guide to Cooperative Collection Development*, Collection Management and Development Guides no. 6 (Chicago: American Library Association, 1994), 22, 24.

40. National Information Standards Organization, Information Services and Use: Metrics and Statistics for Libraries and Information Providers—Data Dictionary, Section 2.1.8, Library Cooperatives (2004), NISO Z39.7-2004, www.niso.org/dictionary/.

41. Denise M. Davis, Office for Research and Statistics, American Library Association, "Library Networks, Cooperatives and Consortia: A National Survey" (Dec. 3, 2007), www.ala.org/ala/ors/lncc/Final%20report.pdf.

42. James J. Kopp, "Library Consortia and Information Technology: The Past, the Present, the Promise," *Information Technology and Libraries* 17, no. 7 (1998): 7–12.

43. George Bobinski, *Libraries and Librarianship: Sixty Years of Challenge and Change, 1945–2005* (Lanham, Md.: Scarecrow, 2007).

44. Carlos A. Cuadra and Ruth J. Patrick, "Survey of Academic Library Consortia in the U.S.," *College and Research Libraries* 33 (July 1972): 271–83.

45. Dave Bogart, ed., *Bowker Annual Library and Book Trade Almanac: Facts, Figures, and Reports* (Medford, N.J.: Information Today, 2007).

46. Davis, "Library Networks, Cooperatives and Consortia."

47. Primary Research Group, *The Survey of Library Database Licensing Practices* (New York: Primary Research Group, 2007).

48. Tim Bucknall, "The Virtual Consortium," *Library Journal netConnect* (Spring 2005): 16–19.

49. Nancy Chipman Shlaes, "Cooperative Collection Management Succeeds in Illinois," *Resource Sharing and Information Networks* 12, no. 1 (1996): 49–53.

50. Naomi J. Goodman and Carole L. Hinchcliff, "From Crisis to Cooperation and Beyond: OhioLINK's First Ten Years," *Resource Sharing and Information Networks* 13, no. 1 (1997): 21–38.

51. Joseph J. Branin, "Shaping Our Space: Envisioning the New Research Library," *Journal of Library Administration* 46, no. 2 (2007): 27–53.

52. George J. Soete, comp., *Collaborative Collections Management Programs in ARL Libraries,* SPEC Kit no. 235 (Washington, D.C.: Association of Research Libraries, 1998).

53. Primary Research Group, *Survey of Library Database Licensing Practices.*

54. OhioLINK, Fast Facts: OhioLINK Electronic Journal Center (EJC; March 2008), www.ohiolink.edu/about/news/ejcff.html.

55. Kimberly L. Armstrong, Assistant Director, Center for Library Initiatives, Committee on Institutional Cooperation, "Re: Cost Savings," e-mail message to the author, March 17, 2008.

56. Douglas Anderson, "Allocation of Costs for Electronic Products in Academic Library Consortia," *College and Research Libraries* 67, no. 2 (2006): 123–35.

57. Barbara McFadden Allen and Arnold Hirshon, "Hanging Together to Avoid Hanging Separately: Opportunities for Academic Libraries and Consortia," *Information Technology and Libraries* 17, no. 1 (1998): 40.

58. International Coalition of Library Consortia, "Statement of Current Perspective and Preferred Practices for the Selection and Purchase of Electronic Information" (1998), www.library.yale.edu/consortia/statement.html; International Coalition of Library Consortia, "Statement of Current Perspective and Preferred Practices for the Selection

and Purchase of Electronic Information: Update No. 1: New Developments in E-Journal Licensing" (Dec. 2001), www.library.yale.edu/consortia/2001currentpractices .htm; "Update No. 2: Pricing and Economics" (Oct. 2004), www.library.yale.edu/ consortia/2004currentpractices.htm.

59. Cynthia Shelton, "Best Practices in Cooperative Collection Development: A Report Prepared by the Center for Research Libraries Working Group in Best Practices in Cooperative Collection Development," *Collection Management* 28, no. 3 (2003): 191–222.

60. Kachel, *Collection Assessment and Management.*

61. Martin Runkle, "What Was the Original Mission of the Center for Research Libraries and How Has It Changed?" in *CRL's Role in the Emerging Global Resources Program, 1997 Symposium, Chicago, Illinois, April 25, 1997, 1–4* (Chicago: Center for Research Libraries, 1997), 3.

62. Branin, "Cooperative Collection Development," 104.

63. Atkinson, "Crisis and Opportunity."

64. James Burgett, John Haar, and Linda L. Phillips, *Collaborative Collection Development: A Practical Guide for Your Library* (Chicago: American Library Association, 2004), 160.

65. Anthony W. Ferguson and Kathleen Kehoe, "Access versus Ownership: What Is More Cost-Effective in the Sciences?" *Journal of Library Administration* 19, no. 2 (1993): 89–99.

66. Jane P. Kleiner and Charles A. Hamaker, "Libraries 2000: Transforming Libraries Using Document Delivery, Needs Assessment, and Networked Resources," *College and Research Libraries* 58, no. 4 (1997): 355–74.

67. Bruce Kingma, "The Economics of Access versus Ownership: The Costs and Benefits of Access to Scholarly Articles via Interlibrary Loan and Journal Subscriptions." *Journal of Library Administration* 26, nos. 1/2 (1998): 145–57.

68. Donald W. King et al., "Library Economic Metrics: Examples of the Comparison of Electronic and Print Journal Collections and Collection Services," *Library Trends* 51, no. 3 (2003): 377.

69. Susan Imholz and Jennifer Weil Arns, *Worth Their Weight: An Assessment of the Evolving Field of Library Valuation* (New York: Americans for Libraries Council, 2007), www .actforlibraries.org/pdf/WorthTheirWeight.pdf.

70. Ian J. Bateman et al., *Economic Valuation with Stated Preference Techniques: A Manual* (Cheltenham: Edward Elgar, 2002).

71. King et al., "Library Economic Metrics."

72. Peter Scholten, *SROI: A Guide to SROI Analysis* (Amsterdam: Lenthe, 2006); Jeremy Nichols, Susan Mackenzie, and Ailbeth Somers, *Measuring Real Value: A DIY Guide to Social Return on Investment* (London: New Economics Foundation, 2007), www.neweconomics.org/gen/uploads/4qcbgz45bk3t5e552edflr2d04072007200455.pdf.

73. Stephen Bosch, Lucy Lyons, and Mary H. Munroe, "Measuring Success of Cooperative Collection Development: Report of the Center for Research Libraries/Greater Western Library Alliance Working Group for Quantitative Evaluation of Cooperative Collection Development Projects," *Collection Management* 28, no. 3 (2003): 223–39.

Suggested Readings

Alexander, Adrian W. "Toward 'The Perfection of Work': Library Consortia in the Digital Age." *Journal of Library Administration* 28, no. 2 (1999): 1–14.

Armstrong, Kim, and Bob Nardini. "Making the Common Uncommon? Examining Consortial Approval Plan Cooperation." *Collection Management* 25, no. 3 (2001): 87–105.

Atkinson, Ross. "Toward a Redefinition of Library Services." In *Virtually Yours: Models for Managing Electronic Resources and Services,* edited by Peggy Johnson and Bonnie MacEwan, 1–12. Chicago: American Library Association, 1999.

Ball, David, and Jo Pye. "Library Purchasing Consortia: Their Activity and Effect on the Marketplace." In *Collection Management,* edited by G. E. Gorman, 199–220. International Yearbook of Library and Information Management, 2000–2001. London: Library Association Publishing, 2000.

Beaubien, Anne K. "ARL White Paper on Interlibrary Loan" (June 2007). www.arl.org/ bm~doc/ARL_white_paper_ILL_june07.pdf.

Bosch, Stephen, Patricia A. Promis, and Chris Sugnet. *Guide to Licensing and Acquiring Electronic Information.* ALCTS Collection Management and Development Guides no. 13; ALCTS Acquisitions Guides no. 13. Lanham, Md.: Scarecrow, 2005.

Chrzastowski, Tina E., et al. "Feast AND Famine: A Statewide Science Serial Collection Assessment in Illinois." *College and Research Libraries* 68, no. 6 (2007): 517–32.

Clements, Suzanne. "Skills for Effective Participation in Consortia: Preparing for Collaborating and Collaboration." *Collection Management* 32, nos. 1/2 (2007): 191–204.

Conger, Joan E. *Collaborative Electronic Resource Management: From Acquisitions to Assessment.* Westport, Conn.: Libraries Unlimited, 2004.

Edwards, Phillip M. "Collection Development and Maintenance across Libraries, Archives, and Museums: A Novel Collaborative Approach." *Library Resources and Technical Services* 48, no. 1 (2004): 26–33.

Gammon, Julia A., and Michael Zeoli. "Practical Cooperative Collecting for Consortia: Books-Not-Bought in Ohio." *Collection Management* 28, nos. 1/2 (2003): 77–105.

Gherman, Paul. "The North Atlantic Storage Trust: Maximizing Space, Preserving Collections." *portal: Libraries and the Academy* 7, no. 3 (2007): 273–75.

Haar, John. "Assessing the State of Cooperative Collection Development: Report of the Working Group to Map Current Cooperative Collection Development Projects." *Collection Management* 28, no. 3 (2003): 183–90.

Hayes, Robert M. "Cooperative Game Theoretic Models for Decision-Making in Contexts of Library Cooperation." *Library Trends* 51, no. 3 (2003): 441–61.

Hazen, Dan C. "The Cooperative Conundrum in the Digital Age." *Journal of Library Administration* 46, no. 2 (2007): 101–18.

———. "Dancing with Elephants: International Cooperation in an Interdependent (but Unequal) World." *Collection Management* 24, nos. 3/4 (1999): 185–213.

Hiremath, Uma. "Electronic Consortia: Resource Sharing in the Digital Age." *Collection Building* 20, no. 2 (2001): 80–87.

Hirshon, Arnold. "Libraries, Consortia, and Change Management." *Journal of Academic Librarianship* 25, no. 2 (1999): 124–26.

Hoffert, Barbara. "The United Way: Will Public Libraries Follow Academics as They Take Collaborative Collection Development One Step Further?" *Library Journal* 131, no. 8 (2006): 38–41.

Kairis, Rob. "Tools for Small Colleges: Using Yankee Book Peddler to Facilitate Cooperative Collection Development." *Library Collections, Acquisitions, and Technical Services* 27, no. 2 (2003): 173–78.

Kingma, Bruce R. *The Economics of Information: A Guide to Economic and Cost-Benefit Analysis for Information Professionals.* 2nd ed. Englewood, Colo.: Libraries Unlimited, 2001.

Lamborn, Joan, and Michael Levine-Clark. "Cooperative Monographic Collection Development, Part II: The Colorado Not-Bought Project—Cooperative Collection Development without a Share Approval Plan." In *Charleston Conference Proceedings 2005*, edited by Beth R. Bernhardt, Tim Daniels, and Kim Steinle, 27–29. Westport, Conn.: Libraries Unlimited, 2006.

Landesman, Margaret, and Johann Van Reenen. "Consortia vs. Reform: Creating Congruence." *Journal of Electronic Publishing* 6, no. 2 (2000). http://quod.lib .umich.edu/cgi/t/text/text-idx?c=jep;view=text;rgn=main;idno=3336451.0006.203.

Medeiros, Norm. "Accommodating Consortia within Electronic Resource Management Systems: Extending the ERMI Specifications." *OCLC Systems and Services* 22, no. 4 (2006): 238–40.

Metz, Paul, and Sharon Gasser. "Analyzing Current Serials in Virginia: An Application of the Ulrich's Serials Analysis System." *portal: Libraries and the Academy* 6, no. 1 (2006): 5–21.

Oder, Norman. "Consortia Hit Critical Mass." *Library Journal* 125, no. 2 (2000): 48–51.

Payne, Lizanne. "Depositories and Repositories: Changing Models of Library Storage in the USA." *Library Management* 26, nos. 1/2 (2005): 10–17.

Perrault, Anna H. "The Role of WorldCat in Resources Sharing." *Collection Management* 28, nos. 1/2 (2003): 63–75.

Reilly, Bernard F. *Developing Print Repositories: Models for Shared Preservation and Access.* CLIR Reports no. 117. Washington, D.C.: Council on Library and Information Resources, 2003. www.clir.org/pubs/reports/pub117/pub117.pdf.

———. "Preserving American Print Resources." *Library Management* 26, nos. 1/2 (2005): 102–5.

Rethinking Resource Sharing. "It's Time to Think Again about Resource Sharing: A Discussion Paper" (rev. June 1, 2005). www.rethinkingresourcesharing.org/docs/ rrs-whitepaper2005.pdf.

Sauer, Cynthia K. "Doing the Best We Can? The Use of Collection Development Policies and Cooperative Collecting Activities at Manuscript Repositories." *American Archivist* 64, no. 2 (2001): 308–49.

Schottlaender, Brian E. C. "'You Say You Want an Evolution . . .': The Emerging UC Libraries Shared Collection." *Library Collections, Acquisitions, and Technical Services* 28, no. 1 (2004): 13–24.

Shreeves, Edward, ed. *The New Dynamics and Economics of Cooperative Collection Development: Papers Presented at a Conference Hosted by the Center for Research Libraries.* Binghamton, N.Y.: Haworth, 2003.

Simpson, Donald B., ed. *Cooperative Collection Development: Significant Trends and Issues.* New York: Haworth, 1998.

Stern, David. "Comparing Consortial and Differential Pricing Models." *Bottom Line* 16, no. 4 (2003): 154–56.

Thornton, Glenda. "Back to the Future of Cooperative Collection Development." *Collection Management* 29, no. 2 (2004): 3–6.

Walters, William H. "Should Libraries Acquire Books That Are Widely Held Elsewhere? A Brief Investigation with Implications for Consortial Book Selection." *Bulletin of the American Society for Information Science and Technology* 32, no. 1 (2006): 25–27. http://asis.org/Bulletin/Feb-06/watters.html.

Wood, Richard J. "The Axioms, Barriers, and Components of Cooperative Collection Development." In *Collection Management for the Twenty-first Century: A Handbook for Librarians,* edited by G. E. Gorman and Ruth H. Miller, 221–48. Westport, Conn.: Greenwood, 1997.

CHAPTER NINE

Scholarly Communication

The process of exchanging discoveries, ideas, and information is being transformed. These changes are of critical importance to academic and research librarians with collections responsibilities, but they are also important for collections librarians in other types of libraries. Libraries are in the knowledge business, with core functions to select and acquire resources, facilitate their discovery, support their access and dissemination, archive and preserve them, and support their community of users as they do their work. Changes in the process of information dissemination have obvious effects in all these areas. The results of research are increasingly perceived as both a public good and a common good as the Internet makes a tremendous amount of research and scholarship freely available and discoverable. The dissemination of these results and access to them should be of concern to all librarians because all library users, regardless of the type of library they use, are seeking, finding, and using information and resources located through the Internet. This chapter begins by exploring the scholarly communication system and its origins, changing nature, and role in the promotion and tenure system. The open access initiative and strategies and policies that support it are identified. The chapter concludes with issues for libraries and librarians. Readers are strongly encouraged to view this chapter as a starting point for understanding a quickly changing landscape and then to monitor new events, initiatives, and publications on this topic.

What Is the Scholarly Communication System?

Scholarship is the craft of learning and teaching, activities encompassing research and creative expression.[1] *Scholarly communication* is the process of disseminating research and providing continuing access to the scholarly record in print and digital format to the broader academic community. Scholarship is as much a process of communication as it is investigation and discovery. The *scholarly communication system* refers to the interactions of participants who create, transform, distribute, collect, preserve, make available, and use the research of scholars and scientists for teaching, additional research, and other scholarly activities. *Schol-*

arly publishing is part of scholarly communication. Karla L. Hahn defines it as "a subset of communication activities mediated through the use of a durable medium to fix knowledge."[2]

Through the Internet, scholarship has become a global activity conducted in real time. Technology reduces barriers and results in increased access both to the scholarly literature and to the underlying research data and source materials. Paul Courant writes that collaboration (across time and space) is the fundamental method of scholarship.[3] Through the Internet, researchers "have been able to expand the conversation at an earlier point in the research process and to explore the content of these exchanges to observers."[4] Scholarly communication occurs via e-mail, blogs, online laboratory notebooks, electronic discussion groups, and websites as well as through electronic journals and digital repositories.

Issues of scholarly communication are more than simply publishing or even technology issues. Key topics in the emerging system of scholarly communication include dissemination using new models of publishing, the changing economics of scholarly resources, open access and public access to research, author copyright management, preservation of intellectual assets, and changes in the libraries' role in the system. Scholarly communication is of critical interest to academic and research librarians and of importance to all librarians, whose mission is to collect, preserve, and provide access to information.

In the scholarly communication system, publishing scholarly books and journals has provided an efficient way to disseminate scholarly findings, secure the final version of a work, and make it accessible to future generations. For scholars and researchers, publishing serves as a means of conferring qualitative evaluation and judgment on the scholar's or researcher's work through the practice of peer review and is an essential mechanism for establishing their reputation. Journal articles are the most common venue. Ulrichsweb (www.ulrichsweb.com/ulrichsweb/) lists more than 26,000 peer-reviewed journals worldwide publishing approximately 2.5 millions articles per year. This sort of formal publication has been an essential component of promotion and tenure decisions.

The pre-Internet system of scholarly publishing can be viewed as a continuous cycle. Universities and external funding agencies subsidize and pay the costs of research. Faculty members and researchers create works to report their findings and then transfer this intellectual property through copyright assignment to publishers. Faculty members and researchers serve (seldom receiving financial compensation) on editorial boards and review papers submitted for publication. Publishers usually handle copyediting and typography and are responsible for production and distribution of the printed work. Academic and research libraries buy back the final products to fulfill their role of organizing, disseminating, and archiving scholarly works. The cycle continues as researchers consult publications to further new research. Figure 9-1 offers a visual representation of this traditional cycle.

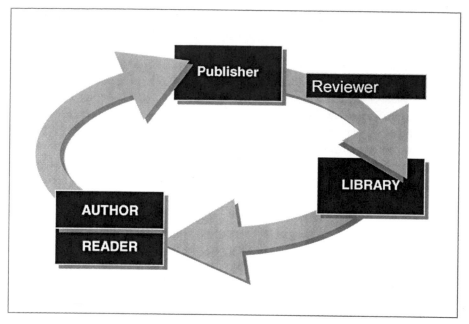

FIGURE 9-1 Cycle of scholarly publishing. Reprinted with the permission of the Association of Research Libraries.

Scholarly Publishing before the Internet

Today's scholarly communication system has its roots in the 1600s, when European scholarly societies were first established. Their purpose was to provide a forum in which independent scholars could share and discuss their research. Scholarly publishing was born when these societies began to publish their findings in serial publications with names like *Comptes rendus*, *Transactions*, and *Abhandlungen*. These periodicals were issued by the societies, and their content was vetted by the society members or a small group selected to serve that role—the origins of peer review. In the United States, as in Europe, the original system of scholarly communication was the realm of the wealthy; the creators and the consumers of scholarship were the same people, with virtually no middlemen involved.

This arrangement began to change in America with the Morrill Act (1862), which established funding for land-grant universities and placed obligations on the faculties at these institutions to conduct research that would benefit society. A direct result was a tremendous increase in publication of journals and monographs. After the Second World War, when college and university enrollments swelled and the U.S. government began to direct large amounts of money to higher education for research, the volume of scholarly publications grew exponentially. Unable to keep pace or absorb the expensive costs, many professional and scholarly societies turned to the for-profit sector to absorb the growth in publishing activities. Commercial publishers quickly saw the profit potential in controlling this unique content. Journal prices rose rapidly and commercial publishers began an ongoing program of consolidation. The result was a journal publishing system with a few large publishers of extensive journal lists and many professional and scholarly societies publishing single journals or small lists of titles.

Scholarly monographs have fared differently with changes in the economics of scholarly publishing. They traditionally have been published by university presses and scholarly societies and associations. Although these bodies were willing to subsidize the costs of publishing to advance scholarship, most of their parent organizations now expect these presses to generate a profit or, at a minimum, sustain no losses. The result is that university, scholarly society, and scholarly association presses are more market-sensitive and publish fewer economically marginal books. Sales increasingly trump scholarship in the decisions presses make about which books to publish. The market for scholarly monographs has suffered as academic and research libraries struggle to cope with increasing serial costs and consequently buy fewer books. Many presses have been shut down by their universities. The result has been a significant decrease in opportunities for scholars to publish monographs, according to the Modern Language Association's 2006 report on evaluating scholarship for tenure and promotion.[5]

Rapidly escalating prices and the library's financial difficulty in acquiring the materials needed to support the research and teaching missions of their educational institutions were seen initially as "the library's problem." Academic libraries started addressing increasing serial costs in the 1980s and began to talk about the "the serials crisis." Over time, librarians realized that they alone could not bring about the changes needed in a system driven largely by tenure considerations and profit-making concerns outside the control of libraries, and so they began talking about the "crisis in scholarly communication." Librarians have sought to educate faculty, college and university administrators, and government officials to understand scholarly communication as a complex system with many stakeholders, each with responsibilities and roles to play.

Changing the Nature of Scholarly Communication

During the past twenty years, the Internet has profoundly changed how scholars communicate, both formally and informally. Earlier chapters in this book consider the range of new kinds of digital publications that have emerged. An important alternative approach has arisen—open access.

One of the first events to give formal shape to the open access movement was the Budapest Open Access Initiative (www.soros.org/openaccess/), born

at an international conference convened by the Open Society Institute (www
.soros.org) in December 2001. According to Peter Suber, the Budapest Open
Access Initiative "was the first [initiative] to offer a public definition of OA [open
access], the first to use the term 'open access,' the first to call for OA journals
and OA archives as complementary strategies, the first to call for OA in all disciplines and countries, and the first to be accompanied by significant funding."[6]
The statement of principles that defined the initiative was released on February
14, 2002, and begins:

> An old tradition and a new technology have converged to make possible an
> unprecedented public good. The old tradition is the willingness of scientists
> and scholars to publish the fruits of their research in scholarly journals without
> payment, for the sake of inquiry and knowledge. The new technology is the
> internet. The public good they make possible is the world-wide electronic dis-
> tribution of the peer-reviewed journal literature and completely free and unre-
> stricted access to it by all scientists, scholars, teachers, students, and other curi-
> ous minds. Removing access barriers to this literature will accelerate research,
> enrich education, share the learning of the rich with the poor and the poor with
> the rich, make this literature as useful as it can be, and lay the foundation uniting
> humanity in a common intellectual conversation and quest for knowledge.[7]

Two further statements followed—the Bethesda Statement on Open Access
Publishing (June 2003) and the Berlin Declaration on Open Access to Knowledge in the Sciences and Humanities (October 2003).[8] Both statements include
the same definition of an open access publication as one that meets the two following conditions:

1. The author(s) and copyright holder(s) grant(s) to all users a free,
   irrevocable, worldwide, perpetual right of access to, and a license to
   copy, use, distribute, transmit and display the work publicly and to
   make and distribute derivative works, in any digital medium for any
   responsible purpose, subject to proper attribution of authorship, as
   well as the right to make small numbers of printed copies for their
   personal use.

2. A complete version of the work and all supplemental materials,
   including a copy of the permission as stated above, in a suitable
   standard electronic format is deposited immediately upon initial
   publication in at least one online repository that is supported by
   an academic institution, scholarly society, government agency, or
   other well-established organization that seeks to enable open access,
   unrestricted distribution, interoperability, and long-term archiving.

Another formative response grew out of recognition that a proactive
approach to change was needed. An international group of librarians, academic administrators, and representatives from professional associations met

in Tempe, Arizona, in March 2000 and agreed to the Principles for Emerging Systems of Scholarly Publishing.[9] The meeting was held to facilitate discussion among the various academic stakeholders in the scholarly publishing process and to build consensus on a set of principles that could guide the transformation of the scholarly publishing system. The Tempe Principles, as they came to be known, suggested three approaches: increased use of electronic capabilities, review of promotion and tenure practices, and responsible copyright management. These are not three separate strategies; they are related. Increased use of electronic capabilities may seem an obvious approach to developing an efficient and effective communication system, but the relationships between tenure and promotion practices and author copyright management practices are less self-evident and deserve discussion.

Promotion and Tenure Practices

Scholarly publication in books and journals is a cornerstone of the current promotion and tenure system, yet this academic reward system in U.S. institutions is less than one hundred years old.[10] In 1915, the American Association of University Professors' (AAUP) formed and issued its Declaration of Principles, which justified academic freedom and tenure.[11] At that time, faculty members were open for dismissal by trustees and presidents, who sought to control what faculty taught, said, and wrote. One key recommendation from the AAUP was that only committees of other faculty could judge a member of the faculty—early peer review. Colleges and universities were slow to adopt the AAUP's resolution, and the processes for promotion and tenure varied from institution to institution until after the Second World War. After the war, the tremendous increase in students under the GI Bill resulted in faculty shortages. Only at this point did most institutions of higher education begin offering formal tenure as a benefit and create an official process for promotion and tenure review.

Scholarly publication is a crucial component of research and of promotion and tenure processes. A key element of scholarly publication is validating the research through a peer review process, intended to confirm that the paper is of high quality and scholarly merit. Faculty members aspire to publish their work in the most prominent journal and with the most prominent presses, thereby signifying its merit as corroborated by equally prominent researchers in the discipline through the peer review process.

The peer review process is what Diane Harley and colleagues call "the coin of the realm," essential to ensuring quality.[12] Publication brings recognition to the authors and visibility to the institution, and it supports future research. Faculty members are usually evaluated in part by their academic output, demonstrated in publications. Promotion and tenure decisions normally take into account the number of publications and the prestige of the journals in which a faculty member's papers are published and (particularly in the humanities) the books a faculty member publishes and the prestige of the books' publishers.

A tension exists between the traditional system of scholarly publication, which provides what Friedlander calls "a collective trusted persistent record for multiple audiences," and the evolving new system, which is viewed with apprehension by some.[13] Research conducted in 2006 by the University of California indicates that faculty, though actively concerned about scholarly communication issues, are slow to change their behavior. Findings revealed that University of California faculty members view publishing as the critical currency of scholarship and academic success, overwhelmingly continue to rely on traditional forms of publishing, and are concerned that changes in the current system may undermine the quality of scholarship. The study found that 70 percent of faculty respondents expect their publishing activities to remain largely unchanged, and that most faculty members still readily transfer their copyrights to scholarly societies and commercial publishers.

Research conducted at the University of California Berkeley in 2005/6 found that faculty members perceive open access models as having little or no means of quality control (e.g., peer review).[14] Faculty members worry that the new system will not have the same credibility for measuring productivity and impact in promotion and tenure reviews. Junior researchers and faculty's unease and anxiety about the new modes of dissemination are not surprising.[15]

Authors' Copyright Management

A major thrust of the movement to reform scholarly publishing focuses on authors' rights. When authors retain some or all of their rights, they can keep control of how their work is distributed and used. They can maximize their work's availability and impact by reducing barriers between their work and its potential readers. They can retain the legal rights to

- post their articles on their own websites
- deposit in institutional and discipline-based digital repositories
- distribute copies to students and use in classes
- distribute to colleagues for noncommercial purposes
- distribute copies at conference presentations and lectures
- use their work in future efforts (e.g., new books, revised editions, or studies building on the original work)

Copyright law defines the ownership of a work of intellectual property (published and unpublished) and the control owners can exercise over access to and use of the work. Copyright owners can choose to keep their rights, give them over to another party, or share them as they see fit. The Copyright Law of the

United States defines copyright as a group of rights that can be individually granted or withheld.[16] Copyright owner rights are the exclusive rights to reproduce the copyrighted work; prepare derivative works based on the copyrighted work; distribute copies to the public by sale or other transfer of ownership, or by rental, lease, or lending; perform or display the copyrighted work publicly (in the case of literary, musical, dramatic, and choreographic works, pantomimes, motion pictures, and other audiovisual works); and perform the work publicly by means of digital audio transmission (in the case of sound recording).

Authors can retain all or some rights; for example, an author can transfer to the publisher the single right of first publication. Publishers usually use a legal document (often called a copyright transfer agreement or publication agreement) to specify the rights the author transfers to the publisher and any rights the author retains. For decades, authors routinely assigned all copyrights to publishers, often not realizing what they were signing away. The 2003 RoMEO copyright transfer survey found that, even though 90 percent of responding authors assigned their copyright, 61 percent thought they still had ownership.[17] For example, many faculty authors assumed they had the right to distribute copies of their articles to students in their classes or to post them on their websites, when they had no legal standing to do so.

Authors seeking to manage their rights have several options. They can opt to publish only with publishers that have "open" copyright policies. An assertive author may find that some publishers offer a variety of agreements; some are more restrictive (i.e., transfer all rights exclusively to the publishers), and some permit the author to assign specific rights to the publisher while retaining others . If the publisher has a single agreement that assigns, conveys, grants, or transfers all rights, copyright interest, copyright ownership, and/or title exclusively to the publisher, the author can propose changing the publisher's agreement by preparing an addendum that allows retention of some rights; an author addendum is attached to the publisher's standard copyright transfer agreement and modifies it to allow the author to retain those rights he or she identifies. Because it is a proposed modification, the publisher can accept or reject it; many publishers are willing to negotiate publication terms when asked.

Various model addenda, prepared by lawyers, are available. One example is the SPARC (Scholarly Publishing and Academic Resources Coalition) and Science Commons Author's Addendum (www.arl.org/sparc/author/addendum .html). This addendum secures the author's rights to reproduce, distribute, publicly perform, and publicly display the article for noncommercial purposes; prepare derivative works; make and distribute copies in the course of teaching and research; and post the article on personal and institutional websites and other open access digital repositories. In addition this addendum requires the publisher to provide the author an electronic copy of the published article within fourteen days of first publication at no charge.

Another source for model licenses is the Creative Commons, a nonprofit organization that provides free tools to help authors, scientists, artists, and educators control their creative works. The Creative Commons provides a set of copyright licenses (http://creativecommons.org/about/licenses/meet-the-licenses) for public use. For example, creators can retain their copyright while licensing works as free for certain uses in certain conditions.

Open Access: Putting the Pieces Together

Open access to scholarly publications involves leveraging new technology and author rights management to enhance the benefits of new knowledge and to reward scholars. A key goal of many efforts to reenvision the system of scholarly publishing to enhance scholarly communication is to create peer-reviewed, scholarly literature that is openly accessible—this means both available at no cost and easily accessible online. The Budapest Open Access Initiative defines open access to the literature as

> its free availability on the public internet, permitting any users to read, download, copy, distribute, print, search, or link to the full texts of these articles, crawl them for indexing, pass them as data to software, or use them for any other lawful purpose, without financial, legal, or technical barriers other than those inseparable from gaining access to the internet itself. The only constraint on reproduction and distribution, and the only role for copyright in this domain, should be to give authors control over the integrity of their work and the right to be properly acknowledged and cited.[18]

Open access literature is digital, online, free of charge, and free of copyright and licensing restrictions on access and use, and it ensures appropriate credit to authors and publishers for their efforts.

Open access does not mean forgoing peer review to obtain accessibility, nor does it mean abandoning copyright and its protections for authors. Despite many misconceptions, open access is entirely compatible with the peer review process. The same quality and control found in traditional scholarly publishing can apply. Peer review does not depend on the medium (print or digital) or on the means of access permitted. What open access does is remove the barriers to accessing peer-reviewed literature and other high-quality content.

Open access does not depend on putting online works into the public domain, though this does make them accessible. Works in the public domain have none of the rights that authors can retain through managing their copyrights. Among these are the rights to prevent plagiarism, prevent publication of corrupted versions of the work, protect the integrity of the work, and require appropriate citation of the source, thereby recognizing the creator or the work.

Open access is not the same as open content. *Open content* is usually understood to describe any freely available work that explicitly allows copying and modifying by anyone; thus, it is not protected by copyright. The largest open content-project is Wikipedia (http://en.wikipedia.org).

Numerous studies have shown that open access scholarly articles have a higher impact factor—they are more likely to be cited than those that are not open access. Stevan Harnad and Tim Brody describe the benefits of open access succinctly:

> OA [open access] dramatically increases the number of potential users of any given article by adding those users who would otherwise have been unable to access it because their institution could not afford the access-tolls of the journal in which it appeared; therefore, it stands to reason that OA can only increase both usage and impact.[19]

A 2001 study by Steve Lawrence on literature use in computer science and related disciplines reported that the mean number of citations to offline articles was 2.74 and the mean number of citations to online articles was 7.03, an increase of 157 percent.[20] Lawrence drew no conclusions about the cause of the correlation between high citation rates and online availability, though he did posit that the easier availability and improved visibility of online articles were significant. Subsequent studies of individual journals and of behavior in specific disciplines confirm that an open access article is more likely to be used and cited than one behind subscription barriers.[21] A 2006 study in *PLoS Biology* found that articles published as immediate open access in the *Proceedings of the National Academy of Sciences (PNAS)* were three times more likely to be cited than non-open-access papers, were cited earlier, and were cited more frequently than *PNAS* articles that were only self-archived.[22]

Open access journals, open access monographs, and self-archiving and open access repositories are three strategies supporting open access.

Open Access Journals

Open access journals are available online to the reader without financial or other barriers other than access to the Internet. Regardless of whether the author or the publisher holds copyright, the copyright holder consents to open access for the published work. Different approaches to funding open access journals are used—some are subsidized by the publisher, and some require payment on behalf of the author—by either the author or the author's institution.

Peter Suber reports that a minority of open access journals charge author-side fees, sometimes called the *dissemination-fee model*.[23] This was confirmed in December 2007 by Bill Hooker, who reports that 67 percent of fully open access journals listed in OpenDOAR do not charge author fees, 18 percent do charge, and 15 percent of the titles lack information on this question.[24] Many academic journals, especially in the science, medical, and technical disciplines, have levied page charges for publishing, even before the open access movement to subsidize publication. An author-side fee may be paid by the author, by his or her institution or employer, or from the author's research grant. Many open access journals that charge fees waive them in whole or part in cases of financial hardship. According to Suber,

> Some no-fee OA journals have direct or indirect subsidies from institutions like universities, laboratories, research centers, libraries, hospitals, museums, learned societies, foundations, or government agencies. Some have revenue from a separate line of non-OA publications. Some have revenue from advertising, auxiliary services, membership dues, endowments, reprints, or a print or premium edition. Some rely, more than other journals, on volunteerism. Some undoubtedly use a combination of these means.[25]

BioMed Central (www.biomedcentral.com)—not to be confused with PubMed Central—is another for-profit publisher that charges author-side fees to sustain its business model. BioMed Central offers close to two hundred open access, peer-reviewed biomedical research journals. BioMed Central's standard article-processing charge is $1,710; fees for some journals differ. Some discounts are available, including discounts when an author uses Endnote or Ref Manager (software for managing bibliographies) and if the author is affiliated with a BioMed Central supporting member institution.

An example of a nonprofit publisher is Public Library of Science (www.plos.org), which charges author-side fees ($2,000–$2,500) and also generates revenue through individual and institutional members. Public Library of Science publishes seven journals (as of March 2008) and uses the Creative Commons Attribution License for all works it publishes.

The "SAGE Open" publishing model from Sage Publications is an example of the author-pays model. Offered so that authors can comply with new funding body requirements, SAGE Open charges a per-article fee of $3,000 and excludes any other potential author fees (such as color charges) and taxes. Payment of the SAGE Open fee enables articles to be available immediately through SAGE Journals Online to journal nonsubscribers as well as subscribers. It also permits authors to submit the final manuscript to their funding agency's preferred archive if applicable.

Although faculty members and researchers use open access journals heavily, they continue to have concerns about their quality.[26] Because the quality of scholarly journals is a function of the quality of their editors, editorial boards, and referees, all journals (print or online, priced or free) can have the same quality controls. Open access scholarly journals can, therefore, have the same commitment to peer review and quality and the same methods for attaining them as priced journals.

Open Access Monographs

Some academic publishers are experimenting with *open access monographs*. Although thousands of journals are fully open access and many more allow open access for individual articles, open access monographs are developing more slowly. The challenges to developing effective open access strategies for monographs appear to be greater.

The National Academies Press (www.nap.edu), created by the U.S. National Academies to publish reports issued by the National Academy of Sciences, the National Academy of Engineering, the Institute of Medicine, and the National Research Council, provides free page-by-page online access to all of its books. Many books can be downloaded in their entirety or by chapter. Because the publisher depends on a revenue stream to offset the cost of offering free PDF files, it continues to charge for some books in PDF format.

The Gutenberg-e Project was launched in 1999 with a grant from the Andrew W. Mellon Foundation to explore and promote the electronic publication of scholarly writing. Between 1999 and 2004, the American Historical Association awarded Gutenberg-e prizes to high-quality dissertations in history. A panel of scholars judged the dissertations and selected award recipients based on the scholarly merits of the dissertations. Each prize consisted of a $20,000 fellowship to be used by the author to convert the dissertation into an electronic monograph to be published by Columbia University Press. The goal of this project was to legitimize electronic publishing and change attitudes of academics toward e-books. Initially available through subscription, in late 2007 the thirty-six Gutenberg-e titles became open access because the original financial model was not sustainable. Robert Townsend wrote:

> Unfortunately, despite the hopes of many in the open access movement, we have not been able to create a sustainable financial model for the publication of these online scholarly monographs. . . . Quite apart from the fellowships given to the authors and the costs of administering the selection process for these books, it appears that the basic costs of preparing the Gutenberg-e titles for online publication were not sustainable without a significant revenue stream or outside support.[27]

Another new approach to publishing scholarly monographs was premiered by the Pennsylvania State University Press and Penn State's Libraries, Department of French and Francophone Studies, and Department of Italian, Spanish, and Portuguese in 2007. Called Romance Studies (www.romancestudies.psu.edu), it is described as an open access experiment that gives readers the options to view the content freely online and to purchase a print edition. Though access to the material is free, use of monographs in the series is governed by copyright laws. Materials may be used for noncommercial, educational, and research purposes. Redistribution of materials is restricted and requires permission of Penn State Press.

According to the website, all books chosen for publication in the series undergo full peer review, ensuring the same commitment to quality as with any other university press series. An individual or library that wishes to purchase a book can request a print-on-demand copy, and the book is usually shipped in forty-eight hours. The goal is to generate enough revenue through sales to recover costs. As Sanford G. Thatcher, Penn State Press director, puts it, "Whether this model will succeed and prove sustainable, of course, is the big question."[28]

Self-Archiving and Open Access Repositories

Self-archiving is the deposit of articles, sometimes called e-prints, by authors (or directly by publishers as part of the agreement with an author) in free, open electronic archives or repositories, usually either discipline-based repositories (e.g., PubMed Central, www.pubmedcentral.nih.gov) or institutional repositories (e.g., Massachusetts Institute of Technology DSpace, http://dspace.mit .edu). Open access self-archiving was first formally proposed by Stevan Harnad in 1995.[29]

The development of digital repositories became possible with the decline in online storage costs, development and adoption of standard metadata harvesting protocols, and maturity of digital preservation. To deposit articles, authors must retain the right to self-archive in the copyright agreement with the publisher. Deposit can be in the form of a peer-reviewed postprint following publication in a journal or a non-peer-reviewed preprint.

The history of self-archiving dates to the 1980s when computer scientists were posting their papers on their anonymous-FTP sites.[30] High-energy physicists have been self-archiving in arXiv (http://arxiv.org), a shared discipline-based repository, since 1991. Developed by Paul Ginsparg and now hosted at Cornell University, arXiv started as an archive for preprints in physics and later expanded to include astronomy, mathematics, computer science, nonlinear science, quantitative biology, and statistics. Another early discipline-based archive is AgEcon Search: Research in Agricultural and Applied Economics (http://agecon.lib.umn .edu), developed and maintained by the University of Minnesota Libraries and Department of Applied Economics. The majority of items in AgEcon Search are working papers, conference papers, and journal articles. Full issues of twenty journals, some going back to volume 1, are also part of the archive.

Self-archiving in digital repositories does not simply provide open access. When these archives conform to the Open Archives Initiative Protocol for Metadata Harvesting (OAI-PMH), the interoperability standards created by the Open Archives Initiative (www.openarchives.org), search engines can treat the separate archives as one and harvest data across a wide range of digital resources.[31] Users do not need to know which archives exist or where they are located in order to find and use their contents.

The Scientific Commons (http://en.scientificcommons.org), for example, uses OAI-PMH to identify and retrieve "scientific knowledge products" from distributed digital repositories. It indexes these resources and makes them searchable through a single interface. Many of these resources are located in what is known as the "Deep Web" because they are hidden behind web scripts, and search engines like Google and Yahoo do not pick up information about them. The Scientific Commons identifies authors and makes their social and professional relationships transparent and visible to anyone across disciplinary, institutional, and technological boundaries. In March 2008, the Scientific Commons indexed 17,989,731 papers, 7,339,885 authors, and 901 repositories.

OAIster (www.oaister.org), another online catalog of digital resources that harvests data using OAI-PMH, is not limited to a single discipline or subject area. In March 2008, it listed 15,475,946 resources from 935 contributors. The digital resources include digitized books and articles, born-digital texts, audio files, images, movies, and data sets (e.g., downloadable statistics files). Science Commons and OAIster serve to collocate resources through a single interface, much like a traditional library catalog, but they still face the same problems that library catalogs do: the information seeker needs to know to look in them. They are not necessarily in the flow where researchers do their work.

To assist authors and users in identifying journals' support for various forms of self-archiving and open access, a color code has been developed to classify open access journals. Gold journals make all their contents freely accessible online. Green journals permit some form of author self-archiving, which may be postprint, preprint, or both. Gray is used for journals that allow no form of self-archiving. The Directory of Open Access Journals (DOAJ; www.doaj.org) listed 3,262 gold journals in March 2008, or approximately 12 percent of the scholarly journals published worldwide. Heather Morrison reported in February 2008 that the DOAJ was adding titles at the rate of 4.5 per day.[32] The DOAJ covers all open access scientific and scholarly journals that use a quality-control system, usually the traditional peer-review system, to guarantee the content's quality.

SHERPA RoMEO (www.sherpa.ac.uk/romeo.php) lists publishers and their copyright policies and self-archiving permissions normally given as part of each publisher's copyright transfer agreement. SHERPA RoMEO uses a four-color code to categorize publishers; it differs slightly from the gold and green categories used for journals. RoMEO classifies publishers as green (authors can archive preprint and postprint), blue (authors can archive postprint, i.e., final draft post-refereeing), yellow (authors can archive preprint, i.e., pre-refereeing), and white (archiving not formally supported). In March 2008, RoMEO listed copyright and self-archiving policies for 378 publishers, representing several thousand journals. Of them, 129 were green (34 percent), 86 were blue, 38 were yellow, and 125 were white.

Policies Promoting Open Access Publishing

Open access publishing and self-archiving can result from decisions individual scholars and researchers make about where and how to publish their works, but a different strategy for encouraging open access and self-archiving is through development of open access and public access policies.

A historic step toward large-scale self-archiving in the United States was taken when Public Law 110-161 (consolidated Appropriations Act, 2008) was signed by President George W. Bush on December 26, 2007. The law states:

> The Director of the National Institutes of Health shall require that all investigators funded by the NIH submit or have submitted for them to the National Library of Medicine's PubMed Central an electronic version of their final, peer-reviewed manuscripts upon acceptance for publication, to be made publicly available no later than 12 months after the official data of publication: Provided, That the NIH shall implement the public access policy in a manner consistent with copyright law.[33]

With this law, the National Institutes of Health (NIH) voluntary Public Access Policy became mandatory. Prior to its passage, less than 5 percent of researchers complied with the voluntary policy. Under the new policy, NIH grant recipients and their institutions (as the grantees) must ensure that any agreements made with publishers grant them the right to make their work publicly accessible via PubMed Central, the NIH publicly accessible digital archive (or repository) of full-text, peer-reviewed journal articles. Compliance is a statutory requirement. Effective May 25, 2008, anyone submitting an application, proposal, or progress report to the NIH must include the PubMed Central or NIH manuscript submission reference number when citing articles that arise from their NIH-funded research. The policy permits an embargo of up to twelve months following publication. According to Ray English and Heather Joseph, the NIH public access mandate is "the largest such policy—both in terms of the size of the research budget it covers [$29 million per year] and the number of articles [80,000 per-reviewed journal articles annually] that result from funded projects—to be implemented by any government agency in the world."[34]

Some journals automatically deposit articles in PubMed Central on behalf of their authors.[35] In addition, some publishers do not participate in PubMed Central but do submit manuscripts for authors if the author completes a release form with the publisher. When contracting to publish with other journals, the author must retain the rights necessary to comply with the law, either through the use of a contract addendum or by negotiating a revised agreement.[36]

Though it was the first with a deposit mandate based on U.S. law, the NIH was not the first funding agency to require open access archiving. For example, the Britain's Wellcome Trust, which funds biomedical research, began requiring open access archiving in 1995. SHERPA Juliet (www.sherpa.ac.uk/juliet/) lists a summary of policies given by various research funders as part of their grant awards and covers open access archiving, open access publishing, and data archiving.

A second historic development in the United States, also in 2008, was the unanimous approval of a motion by the Harvard University Faculty of Arts and Sciences mandating that Harvard faculty and researchers deposit their scholarly articles in an open access repository to be managed within the library and to be made freely available via the Internet. Faculty members can opt out of compliance by obtaining a waiver from the dean or dean's designee. The motion states,

> In legal terms, the permission granted by each Faculty member is "a nonexclusive, irrevocable, paid-up, worldwide license to exercise any and all rights under copyright relation to each of his or her scholarly articles, in any medium and to authorize others to the same, provided that the articles are not sold for profit."[37]

Stuart Shieber, professor of computer science at Harvard, who put forth the motion, cited the astronomical increase in serial costs that had forced the library to cancel subscriptions and reduce access to scholars' works and stated that the motion was intended to "be a very powerful message to the academic community that we want and should have more control over how our work is used and disseminated."[38]

Institutional Repositories

An *institutional repository* is defined as "a permanent, institution-wide repository of diverse, locally produced digital works (e.g., article preprints and postprints, data sets, electronic theses and dissertations, learning objects, and technical reports) that is available for public use and supports metadata harvesting."[39] Institutional repositories usually offer several services: document ingest, storage, management, retrieval and access, and preservation; system management; and user support. Some provide consultation, digitization of print materials, file conversion, and metadata services and may or may not charge fees for these functions. In 2003, Clifford A. Lynch proposed that

> a mature and fully realized institutional repository will contain the intellectual works of faculty and students—both research and teaching materials—also documentation of the activities of the institution itself in the form of records of events and performances and of the ongoing intellectual life of the institutions. It will also house experimental and observational data captured by members of the institution that support their scholarly activities.[40]

He wrote that institutional repositories could serve as an engine of change for institutions of higher education and the landscape of scholarly communication—and this was the goal and hope of many.

The earliest open access institution-based repository that Peter Suber has been able to identify is the IUBio-Archive (http://iubio.bio.indiana.edu), launched in 1989 at the Indiana University Biology department and still serving as an open archive of biology data, open software, biology news, and documents.[41] Although not an institutional repository in the comprehensive sense, it is an institution-based repository focused on a discipline. The IUBio-Archive "About" page states, rather charmingly, that "access to the archive is via HTTP (world wide web), Internet Gopher, anonymous FTP (file transfer), and e-mail programs that connect to computers on the Internet."

This and other early institutional repositories preceded the release of the Open Archives Initiative protocol in 1999 and the first Initiative-compliant software designed for open access archiving (EPrints, released by Southampton University in September 2000, and DSpace, released by MIT in November 2002). The release of open-source software served as a catalyst for the implementation of digital repositories. SPARC, an early proponent of institutional repositories, released the *SPARC Institutional Repository Checklist and Resources Guide* in 2002 to assist in their development and management.[42]

Together the EPrints and DSpace software packages are used by nearly half of the institutional and disciplinary repositories listed by OpenDOAR.[43] In March 2008, OpenDOAR reported 1,087 repositories worldwide, 288 of which were in the United States and thirty-eight in Canada. Of the U.S. repositories, 176 were affiliated with colleges and universities. ROAR (Registry of Open Access Repositories; http://roar.eprints.org) listed 1,019 repositories in March 2008; 53 percent of these were categorized as research institutional or departmental.

In 2002, Raym Crow suggested four characteristics of an institutional repository: it should be institutionally defined, contain scholarly content, be cumulative and perpetual, and support interoperability and open access.[44] In the intervening years, most institutional repositories have grown to contain a variety of materials. According to research published by Cat S. McDowell in fall 2007, approximately 41.5 percent of all items in American academic institutional repositories were student produced, including 93,000 electronic theses and dissertations. McDowell further reports that only approximately 37 percent of the items were faculty scholarly output and only about 13 percent were peer-reviewed works. This is especially interesting when one considers that scholarly works were the primary content most institutional repositories were designed to collect. McDowell concludes that "it is doubtful that [institutional repositories] will prove to alleviate the crisis in scholarly communication, at least the way we initially expected, any time some."[45]

Many institutional repositories explicitly seek to be the digital equivalent of college or university archives, collecting, preserving, and providing access to the institutional information of enduring value that supports both historical research and administrative planning, policy setting, and decision making. Fulfilling this mission requires close working relationships with administrators and their offices, trustee boards, records managers, financial officers, registrars, and others in key positions on campus.

Most definitions of institutional repositories, including Crow's above, state that an institutional repository provides open access to its content. Findings reported in 2007 in the *International Survey of Institutional Digital Repositories* show that many repositories do not meet this criterion: at that time, 8 percent of U.S. repositories restricted access to the institution itself, 20 percent restricted access to the consortium, and 72 percent provided open access to all. Worldwide, 11.11 percent restricted access to the institution, 14.81 percent restricted access to the consortium, and 74.07 percent provided open access.[46]

Much of the library literature has focused on how to encourage faculty to deposit their scholarly works in institutional depositories.[47] In the 2006 ARL study, 63 percent of the respondents reported that recruiting content was either "somewhat difficult" or "very difficult."[48] Several approaches have been proposed. These include

- improving content recruitment mechanisms
- reaching out to individual faculty, who may be likely depositors, by library liaisons
- offering to deposit electronic materials for authors
- sending electronic announcements
- recruiting early adaptor faculty to recruit content
- holding awareness-raising symposiums
- Seeking institutional (or academic department) mandates that require deposit

Institutional repositories are rare in public libraries. OpenDOAR listed only one in the United States in March 2008: Education by Design: Educational Visual Aids from the Bienes Center's WPA Museum Extension Project Collection (http://digital.browardlibrary.org/wpa/), at the Broward County Library in Fort Lauderdale, Florida. This is an online exhibit and digitized image database of educational visual aids produced by the Works Progress Administration. Digitization was funded through a grant from the Institute for Museum and Library Services.

Richard W. Boss explores the role public libraries might have in creating and maintaining institutional repositories in a paper written for the Public Library Association Technology Committee.[49] He suggests that the challenge for public libraries is defining the community for which it would assume a digital repository role. A public library institutional repository might be a combination of a community repository and links to other repositories. It might serve as a repository for the digital output of its parent government entity. The critical first step for a public library is a needs assessment and analysis of the benefits to be obtained and the implementation and maintenance costs, especially to serve the preservation goals of a digital repository. The challenge for most public libraries is funding. Boss concludes that the most likely sources of funds are grants, leaving sustainability a significant issue.

Issues for Libraries and Roles for Collections Librarians

Libraries and their librarians, especially those charged with collections responsibilities, have significant responsibilities as the nature of scholarly communication evolves. Paul N. Courant has written:

> Both locally and collectively, there is an enormous amount of work to be done to make digitized materials easy to use, to create extensive, virtual archives and collections across space, to link working notes together, to develop and employ all sort of collaborative tools. The new technologies make collaboration much easier, and make it much easier for users to find what they are looking for, for materials across the world. Universities and their libraries that are best and most creative about usability will still have a competitive advantage. And the main business of the university—turning information into understanding and knowledge—understanding what is good and not so good, separating the wheat from the chaff, being smart about collections of materials, albeit "virtual collections," will still be vital—even more so in a world of ubiquitous information. So we will need good librarians, and they will be a continuing source of competitive advantage for individual universities.[50]

Supporting Open Access Models

Collections librarians can support the evolution of open access by selecting materials available through new publishing and economic models that offer open access. They can apply the same rigorous standards for selection regardless of format or publishing venue. They can seek partnerships with publishers that offer open access models.

Developing and Managing the Content of Institutional Repositories

Some selection and acquisition roles are changing with the advent of institutional repositories. Academic library liaisons actively solicit deposit in institutional repositories and encourage the user community to self-archive materials. In one sense, faculty authors are assuming responsibility for selecting the items to be added to the collection. Librarians can help the community define what is appropriate for the institutional repository through a clear repository mission statement and collection development policies and guidelines that are consistent with this mission.

The University Conservancy, the institutional repository at the University of Minnesota managed by the University Library, has developed content guidelines that state:

> The University Digital Conservancy (UDC) is a program of the University of Minnesota Libraries that provides long-term open access to a wide range of University works in digital formats. It does so by gathering, describing, organizing, storing, and preserving that content.
>
> Works produced or sponsored by the University of Minnesota faculty, researchers, staff, and students are appropriate for deposit in the UDC. Works might include pre- and post-prints, working papers, technical reports, conference papers and theses.
>
> Works produced or sponsored by administrative and academic units may also be appropriate for deposit in the UDC; see Regents' policy on University Archives. Works might include digital departmental newsletters, administrative reports, compilations of University data, meeting agendas and minutes.
>
> The following statements are meant to guide contributors in determining appropriate types of submissions for the UDC.
>
> The UDC welcomes works in most digital formats. Digital preservation support will be provided at different levels for specific formats as specified in the UDC preservation policy.
>
> - Contributors must have authorization to place the works they deposit in the UDC.
> - The UDC must be granted permission to distribute and preserve all works placed in the UDC. The author/original copyright owner retains copyright on all works.
> - Works should be free from access restrictions and appropriate for open access by all users of the UDC.[51]

Fostering Easy Access

Librarians can facilitate discovery and access by ensuring that finding digital resources is easy for users. Approaches can include offering local tools that simplify finding e-resources, such as A-to-Z e-journal lists, live links in catalogs to online resources, link resolvers within catalogs, and open access materials integrated into normal library operations so that they get the same kinds of description. Another is to ensure that the descriptive metadata created for materials in institutional repositories can be harvested by OAI-PMH. Institutional repositories often create metadata for deposited materials or provide simple templates for depositors to use. They frequently describe best practices and the rationale for creating metadata that facilitates discovery and access.

Preserving Digital Content

The collections librarian has a critical role as steward of the collection and its preservation. The issue of digital preservation is intertwined with issues of access. When licensing e-content for the collection, the librarian should prefer providers that guarantee perpetual access. Libraries can participate in and support projects like LOCKSS and shared digital repositories. Libraries can digitize open access versions of works in the public domain, making them available online to support international scholarship. Librarians can work to ensure that their institutional repositories are committed to providing long-term access to the digital works they contain, and that the repositories adhere to digital preservation best practices. These practices should support data accessibility through the use of persistent identifiers, stability (bitstream integrity), and usability (through format migration, emulation, and normalization) in perpetuity. Many institutional repositories have explicit preservation policies that spell out the commitment to perpetual access, along with policies about withdrawal and when it might be permitted. Just as collections librarians seek secure and safe facilities for print collections, they should aim for secure e-content storage, backup, and recovery services.

Outreach and Liaison Activities

Through their outreach and liaison activities, academic librarians can help faculty members understand the changing nature of scholarly communication, especially the benefits it can bring. Nancy Fried Foster and Susan Gibbons observe that what faculty members care most about is their research—and how they locate and organize their resources, work with coauthors, and do their writing. Though Foster and Gibbons were writing specifically about promoting the benefits of institutional repositories to faculty, the list they developed to promote repositories applies to the open access environment. Through open access, scholars can [52]

- make their own work easily accessible to others online
- preserve their own digital items
- provide online links to their work
- maintain ownership of their own work and control who sees it
- avoid having to maintain their work on a local server

A key component of open access is making appropriate choices about copyright ownership. Librarians can help faculty members and researchers understand the rights they often sign away in standard publisher agreements along, with their copyright options. Many academic libraries have developed websites and proactive education programs to reach faculty and to answer their questions. Institutional repositories typically have policies addressing copyright and require deposit agreements in which the depositor confirms that he or she is the creator of the work and either owns all rights of copyright or has the right to deposit the work in a digital archive.

Engaging in Public Policy and Legal Issues

Librarians should be actively engaged in public policy and legal matters that have the power to inhibit or enable scholarship and scholarly communication. Librarians can monitor new initiatives and developments in scholarly communication through pertinent websites, including

- Association of College and Research Libraries, Scholarly Communication Initiative: www.ala.org/ala/acrl/acrlissues/scholarlycomm/scholcomm initiative.cfm
- ARL Office of Scholarly Communication: www.arl.org/sc/index.shtml
- SPARC: The Scholarly Publishing and Academic Resources Coalition: www.arl.org/sparc/

Summary

Scholarly communication, the process of disseminating research and providing continuing access to the scholarly record in print and digital format to the broader academic community, is being transformed. Scholarly publishing can be traced to the 1600s, when European scholarly societies began to publish their findings in serial publications. Over time, scholarly publishing shifted to commercial publishers. In the past twenty-five years, many of these publishers have merged and journal prices have escalated. As libraries have canceled subscriptions, access to scholarly publishing has declined.

Initially viewed as the libraries' problem ("the serials crisis"), the more encompassing crisis in scholarly publication gained attention in the academic and research communities in the early twenty-first century. Free and open access via the Internet was seen as one obvious solution to the scholarly communication crisis. The Budapest Open Access Initiative issued the first call for open access journals and archives.

Scholarly publication (formal dissemination) is a crucial component of research and promotion and tenure processes. The peer review process is seen to ensure quality. Publication brings recognition to authors and visibility to their institutions and supports future research. Faculty members are usually evaluated in part by their academic output, as demonstrated in publications. A tension exists between the traditional system of scholarly publication and the evolving new system, which is seen by some faculty as lacking quality control. In reality, open access is simply a model for access and delivery and can be consistent with both peer review and copyright law.

Copyright law defines the ownership of a work and the control owners can exercise over access to and use of the work. A major thrust of the movement to reform scholarly publishing focuses on authors' rights. When authors retain some or all of their rights, they can keep control of how their work is distributed and used and advance a central goal of the movement to reform scholarly publishing—open access to peer-reviewed, scholarly literature.

Three strategies support open access: publishing in open access journals, publishing open access books, and self-archiving in open access repositories. Self-archiving is the deposit of articles by authors in free, open electronic archives or repositories, usually either discipline-based repositories or institutional repositories. The development of digital repositories became possible with the decline in online storage costs, development and adoption of standard metadata harvesting protocols, and maturity of digital preservation.

Librarians have important roles in the transformation of scholarly communication. These include selecting and acquiring resources that support open access, facilitating their discovery, supporting their access and dissemination, archiving and preserving them, and supporting their community of users as they do their work. Through outreach and liaison activities, academic librarians can help faculty members understand their copyright options and the changing nature of scholarly communication, especially the benefits it can bring.

CASE STUDY

Briddle College is a small, comprehensive, private, four-year college located in the Northeast. It partners with two similar schools in a shared automated system, collaborative collection building, and resource sharing. Together, the three colleges have received a major grant to develop a shared institutional repository. The colleges' trustee boards have committed to ongoing financial support to maintain the repository. They see the new digital repository as addressing campus needs for digital asset management, including digital assets for instruction. In addition, they see the shared repository as critical to preservation of central administrative and departmental documents, many of which are available only digitally and are often fugitive. These include college committee materials (minutes, agendas, and attachments), task force reports, departmental newsletters, policy documents, course catalogs, statistical information, and budget documents. They also expect the institutional repository to serve as an open access archive for faculty research and associated publications. The college presidents have appointed a steering committee composed of the college library directors and heads of campus computing services. The library directors have identified librarians at each of their colleges to draft various documents for consideration by the steering committee.

The library director at Briddle College has asked Charles, Briddle's collections coordinator, to identify areas that should be addressed in policies and best practices for the repository, to propose the core services the repository should offer, and to identify additional campus partners who should be involved in planning and implementing the repository.

Activity

Suggest the key areas that policies for the institutional repository should address. Identify where best practices are appropriate. Describe the core services the repository should offer. This could be supplemented with a list of additional services that might be offered, perhaps on a fee basis. Suggest others on the campuses who should be involved in planning and implementing the repository. Identify additional stakeholders whose support is essential. Suggest ways to encourage their support and participation in the institutional repository.

Notes

1. Paul N. Courant, "Scholarship and Academic Libraries (and Their Kin) in the World of Google," *First Monday* 11, no. 8 (2006), http://firstmonday.org/issues/issue11_8/courant/index.html.
2. Karla L. Hahn, "Talk about Talking about New Models of Scholarly Communication," *Journal of Electronic Publishing* 11, no. 1 (2008), http://hdl.handle.net/2027/spo.3336451.0011.108.
3. Courant, "Scholarship and Academic Libraries."
4. Amy Friedlander, "The Triple Helix: Cyberinfrastructure, Scholarly Communication, and Trust," *Journal of Electronic Publishing* 11, no. 1 (2008), http://hdl.handle.net/2027/spo.3336451.0011.109.
5. Modern Language Association, *Report of the MLA Task Force on Evaluating Scholarship for Tenure and Promotion* (New York: MLA, 2007), www.mla.org/pdf/task_force_tenure_promo.pdf.
6. Peter Suber, "Happy Birthday BOAI," *Open Access News: News from the Open Access Movement*, Feb. 14, 2008, www.earlham.edu/~peters/fos/2008/02/happy-birthday-boai.html.
7. Budapest Open Access Initiative (Feb. 14, 2002), www.soros.org/openaccess/read.shtml.

8. "Bethesda Statement on Open Access Publishing" (June 20, 2003), www.earlham
.edu/~peters/fos/bethesda.htm; "Berlin Declaration on Open Access to Knowledge in
the Sciences and Humanities" (Oct. 22, 2003), http://oa.mpg.de/openaccess-berlin/
berlindeclaration.html.

9. Association of Research Libraries, "Principles for Emerging Systems of Scholarly
Publishing" (May 10, 2000), www.arl.org/bm~doc/tempe1.pdf.

10. Ryan C. Amacher and Roger E. Meiners, *Faulty Towers: Tenure and the Structure of
Higher Education* (Oakland, Calif.: Independent Institute, 2004); Richard P. Chait,
ed., *The Questions of Tenure* (Cambridge: Harvard University Press, 2002); Frederick
Rudolph, *The American College and University: A History* (New York: Knopf, 1962).

11. American Association of University Professors, "AAUP's 1915 Declaration of
Principles" (Dec. 31, 1915), www.campus-watch.org/article/id/566.

12. Diane Harley et al., "The Influence of Academic Values on Scholarly Publication and
Communication Practices," *Journal of Electronic Publishing* 10, no. 2 (2007), http://hdl
.handle.net/2027/spo.3336451.0010.204.

13. Friedlander, "Triple Helix."

14. Harley et al., "Influence of Academic Values."

15. Jeremy Birnholtz, "When Authorship Isn't Enough: Lessons from CERN on the
Implications of Formal and Informal Credit Attribution Mechanisms in Collaborative
Research," *Journal of Electronic Publishing* 11, no. 1 (2008), http://hdl.handle.net/2027/
spo.3336451.0011.105.

16. U.S. Copyright Office, U.S. Copyright Law (Oct. 2007), www.copyright.gov/title17/.

17. Elizabeth Gadd, Charles Oppenheim, and Steve Probets, "RoMEO Studies 1: The
Impact of Copyright Ownership on Academic Author Self-Archiving," *Journal of
Documentation* 59, no. 3 (2003): 243–77.

18. Budapest Open Access Initiative, www.soros.org/openaccess/read.shtml.

19. Stevan Harnad and Tim Brody, "Comparing the Impact of Open Access (OA) vs. Non-
OA Articles in the Same Journals," *D-Lib Magazine* 10, no. 6 (2004), www.dlib.org/dlib/
june04/harnad/06harnad.html.

20. Steve Lawrence, "Free Online Availability Substantially Increases a Paper's Impact,"
Nature 411, no. 6837 (2001): 521.

21. See, e.g., Hajar Sotudeh Abbas Horri, "The Citation Performance of Open Access
Journals: A Disciplinary Investigation of Citation Distribution Models," *Journal of
the American Society for Information Science and Technology* 58, no. 13 (2007): 2145–56;
Yanju Zhang, "The Effect of Open Access on Citation Impact: A Comparison Study
Based on Web Citation Analysis," *Libri* 56, no. 3 (2006): 145–56; David Nichols, Paul
Huntington, and Hamid R. Jamali, "The Impact of Open Access Publishing (and Other
Access Initiatives) on Use and Users of Digital Scholarly Journals," *Learned Publishing*
20, no. 1 (2007): 11–15; Kayvan Kousha and Mike Thelwall, "The Web Impact of Open
Access Social Science Research," *Library and Information Science Research* 29, no. 4 (2007):
495–507; Thomson ISI, "The Impact of Open Access Journals: A Citation Study from
Thomson ISI" (2004), http://scientific.thomson.com/media/presentrep/acropdf/impact-
oa-journals.pdf.

22. Gunther Eysenbach, "Citation Advantage of Open Access Articles," *PLoS Biol* 4, no. 5
(2006): e157, http://dx.doi.org/10.1371/journal.pbio.0040157.

23. Peter Suber, "No-Fee Open-Access Journals," *SPARC Open Access Newsletter*, no. 103 (Nov. 2, 2006), www.earlham.edu/~peters/fos/newsletter/11-02-06.htm#nofee.

24. Bill Hooker, "If It Won't Sink In, Maybe We Can Pound It In," *Open Reading Frame*, Dec. 2, 2007, www.sennoma.net/main/archives/2007/12/.

25. Suber, "No-Fee Open-Access Journals."

26. University of California Office of Scholarly Communication and the California Digital Library eScholarship Program, in association with Greenhouse Associates, Inc., "Faculty Attitudes and Behaviors Regarding Scholarly Communication: Survey Findings from the University of California" (August 2007), http://osc.universityofcalifornia.edu/responses/materials/OSC-survey-full-20070828.pdf.

27. Robert B. Townsend, "Gutenberg-e Books Now Available Open Access and through ACLS Humanities E-Book," *AHA Today*, Feb. 13, 2008, http://blog.historians.org/publications/454/gutenberg-e-books-now-available-open-access-and-through-acls-humanities-e-book.

28. Sanford G. Thatcher, "Print-on-Demand from University Press," LIBLICENSE-L, Jan. 25, 2008, www.library.yale.edu/~llicense/ListArchives/0801/msg00076.html.

29. Stevan Harnad, "1. Overture: The Subversive Proposal," in *Scholarly Journals at the Crossroads: A Subversive Proposal for Electronic Publishing; An Internet Discussion about Scientific and Scholarly Journals and Their Future*, ed. Ann Shumelda Okerson and James J. O'Donnell, 1–2 (Washington, D.C.: Association of Research Libraries, 1995), www.arl.org/bm~doc/subversive.pdf.

30. Stevan Harnad, "Re: When Did the Open Access Movement 'Officially' Begin," American Scientist Open Access Forum, June 27, 2007, http://users.ecs.soton.ac.uk/harnad/Hypermail/Amsci/6519.html.

31. Open Archives Initiative, The Open Archives Initiative Protocol for Metadata Harvesting, Protocol Version 2.0 of 2002-06-14, Document Version 2004/10/12T15:31:00Z, www.openarchives.org/OAI/openarchivesprotocol.html.

32. Heather Morrison, "Happy Birthday, BOAI! and Confirmation of Acceleration of Growth in DOAJ" (Feb. 14, 2008), *Imaginary Journal of Poetic Economics*, http://poeticeconomics.blogspot.com/2008/02/happy-birthday-boai-and-confirmation-of.html.

33. U.S. Congress, Consolidated Appropriations Act, 2008, Pub. L. No. 110-161 Div. G. Titl. II Sec. 218.

34. Ray English and Heather Joseph, "The NIH Mandate: An Open Access Landmark." *College and Research Libraries News* 69, no. 2 (2008), www.ala.org/ala/acrl/acrlpubs/crlnews/backissues2008/february08/nihupdate.cfm.

35. National Institutes of Health Public Access, Journals That Submit Articles to PubMed Central, http://publicaccess.nih.gov/submit_process_journals.htm.

36. Michael W. Carroll, "Complying with the National Institutes of Health Public Access Policy: Copyright Considerations and Options," joint SPARC/Science Commons/ARL white paper (Feb. 2008), www.arl.org/sparc/bm%7Edoc/NIH_Copyright_v1.pdf.

37. [Harvard University] Faculty of Arts and Sciences, Regular Meeting, Tuesday, February 12, 2008, 4 p.m. . . . . Agenda, www.fas.harvard.edu/~secfas/February_2008_Agenda.pdf.

38. "A Shot Heard 'Round the Academic World: Harvard FAS Mandates Open Access," *Library Journal Academic Newswire* (Feb. 14, 2008), www.libraryjournal.com/info/CA6532658.html#news1.

39. University of Houston Libraries Institutional Repository Task Force, Charles W. Bailey Jr., Chair, *Institutional Repositories*. SPEC Kit no. 292 (Washington, D.C.: Association of Research Libraries, 2006), 13.

40. Clifford A. Lynch, "Institutional Repositories: Essential Infrastructure for Scholarship in the Digital Age," *ARL: A Bimonthly Report*, no. 226 (Feb. 2003), www.arl.org/bm~doc/br226ir.pdf.

41. Peter Suber, "Re: IR Question," e-mail message to the author, March 8, 2008.

42. Raym Crow, preparer, *SPARC Institutional Repository Checklist and Resource Guide* (Washington, D.C.: SPARC, 2002).

43. OpenDOAR, Repository Statistics, www.opendoar.org/find.php?format=charts.

44. Raym Crow, "The Case for Institutional Repositories: A SPARC Position Paper" (Washington, D.C.: SPARC, 2002), www.arl.org/sparc/bm~doc/ir_final_release_102.pdf.

45. Cat S. McDowell, "Evaluating Institutional Repository Deployment in American Academe since Early 2005: Repositories by the Numbers, Part 2," *D-Lib Magazine* 13, nos. 9/10 (2007), www.dlib.org/dlib/september07/mcdowell/09mcdowell.html.

46. Primary Research Group, *The International Survey of Institutional Digital Repositories* (New York: Primary Research Group, 2008).

47. See, e.g., Nancy Fried Foster and Susan Gibbons, "Understanding Faculty to Improve Content Recruitment for Institutional Repositories," *D-Lib Magazine* 11, no. 1 (2005), www.dlib.org/dlib/january05/foster/01foster.html; Carol Hixson, "If We Build It, Will They Come (Eventually)? Scholarly Communication and Institutional Repositories," *Serials Librarian* 50, nos. 1/2 (2006): 197–209; Richard K. Johnson, "Institutional Repositories: Partnering with Faculty to Enhance Scholarly Communication," *D-Lib Magazine* 8, no. 11 (2002), www.dlib.org/dlib/november02/johnson/11johnson.html; Tyler O. Walters, "Strategies and Frameworks for Institutional Repositories and the New Support Infrastructure for Scholarly Communications," *D-Lib Magazine* 12, no. 10 (2006), www.dlib.org/dlib/october06/walters/10walters.html.

48. University of Houston Libraries, *Institutional Repositories*.

49. Richard W. Boss, "Institutional Repositories" (April 29, 2006), www.ala.org/ala/pla/plapubs/technotes/Institutionalrepositories.doc.

50. Courant, "Scholarship and Academic Libraries."

51. University of Minnesota Digital Conservancy, Content Guidelines, http://conservancy.umn.edu/pol-content.jsp.

52. Foster and Gibbons, "Understanding Faculty."

Suggested Readings

Allard, Suzie, Thura R. Mack, and Melanie Feltner-Reichert. "The Librarian's Role in Institutional Repositories: A Content Analysis of the Literature." *Reference Services Review* 33, no. 3 (2005): 325–36.

Andersen, Deborah Lines, ed. *Digital Scholarship in the Tenure, Promotion, and Review Process*. Armonk, N.Y.: M. E. Sharpe, 2004.

Antelman, Kristin. "Do Open Access Articles Have a Greater Research Impact?" *College and Research Libraries* 65, no. 5 (2004): 372–82.

Armbruster, Chris. "Moving Out of Oldenbourg's Long Shadow: What Is the Future for Society Publishing?" *Learned Publishing* 20, no. 4 (2007): 259–66.

Association of College and Research Libraries Scholarly Communication Committee. "Establishing a Research Agenda for Scholarly Communication: A Call for Community Engagement" (Nov. 5, 2007). www.ala.org/ala/acrl/acrlissues/scholarlycomm/SCResearchAgenda.pdf.

Association of Learned and Professional Society Publishers. *The Facts about Open Access: A Study of the Financial and Non-Financial Effects of Alternative Business Models for Scholarly Journals.* Researchers: Kaufman-Wills Group, LLC: Sponsors: ALPSP, HighWire Press, and AAAS Project on Science and Intellectual Property in the Public Interest. Worthington, England: Association of Learned and Professional Society Publishers, 2005.

Atkins, Daniel E., John Seely Brown, and Allen L. Hammond. "A Review of the Open Educational Resources (OER) Movement: Achievements, Challenges, and New Opportunities," report to the William and Flora Hewlett Foundation (Feb. 2007). www.oerderves.org/wp-content/uploads/2007/03/a-review-of-the-open-educational-resources-oer-movement_final.pdf.

Atkinson, Ross. "A Rationale for the Redesign of Scholarly Information Exchange." *Library Resources and Technical Services* 44, no. 2 (2000): 59–69.

Bailey, Charles W. "Open Access and Libraries." *Collection Management* 32, nos. 3/4 (2007): 351–83.

———. The Scholarly Electronic Publishing Bibliography. www.digital-scholarship .org/sepb/sepb.html.

Bankier, Jean-Gabriel, and Irene Perciali. "The Institutional Repository Rediscovered: What Can a University Do for Open Access Publishing?" *Serials Review* 34, no. 1 (2008): 21–26.

Barjak, Franz. "The Role of the Internet in Informal Scholarly Communication." *Journal of the American Society for Information Science and Technology* 57, no. 10 (2006): 1350–67.

Baudoin, Patsy, and Margret Branschofsky. "Implementing an Institutional Repository: The DSpace Experience at MIT." *Science and Technology Libraries* 24, nos. 1/2 (2003): 31–45.

Bergman, Sherrie S. "The Scholarly Communication Movement: Highlights and Recent Developments." *Collection Building* 25, no. 4 (2006): 108–28.

Boyle, James. "Expanding the Public Domain." *ARL: A Bimonthly Report*, no. 241 (Aug. 2005): 1–4.

Brown, Laura, Rebecca Griffiths, and Matthew Rascoff. "University Publishing in a Digital Age" (July 26, 2007). www.ithaka.org/strategic-services/Ithaka%20University%20Publishing%20Report.pdf.

Byrd, Gary D., et al. "The Status of Open Access Publishing by Academic Societies." *Journal of the Medical Library Association* 93, no. 4 (2005): 423–24.

Carter, Howard. "Library Faculty Publishing and Intellectual Property Issues: A Survey of Attitudes and Awareness." *portal: Libraries and the Academy* 7, no. 1 (2007): 65–79.

Davis, Hilary M., and John N. Vickery. "Datasets: A Shift in the Currency of Scholarly Communication: Implications for Library Collections and Acquisitions." *Serials Review* 33, no. 1 (2007): 26–32.

Downes, Daniel M. "New Media Economy: Intellectual Property and Cultural Insurrections." *Journal of Electronic Publishing* 9, no. 1 (2006). http://hdl.handle .net/2027/spo.3336451.0009.103.

Esposito, Joseph. "The Wisdom of Oz: The Role of the University Press in Scholarly Communications." *Journal of Electronic Publishing* 10, no. 1 (2007). http://hdl .handle.net/2027/spo.3336451.0010.103.

Estabrook, Leigh, with Bijan Warner. "The Book as the Gold Standard for Tenure and Promotion in the Humanistic Disciplines" (2003). http://lrc.lis.uiuc.edu/reports/ CICBook.html.

Gillespie, Tarleton. *Wired Shut: Copyright and the Shape of Digital Culture.* Cambridge, Mass.: MIT Press, 2007.

Guédon, Jean-Claude. "The 'Green' and 'Gold' Roads to Open Access: The Case for Mixing and Matching." *Serials Review* 30, no. 4 (2004): 315–28.

———. "In Oldenburg's Long Shadow: Librarians, Research Scientists, Publishers, and the Control of Scientific Publishing." Washington, D.C.: Association of Research Libraries, 2002. www.arl.org/resources/pubs/mmproceedings/138guedon.shtml.

Hahn, Karla L. *Electronic Ecology: A Case Study of Electronic Journals in Context.* Washington, D.C.: Association of Research Libraries, 2001.

———. "New Tools for New Times: Remodeling the Scholarly Communication System." *College and Research Libraries News* 67, no. 10 (2006): 608–10, 614.

Harnad, Stevan, et al. "The Access/Impact Problem and the Green and Gold Roads to Open Access." *Serials Review* 30, no. 4 (2004): 310–14.

Hawkins, Brian L. "Advancing Scholarship and Intellectual Productivity: An Interview with Clifford A. Lynch: Part 1." *EDUCAUSE Review* 41, no. 2 (2006): 46–56. http://connect.educause.edu/Library/EDUCAUSE+Review/AdvancingScholarship andIn/40618.

———. "Advancing Scholarship and Intellectual Productivity: An Interview with Clifford A. Lynch: Part 2." *EDUCAUSE Review* 41, no. 3 (2006): 44–56. http:// connect.educause.edu/Library/EDUCAUSE+Review/AdvancingScholarshipandIn/ 40630.

Hirtle, Peter B. "Author Addenda: An Examination of Five Alternatives." *D-Lib Magazine* 12, no. 11 (2006). www.dlib.org/dlib/november06/hirtle/11hirtle.html.

Holley, Robert P. "The Ethics of Scholarly Research and the Internet: Issues of Publication, Privacy, and the Right to Speak." *Journal of Information Ethics* 15, no. 1 (2006): 27–34.

Hood, Anna K. *Open Access Resources.* SPEC Kit no. 300. Washington, D.C.: Association of Research Libraries, 2007.

Hughes, Carol Ann. "The Case for Scholars' Management of Author Rights." *portal: Libraries and the Academy* 6, no. 2 (2006): 123–26.

Jeon-Slaughter, Haekyung, Andrew C. Herkovic, and Michael A. Keller. "Economics of Scientific and Biomedical Journals: Where Do Scholars Stand in the Debate of Online Journal Pricing and Site License Ownership between Libraries and Publishers?" *First Monday* 10, no. 3 (2005). www.firstmonday.org/issues/issue10_3/ jeon/.

Johnston, Wayne. "The Library as an Agent for Transforming Scholarly Communications." *IATUL Proceedings,* part n.s. 17 (2007): 1–13.

Jones, Catherine. *Institutional Repositories: Content and Culture in an Open Access Environment.* Oxford: Chandos, 2007.

Jones, Richard, Theo Andrew, and John MacColl. *The Institutional Repository.* Oxford: Chandos, 2006.

Kaur, Amritpal. "Electronic Journals and Scholarly Communication." *Information Studies* 13, no. 4 (2007): 227–39.

Kennan, Mary Anne, and Concepción Wilson. "Institutional Repositories: Review and an Information Systems Perspective." *Library Management* 27, nos. 4/5 (2006): 236–48.

Kim, Jihyun. "Motivating and Impeding Factors Affecting Faculty Contribution to Institutional Repositories." *Journal of Digital Information* 8, no. 2 (2007). http://journals.tdl.org/jodi/article/view/193/177.

King, C. Judson, et al. *Scholarly Communication: Academic Values and Sustainable Models.* Berkeley: University of California, Center for Studies in Higher Education, 2006. http://cshe.berkeley.edu/publications/publications.php?id=23.

Lewis, David W. "A Strategy for Academic Libraries in the First Quarter of the 21st Century." *College and Research Libraries* 68, no. 5 (2007): 418–34.

Markey, Karen, et al. *Census of Institutional Repositories in the United States: MIRACLE Project Research Findings.* CLIR Publication no. 140. Washington, D.C.: Council on Library and Information Resources, 2007. www.clir.org/pubs/reports/pub140/contents.html.

———. "Nationwide Census of Institutional Repositories: Preliminary Findings." *Journal of Digital Information* 8, no. 2 (2007). http://journals.tdl.org/jodi/article/view/194/170.

Marshall, Catherine C. "Rethinking Personal Digital Archiving, Part 1." *D-Lib Magazine* 14, nos. 3/4 (2008). www.dlib.org/dlib/march08/marshall/03marshall-pt1.html.

———. "Rethinking Personal Digital Archiving, Part 2." *D-Lib Magazine* 14, nos. 3/4 (2008). www.dlib.org/dlib/march08/marshall/03marshall-pt2.html.

McKiernan, Gary. "Open Access and Retrieval: Liberating the Scholarly Literature." In *E-Serials Collection Management: Transitions, Trends, and Technicalities,* edited by David C. Fowler, 197–220. Binghamton, N.Y.: Haworth, 2004.

Morrison, Heather, and Andrew Waller. "Open Access for the Medical Librarian." *Journal of the Canadian Health Libraries Association* 27, no. 3 (2006): 69–73.

Nelson, Mark R. "Digital Content Delivery Trends in Higher Education." *EDUCAUSE Center for Applied Research Bulletin,* no. 9 (2006): 1–12. http://net.educause.edu/ir/library/pdf/ERB0609.pdf.

Newman, Kathleen A., Deborah D. Blecic, and Kimberly L. Armstrong. *Scholarly Communication Education Initiatives.* SPEC Kit no. 299. Washington, D.C.: Association of Research Libraries, 2007.

Ober, John. "Facilitating Open Access: Developing Support for Author Control of Copyright." *College and Research Libraries News* 67, no. 4 (2006): 219–21, 255.

Ober, John, Catherine Candee, and Beverlee French. "Reshaping Scholarly Communication." *Against the Grain* 16, no. 3 (2004): 42, 44, 46, 48.

Odlyzko, Andrew. "The Rapid Evolution of Scholarly Communication." *Learned Publishing* 15, no. 1 (2002): 7–19. http://alpsp.publisher.ingentaconnect.com/content/alpsp/lp/2002/00000015/00000001/art00002.

Ogburn, Joyce L. "Defining and Achieving Success in the Movement to Change Scholarly Communication." *Library Resources and Technical Services* 52, no. 2 (2008): 44–53.

Plutchak, T. Scott. "The Impact of Open Access." *Journal of the Medical Library Association* 93, no. 4 (2005): 419–21.

Primary Research Group. *The International Survey of Institutional Digital Repositories.* New York: Primary Research Group, 2008.

Public Library of Science. "Publishing Open-Access Journals: A Brief Overview from the Public Library of Science" (Feb. 2004). www.plos.org/downloads/oa_whitepaper.pdf.

Rieger, Oya Y. "Select for Success: Key Principles in Assessing Repository Models." *D-Lib Magazine* 13, nos. 7/8 (2007). www.dlib.org/dlib/july07/rieger/07rieger.html.

Rieh, Soo Young, et al. "Census of Institutional Repositories in the U.S.: A Comparison across Institutions at Different Stages of IR Development." *D-Lib Magazine* 13, nos. 11/12 (2007). www.dlib.org/dlib/november07/rieh/11rieh.html.

Sale, Arthur. "The Patchwork Mandate." *D-Lib Magazine* 13, nos. 1/2 (2007). www.dlib.org/dlib/january07/sale/01sale.html.

Schonfeld, Roger C., and Kevin M. Guthrie. "The Changing Information Services Needs of Faculty." *EDUCAUSE Review* 42, no. 4 (2007): 8–9. http://connect.educause.edu/Library/EDUCAUSE+Review/TheChangingInformationSer/44598.

Schulenburger, David. "Improving Access to Publicly Funded Research: What's in It for the Institution? Can We Make the Case?" *ARL: A Bimonthly Report,* no. 248 (Oct. 2005): 1–4.

Seadle, Michael. "Copyright in the Networked World: Author's Rights." *Library Hi Tech* 23, no. 1 (2005): 130–36.

Skomal, Susan. "Transformation of a Scholarly Society Publishing Program." *ARL: A Bimonthly Report,* no. 242 (Oct. 2005): 1–5.

Smith, Abby. *New Model Scholarship: How Will It Survive?* Washington, D.C.: Council on Library and Information Resources, 2003. www.clir.org/pubs/reports/pub114/pub114.pdf.

Smith, Kevin L. "Managing Copyright for NIH Public Access: Strategies to Ensure Compliance." *ARL: A Bimonthly Report,* no. 258 (June 2008): 1–5.

Solomon, David J. "The Role of Peer Review for Scholarly Journals in the Information Age." *Journal of Electronic Publishing* 10, no. 1 (2007). http://hdl.handle.net/2027/spo.3336451.0010.107.

Struik, Christina, et al. "Transitioning to Open Access (OA)." *First Monday* 12, no. 10 (2007). www.uic.edu/htbin/cgiwrap/bin/ojs/index.php/fm/article/view/1996/1871.

Suber, Peter. "Open Access in 2007." *Journal of Electronic Publishing* 11, no. 1 (2008). http://hdl.handle.net/2027/spo.3336451.0011.110.

Susman, Thomas M., David J. Carter, and the Information Access Alliance. "Publisher Mergers: A Consumer-Based Approach to Antitrust Analysis." Washington, D.C.: Information Alliance, 2003. www.arl.org/bm~doc/whitepaperv2final.pdf.

Thibodeau, Kenneth. "If You Build It, Will It Fly? Criteria for Success in a Digital Repository." *Journal of Digital Information* 8, no. 2 (2007). http://journals.tdl.org/jodi/article/view/197/174.

Thomas, Chuck, and Robert H. McDonald. "Measuring and Comparing Participation Patterns in Digital Repositories." *D-Lib Magazine* 13, nos. 9/10 (2007). www.dlib.org/dlib/september07/mcdonald/09mcdonald.html.

Thompson, John B. *Books in the Digital Age: The Transformation of Academic and Higher Education Publishing in Britain and the United States.* Cambridge, England: Polity, 2005.

Thorin, Suzanne E. "Global Changes in Scholarly Communication" (2003). www.arl.org/bm~doc/thorin.pdf.

Urs, Shalini R. "Gutenberg to Google: Changing Facets of Libraries." *Information Studies* 12, no. 4 (2006): 197–204.

Van de Sompel, Herbert. "Rethinking Scholarly Communication: Building the System that Scholars Deserve." *D-Lib Magazine* 10, no. 9 (2004). www.dlib.org/dlib/september04/vandesompel/09vandesompel.html.

Van Orsdel, Lee C. "The State of Scholarly Communications: An Environmental Scan of Emerging Issues, Pitfalls, and Possibilities." *Serials Librarian* 52, nos. 1/2 (2007): 191–209.

Walters, Tyler O. "Reinventing the Library: How Repositories Are Causing Librarians to Rethink Their Professional Roles." *portal: Libraries and the Academy* 7, no. 2 (2007): 213–25.

Waters, Donald J. "Managing Digital Assets in Higher Education: An Overview of Strategic Issues." *ARL: A Bimonthly Report*, no. 244 (Feb. 2006): 1–10.

———. "Open Access Publishing and the Emerging Infrastructure of 21st Century Scholarship." *Journal of Electronic Publishing* 11, no. 1 (2008). http://hdl.handle.net/2027/spo.3336451.0011.106.

Willinsky, John. *The Access Principle: The Case for Open Access to Research and Scholarship.* Boston: MIT Press, 2006.

APPENDIX A

Professional Resources for Collection Development and Management

Journals

Against the Grain: Linking Publishers, Vendors, and Librarians (Charleston, S.C.: Against the Grain, v. 1, 1989–).

> Provides news about libraries, publishers, book jobbers, and subscription agents; covers library-vendor and publisher-library relations, acquisition business, publisher profiles, prices, studies, and collection development.

ALCTS Newsletter Online (ANO) (Chicago: Association for Library Collections and Technical Services, v. 10, 1998–). www.ala.org/ala/alcts/pubs/alctsnewsletter/.

> Official online newsletter of the Association for Library Collections and Technical Services; discusses topics of interest to persons involved in library collections and technical services.

The Bottom Line: Managing Library Finances (Bradford, U.K.: Emerald, v. 1, 1987–).

> Peer-reviewed journal providing practical information on planning, budgeting, managing cash, purchasing, investment, cost analysis, new technology, and other financial tools and techniques.

Children and Libraries (Chicago: Association for Library Service to Children, v. 1, 2003–).

> Official, peer-reviewed journal of the Association for Library Service to Children, publishing current scholarly research and practice in library service to children and spotlighting significant activities and programs of the Association.

Collection Building (Bradford, U.K.: Emerald, v. 1, 1978–).

> Peer-reviewed journal addressing collection maintenance and development for librarians in all types of libraries. Coverage includes resource development and sharing, technology, evaluation of electronic resources, and collection development policy issues.

Collection Management (New York: Haworth, v. 1, 1978–).

> Peer-reviewed journal covering all aspects of collection management and development that affect college and research libraries of all types, including resource sharing, staff training and development, management and analysis of administrative data associated with collections, usage, licensing, rights, access, and financial issues.

Journal of Electronic Publishing (Ann Arbor, Mich.: University of Michigan Press, v. 1, 1995–). www.journalofelectronicpublishing.org.

> Online, peer-reviewed journal covering all facets of publishing material in an electronic environment and the impact of those practices on users.

Journal of Electronic Resources Librarianship (Binghamton, N.Y.: Haworth, no. 1, 1989–). Formerly *The Acquisitions Librarian.*

> Peer-reviewed journal covering work-related processes and procedures, current research, and the latest news about electronic resources and the impact of the digital environment on collecting, acquiring, and making accessible library materials.

Journal of Interlibrary Loan, Document Supply and Electronic Reserve (Binghamton, N.Y.: Haworth, v. 1, 1990–). Formerly *Journal of Interlibrary Loan, Document Delivery and Information Supply.*

> Peer-reviewed journal covering interlibrary loan, document delivery, and electronic reserve.

Journal of Scholarly Publishing (Toronto: University of Toronto Press, v. 1, 1969–).

> Peer-reviewed journal for authors, editors, librarians, marketers, and publishers, covering publishing and the new challenges resulting from changes in technology and funding.

Knowledge Quest (Chicago: American Association of School Librarians, v. 1, 1951–).

> Official, peer-reviewed journal of the American Association of School Librarians, publishing news and articles of interest to K–12 library media specialists, supervisors, library educators, and other decision makers concerned with the development of school library media programs and services, education, learning theory, and relevant disciplines. KQWeb, the online component of *Knowledge Quest*, is dedicated to enhancing the print publication with expanded articles and original content.

Library Collections, Acquisitions and Technical Services (Amsterdam: Elsevier, v. 23, 1999–).

> Peer-reviewed journal covering library collection management, technical services, vendors, and publishing.

Library Resources and Technical Services (Chicago: Association for Library Collections and Technical Services, v. 1, 1947–).
> Official, peer-reviewed journal of the Association for Library Collections and Technical Services, covering bibliographic access and control, preservation, conservation and reproduction of library materials, serials and continuing resources, and collection development and management.

LMC: Library Media Connection (Columbus, Ohio: Linworth, v. 1, 1982–).
> Magazine providing articles, tips, and ideas for school library media specialists and technology specialists.

Publisher's Weekly (New York: Reed, v. 1, 1872–).
> Trade news magazine of interest to publishers, booksellers, literary agents, and librarians, covering publishing trends, mergers and acquisitions, other trade news, and book reviews.

Resource Sharing and Information Networks (Binghamton, N.Y.: Haworth, v. 1, 1981–).
> Peer-reviewed journal covering both theoretical and practical issues for planners, practitioners, and users of network services, library consortia, and systems for interlibrary cooperation.

School Libraries Worldwide (Kalamazoo, Mich.: International Association of School Librarianship, v. 1, 1995–).
> Official, peer-reviewed journal of the International Association of School Librarianship, publishing current research and scholarship on all aspects of school librarianship.

School Library Journal (New York: Reed, v. 8, 1961–).
> Magazine directed to librarians serving children and young adults in schools and public libraries, offering articles, advertising, bibliographies, trade literature, and reviews.

School Library Media Activities Monthly (Westport, Conn.: Libraries Unlimited, v. 1, 1984–).
> Magazine for K–8 library media specialists, focusing on teaching library and information skills.

School Library Media Research (Chicago: American Association of School Librarians, v. 1, 1998–). Formerly *School Library Media Quarterly Online*. www.ala.org/ala/aasl/aaslpubsandjournals/slmrb/schoollibrary.cfm
> Official, peer-reviewed online journal of the American Association of School Librarians; covers research on the management, implementation, and evaluation of school library media programs as well as instructional theory, teaching methods, and critical issues relevant to school library media.

Serials Review (Amsterdam: Elsevier, v. 1, 1975–).

> Peer-reviewed journal covering the practical aspects of collecting, managing, and publishing serials as well as emerging and theoretical issues of importance to librarians, publishers, and others in the serials community.

Technical Services Quarterly (Binghamton, N.Y.: Haworth, v. 1, 1983–).

> Peer-reviewed journal covering new developments and trends in computer automation and advanced technologies in the operation of libraries and information centers.

Electronic Discussion Groups

ACQNET. www.acqweb.org/acqnet.html

> Moderated, archived list that facilitates the exchange of information, ideas, and solutions to common problems in the areas of acquisitions and collection development and management.

COLLDV-L: Library Collection Development List. www.infomotions.com/serials/colldv-l/

> Moderated, archived list directed to collection development librarians and others (including publishers and vendors) interested in library collection development and management.

LIBLICENSE-L. www.library.yale.edu/~llicense/mailing-list.shtml

> Moderated, archived list for the discussion of issues related to the licensing of digital information by academic and research libraries.

LM_NET. www.eduref.org/lm_net/

> Moderated, archived list for school library media specialists worldwide and others involved with the school library media field.

SERIALST. www.uvm.edu/~bmaclenn/serialst.html

> Moderated, archived list intended to serve as a forum for most aspects of serial processing in libraries, including collection management and development, serial budgets, and pricing concerns.

Professional Associations

American Library Association: Divisions, Sections, and Committees within Those Divisions

American Association of School Librarians (AASL). www.ala.org/aasl/

> The mission of the American Association of School Librarians is to advocate excellence, facilitate change, and develop leaders in the school library media field.

Association for Library Collections and Technical Services, Collection Management and Development Section (CMDS). www.ala.org/ala/alcts/sections/collections/

> The mission of CMDS is to contribute to library service and librarianship through encouragement, promotion of, and responsibility for those activities of ALCTS related to collection management and development, selection, and evaluation of library materials in all types of institutions.

Association for Library Service to Children (ALSC). www.ala.org/alsc/

> ALSC is dedicated to the support and enhancement of service to children in all types of libraries and committed to a better future for children through libraries.

Public Library Association, Collection Management Committee. www.ala.org/ala/pla/committeework/collectionmanagement.cfm

> The mission of this committee is to collect and disseminate information on all aspects of collection management, including issues related to resource allocation, collection policies and practices, vendor relations, and special collections.

Reference and User Services Association, Collection Development and Evaluation Section (CODES). www.ala.org/ala/rusa/rusaourassoc/rusasections/codes/codes.cfm

> CODES addresses the collection development interests of reference and user services librarians in libraries of all types.

Reference and User Services Association, Cooperative Collection Development Committee, Joint Committee of Collection Development and Evaluation Section (CODES) and Sharing and Transforming Access to Resources Section STARS. www.ala.org/ala/rusa/rusaourassoc/rusasections/stars/starssections/committeesa/cooperativecollectiondevelopmentcommittee/CCD.cfm

> This committee is charged to study, promote, and support cooperative collection development and related user services.

Canadian Library Association

Canadian Association of School Librarians (CASL). www.cla.ca/casl/

> CASL provides a national forum for promoting school library programs as an essential element in the educational process, through advocacy, continuing education, and leadership.

Collection Development and Management Interest Group. www.cla.ca/Content/NavigationMenu/CLAatWork/InterestGroups/CollectionDevelopmentandManagement/

> This interest group's mission is to represent the interests of librarians involved in collection development and management, arrange opportunities for continuing education, provide a means of communication between librarians involved in collection development and management, and raise the awareness of the library community at large with regard to the issues of concern to librarians involved in collection development and management.

International Organizations

International Reading Association (IRA). www.reading.org

> The IRA is aimed at those involved in teaching reading to learners of all ages and is dedicated to promoting high levels of literacy for all by improving the quality of reading instruction, disseminating research and information about reading, and encouraging the lifetime reading habit.

International Federation of Library Associations and Institutions (IFLA), Division of Collections and Services. www.ifla.org/VII/d5/dcs.htm

> This division of the IFLA focuses on acquiring information for the improvement of collection building of specific types of materials such as rare books, serials, newspapers, and government publications.

APPENDIX B

Selection Aids

Bibliographical Tools and Directories

Most of the tools listed here are updated through new editions and supplements. Many are available in electronic format, on CD-ROMs, via the Internet, or both. Selectors should consult the most recent resources available and be aware that publications cease and change names over time.

ALA's Guide to Best Reading. Chicago: American Library Association. (annual)

American Book Publishing Record: Arranged by Dewey Decimal Classification and Indexed by Author, Title, and Subject. New Providence, N.J.: R. R. Bowker. (monthly)

American Reference Books Annual. Westport, Conn.: Libraries Unlimited. (annual)

Best Books for Children: Preschool through Grade 6. Westport, Conn.: Greenwood. (annual)

Best Books for Young Adults. 3rd ed., ed. Holly Koelling. Chicago: American Library Association, 2007.

Best Free Reference Web Sites. Reference and User Services Association, Machine-Assisted Reference Section. www.ala.org/rusa/mars/best2001 .html. (annual)

Books in Print. New Providence, N.J.: R. R. Bowker. (annual)

Books Out Loud: Bowker's Guide to Audiobooks. New Providence, N.J.: R. R. Bowker. (annual)

Bowker's Complete Video Directory: Combining Variety's Extensive Listing of Currently Available Entertainment Titles with Education and Special Interest Videos for Home, School, and Business. New Providence, N.J.: R. R. Bowker. (annual)

Bowker's Global Books in Print. New Providence, N.J.: R. R. Bowker. (online, updated daily)

C&RL NewsNet: Internet Reviews. www.bowdoin.edu/~samato/IRA/. (monthly)

CD Guide. Peterborough, N.H.: Connell Communications. (semiannual)

CD-ROMs in Print. Detroit: Mich.: Gale Research. (annual)

Children's Books in Print: An Author, Title, and Illustrator Index to Books for Children and Young Adults. New Providence, N.J.: R. R. Bowker. (annual)

Children's Core Collection, A Selection Guide (formerly *Children's Catalog*). New York: H. W. Wilson. (quadrennial, plus annual supplements)

The Complete Directory of Large Print Books and Serials. New Providence, N.J.: R. R. Bowker. (annual)

Directory of Published Proceedings, issues in three sections: OCE—Pollution Control and Ecology; SEMT—Science/Engineering/ Medicine/Technology; SSH—Social Sciences/Humanities. Harrison, N.Y.: InterDok Corp. (ten per year with quarterly and annual compilations)

El-Hi Textbooks and Serials in Print: Including Related Teaching Materials K–12. New Providence, N.J.: R. R. Bowker. (annual)

Film and Video Finder. Medford, N.J.: National Information Center for Educational Media. (irregular)

Forthcoming Books. New Providence, N.J.: R. R. Bowker. (three per year)

Fulltext Sources Online. Medford, N.J.: Information Today. (semiannual)

Gale Directory of Databases. Detroit, Mich.: Gale Research. (annual)

Gale Directory of Publications and Broadcast Media. Detroit, Mich.: Gale Research. (annual)

Graphic Novels Core Collection. New York: H. W. Wilson. (online, updated regularly)

Great Web Sites for Kids. American Library Association. www.ala.org/greatsites/. (updated frequently)

Guide to Microforms in Print. Munich: K. G. Saur. (annual)

Guide to Reference. Chicago: American Library Association.

Guide to Reference Books for School Media Centers. Westport, Conn.: Libraries Unlimited. (irregular)

Guide to Reference Materials for School Library Media Centers. Westport, Conn.: Libraries Unlimited. (irregular)

Guide to Reprints. Munich: K. G. Saur. (annual)

Guide to the American Left: Directory and Bibliography. Olathe, Kans.: Laird Wilcox. (annual)

Guide to the American Right: Directory and Bibliography. Olathe, Kans.: Laird Wilcox. (annual)

Guide to U.S. Government Publications. Detroit, Mich.: Gale Research. (annual)

Index to Current Urban Documents. Westport, Conn.: Greenwood. (quarterly)

Index to Social Sciences and Humanities Proceedings. Philadelphia: Thomson. (quarterly)

International Books in Print. Munich: K. G. Saur. (annual)

International Directory of Little Magazines and Small Presses. Paradise, Calif.: Dustbooks. (annual)

The Internet Scout. Madison, Wis.: University of Wisconsin, Department of Computer Sciences. http://scout.cs.wisc.edu/report/sr/current/. (updated weekly)

Magazines for Libraries. New Providence, N.J.: R. R. Bowker. (annual)

Middle and Junior High Core Collection: A Selection Guide (formerly *Middle and Junior High School Library Catalog*). New York: H. W. Wilson. (quadrennial, plus annual supplements)

Monthly Catalog of United States Government Publications. Washington, D.C.: U.S. Government Printing Office. (monthly)

Newbery and Caldecott Medal Books, 1986–2000: A Comprehensive Guide to the Winners. Chicago: American Library Association. (irregular)

NewJour: Electronic Journals and Newsletters [announcement list for new serials on the Internet]. http://library.georgetown.edu/newjour/. (updated frequently)

Newsletters in Print. Detroit, Mich.: Gale Research. (irregular)

Notable Trade Books for Young People. New York: National Council for the Social Studies. (annual)

Outstanding Science Trade Books for Students K–12. New York: Children's Books Council. (annual)

Oxbridge Directory of Newsletters. New York: Oxbridge Communications. (annual)

Public Library Core Collection: Fiction, a Selection Guide (formerly *Fiction Catalog*). New York: H. W. Wilson. (quadrennial, plus annual supplements)

Public Library Core Collection: Nonfiction, a Selection Guide (formerly *Public Library Catalog*). New York: H. W. Wilson. (quadrennial, plus annual supplements)

Recommended Reference Books for Small and Medium-Sized Libraries and Media Centers. Westport, Conn.: Libraries Unlimited. (annual)

Reference and User Services Notable Books [lists of fiction, nonfiction, and poetry books]. www.ala.org/ala/rusa/protools/notablebooks/thelists/notablebooks.cfm. (annual)

Resources for College Libraries. New Providence, N.J.: R. R. Bowker. (irregular)

Senior High Core Collection: A Selection Guide (formerly *Senior High School Library Catalog*). New York: H. W. Wilson. (quadrennial, plus annual supplements)

Serials Directory: An International Reference Book. Birmingham, Ala.: EBSCO Publishing. (quarterly)

Software Encyclopedia: A Guide for Personal, Professional, and Business Users. New Providence, N.J.: R. R. Bowker. (annual)

Standard Periodical Directory. New York: Oxbridge Communications. (annual)

Statistical Reference Index: A Selective Guide to American Statistical Publications from Sources Other Than the U.S. Government. Washington, D.C.: Congressional Information Service. (monthly)

Ulrich's Periodicals Directory: International Periodicals Information. New Providence, N.J.: R. R. Bowker. (annual, with triennial supplements)

The Video Sourcebook. Detroit, Mich.: Gale Research. (annual with semiannual supplements)

Review Sources and Guides to Reviews

Many titles listed here are online resources or have an online version and associated website with indexed reviews.

ALAN Review. Assembly on Literature for Adolescents of the National Council for Teachers of English. (three per year)

Audiofile: The Magazine for People Who Love Audiobooks. Portland, Maine: Audiofile. (bimonthly)

Billboard: The International Newsweekly of Music, Video, and Home Entertainment. New York: Nielsen Business Publications. (weekly)

Book Links: Connecting Books, Libraries, and Classrooms. Chicago: American Library Association. (bimonthly)

Book Review Digest: An Index to Reviews of Current Books. New York: H. W. Wilson. (monthly except February and July; annual cumulation)

Book Review Index. Detroit, Mich.: Gale Research. (three per year)

Booklist. Chicago: American Library Association. (bimonthly)

Bookwire: The Book Industry Resource. www.bookwire.com. New Providence, N.J.: R. R. Bowker.

Bulletin of the Center for Children's Books. Baltimore, Md.: Johns Hopkins University Press. (monthly except August)

Children's Magazine Guide: Subject Index to Children's Magazines and Web Sites. Westport, Conn.: Greenwood. (nine per year)

Children's Technology Revue. Flemington, N.J.: Active Learning Association. (monthly)

Children's Video Report. Brooklyn, N.Y.: Great Mountain Proeditions. (eight per year)

Choice: Current Reviews of Academic Books. Middleton, Conn.: Association of College and Research Libraries. (monthly, except bimonthly in July/August)

Chronicle of Higher Education. Washington, D.C.: The Chronicle. (49 per year)

CM Magazine: Canadian Review of Materials. Manitoba: Manitoba Library Association. (biweekly)

The Comics Journal: The Magazine of Comics News and Criticism. Seattle: Fantagraphics Books. (monthly)

Counterpoise: For Social Responsibilities, Liberty and Dissent. Gainesville, Fla.: Civic Media Center and Library. (quarterly)

Criticas Magazine: An English Speaker's Guide to the Latest Spanish-Language Titles. New York: Reed (two per year)

Down Beat: Jazz, Blues, and Beyond. Elmhurst, Ill.: Maher Production. (monthly)

EContent: Digital Content Strategies and Resources. Wilton, Conn.: Information Today. (ten per year)

Educational Media Reviews Online (EMRO). http://libweb.lib.buffalo.edu/emro/search.asp. Buffalo, N.Y.: University at Buffalo Libraries.

The Electronic Library: The International Journal for the Application of Technology in Information Environments. Bradford, England: Emerald. (bimonthly)

Factsheet 5: The Definitive Guide to the Zine Revolution. San Francisco: F5. (six per year)

Five Owls: A Publication for Readers, Personally and Professionally Involved in Children's Literature. Marathon, Tex.: Jara Society. (quarterly)

Government Information Quarterly. Amsterdam: Elsevier. (quarterly)

Harvard Gay and Lesbian Review Worldwide. Boston, Mass.: Harvard Gay and Lesbian Review. (quarterly)

Horn Book Magazine: Recommending Books for Children and Young Adults. Boston, Mass: Horn Book. (bimonthly)

The Independent. New York: Independent Media Publications. (quarterly)

Kirkus Reviews: Adult, Young Adult, and Children's Book Reviews. New York: Nielsen Business Media. (monthly)

Kliatt: Reviews of Selected Current Paperbacks, Hardcover Fiction, Audiobooks, and Educational Software. Wellesley, Mass.: Kliatt. (bimonthly)

Knowledge Quest. Chicago: American Library Association (five per year)

Lambda Book Report. Washington, D.C.: Lambda Literary Foundation. (eleven per year)

Library Journal. New York: Reed. (22 per year)

Library Media Connection: Magazine for Secondary School Library Media and Technology Specialists. Worthington, Ohio: Linworth. (seven per year)

Literature Film Quarterly. Salisbury, Md.: Salisbury State College. (quarterly)

Media and Methods. Philadelphia: American Society of Educators. (five per year)

Microform and Imaging Review. Munich: K. G. Saur. (quarterly)

Multicultural Review: Dedicated to a Better Understanding of Ethnic, Racial, and Religious Diversity. Tampa, Fla.: Goldman. (quarterly)

New Technical Books. New York: New York Public Library. (bimonthly)

New York Review of Books. New York: New York Review. (20 per year)

New York Times Book Review. New York: New York Times Company. (weekly)

Notes. Canton, Mass.: Music Library Association. (quarterly)

Parents' Choice: Reviewing Children's Media since 1978. Timonium, Md.: Parents' Choice Foundation. www.parents-choice.org.

Publishers' Weekly: The Journal of the Book Industry. New York: Reed. (weekly)

Quarterly Review of Film and Video. Philadelphia: Taylor and Francis. (five per year)

Rolling Stone. New York: Rolling Stone. (biweekly)

SB & F: Your Guide to Science Resources for All Ages. Washington, D.C.: American Association for the Advancement of Science. (bimonthly)

School Library Journal: The Magazine of Children, Young Adults and School Librarians. New York: Reed. (monthly)

School Library Media Activities Monthly. Westport, Conn.: Libraries Unlimited. (ten per year)

Serials Review. Amsterdam: Elsevier. (quarterly)

Sing Out. Bethlehem, Pa.: Sing Out Corp. (quarterly)

Small Press Book Review. Southport, Conn.: Greenfield. (quarterly)

Small Press Review. Paradise, Calif.: Dustbooks. (bimonthly)

Software Encyclopedia: A Guide for Personal, Professional, and Business Users. New Providence, N.J.: R. R. Bowker. (quarterly)

Sound and Vision: Home Theater—Audio—Video—Multimedia—Movies—Music. New York: Hachette Filipacchi. (ten per year)

Teacher Librarian: The Journal for School Library Professionals. Lanham, Md.: Scarecrow. (five per year)

Technology and Learning. New York: Newbay Media. (ten per year)

TLS: The Times Literary Supplement. London: TLS Education. (weekly)

Video Choice. Peterborough, N.H.: Connell Communications. (monthly)

Video Librarian: The Video Review Guide for Libraries. Seabeck, Calif.: Video Librarian. (bimonthly)

VOYA: Voice of Youth Advocates. Lanham, Md.: Scarecrow. (bimonthly)

APPENDIX C

Sample Collection Development Policy Statements

Saint Paul Public Library Collection Development Policy

The mission of the Saint Paul Public Library is to anticipate and respond to the community's need for information; to facilitate lifelong learning; to stimulate and nurture a desire to read in young people; to provide materials to meet the interests of all ages; and to enrich the quality of life in the community.

Purpose of the Collection Development Policy

The policy reflects the mission of the Library and a commitment to intellectual freedom. The policy serves as a blueprint to guide staff in the selection and retention of materials and to inform the public of the principles supporting selection decisions. The Library serves a diverse population possessing an unlimited range of interests and tastes but the Library has limited means and must make choices to serve all said interests. Therefore, the Library partners with other libraries through consortia and organizational commitments in order to expand its capacity to make more information and materials available to citizens than would otherwise be possible.

Basic to this policy is the Library Bill of Rights as adopted by the American Library Association. This statement, together with other official interpretations by the American Library Association, is considered to be adopted by reference in this document. Final responsibility for materials selection lies with the Director of the Saint Paul Public Library who delegates to the Collection Management Librarian and other staff selectors the authority to make individual selections. The Library seeks to meet the needs of the total community, recognizing that some materials may be controversial. It is the responsibility of the individual library users to choose materials which suit his or her tastes and needs. Users are free to restrict for themselves materials of which they do not approve, but they may not restrict the freedom of others to read what they desire. Responsibility for children's use of library materials rests with their parents or legal guardians. Selection of materials for adults will not be inhibited by the possibility that such materials may be accessible to children. For more complete explanation of this policy see the section of this policy, Intellectual Freedom.

The Roles of the Library's Public Agencies

The Saint Paul Public Library system comprises a Central Library, 12 branches and Bookmobile service. The Central Library is the system's primary reference and resource center. The branch libraries primarily serve their neighborhoods, with collections and services tailored to the characteristics and information needs of the various communities. All these resources are easily accessible to users systemwide through interlibrary delivery, fax transmission, online holds, and reserves for customer pickup.

As the primary reference and resource center of the Saint Paul Public Library system, the Central Library collection is the most inclusive and comprehensive. However, the Central Library does not necessarily collect a copy of every title that is held in the system. Often the Central Library will be the first site in the library system to initiate a new service, such as new databases offered through computer access or other technological advances. The Central Library houses very expensive resources which cannot be widely purchased and materials which are less frequently used. Both reference and circulating materials are available at Central since it is the neighborhood library for those who live, work, go to school or day care in the downtown area. Included in this neighborhood base are those on job assignments for city agencies.

Branch libraries collect and access materials to meet the informational, educational, and recreational needs of their communities. These needs are continually assessed by studying population demographics; evaluating the use of the collection; monitoring community interests and activities; monitoring other services and programs available in the community; and collaborating with appropriate neighborhood organizations and schools.

Collection Priorities and Objectives

The Library's primary collection priority is to support its mission and the roles it serves in the community. Specifically these include

- To provide popular and factual materials, reference tools, materials that assist in life-long learning and multi-lingual collections. Materials will be purchased in multiple formats and will always strive to reflect the diversity of the communities the Library serves.

- To defend the Library's commitment to the protection of every person's freedom to read, establishing a balanced collection that reflects many aspects of our society and not avoiding acquiring materials that some may find controversial.

- To continue the Library tradition of meeting new demands with thoughtful innovations that respectfully build on past achievements.

Basic Selection Principles

Selectors use their training, knowledge and expertise along with [the] following standard criteria to select materials. An item need not meet all criteria to be selected.

GENERAL CRITERIA

- Relevance to current and anticipated community needs
- Suitability of subject and style for intended audience
- Critical reviews
- Reputation and qualifications of the author and/or publisher
- Cost
- Relation to the current collection and other materials on the subject
- Local significance of the author or topic
- Potential user appeal

CONTENT CRITERIA

The selection of materials includes, but is not limited to

- Comprehensiveness of treatment
- Authority, competence, reputation and purpose of the author
- Currency and accuracy of the information
- Long-term significance or interest
- Representation of diverse points of view

Selectors decide how many copies to purchase based on anticipated demand, the interests of library users in our many neighborhoods, physical space available in branches and total cost of the materials. The Library recognizes that users have differing abilities and backgrounds and thus provides materials on varying levels of difficulty and scholarship. The library does not attempt to be a historical repository of all materials which have contributed to the development of various fields of interest. The Library does not serve as an archive for the city of Saint Paul or any organization. It maintains a selective, not complete, collection of materials which document local history. Some of that material is featured in the Saint Paul Collection.

ELECTRONIC FORMATS CRITERIA

- Ease of use of the product
- Availability to multiple users, usually simultaneously
- Equipment, technology and training requirements
- Enhancement of the print equivalents in terms of speed, flexibility, combinations of search terms, full text
- Access to retrospective information
- Reduction of space requirements over print products

- Reduction or elimination of need to purchase multiple copies of a print source for multiple locations
- Cost

Gifts

The Library welcomes gifts of materials, with the understanding that the same standards of selection are applied to gifts as to materials purchased for the collection. If gifts are accepted, they will be accepted without commitment as to their final disposition and with the understanding that they may not necessarily be added to the collection. The library may choose not to accept some gifts. Those gifts added to the collection will be housed in the agency the library deems most appropriate. They may be sold if not needed in the collection.

Prospective donors should contact the library to discuss appropriate donations and procedures before dropping off gifts. A general guideline is that materials should be less than three years old. All material should be in good condition. The library will give a donor an acknowledgment of receipt, which may be used for income tax purposes, stating the number and type of materials donated. The library does not assign a value to the materials. It is a donor's responsibility to determine the value of the donated materials.

Intellectual Freedom

As the Library meets its mission it is expected that some of the materials acquired will be controversial, not suiting everyone's taste, interest or code of ethics. The Library does not select its materials on the basis of anticipated approval or disapproval. It considers the merits of the works and the need for the material in its collection. Users are free to choose what they like from the collection, to reject what they don't like, but not to restrict the freedom of others to read what they desire. Selection of materials for adults is not inhibited by the possibility that such materials are accessible to children. Moreover, the responsibility for children's use of library resources rests with their parents or legal guardians who are free to guide their children according to their particular family values.

Library selectors make a concerted effort to present various points of view on controversial subjects and to have a balanced collection. The fact that an item is included in the collection does not mean that the Library endorses any theory or statement contained in it.

The Library may include proselytizing works representing political, economic, moral, religious or other vested positions when they meet the selection criteria and the needs of the collection.

The Library does not remove, restrict or withdraw materials solely because they are regarded as discriminatory or inflammatory by an individual group.

The Library does not label materials to indicate approval or disapproval of the content or philosophy of the author, nor does it expurgate any material in the collection. Access to materials is restricted only to ensure they are available to all. For example, materials may be designated reference to ensure a copy is always available.

Because the Library is committed to freedom of information, and because information is neither intrinsically good or bad, materials are not excluded from the collection because they describe an illegal act or explain how to commit an illegal act. Materials that argue that the law is bad and should be changed are not excluded. However the Library does not collect materials which are intended to persuade the reader to commit an illegal act.

All that being said, the library staff welcome input from library users on the quality, balance, and responsiveness of the collection. Suggestion for Purchase forms are available at all library agencies to recommend books or subject areas of importance to the user.

Reprinted with the permission of the Saint Paul Public Library, Saint Paul, Minnesota. www.stpaul.lib.mn.us/userguide/collection-policy.html.

Dentistry/Dental Hygiene Collection Scope Policy

Selector

[name and contact information]

Web Page

- Subject Resources on the Bio-Medical Library web page: Dentistry www
  .biomed.lib.umn.edu/bmslist.html?id=47
- Research QuickStart—Dentistry: http://research.lib.umn.edu/rqs.phtml?
  subject_id=47&x=22&y=18
- Research QuickStart—Dental Hygiene: http://research.lib.umn.edu/rqs
  .phtml?subject_id=46&x=70&y=11

Background/Overview

The dentistry fund (1004) at the Bio-Medical Library covers acquisition of materials on dentistry and dental hygiene topics.

Primary Departments and Research Centers Profile(s)

Among the primary users of this collection are the faculty, staff, and students affiliated with the Academic Health Center, and specifically the School of Dentistry. School of Dentistry academic units include

Diagnostic and Surgical Sciences

- Oral Medicine and Diagnosis
- Oral and Maxillofacial Surgery
- Orthodontics
- TMJ and Orofacial Pain

Restorative Sciences

- Endodontics
- Operative Dentistry
- Oral Anatomy
- Patient Management
- Maxillofacial Prosthodontics
- Prosthodontics

Preventive Sciences

- Cleft Palate
- Dental Hygiene
- Health Ecology
- Neurosystems Center
- Oral Health Clinical Research Center
- Pediatric Dentistry
- Periodontology

Degree Programs Supported/Types of Degrees Offered

- B.S. (dental hygiene)
- M.S. (endodontics, orthodontics, pediatric dentistry, periodontics, prosthodontics, temporomandibular disorders and orofacial pain, oral biology, dentistry [for dentists or hygienists])
- D.D.S
- Ph.D.

Departmental Demographics

- Spring 2006 Registration for School of Dentistry—590 students.

Research Focus/Research Interest

- Minnesota Oral Health Clinical Research Center supports research projects in the areas of oral surgery, dental materials, restorative procedures, facial pain, neuroscience, caries, periodontal diseases, and oral medicine

Areas of Emphasis/Specific Areas of Emphasis

NLM Classification: WU Dentistry, Oral Surgery

- WU1-49: Reference and general works
- WU50-95: Ethics. Professional practice, and Personnel records
- WU100-113: Anatomy. Physiology. Hygiene
- WU140-166: Diseases. Injuries. Technologies. Therapeutics
- WU170-190: Dental Chemistry and Materials
- WU210-290: Dental Anatomy. Diseases
- WU300-360: Operative Dentistry
- WU400-440: Orthodontics

- WU460-495: Special Patient Groups
- WU500-530: Prosthodontics
- WU600-640: Oral Surgery

Level of Coverage

- Print and electronic journals
- Books
- Reference materials

General Exclusions/Exclusions

- Course textbooks
- Board exam preparation materials

Core Databases

- MEDLINE
- CINAHL

Reprinted with the permission of the University of Minnesota Libraries.

Pennsylvania State University Libraries

Collection Development Policy

History (HIST fund)

Latest revision: July 1, 2007

Principal Selector

[name and contact information]

I: Purpose and Programs Supported

The History fund provides primary support for the curricular and research needs of faculty and students in the History Department. The Department offers an undergraduate major and minor, and an M.A. degree en route to a Ph.D. The fund supports 40–50 faculty, 60–70 graduate students, and over 300 undergraduate minors in the History Department, as well as an indeterminate number of scholars in other disciplines whose research employs historical materials including African-American Studies, American Literature, Classics and Ancient Mediterranean Studies, Communication Arts and Sciences, Comparative Literature, Film, History of the Book, Philosophy, Political Science, Science, Medicine, and Technology in Culture, and Women's Studies. The Religious Studies Program, administratively housed within the Department of History, is primarily supported by the Religion fund.

The History Department offers a broad curriculum of undergraduate and graduate courses, and sustains a robust program of faculty and student research. In addition to national and region-based history, subjects include

> History of Religion, Diaspora Studies, Comparative Colonialism, Women and Gender History, Political and Diplomatic History, Cultural and Social History, Military History, Economic History, Labor History, Environmental History, and History of Science, Technology, and Society

Collection development is focused on acquiring materials that match Penn State's History course offerings and research interests. Current areas of Faculty strength include the early modern period, the U.S. Civil War era, and modern society. The Department has also developed faculty concentrations in thematic areas which cut across geographical or chronological lines, such as gender, the African diaspora (including Latin America and the Caribbean), and empire and colonialism. In conjunction with the Department of Classics and Ancient

Mediterranean Studies, Penn State also has a strong emphasis on Ancient history. The history selector works collaboratively with other selectors to ensure interdisciplinary needs are met.

ADDITIONAL SOURCES OF SUPPORT

Many subject specialists acquire materials related to the history of the discipline they collect for (e.g., Medicine, Anthropology, Education). Additional materials of value to historians are acquired through communication and cooperation with selectors across the libraries, including African and African American Studies, Archaeology, Art, Asian Studies, Classics and Ancient Mediterranean Studies, Comparative Literature, English, Ethnic Studies, Global Studies, Jewish Studies, Latin American Studies, Law, Lesbian, Gay, Bisexual, and Transgender Studies, Middle East Studies, Politics and Government, and Religious Studies.

In addition to subject based funds, historians rely on material purchased by related Penn State libraries including the Business Library, the News and Microforms Library, the Social Sciences Library, the Maps Library, and the Special Collections Library. Certain history of science courses depend upon the science library collections.

II: General Collection Guidelines

Location of Materials: Physical collections acquired using HIST funds are ordinarily housed at University Park. The History subject specialist consults and cooperates with subject specialists at Penn State campus libraries to ensure coverage of needed research materials at all locations.

Languages: English is the most commonly collected language, with important primary and secondary works in modern languages collected including German, French, Spanish, and to a lesser degree, Italian and Russian. Works in Chinese and Japanese are often acquired in cooperation with the Asian Studies librarian (see the collection policy statement for Asian Studies). Other languages are selectively acquired in consultation with researchers working in these areas, with an emphasis on acquiring core works, reference materials such as directories, biographies, etc., and collections of primary source documents.

Chronological Guidelines: Acquiring recent in-print publications takes priority. However, older, out-of-print materials are frequently pursued to fill gaps in the collections as they are discovered. Ordinarily no preference will be given to original printings over reprints.

Geographical Guidelines: Collecting follows the University's research and teaching emphases, with significant current concentrations in Asia, Latin America and the Caribbean, Western Europe, and the United

States. Collecting of materials concerning Eastern Europe, Canada, and modern Africa mirrors the evolving emphases of the Department. Materials related to Pennsylvania history are collected extensively.

Weeding and Deselection: By definition Historians retain an interest in older materials long after they lose value in most other disciplines. To support historical research it is understood that acquired materials will ordinarily be retained indefinitely in the collection. In the event of deselection, preference will be given to retaining works that are unique to Penn State (or held by few other libraries), and works in subject areas where Penn State has developed in-depth collections.

III: Types of Materials Collected

The collection is developed to support teaching and research in higher education. Regardless of format, academic publications are the focus.

Monographs form the largest portion of the collection and include University Press books, trade publications, conference proceedings, etc. Facsimile reproductions, anthologies, and other collections of English-language primary source documents are collected selectively as needed for teaching. These materials may be collected in greater depth for languages other than English where we lack the original documents.

Journals: Scholarly journals publishing research throughout the sub-disciplines of History are acquired in all relevant languages. Subscriptions to new journals are initiated after careful review and in consultation with the History faculty.

Theses and dissertations from institutions other than Penn State are acquired in limited numbers, typically on a case by case basis upon request.

Archival materials including rare books, original manuscripts, broadsides, interviews, and other unpublished materials, which are not in microform, are the primary responsibility of Special Collections and are covered by separate collection statements.

Microforms including primary source materials, manuscript collections, periodical and newspaper backfiles, and other items unavailable or too expensive in hard copy are often acquired on microform (microfilm, microfiche, etc.). Additional microform collections are purchased as funds permit. Often such purchases are possible only when additional funds are available through endowed library funds, Arts and Humanities Group funds, or other sources.

Government documents are acquired and managed by the Government Documents Librarian. See the statement for the U.S. federal government Depository Program.

Maps and atlases are primarily the responsibility of the Maps selector. Additional cartographic materials may be purchased on the History fund.

Historical news sources are typically acquired on microfilm, or more recently, online. The Communications selector has primary responsibility for current newspaper subscriptions. History funds are used to acquire retrospective archives of older publications as funds permit. For online, databases that provide facsimile page images are preferred over those that provide text only.

Reference works including bibliographies, dictionaries and encyclopedias, directories, indexes and abstracts are collected extensively in print and online to support faculty and student research.

Films are acquired primarily to support curricular interests in the Department.

Electronic resources are acquired for most formats, particularly scholarly journals, reference works, and collections of historical documents such as *Early American Imprints* or *Eighteenth Century Collections Online*.

The following types of materials are not ordinarily collected: minor revisions and reprints of works, works on poor quality paper, and juvenile literature. Textbooks, anthologies, and popular level publications are acquired selectively when they relate to research and teaching in the Department. Genealogical materials are not collected excepting resources relevant to historical researchers such as the U.S. Census Manuscripts, or selected items documenting central Pennsylvania history.

IV: Other General Considerations

All selectors are guided by the Collection Development Guideline adopted by the Dean's Library Council in 2001. In addition the Collection Development Council has begun working on Core Principles to guide the overall development of the collection.

V: Collection Levels

The levels below reflect existing collection strengths, which are heavily influenced by the cumulative impact of prior collection decisions. It is not a statement of desirable future collection levels. These will evolve with the interests of historical scholars. Collecting patterns and strengths within the broad categories are in the "Comments" column.

(F = non-English language collection level; E = English language collection level)

Subject	Collection Level	Comments
Auxiliary Sciences of History	3	See also the appropriate collection policy statements for CC (Archaeology), CJ (Numismatics), and CN (Inscriptions, Epigraphy).
History, General	4E, 3F	
Great Britain	4	
France	4E, 3F	
Germany	4E, 3F	
Mediterranean, Greco-Roman World		See the Statement for Classics and Ancient Mediterranean Studies. Modern history of the region is collected at level 3E and level 2F.
Italy	4E, 3F	See also the Collection Statement for Classics and Ancient Mediterranean Studies.
Netherlands and Belgium	3	
Eastern Europe, Balkans	3E, 2F	Acquisitions relating to the Ottoman Empire have recently increased.
Russia, U.S.S.R.	4E, 3F	
Northern Europe, Scandinavia	3	Emphasis on trade and relations in the early modern world.
Spain	4	See also the Spanish Collection Development Policy.
Portugal	3	
Asia	4E, 3F	Acquisitions have strengthened since the 1990s with an emphasis on China, Japan, and India.
Middle East	4E, 3F	
Africa	4	
Indians, North America	4	
United States	4	All time periods, with an emphasis on Slavery and the Civil War Era, African American history, women's history.
New England, Atlantic Coast	4	Pennsylvania history collected at near level 5.
Southern U.S., Gulf States	4	
Midwest, Mississippi Valley	3	
The West	3	Increasing emphasis since early 2000s in conjunction with new Latino/a Studies minor.
Latin America	3	Areas closer to level 4 include Mexico, the Caribbean, and topics such as African Diaspora, colonialism.
Canada	2	

VI: Priorities for Future Collection Efforts

- Continue to pay special attention to Women's history and African American history.
- Support new areas of interest in the Department such as Latino/a Borderlands Studies, and Ottoman History.
- Expand subjects collected at Level 3 and 4 in languages other than English.
- Continued purchase of microform and online primary source materials
- Expand upon current strengths in historical newspapers from the United States and Pennsylvania to include more international titles, and titles from minority populations in the United States.

Reprinted with the permission of the Pennsylvania State University Libraries.

APPENDIX D

Contracts and Licensing Terms

A contract is a formal, legally binding written agreement between two or more parties. At its most basic, a contract consists of an offer, acceptance of the offer, and consideration, which is the exchange of something of value in the eyes of the law (e.g., a good, service, or money). The publisher or vendor (e.g., licensor) offers a product with terms and conditions set forth in the contract, the library accepts the offer, and the vendor provides access to the product for which the library pays a fee. The licensor is free to ask whatever price and set whatever conditions on use the market will bear. A license or license agreement is a legally binding form of contract through which a library (the licensee) pays for the right to use or access a resource, usually for a fixed period of time. A lease is a contract by which one party grants access to another party to use a resource for a specified term and for a specified amount.

The terms that follow are presented in the order in which they usually appear in a contract for an electronic resource.

Content. The contract should describe the product and make clear if the library is acquiring a product or content that it can keep forever, leasing content, or purchasing the rights to access the product. It should state whether or not the library has any permanent rights to the product, perhaps the files in existence at the time the contract is terminated.

Parties. The parties (the licensee and licensor) to the agreement are named or defined. If a library is part of a larger institution or organization, the licensee may be the firm or corporation, the college or the university, or the executive board, board of education, or board of regents.

Definitions. All potentially disputable terms should be defined. The most important of these are *authorized user* and *authorized site*. Authorized users are those individuals authorized under the contract to have access to the product. They may be the citizens of a state; currently enrolled students, faculty, and staff of an educational institution; or current employees of a specific office in a corporation. A college or university may wish to ensure that visiting lecturers, emeriti, and part-time students are also authorized users. Many academic libraries seek to permit insubstantial use by unaffiliated, walk-in users; these are part of the definition of *authorized users*. If the library expects to provide the resource to remote users, this should be addressed in the definition. The authorized site is the physical location where the licensee provides access to the e-resources. Libraries with several branches or located on several campuses or in several buildings should ensure that the authorized site(s) defines these.

Authentication. This is the process through which the identity of authorized users is verified before access is granted and often is specified in the agreement. Some common methods are passwords and user IDs, Internet protocol (IP) addresses, and public keys and digital certificates.

Grant of rights and restrictions. Rights are the permitted uses of the licensed digital information. By contract law, any rights not expressly granted in the license agreement are reserved to the licensor. Typical rights are user rights to search, browse, retrieve, view, display, download, and print the search results; store or save them to disk for a specific period; forward electronically to others or to oneself; fax to oneself and to others; and library rights to use the product in interlibrary loan transactions, distance education, and course reserves. Most contracts explicitly prohibit copying substantial portions of the database, downloading or printing issues of a journal, or modifying the search software or content. Type of use may be restricted to, for example, academic or noncommercial use. Some may grant the right to the library to make and save a copy of the e-resource and of the software during the duration of the contract.

Contractual obligations. Contracts typically assign obligations to both parties. Obligations of the licensor may include training staff, providing user support updates, replacing defective products, guaranteeing hours of access and service for a remote resource, and protecting the privacy of users. The library may seek to obligate the licensor to provide use statistics. Library obligations most often have to do with the level and type of security provided. Care must be taken so that the library does not promise a level of control it cannot provide. Another common contractual obligation is to keep financial aspects of the agreement confidential. A breach is the failure of a party to perform a contractual obligation.

Penalties. Penalties are applied when contractual obligations are not fulfilled. Examples are a penalty fee charged a library for a late payment or immediate cancellation of access if contractual obligations are breached.

Warranties. Warranties are promises or assurance made by parties to the contract. The licensor may guarantee hours of access or server performance for a remote resource. Another typical warranty is the assurance that the licensor legally owns the copyright to or the content of the product.

Payment and cost. This section lays out the terms of payment—cost, how it is determined, and payment schedule.

Contract term and termination. The term of the contract is its duration, which may or may not match the term of the subscription. It may be automatically renewed unless the licensee notifies the licensor. The section dealing with termination specifies under what conditions the contract can be terminated—for failure to fulfill obligations or deception in the warranties. For example, the licensor may specify immediate termination of access in the case of a security breach. Libraries usually ask for a cure period in which to remedy a breach.

Indemnity and limitation of liability. Indemnification is one party's agreement to insure or otherwise defend another party against any claims by third parties resulting from performance under the agreement. It can, for example, provide for financial compensation should the warranties made in the contract prove false. A limit of liability clause sets out how much and what kind of damages are to be paid for remedies. Many libraries have policies that forbid them from indemnifying a licensor or holding them harmless to other parties.

Force majeure. This clause excuses the licensor from poor performance or nondelivery in the case of conditions beyond the reasonable control of the vendor. Typical instances are war, postal strikes, and acts of terrorism.

Governing law. Governing law identifies the state's or country's law or courts under which a dispute relating to the contract are to be adjudicated. Libraries usually negotiate for the laws of the state in which they are located; the licensor prefers the state or country in which its primary office is located. A reasonable compromise is to agree to adjudicate the dispute in the state or country in which the grieving party is located.

Amendments. These are any modifications to the original contract. They should be dated and signed by all parties who signed the original agreement.

Authorized signature. The contract is signed by an individual authorized to represent the parties to the contract. Care should be taken in a library that signatory authority is carefully controlled; this helps ensure thoughtful review of contracts by focusing responsibility within the library. All parties to the contract should receive signed and countersigned copies.

Archives and perpetual access. Libraries signing contracts should consider the importance they are willing to place on access to archived materials, if such an archive exists. Most contracts provide access to or use of a product only during the duration of the agreement. Some may include a provision to provide files created during the term of the contract in a specified format (perhaps CD-ROM) or a format yet to be determined. A perpetual license guarantees access to those files after the contract is terminated.

A-Z serials list. Listing of a library's **serial** holdings, usually available via the library's website and providing direct links from the entry to the serial.

Accrual method. Accounting method that focuses on the passage of time (usually a fiscal year) to recognize revenues and expenses.

Acid-free. Materials with a pH value of 7.0 (neutral) or greater (alkaline).

Acidic. Having a pH value less than 7.0 (neutral).

Acquisition. (1) Process of obtaining and receiving physical library materials or access to online resources. (2) Organizational unit within a library that handles the acquisitions function.

Agent. Individual or company that acts as an intermediary between a library and a **publisher** in the purchase of materials, such as a **subscription** service that manages **periodical** subscriptions. *See also* **vendor.**

Aggregation. Process of gathering information from multiple websites.

Aggregator. (1) Service or intermediary that provides access to a large number of **electronic journals** and, perhaps, other electronic resources from different **publishers** and offers the end user access to these journals through a single interface. (2) More broadly, organization, individual, or application that gathers content from multiple sources for presentation elsewhere.

Agreement. Understanding between two or more parties. *See also* **contract.**

Allocation. (1) The amount distributed to **fund lines** in the **budget.** (2) The process of distributing financial resources.

Alternative literature. Publications not part of the dominate culture and not sharing the perspectives and beliefs of that culture.

Alternative press. Small, independent **publisher.** Alternative presses often address social issues and the interests of minority and diverse populations and publish innovative and experimental works.

Amendment. Addition to the terms of an **agreement.**

American National Standards Institute (ANSI). Private, nonprofit organization that administers and coordinates the U.S. voluntary standardization and conformity assessment system.

Analog. Pertaining to data represented by a continuous, physically measurable quantity. Analog data cannot be processed by computer unless it is first translated into **digital** format.

Appropriation. Funds granted through formal action by a controlling or funding authority.

Approval plan. Method of acquiring library materials, usually books. The **vendor** supplies books automatically, according to a **profile** from the library, which may keep or return the books to the vendor. Some plans provide advance **notification slips** instead of sending the physical item. *See also* **blanket order.**

Approval profile. *See* **profile.**

Archivally sound. Nontechnical term describing a material or product that is permanent, durable, free of contaminates, and chemically stable. No formal standards exist to specify how long "archivally sound" material will last.

Area specialist. *See* **subject specialist.**

Artifact. Physical object made or modified by a person.

Assessment. *See* **collection assessment.**

Association for Library Collections and Technical Services (ALCTS). Division of the American Library Association that serves the needs of those who are responsible for the following activities: **selection, evaluation** and **assessment, acquisition,** cataloging, classification, management, and **preservation** of library materials.

Association of American Publishers (AAP). Principal trade association of the book publishing industry.

Association of Research Libraries (ARL). Organization of approximately 120 leading university and research libraries in the United States and Canada.

Audit. Systematic evaluation of procedures, operations, and cash records to determine whether they conform to established financial criteria.

Authentication. Process that verifies the identity of a person or process, usually through a user name and password. In security systems, authentication is distinct from **authorization.** Authentication confirms that the individual is who he or she claims to be but does not address authorization.

Authorization. Process that gives or denies an individual access rights to an online resource based on his or her identity, which often is matched against a directory with various profiles granting various types of access. Most computer security systems are based on a two-step process: **authentication,** followed by authorization.

Authorized signature. Signature of a person legally empowered to represent a party to a **contract.**

Authorized user. Person having permission, under a **contract,** to access or use an electronic resource.

Back file or **back run.** Issues of a periodical that precede the current issue.

Balanced scorecard. Management and measurement system that links strategic objectives to a comprehensive range of key performance indicators, to provide a balanced view.

Banned book. Book that has been prohibited or suppressed by a governing or religious authority because its content is considered objectionable or dangerous (or both), usually for moral, political, or cultural reasons. *See also* **censorship** and **intellectual freedom.**

Bibliographer. Usually, a **subject specialist** in a larger library, whose primary or sole responsibility is selecting for and managing a collection; may be used interchangeably with **selector.**

Bibliographic utility. Online service that provides a shared **database** of cataloging records created by member libraries. The database may be used for copy cataloging, **interlibrary loan, selection,** and bibliographic verification.

Bibliography. (1) Systematic list of works by an individual author on a given subject, or of works that share one or more characteristics. (2) List of references to sources cited in the text of an article or book, or for further reading.

Bibliometrics. Use of mathematical and statistical methods to study the usage of materials and services within a library or to analyze the historical development of a specific body of literature. *See also* **citation analysis.**

Big Deal. License agreement, often multiyear, that provides access to all or a substantial portion of titles from a single publisher. Libraries participating in such an agreement usually have limited ability to select titles, and canceling titles before the end of the contract period results in financial penalties.

Blanket order. Order placed with a **publisher, vendor,** or distributor to supply automatically all publications that match a **profile.** Blanket orders can be for a single publisher's series, all publications of an individual publisher, or all materials of a particular type or subject. Most blanket orders do not allow returns.

Blog. Web log functioning as a journal or newsletter of short, dated entries posted on the Web; frequently updated and intended for general public consumption.

Bookseller. Person in the business of selling new or used books and related materials to the retail trade. *See also* **dealer** and **jobber.**

Born digital. Created originally in digital format.

Breach. Failure to perform an obligation set forth in a **contract.**

Brittleness. Fragility of paper due to acid-caused deterioration. The standard test for brittleness in paper is whether a corner can withstand folding in each direction twice.

Budget. (1) Plan for the use of money available during a **fiscal year,** reflecting **allocations,** expected revenues, and projected expenditures. (2) Total amount of funds available to meet a library's expenditures over a fixed period of time. *See also* **fund line** and **materials budget.**

Bundling. (1) Practice of providing a group of serial titles to a library. (2) Practice of providing access to an online version packaged with subscription to the print version, or vice versa.

Cancellation. Termination of a subscription, a standing order, or firm order.

Capital expenditure or **capital expense.** One-time **expenditure,** expected to benefit more than the current period and recorded as an asset. Library materials expenditures are usually capitalized, except in the case of expenditures for the rights to access an online resource.

Cash accounting method. Method of bookkeeping that records transactions when a cash exchange has taken place, that is, when an account is paid, not when an expense in incurred.

Censorship. Suppression or prohibition of the production, distribution, circulation, or display of a work on grounds that it contains objectionable or dangerous material. Censored materials may be deemed objectionable on moral, political, military, or other grounds. *See also* **banned book.**

Center for Research Libraries (CRL). Cooperative, nonprofit organization of research institutions, located in Chicago, intended to increase research resources available for scholarly use. Members can deposit little-used publications at CRL, which also acquires esoteric, little-used, and expensive materials to lend to members.

Children's Internet Protection Act (CIPA). Federal law that requires public libraries and schools to install filters on their Internet computers to retain federal funding and discounts for computers and computer access.

CIC. *See* **Committee on Institutional Cooperation.**

Circulation analysis. Examination of statistics compiled on the circulation of library materials, usually broken down by classification, material type, category of borrower, time of year, and so on, to determine patterns of usage.

Citation analysis. Technique in **bibliometrics** that examines the works cited in publications to determine patterns. Two methods are counting the number of times a **journal** title appears in footnotes and bibliographies, and counting the number of times a title is cited by local faculty.

Clapp-Jordan formula. Quantitative method, developed by Verner W. Clapp and Robert T. Jordan, to calculate the total number of volumes required for minimum-level collection adequacy in an academic library.

Classed analysis. Format for collection analysis that describes the collection and, perhaps, current collecting levels and desired future collecting levels in abbreviated language and numerical codes, according to a classification scheme.

Client-centered. *See* **user-centered.**

CLOCKSS (Controlled LOCKSS). Partnership of publishers, libraries, and OCLC that provides a **dark archive,** for **electronic journal** content. *See also* **LOCKSS.**

Closed stacks. Shelving area in a library to which only library staff members have access.

Collection. Group of materials assembled by a library or a private individual. A library collection consists of both physical items held by the library and digital resources (local and online) selected and organized by the library and accessed by library users and staff members.

Collection assessment. Systematic quantitative and qualitative measurement of the degree to which a library's collections meet the library's goals and objectives and the needs of its users. *See also* **collection evaluation.**

Collection-centered analysis. Analytical method that focuses on the collection itself, not on its users.

Collection condition survey. Detailed survey of the physical nature and condition of the collection.

Collection development. Originally used to mean activities involved in developing a library collection in response to institutional priorities and user needs and interests—that is, the **selection** of materials to build a collection. Collection development was understood to cover several activities related to the development of library collections, including selection, determination and coordination of policies, needs assessment, collection use studies, collection analysis, **budget** management, community and user **outreach** and **liaison,** and planning for **resource sharing.** Now the term is often used interchangeably with or in combination with **collection management.**

Collection Development and Evaluation Section (CODES). Section of the References and User Services Association, a division of the American Library Association, that addresses the collection development interests of reference and user services librarians in libraries of all types.

Collection development officer (CDO). Individual within a library charged with managing or overseeing collections-related activities. This person may also have an organizational title, such as assistant university librarian for collection development, deputy librarian for collections, or collections coordinator.

Collection development policy, collection development and management policy, or **collection policy.** Formal written statement of the principles guiding a library's **selection** of books and other materials, including the criteria used in selection, **deselection,** and acceptance of gifts. It may also address **intellectual freedom,** future goals, and special areas of attention.

Collection evaluation. Systematic consideration of a collection to determine its intrinsic merit. Evaluation seeks to examine or describe collections either in their own terms or in relation to other collections and checking mechanisms (lists, standards, etc.). *See also* **collection assessment.**

Collection management. Proposed in the 1980s as a term under which **collection development** was to be subsumed. In this construct, collection management includes collection development and an expanded suite of decisions about **withdrawal,** transfer, canceling **serials, storage,** and **preservation.** Collection development and collection management tend to be used synonymously or in tandem.

Collection mapping. Technique for graphically representing the strengths and weaknesses of a library collection, used primarily in school library media centers. The categories of the collection map are usually based on the curricular needs of the school, often presented through **curriculum mapping.** *See also* **Conspectus.**

Collection profile. Statistical picture of a collection at one point in time.

Collections librarian. *See* **selector.**

Committee on Institutional Cooperation (CIC). Academic consortium of twelve major teaching and research universities in the Midwest, with programs and activities in all aspects of university activity except intercollegiate athletics. The Center for Library Initiatives, a unit of the CIC, focuses on the activities of the libraries at CIC member institutions.

Common good. Something shared and beneficial for all (or most) members of a given community. *See also* **public good.**

Compact storage or **compact shelving.** Storage area for less used materials in stacks that are either designed with narrower aisles and higher-than-normal shelves or mobile and compacted by being moved together. Compact storage accommodates more materials than conventional stack arrangements.

Concurrent use. Simultaneous use of digital information by more than one user.

Conservation. Noninvasive physical or chemical methods employed to ensure the survival of manuscripts, books, and other **documents.** *See also* **preservation** and **restoration.**

Consortium. Two or more libraries that have formally agreed to coordinate, cooperate in, or consolidate certain functions. Consortia may be formed on the basis of locality, function, type, format, or subject.

Conspectus. Comprehensive collection survey instrument, first developed by the Research Libraries Group, to record existing collection strengths, current collecting intensities, and intended future intensities. The Conspectus is arranged by subject, classification, or a combination of these two and contains standardized codes for languages of materials collected and for collection or collecting levels.

Constituency. Users and potential users of a library.

Contingency fund. Amount set aside, usually at the beginning of the **allocation** process, in a **budget** to cover unexpected or unplanned **expenditures** and emergencies.

Contingency planning. Process of preparing a plan of action to be put into effect when prior arrangements become impossible or certain preestablished conditions arise.

Continuation order. *See* **standing order.**

Contract. Formal, legally binding written agreement between two or more parties. *See also* **license.**

Cooperative collection development. Sharing responsibilities among two or more libraries for the process of acquiring materials, developing collections, and managing the growth and maintenance of collections in a way that benefits users and leverages investments.

Copyright. Set of exclusive **rights** to permit or forbid particular uses of a work for a specified period of time. In the United States, copyright is defined by statute. Copyright gives the author, the author's employer, or anyone to whom the author transfers his or her right the legal ability to control who may copy, adapt, distribute, publicly perform, or publicly display his or her work, subject to certain legal exceptions.

Copyright Term Extension Act (CTEA). Passed in 1998, this legislation extended the duration of **copyright** an additional twenty years. Also called the Sonny Bono Copyright Term Extension Act.

Core collection. (1) Collection intended to meet the basic information needs of a library's primary user group. (2) Collection that represents the intellectual nucleus of a discipline.

Council on Library and Information Resources (CLIR). Formed by a merger of the Council on Library Resources (CLR) and the Commission on Preservation and Access in 1997, CLIR is an independent foundation that supports initiatives in **preservation** awareness, **digital** libraries, information economics, resources for scholarship, and international developments in library and information science.

Creative Commons. Organization founded in 2001 that has defined an alternative to copyrights by filling in the gap between full copyright, in which no use is permitted without permission, and public domain, where permission is not required at all. Creative Commons' licenses let people copy and distribute the work under specific conditions.

Cure period. Time within which a party to a contract has to fix a contractual **breach.**

Curriculum mapping. Process of documenting by teacher, grade, and class what is taught over an academic year; the structured overview usually contains a time line, content, units or broad activities, and perhaps applicable standards and benchmarks.

Dark archive. Repository that protects digital content as a failsafe measure, to be used only if the content is not available elsewhere. *See also* **light archive.**

Database. (1) Large store of digitized information, consisting of records of uniform format organized for ease and speed of search and retrieval, managed by a database management system. (2) In libraries, usually a set of records that provides bibliographic information from indexes and abstracts; may or may not include full-text articles associated with the bibliographic information.

Deaccession. *See* **withdrawal.**

Deacidification. Process of chemically reducing the acid content of paper to a pH of 7.0 (neutral) or higher. Deacidification may also deposit an alkaline buffer intended to neutralize any acids that develop in the future.

Dealer. Individual or commercial company in the business of buying and selling new books, used books, or rare books for resale to libraries, collectors, and other booksellers. *See also* **bookseller** and **jobber.**

Deed of gift. Signed **document** stating the terms of agreement under which legal title to property, such as a gift to a library or archives, is transferred, voluntarily and without remuneration, by the donor to the recipient institution, with or without conditions.

Democratic planning. Cyclic planning process in which all units are requested to formulate their plans for program development on a regular schedule. The source of ideas rests with individuals and individual units, and these ideas are assembled into a coherent plan for the larger organization.

Depository Library. A U.S. library legally designated to receive, without charge, all or a portion of the government documents provided by the U.S. Government Printing Office and other federal agencies to the superintendent of documents for distribution under the Federal Depository Library Program.

Deselection. Usually applied to the process of identifying serial **subscriptions** for cancellation. *See also* **withdrawal.**

Desiderata file. List of materials needed and wanted by a library, to be purchased when money is available or when the item is located.

Differential pricing. (1) Practice of charging different rates based on the geographic location of the customer library and the number of users, or both. (2) Practice of charging different rates to institutions and individuals.

Digital. Of, pertaining to, or using digits, that is, numbers. Computers are digital machines because, at their most basic level, they distinguish between two values, 0 and 1. *See also* **analog.**

Digital divide. Metaphorical term for the separation between people who have ready access to a personal computer and those who do not.

Digital Library Federation (DLF). **Consortium** of major libraries and library-related agencies dedicated to establishing, maintaining, expanding, and preserving a distributed collection of **digital** materials accessible to scholars, students, and a wider public.

Digital materials. Both digital **surrogates** created by converting **analog** materials to **digital** format and born-digital materials for which there is no analog equivalent.

Digital Millennium Copyright Act (DMCA). Law updating U.S. copyright law, passed in 1998, intended to protect **rights** to intellectual property in **digital** form.

Digital repository. Computer server where digital content is stored and made accessible to a user community. Digital repositories may be open to all or require **authentication.**

Digital rights management (DRM). Technologies, tools, and processes that protect intellectual property during **digital** content commerce by enabling secure distribution or disabling illegal distribution or both of the data.

Digitization. Process of converting **analog** materials to **digital** format.

Direct order. Order placed with a publisher instead of with a vendor or other intermediate supplier.

Disaster preparedness plan or **disaster response plan.** Procedures prepared in advance by a library to deal with an unexpected occurrence (flood, fire, earthquake, etc.) that has the potential to cause injury to personnel or damage to equipment, collections, and facilities. *See also* **contingency planning.**

Discretionary purchase. Individual order for an item or items placed by a library that is outside any existing **approval plan, blanket order** plan, serial **subscription,** or other **nondiscretionary purchase.** *See also* **firm order.**

Document. Object that comprises intellectual or artistic content or both and is conceived, produced, and/or issued as an entity.

Document delivery. Provision of documents upon request. Commercial document delivery services charge a fee to provide libraries or individuals with the requested item. The commercial service usually manages payments to **publishers** for copying **rights.**

EDI (Electronic Data Interchange). Transfer of data between different entities using a network, usually the Internet.

Electronic book or **e-book.** Book created in **digital** format, or converted from print to digital format, for electronic distribution.

Electronic journal or **e-journal.** Serial publication available in **digital** format.

Electronic resources management system (ERMS). Automated system used to manage the creation, use, and maintenance of information related to electronic resource contracts.

Embargo. Publisher-imposed block on access to current content of electronic journals. The length of the embargo varies by publisher and is called a **moving wall.**

Emergency plan. *See* **contingency planning** and **disaster preparedness plan.**

Emulation. Techniques for imitating obsolete systems on future generations of computers and thus providing continued access to **digital** content formatted on early systems.

En bloc or **en masse.** Acquired at one time or through a single purchase decision, applied, for example, to the acquisition of a large collection of materials.

Encumbrance. Recorded commitment of monies for an anticipated purchase. An encumbrance at the end of a **fiscal year** is carried forward into the next fiscal year as an outstanding commitment.

Endowment. Permanent fund consisting of gifts and bequests invested to earn interest. The interest can be spent, sometimes for purposes specified by the donor(s), leaving the principal intact to generate further income.

Entrepreneurial planning. Laissez-faire, individual approach to planning that relies on individuals coming forward whenever they have an idea for altering or expanding programs. Sometimes called opportunistic planning.

Environmental scanning. Method used to gather information and enhance understanding of an organization's environment and constituents. Its purpose is to detect, monitor, and analyze trends and issues in the environment, both internal and external, in which an organization operates.

Ephemera. Materials of everyday life not normally retained because they are perceived to have little or no permanent value. Pamphlets, leaflets, fliers, performance programs, and comic books often are considered ephemera. Sometimes called fugitive material. *See also* **gray literature.**

Ethics. Principles of conduct or standards of behavior governing an individual or a profession. These standards may be legal, moral, personal, or institutional.

Evaluation. *See* **collection evaluation.**

Exchange. (1) Arrangement in which a library sends items it owns to another library and receives in return items owned by the other library or sends duplicate copies to another library and receives duplicate materials in return. (2) Any publication given or received in this manner.

Expenditure. Payment made during the current fiscal period.

Fair Use. The legal right, codified in Section 107 of the 1987 U.S. Copyright Act, which permits use of copyrighted work for education, scholarship, teaching, news reporting, commentary, and research purposes.

Farmington Plan. A federally funded program (1948–72) intended to ensure that at least one copy of every book important for research, regardless of place of publication, is available in at least one U.S. library.

Firm order. Purchase order for an item submitted to a **publisher** or **vendor.** Money is encumbered for these orders, and the materials cannot normally be returned unless defective or damaged. Firm orders normally are placed for materials requested by individual selectors. *See also* **discretionary purchase.**

Fiscal year. Accounting or **budget** twelve-month cycle.

Fixed asset. Item with a determined and continuing value owned by the organization.

Focus group. Technique for gathering opinions and perspectives on a specific topic. A small group of people, with common interests or characteristics, is led by a moderator, who asks questions and facilitates group interaction on the topic being investigated.

Folksonomy. Collaborative approach to describing content, usually on the Web, by assigning descriptive words that are selected by individuals and not associated with a thesaurus or established subject term source.

Force majeure ("greater force"). Clause that protects a party to a **contract** against failures to perform contractual obligations caused by unavoidable events beyond the party's control.

Free balance. Money available for purchasing. The free balance is the **allocation** minus payments made and any **encumbrances.**

FTP (file transfer protocol). Communication method for transferring data between computers on the Internet.

Fund or **fund line.** Self-balancing account in a **budget** with monies set aside for a specific purpose.

Fund accounting. Process of dividing an organization's budget into categories, usually according to prescribed regulations, restrictions, and limitations.

Fund balance. Amount remaining in a **fund** that is the difference between assets (**allocations** or revenue or both) and liabilities (expenses and **encumbrances**). For most funds, a fund balance is available for additional **allocation** or spending.

Fund-raising. Programs and activities intended to encourage benefactors to contribute to a library or library system.

Gift. Items or money donated to a library, usually by an individual but sometimes by a group, organization, estate, or other library.

Governing law. Jurisdiction under which a dispute related to a **contract** is adjudicated.

Graphic novel. Book-length illustrated story.

Gray (or Grey) literature. Printed works such as reports, internal documents, dissertations, and conference proceedings, not usually available through regular market channels because they were never commercially published, listed, or priced. *See also* **ephemera.**

Historical budgeting. *See* **incremental budgeting.**

Holdings. The entire **collection** of materials owned by a library or library system, usually listed in a catalog.

HTML (hypertext markup language). Tagging scheme used to create **hypertext** documents accessible via the Web. Tags imbedded in the text control formatting.

Hypertext. Method of presenting **digital** information that allows related files and elements of data to be interlinked dynamically rather than viewed in linear sequence.

Impact factor. Measure of the importance of a journal in a subject field: the number of times an article is cited within a given time period divided by the number of articles published during that period.

Incentive planning. Planning model that views an organization in economic terms and has an incentive structure that rewards particular types of activities. Incentives are frequently financial—increased budget **allocations** or the opportunity to retain funds generated through various activities or operations.

Incremental budgeting. Process by which historical **allocations** are added to or subtracted from a standard amount or percentage.

Indemnity. One party's agreement to insure or otherwise defend another party against any claims by third parties resulting from performance or nonperformance under the **contract.**

Inflation rate. Percentage the level of prices rises, usually in one year.

Infringement. Unauthorized use of materials protected by copyright, patent, trademark law, or contract.

Inputs. Resources (e.g., money, staff, collections) that provide a service or program.

Integrated library system (ILS). Group of automated library subsystems working together and communicating within the same set or system of software to control such activities as circulation, cataloging, acquisitions, and serials control.

Integrating resource. Library information resource that is added to or changed by means of updates that do not remain discrete but rather are integrated into the whole.

Intellectual freedom. The **right** granted in the First Amendment to the U.S. Constitution that permits a person to read or express views that may be unpopular or offensive to some people, within certain limitations. *See also* **banned book** and **censorship.**

Intellectual Freedom Round Table (IFRT). A round table in the **American Library Association** that advocates freedom of access and expression in libraries, provides support to librarians and other library employees who may be facing **censorship,** and monitors legal and other developments in **intellectual freedom** that affect libraries.

Intellectual property. Products of the human mind, creativity, and intelligence that are entitled to the legal status of personal property, especially works protected by **copyright,** patented inventions, and registered trademarks.

Interlibrary loan or **interlibrary lending** (ILL). Transaction in which one library requests and another library lends an item from its collections (a returnable) or furnishes a copy, either paper or **digital,** of the item (a nonreturnable) to another library.

International Coalition of Library Consortia (ICOLC). Informal, self-organized group established in 1997, composed of more than 150 library consortia from around the world, and intended to facilitate discussion among consortia on issues of common interest.

Interoperability. Condition achieved when two or more technical systems can exchange information directly.

Inventory profiling. *See* **Conspectus.**

Invoice. Report sent to a purchaser by a **vendor** or other supplier indicating the total amount owed for items sold and services rendered. An invoice includes sufficient descriptive information to identify the item or service clearly.

Invoice download. Electronic transmission of invoice data from a supplier's automated system to the library's system.

IP (Internet protocol) address. Physical address of a computer attached to a **network** governed by the **TCP/IP** protocol.

ISO (International Organization for Standardization). Network of national standards institutes from 140 countries working in partnership with international organizations, governments, industry, and business and consumer representatives.

Jobber. Wholesale **dealer** who stocks new books and nonprint materials issued by various **publishers** and supplies them to bookstores or libraries on order, usually at a discount. Some jobbers offer customized services such as **continuation orders, approval plans,** cataloging, and technical processing.

Journal. Serial that disseminates original research and commentary on current developments within a specific subject area, discipline, or field of study. Librarians distinguish between journals and magazines, but **publishers** and users often use the terms interchangeably; for example, *Ladies Home Journal* is considered a **magazine** by librarians.

JSTOR. Nonprofit organization that provides searchable bibliographic **databases** containing the complete full-text **back files** of core scholarly journals in a wide range of disciplines, current to two to five years.

Lease. Contract by which one party grants access to or the use of real estate, equipment, or a resource for a specified term and for a specified dollar amount to another party.

Liability. Legal responsibility for an act or failure to act.

Liaison. Communication for establishing and maintaining mutual understanding and cooperation; in academic libraries, denotes librarians' responsibilities to work with and reach out to academic departments in order to better meet their needs. *See also* **outreach.**

Library binding. Especially strong and durable binding, usually conforming to the **ANSI** standard for library binding.

Library cooperation. Methods by which libraries and library systems work together for mutual benefit, including **cooperative collection development,** cooperative cataloging, exchange of bibliographic information, **resource sharing,** and union catalogs.

Library network. Mechanism that links libraries through shared bibliographic utilities or other formal arrangements.

Library survey. Written or oral question-and-answer instrument designed to elicit feedback from library users.

License or **licensing agreement.** Permission to do something which, without such permission, would be illegal. A license is a **contract** that presents the terms under which a **vendor** grants a license to a library, granting the **rights** to use one or more proprietary bibliographic **databases** or online resources, usually for a fixed period of time in exchange for payment.

Licensee. Party to a **contract** receiving permission or the **rights** to access or use an electronic resource.

Licensor. Party to a **contract** granting permission or the **rights** to use or access an electronic resource.

Light archive. Data storage site that can be accessed by authorized users.

Line-item budget. Detailed financial plan or method of tracking allocation and expenditures by categories.

Link resolver. Tool that enables users of online library resources to navigate from a cited resources (e.g., journal article or abstract) to a full-text copy of the cited item.

LOCKSS (Lots of Copies Keep Stuff Safe). **Open-source** software, developed at Stanford University, that enables participating libraries to store and manage digital content.

Macro selection. Adding large quantities of materials to the library or access to numerous resources through a single decision. *See also* **micro selection.**

Magazine. Popular-interest **serial** publication usually containing articles on a variety of topics, written by various authors in a nonscholarly style. *See also* **journal.**

Management report. Term used in libraries for statistical and informational reports, typically used in acquisitions and collection management activities, produced by vendors or locally by libraries.

Manga (lit. "whimsical pictures"). Commonly used in reference to all Japanese comics, or those created in that style, particularly **graphic novels.**

Marketing. Umbrella term denoting several activities: understanding an entity's market (in the case of a library—its present and future users), planning how best to serve that market, implementing the plan, and assessing its effectiveness.

Master planning. Top-down planning that begins in the administrative offices of an organization.

Materials budget. Portion of a library's budget allocated for the purchase of books, media, **serials,** and other information resources. Some libraries include electronic resources, postage and service charges associated with acquiring materials, and **conservation** and **preservation** in the materials budget; others have separate allocations for them. This part of the budget may also be called the acquisition budget, access budget, or collections budget.

Mending. Minor **restoration** of a book's condition, not requiring replacement of material or removal of the text block from the cover. *See also* **repair** and **rebinding.**

Metadata (lit. "data about data"). Metadata are used for different purposes: (1) Resource description or resource discovery metadata serve to identify and locate a piece of information. Library cataloging is one specific use of a subset of resource discovery metadata; Dublin Core is an example of this descriptive metadata. The Dublin Core contains a **rights** element as well as descriptive elements. (2) Rendering is the process of realizing a specific information object on the user's computer. To do this, the receiving computer needs technical information, transmitted by metadata, about the characteristics of the object; for example, the need to open Adobe Acrobat to access a web-based **document** is conveyed in metadata imbedded in that document in the file extension. (3) Rights management is related to the ownership of content and the right of a user to carry out any operation on that informational object. This may involve making a payment to the owner of the right, or the operation (e.g., viewing, downloading, printing) may be carried out free of charge under an existing license agreement.

Micro selection. Selecting titles to acquire or to which a library will provide access individually, one title at a time. *See also* **macro selection.**

Migration. Transferring **digital** resources from one hardware or software configuration to another or from one generation of computer technology to another.

Monograph. Any nonserial publication, either complete in one volume or intended to be completed in a finite number of successive parts issued at regular or irregular intervals, consisting of a single work or collection of works.

Monographic series. Group of individual **monographs** that have a collective title applying to the group as a whole. Monographic series may be numbered or unnumbered; publication is expected to continue indefinitely.

Monographic set. Multipart title with a predetermined last volume; the date of the last volume may or may not be specified. Examples include encyclopedias and collected letters of historical or literary figures.

Moving wall. Fixed period of time, usually ranging from two to five years, that defines the gap between the most recently published issue and the date of the most recent issues available in a given online database.

Mutilation. Intentional damage of library materials, either out of malicious intent or to mark or obtain parts of the items for personal use.

Narrative collection policy. Prose-based collection policy. See also **classed analysis.**

National Endowment for the Humanities (NEH). Independent grant-making agency of the U.S. government that supports research, education, **preservation,** and public programs in the humanities.

National Information Standards Organization (NISO). Organization accredited by the **American National Standards Institute** to identify, develop, maintain, and publish technical standards for libraries, information sciences, and the publishing community.

Needs analysis or **needs assessment.** Systematic process that gathers information about a user community and then analyzes that data for planning.

Network. Two or more connected computers. *See also* **library network.**

Newsreader. Automated service that gathers news from multiple **blogs** or online news sites via **RSS,** allowing readers to access all their news from a single website or program.

Nondisclosure. Agreement to treat certain information as confidential, often specified in a contract.

Nondiscretionary purchase. Any purchase that happens automatically. Examples are serial **subscriptions, approval plans,** and **blanket orders.**

Nondiscretionary purchases imply a continuing annual commitment against the acquisitions **budget.**

Notification slip. Online or printed form provided by the library's **approval plan** vendor announcing a new book that meets the library's **profile.** In most cases, a title is supplied only if the **vendor** is notified that the library wishes to order it.

Obscenity. Speech, writing, or artistic expression that appeals to prurient interests with no artistic, literary, or scientific purpose. The courts have had difficulty developing a legal definition of obscenity because of differences in what people find offensive. *See also* **pornography.**

OCLC or **Online Computer Library Center, Inc.** Largest **bibliographic utility** in the world, providing cataloging and acquisitions services, **serial** and circulation control, **interlibrary loan** support, and access to online databases. OCLC maintains OCLC **WorldCat,** an online bibliographic database of member records and holdings.

ONIX (Online Information Exchange). International standard for representing and communicating book industry product information in electronic form to wholesale and retail booksellers, other publishers, and anyone else involved in the sale of books.

OPAC (online public access catalog). Computer catalog of the books and other materials owned by a library; also called an online catalog.

Open access. Resources that are **digital,** online, free of charge, and do not use copyright and licensing restrictions on access and legitimate use.

Open Archives Initiative (OAI). Organization that develops and promotes interoperability standards to facilitate the exchange of information content in **digital** formats.

Open source. Source code freely available to anyone for collaboration, applied to software.

Operating budget. Element of the **budget** allocated to meet the ongoing expenses incurred in running a library or library system.

Orphan work. Original work still protected by its term of copyright but for which the author, creator, or rights holder cannot be found.

Out of print (OP). Publication no longer obtainable through regular market channels because the **publisher** has no more copies and does not plan another printing.

Outcomes. Benefits to the user or user community as a result of a library's **inputs** and **outputs,** that is, the ways library users are changed as a result of contact with a library's resources and programs.

Outputs. Results from the library's **inputs** that can be measured quantitatively (e.g., numbers of books circulated).

Outreach. Act of extending services beyond current or usual limits; usually applied to activities in public and school libraries. *See also* **liaison.**

Outsourcing. Contracting of library services formerly performed in-house to an outside service **provider.** Examples of outsourcing are **conservation** and **preservation** (particularly binding and reformatting), purchasing catalog records in machine-readable form, purchasing cataloging for foreign-language materials, and acquisitions plans (**approval plans, blanket orders,** subscription **agents,** etc.).

PDF (portable document format). Proprietary file format developed by Adobe Systems into which documents formatted by a variety of desktop publishing applications are rendered for ease of delivery.

Peer review. (1) Process by which the job performance and professional contributions of a librarian or other library staff member are reviewed and evaluated by the individual's colleagues, who make recommendations about contract renewal, promotion, and tenure decisions. (2) Process by which experts critically evaluate a work, typically to inform a prospective publisher of the work's worthiness for publication.

Penalty. Specific cost or consequence to be assessed against a contractual party for breach of a term specified in the contract

Periodical. *See* **serial.**

Perpetual license. Continuing **rights** to access an electronic resource after the termination of a license.

Pittsburgh Study. Major study of the usage of library materials, conducted at the University of Pittsburgh by Allen Kent during the 1970s. It reported that approximately 40 percent of the materials purchased never circulated.

Pornography. Works of no artistic value in which sexuality is depicted with the intention to arouse sexual desire. *See also* **obscenity.**

Portico. Nonprofit service that provides a **dark archive** for digital scholarly literature, to be deposited by publishers.

Postprint. Draft of a research paper that has been peer-reviewed and accepted for publication in a scholarly journal.

Preprint. Draft of a research paper before it has been peer-reviewed.

Preservation. Broad range of activities intended to prevent, retard, or stop deterioration of materials or to retain the intellectual content of materials no longer physically intact. *See also* **conservation.**

Preservation needs assessment. Analysis of the condition of a library collection and the environmental conditions in which it is housed to determine what **preservation** treatments are needed.

Price index. Method of calculating and describing the **inflation rate.** It shows the effects of price change on a fixed group of items over a period of time.

Print on Demand (POD). Technology, made possible through **digital** printing, employed by publishers, in which new copies of a book are not printed until after an order has been received.

Profile. (1) Description prepared by a library for a **publisher** or **agent** that supplies materials on an **approval plan** or through a **blanket order.** The profile usually describes subject areas, levels of specialization and/or difficulty, languages, series, formats, price ranges, and so on. (2) Demographic study of the community served by a library or library system that measures economic, social, and educational variables. *See also* **collection profile.**

Programmatic or **program budgeting.** Approach to budgeting in which categories of funding relate to organizational goals or programs.

Project MUSE. Joint project initiated by the Johns Hopkins University Press and Milton S. Eisenhower Library at Johns Hopkins that offers online access to the full text of more than two hundred scholarly journals by **subscription.**

Provider. Individual or entity that provides access to information and delivery services; includes traditional print and electronic scholarly **publishers,** trade publishers, information **aggregators, vendors,** and other electronic-only information disseminators.

Public domain. In copyright law, the total absence of copyright protection for a creative work (e.g., article, book, painting, photograph, movie, poem, musical composition, or computer program). Works enter the public domain through either deliberate surrendering of the copyright by the creator of the work or the expiration of the copyright after the passage of some legally stipulated period of time.

Public good. In economics, something that is nonrivalrous and nonexcludable: consumption of the good by one individual does not reduce the amount of the good available for consumption by others, and no one can be effectively excluded from using that good. *See also* **common good.**

Publisher. Person, commercial venture, university, or other organization that prepares and issues materials for public sale or distribution, normally on the basis of a legal **contract** in which the publisher is granted certain exclusive **rights** in exchange for assuming the financial risk of publication.

Purchase order (PO). Order placed by a library, authorizing a **publisher, jobber, dealer,** or **vendor** to deliver materials or services at a fixed price. A purchase order becomes a **contract** once it is accepted by the seller.

Qualitative methods. Analytical techniques that measure perceived success or goodness.

Quantitative methods. Analytical techniques that count things (volumes, circulation transactions, etc.).

Rebinding. Complete rehabilitation of a book too worn to be **mended** or **repaired.** Rebinding usually entails removing the case or cover, resewing the sections or regluing the text block, and applying a new cover.

Recasing. Process of regluing a book that has come loose from its cover.

Reference and User Services Association (RUSA). Division of the American Library Association responsible for stimulating and supporting the delivery of reference/information services. The **Collection Development and Evaluation Section** of RUSA addresses the collection development interests of reference and user services librarians in libraries of all types.

Reformat. Process of copying information content from one storage medium to a different storage medium or converting from one file format to a different file format.

Refresh. Copy **digital** information to a new storage medium without changing the data's content or structure.

Remote access. Access and use of digital content from a location other than where the information is physically located or the primary site identified in a **contract.**

Repair. Partial rehabilitation of a worn book or other item, including **restoration** of the cover and reinforcement of the hinges or joints. More extensive than **mending** but less extensive than **recasing** or **rebinding.**

Repository. Central place where data are stored and maintained; often used in place of **digital repository.**

Reprint. New printing of an existing edition, with no changes in the text except the correction of typographical errors.

Request for proposal (RFP). Document listing the requirements for vendor services along with the steps to be followed for vendors that wish to submit proposals to handle a library's account. RFPs are typically issued for services provided by, for example, monographic vendors, serials vendors, binders, and integrated library systems.

Resource sharing. Sharing of resources among a group of libraries. Resource sharing has traditionally referred to the sharing of materials through **interlibrary loan.**

Restoration. Returning a book, **document,** or other archival material as nearly as possible to its original condition. Restoration can include **mending, repairing, rebinding,** and **deacidification.** *See also* **conservation** and **preservation.**

Retrospective selection. Process of selecting materials, which may be old, rare, antiquarian, used, or out of print, to fill in gaps in the collection or to replace missing or damaged items.

Rights. Powers or privileges granted by a **contract** or law.

RSS. Web format for syndicating online information so that the information is readable by different kinds of software. RSS stands for Really Simple Syndication, RDF (Resource Description Framework) Site Summary, or Rich Site Summary.

Scenario planning. Process of developing scenarios that describe alternatives futures and formulating plans or strategies for the library in those various futures.

Scholarly communication. Means by which individuals engaged in academic research and creative endeavors inform their peers, formally or informally, of the work they have accomplished. *See also* **peer review.**

Scholarly Publishing and Academic Resources Coalition (SPARC). International alliance of approximately two hundred universities, research libraries, and library associations that seeks to educate faculty on academic **serials** issues, fosters competition in the **scholarly communication** market, and advocates changes in the system and culture of scholarly communication. *See also* **Open Archives Initiative.**

Search engine. Software that searches a file, **database,** or **network** for a specific character string typed as input by the user.

Selection. Process of deciding which materials should be added to a library collection.

Selection criteria. Set of guidelines used by librarians in deciding whether an item should be added to a **collection.** *See also* **collection development policy.**

Selector. One who selects materials for a library and, usually, makes decisions about collection management (e.g., what to withdraw, preserve, store, transfer). *See also* **bibliographer, liaison,** and **subject specialist.**

Self-archiving. Practice of an author (or a publisher as part of the agreement with an author) to deposit his or her work in free, open electronic archives or repositories, usually either discipline-based repositories or institutional repositories.

Serial. Publication issued over a period of time, usually on a regular basis with some sort of numbering used to identify issues, without a foreseeable end date. Serials may be popular **magazines,** scholarly **journals, electronic journals,** or annual reports. The term is often used interchangeably with the term **periodical** to reflect the periodic nature of its publication.

Serials vendor. *See* **vendor.**

Server. Computer that provides some service for other computers connected to it via a **network.**

SGML (standard generalized markup language). **ISO** standard governing the rules for defining tag sets that determine how machine-readable text **documents** are formatted. Not dependent on a specific computer system or type of software, SGML is widely used in preparing machine-readable text archives. The **HTML** code used to create web pages is an SGML language that uses a fixed set of predefined tags. *See also* **XML.**

Shelf-ready book. Book supplied by a **vendor** received ready to go to the stacks. Shelf-ready books are usually cataloged and processed (with spine labels, book plates, antitheft strips, etc.) by the vendor and supplied with a bibliographic record.

SHERPA. Partnership of U.K. academic and research libraries collaborating to foster the development of institutional repositories and support other open access projects.

Site. As used in a **license,** a physical location affiliated with the licensee where the licensee may permit access to digital information to authorized users.

Site license. License that grants official permission from the producer or **vendor** of an electronic resource to use it, under specified conditions, on all the computers at a specific location, a specific **IP address,** or range of IP addresses.

Small press. Small independent **publisher.**

Social bookmarking. Collaborative process of sharing web browser bookmarks.

Social networking. Process through which people with shared interests link to each other via websites.

Social return on investment (SROI). Measure of the social impact of an organization or agency not included in traditional profit-and-loss accounts.

SPARC (Scholarly Publishing and Academic Resources Coalition). International alliance of libraries, research institutions, and organizations from the academic and research community that encourages competition in the scholarly communication market through the support of high-quality, economical alternatives to high-priced scholarly journals.

Standing order. Order placed by a library with an **agent** or **publisher** to supply automatically until further notice each succeeding issue, volume, or part of a **serial** or series as published. Standing orders usually do not permit returns. *See also* **approval plan.**

Stewardship. Careful management of gifts; may include regular reports to the donor.

Storage. Transfer of lesser-used materials or rare, valuable, and fragile materials to restricted access areas within a library building or to a remote facility. *See also* **compact storage.**

Strategic planning. Systematic, broadly participative process by which an organization formulates policy objectives for future growth and development over a period of years. A strategic plan has an external focus and usually involves an **environmental scan.**

Subject specialist. Librarian responsible for selecting materials, managing a collection, and providing bibliographic instruction and reference services to users in a specific academic discipline or field of study. *See also* **bibliographer, liaison,** and **selector.**

Subscription. Agreement or arrangement through which a library (or individual) receives a **periodical** or the **rights** to access a remote electronic resource for a designated period of time or number of issues upon paying a fee to the **publisher,** subscription **agent,** or **vendor.**

Surrogate. Substitute for an original item. In **preservation,** a surrogate is usually made in another medium that is more durable.

Survey. *See* **library survey.**

Syndication. Process through which content is taken from one place and reused in another.

Tags. Keywords (**metadata**) attached to web pages, photos, documents, and so on that help identify them and make them searchable.

TCP (transmission control protocol). TCP is the most common Internet protocol and enables two hosts on a **network** to connect and exchange data; nearly always used in the combination TCP/IP. *See also* **IP (Internet Protocol) address.**

Term. (1) Period of time during which a contract is in effect. (2) Clause or agreement in a **contract.**

Termination. Cancellation or ending of an agreement.

Transfer. Physically move library materials from one location in a library to another.

Trial. Limited period during which a library may test a new electronic product or resource without paying a fee.

Trueswell's 80/20 Rule. Circulation pattern, first reported by Richard W. Trueswell in the 1960s, in which 20 percent of a library's collection accounts for 80 percent of its circulation.

Unauthorized user. Any person designated in a **contract** as not having permission to access or use the digital information covered in the contract.

User-centered and use-centered. Assessment method that focuses on how a collection is being used and how well it meets user needs.

Utility. In economics, a measure or expression of an individual's expected or anticipated satisfaction.

Vendor. (1) Distributor through which the library obtains books, **serials,** other materials, and services instead of dealing directly with a **publisher.** (2) Company in the business of providing access to one or more electronic resources. *See also* **agent.**

Verification list. Extensive subject-based list of important monographs and serials against which a library's holdings are checked to evaluate the quality of a collection.

Warranty. Promise or guarantee, such as assurances about ownership, quality, and hours of performance.

Web 2.0. The second generation of Internet-based services—such as **social networking** sites, communication tools, and **folksonomy**—that let people collaborate and share information online.

Weeding. Process of selecting items in a library collection for **withdrawal** or relocation to **storage.**

Wide area network (WAN). Computer **network** that spans a relatively large geographic area. The largest WAN in existence is the Internet.

Withdrawal. Removing an item from a library's **collection** and removing the bibliographic record from the library's catalog.

WLN. Originally the Western Library Network, now part of **OCLC** and formally named the OCLC/WLN Pacific Northwest Service Center.

World Wide Web (WWW; the Web). Global **network** of Internet **servers** that provides access to **documents** written in **HTML,** which allows content to be linked, locally and remotely.

WorldCat. Bibliographic **database** of materials cataloged and held by **OCLC** member libraries and institutions. WorldCat.org is the version of WorldCat freely available to anyone via the Web.

XML (extensible markup language). Subset of **SGML** in which tags are unlimited and not predefined.

Zero-based budgeting. Budgeting process in which all **allocations** start at zero, and funding needs and requirements are estimated as if no previous allocation had been made.

'Zine. Small-circulation, narrowly focused, often irregular, noncommercial **magazine,** newsletter, or newspaper, self-published by one person or a small group and usually not available by **subscription.**

Note: Page numbers in italic indicate definitions.

You may also be interested in

Managing Electronic Government Information in Libraries: Managing and providing access to the ever-expanding wealth of electronic government information now available presents a significant challenge for librarians, even those who are government documents specialists. In two parts, this guide from ALA's Government Documents Round Table (GODORT) provides the necessary resources you can use to connect patrons to specific information via government sites and electronic documents.

From A to Zine: Are you eager to serve the underserved teen-to-twenty-year-old market and make the library a cool place to hang out? All it takes are zines, according to the author, young adult librarian Julie Bartel. Zines and alternative press materials provide a unique bridge to appeal to disenfranchised youth alienated by current collections. This guide will help you uncover answers to questions about this growing literary genre.

Collection Management for Youth: As education shifts to a learner-centered environment, collection development must address the dynamic interplay between all stakeholders in the wider school community. Connecting to the guidelines of Information Power, the premier learner-focused model for library media centers, this book is grounded in educational theory to help you connect the "whys" to the "hows."

Analyzing Library Collection Use with Excel®: In this unique guide, two collection development experts show how to use Excel® to translate circulation and collection data into meaningful reports for making collection management decisions. Step-by-step instructions accompanied by screen shots assist you in the use of Excel® to quickly "crunch the numbers" that often bog down library use studies.

For more information, please visit www.alastore.ala.org.

Breinigsville, PA USA
24 August 2009

222854BV00003B/157/P